Confraternities were the most common form of organized religious life in medieval and early modern Europe. They were at once the lay face of the church, the spiritual heart of civic government, and the social kin who claimed the allegiance of peers and the obedience of subordinates.

In this collection, fifteen scholars examine the development of confraternities in Italy, where they emerged first and where they had the greatest social, political, and religious impact. Individual essays explore a common set of themes across Italy from the twelfth to the eighteenth centuries: the ubiquity of confraternities; their social construction, and devotional ethos; their ritual culture and civic religion; their antagonistic and collaborative relations with both civic and ecclesiastical authorities; and their role in social welfare and social control of marginal groups. The authors demonstrate how the ritual kinship expressed in confraternities emerged in the middle ages, was transformed in the sixteenth-century Catholic Reformation, and became a powerful force in 'civilizing' early modern Italian society.

NICHOLAS TERPSTRA is Associate Professor of History, University of Toronto. Previous publications include *Lay Confraternities and Civic Religion in Renaissance Bologna* (Cambridge, 1995).

CAMBRIDGE STUDIES IN ITALIAN HISTORY AND CULTURE

Edited by GIGLIOLA FRAGNITO, Università degli Studi, Parma

CESARE MOZZARELLI, Università Cattolica del Sacro Cuore, Milan

ROBERT ORESKO, Institute of Historical Research, University of London

and GEOFFREY SYMCOX, University of California, Los Angeles

This series comprises monographs and a variety of collaborative volumes, including translated works, which concentrate on the period of Italian history from late medieval times up to the Risorgimento. The editors aim to stimulate scholarly debate over a range of issues which have not hitherto received, in English, the attention they deserve. As it develops, the series will emphasize the interest and vigor of current international debates on this central period of Italian history and the persistent influence of Italian culture on the rest of Europe.

For a list of titles in the series, see end of book

THE POLITICS
OF RITUAL KINSHIP

CONFRATERNITIES AND SOCIAL ORDER IN
EARLY MODERN ITALY

EDITED BY

NICHOLAS TERPSTRA

CAMBRIDGE
UNIVERSITY PRESS

PUBLISHED BY THE PRESS SYNDICATE OF THE UNIVERSITY OF CAMBRIDGE
The Pitt Building, Trumpington Street, Cambridge, United Kingdom

CAMBRIDGE UNIVERSITY PRESS
The Edinburgh Building, Cambridge CB2 2RU, UK http://www.cup.cam.ac.uk
40 West 20th Street, New York NY 10011–4211, USA http://www.cup.org
10 Stamford Road, Oakleigh, Melbourne 3166, Australia

First published 2000

Printed in the United Kingdom at the University Press, Cambridge

Typeset in Bembo 11/12.5 pt [VN]

A catalogue record for this book is available from the British Library
Library of Congress cataloguing in publication data

The politics of ritual kinship: confraternities and social order in
early modern Italy / edited by Nicholas Terpstra.
p.   cm. – (Cambridge studies in Italian history and culture)
Includes bibliographical references and index.
ISBN 0 521 62185 2 (hardback)
1. Confraternities – Social aspects – Italy – History. I. Terpstra,
Nicholas.   II. Series.
BX808.5.I8P65 1999
267'.18245 – dc21   98–43693
CIP
ISBN 0 521 62185 2 hardback

CONTENTS

CONTRIBUTORS

Claudio Bernardi (Milan). Ricercatore associated with the Facoltà di Lettere of the Università Cattolica of Brescia. His research has dealt principally with changes in theatre and ritual in early modern Europe, focusing both on changes in aesthetic form, and on the social and anthropological significance of these changes. Among his publications are *Carnevale, Quaresima, Pasqua. Rito e dramma nell'età moderna (1500–1900)* (Milan, 1995) and *La drammaturgia della settimana santa in Italia* (Milan, 1991).

Christopher F. Black (Oxford). Senior Lecturer in History at the University of Glasgow. Elected Fellow of the Royal Historical Society in 1991, and Socio Aggregato of the Deputazione di Storia Patria per l'Umbria in 1987. Black has worked extensively on relations between the Papal State and its subject communes, and on issues of poverty, philanthropy, and social control in connection with sixteenth-century confraternities. Among his publications are *Italian Confraternities in the Sixteenth Century* (Cambridge, 1989), translated as *Le Confraternite Italiane del Cinquecento* (Milan, 1992), and *A Social History of Early Modern Italy* (London, forthcoming).

Daniel E. Bornstein (Chicago). Professor of History at Texas A & M University. Bornstein has held fellowships from the National Endowment for the Humanities, from the Harvard Center for Italian Renaissance Studies, and the Newberry Library. He has worked extensively on the sociological and anthropological analysis of issues relating to lay and clerical piety, particularly as they regard women, devotional movements, and confraternities. Among his publications are *The Bianchi of 1399: Popular Devotion in Late Medieval Italy* (Ithaca, 1993), and a collection of essays, *Women and Religion in Medieval and Renaissance Italy* (Chicago, 1996).

Giovanna Casagrande (Rome). Ricercatrice confermata in the Dipartimento di Scienze Storiche at the University of Perugia, and elected Socio Corrispondente of the Deputazione di Storia Patria per l'Umbria. Her extensive research into lay and clerical devotional movements in late medieval Umbria has resulted in numerous articles and books, including *Religiosità penitenziale e città al tempo dei comuni* (Rome: 1995).

Konrad Eisenbichler (Toronto). Director of the Centre for Reformation and Renaissance Studies at the University of Toronto, and Professor of Renaissance Studies and Italian at Victoria College, University of Toronto. Among his publications are *The Boys of the Archangel Raphael: A Youth Confraternity in Florence, 1411–1785* (Toronto, 1998) and a number of essay collections, including *Crossing the Boundaries: Christian Piety and the Arts in Italian Medieval and Renaissance Confraternities* (Kalamazoo, 1991).

Anna Esposito (Rome). Ricercatrice confermata with the Department of Medieval Studies, and teaching in the Facoltà di Conservazione dei Beni culturali at the Università di Tuscia-Viterbo. Author of many works on late medieval economic, religious, and cultural history, with particular reference to Rome and to minority groups, confraternities, and women's history. Among her recent works is *Un'altra Roma. Minoranze nazionali e comunità ebraiche tra Medioevo e Rinascimento* (Rome, 1995).

Elliott Horowitz (Yale). Senior Lecturer in Jewish History at Bar-Ilan University. He has held fellowships at the Oxford Centre for Hebrew and Jewish Studies, and at the Center for Jewish Studies at the University of Pennsylvania. Horowitz's research on the social history of early modern Jewish communities in the Veneto and Italy generally has resulted in many articles, including works dealing with youths, women, and death.

Lance G. Lazar (Harvard). Assistant Professor of Religious Studies at the University of North Carolina (Chapel Hill). A former Fulbright Fellow, he has also held fellowships from the Charlotte W. Newcombe Foundation, the Lemmermann Foundation, and Harvard University. His research has dealt with topics in both architecture and history, with a more recent concentration on confraternal charity in Rome, and has resulted in papers on history and art history presented at academic conferences in the United States and Europe.

Mark A. Lewis (Toronto). Director of the Jesuit Historical Institute in Rome, and member of the faculty of Church History at the Pontifical Gregorian University. He has held Fellowships at the University of Toronto and the Jesuit Historical Institute. Lewis has presented papers at academic conferences in the United States on theories of punishment in Aquinas and Augustine, and has focused his research on the early history of the Jesuit order.

Richard S. Mackenney (Cambridge). Reader in the Department of History at the University of Edinburgh. Mackenney's research centers on the history of Renaissance Venice, with its more general implications, and on the development of the modern economy and the modern state, with a documentary basis in guild and confraternal records. Among his publications are *Tradesmen and Traders: The World of the Guilds in Venice and Europe, c. 1250–c. 1650* (London, 1987), and *Sixteenth Century Europe: Expansion and Conflict* (London, 1993).

Lorenzo Polizzotto (London). Professor in the Department of Italian at the University of Western Australia. He has held fellowships from the Harvard Center for Italian Renaissance Studies (Villa I Tatti) and University of Melbourne, and is a member of the Australian Academy of the Humanities. Polizzotto has worked on the issues relating to religion and politics in Medicean Florence, focusing on Girolamo Savonarola and his followers. Polizzotto is the author of numerous books and articles, including *The Elect Nation: The Savonarolan Movement in Florence, 1494–1545* (Oxford, 1995), and *La Missione di G. Savonarola a Firenze. Contributi storici* (Pistoia, 1996).

Jennifer Fisk Rondeau (Cornell). Assistant Professor in History at the University of Oregon. Rondeau's research on issues of gender, spirituality, and discourse has been supported by fellowships at the Newberry Library (Chicago), the University of Oregon Humanities Center, and Cornell University. She is the author of *Spiritual Company: Confraternities and Communes in Late Medieval Italy* (Ithaca, forthcoming).

Nicholas Terpstra (Toronto). Associate Professor of History at the University of Toronto and former Fellow of the Harvard Center for Italian Renaissance Studies (Villa I Tatti). His research has focused on various subjects relating to confraternities, crime, and charitable institutions, particularly conservatories and orphanages. His monograph *Lay Confraternities and Civic Religion in Renaissance Bologna* (Cambridge, 1995) was awarded the Howard R. Marraro Prize of the Society for Italian Historical Studies.

Angelo Torre (Torino). Professore Associato at the University of Genoa and Directeur d'Etudes Associé at the Ecole des Hautes Etudes en Sciences Sociales in Paris. He has worked and published extensively on the relationships between history and the social sciences, on the analysis of political units, and on rural religious life in the Ancien Régime. Among his publications are *Il consumo di devozioni. Religione e comunità nelle campagne dell'Ancien Régime* (Venice, 1995).

Danilo Zardin (Milan). Professore Associato di Storia Moderna at the Università Cattolica del Sacro Cuore in Milan. He has worked extensively on the social impact of Tridentine/baroque Christianity in the Ancien Régime, with a focus on Milan and Lombardy. He is currently at work on the tensions between traditional social and religious structures and the Tridentine reforms introduced by Carlo Borromeo and his successors. Among his many publications are *Donna e religiosa di rara excellenza. Prospera Corona Bascapé, i libri e la cultura nei monasteri milanesi del Cinque e Seicento* (Florence, 1992), *Riforma cattolica e resistenze nobiliari nella diocesi di Carlo Borromeo* (Milan, 1984), and essay collections such as *Corpi, "fraternità", mestieri nella storia della società europea* (Rome, 1998).

ACKNOWLEDGMENTS

This collection began with an invitation from Geoffrey Symcox, who warned me from the beginning that it would be an exercise in "herding cats." I would like to thank both him and Robert Oresko for their early support of the project, and William Davies of Cambridge University Press for his patience and generosity when approached with appeals for more resources and more pages. Stephen Parkin and Rodney Lokaj translated the Italian articles, gamely pursuing the specialized terminology of early modern ritual in pursuit of clarity. Luther College at the University of Regina provided a collegial context in which to work; the College covered associated costs without complaint, and my colleagues generously assumed that the project was worthwhile, if a bit arcane. Jenéa Tallentire imposed order on articles and bibliographies submitted in a variety of styles and programs, and ensured that the manuscript would be ready when all the cats got home. Thanks to her and to the School of Graduate Studies at the University of Regina for the Research Assistantship which underwrote her work.

Angela, Nigel, Christopher, and Alison reminded me daily that life with blood kin gives ritual kinship its persuasive pull.

And the cats who, in the end, *seldom* needed herding. To them, and to the whole body of very congenial scholars who pursue confraternal studies, this collection is dedicated.

THE POLITICS OF RITUAL KINSHIP

NICHOLAS TERPSTRA

Long processions of bleeding flagellants wielding banners and whips, or of sleek be-robed worthies shepherding the orphans they sheltered, the adolescent girls they dowered, or the children they educated. Bread handed out on a corner, public feasts hosted on a holy day, private banquets fueled by legacies. Nocturnal gatherings whose purpose could be devotional (as members claimed) or sexual, or political (as critics suspected). Cadres of marching children whose devotion could either inspire or make uneasy. Groups of women who managed shelters, clothed the Virgin Mary on feast days, and organized parochial devotions.

Early modern Italians encountered confraternities in every town and neighborhood, on every holiday, at every rite of passage. But just what did they experience, whether from inside or out? The rituals noted above generated a host of contradictory impressions. Brotherhoods were the most public face of the church, yet were almost entirely lay. They originated to promote civic peace, yet were factious and partisan. Their internal ordering was to reflect the equality of souls in the eyes of God, yet everything from seats in the oratory to place in procession was ranked hierarchically. Distinct groups expressed the finely graded calibrations by which a boundary- and role-conscious society kept genders, ages, classes, and races distinct, though always with boundary-crossing exceptions to prove the rule. Above all, it was their very ubiquity that made conflict and contradiction inevitable: shrines, altars, hospitals, schools, and orphanages testified to the beneficent patronage of *confratelli*, every civic-religious event brought them out in streams behind their banners, and loyalties to neighborhood, craft, parish, religious order, or devotional preference could be magnified through the lens of confraternal ritual kinship.

While the brotherhoods and their rituals were woven into the fabric of early modern life, it has been less clear to historians whether they were central or fringe elements of the tapestry. Traditional political historiography of the early modern state developed its narratives with little if any reference to confraternities. From its nineteenth-century positivist roots, this history tended to disregard ritual, theatre, and social kinship as decorative marginalia to the big narrative of institutional and constitutional development. If religion were of any interest – and this was a debatable point at best – it was better analyzed through the offices, possessions, politics, and doctrines of the institutional church. This approach assumed that early modern states worked much like modern ones in their fundamentals, because early modern individuals pursued their self-interest much like moderns.

Early confraternal studies took their shape from these assumptions. In the nineteenth and early twentieth centuries, they were largely the province of antiquarians and local historians who respectfully plotted the piety of their subjects through every oratory, altarpiece, and memorial plaque acquired in a two- or three- or four-hundred-year history. Few escaped the parish boundaries or city walls, and fewer yet saw any broader significance in their subject. Those rare studies which did transcend locality often fixed attention on the peninsular development of cultural forms like theatre, on the spread of common groups like the Holy Sacrament confraternities or, in the case of histories of the religious orders, on confraternities as the loyal and obedient auxiliaries of the regular clergy. A few anti-clerical histories offered more sardonic readings of their subjects, but could not free themselves from the local-institutional mindset.

In the 1960s, social history offered the first avenue for taking confraternal studies out of the local-antiquarian backwater, and brought greater rigor to the work of administrative, economic, and religious historians. Yet a functionalist mindset initially governed subject and approach. Historians began to see confraternities behind funerary rituals and so approached them as burial clubs aimed at securing subscribers a plot in the ground for the body, and a path into heaven for the soul. Brotherhoods were recognized in the administrative offices at many charitable institutions, and so were written up as altruistic boards of governors rolling up the sleeves of their robes to secure bread for the hungry and beds for the sick. These histories helped explain how things got done in early modern society, but left many questions unasked. How did confraternities affect the temporal, spatial, and communal rhythms of faith? Were frequent evocations of confraternal kinship more than just rhetoric? What motivated membership and how did it shape lives?

These questions emerged in the past few decades as the historical gaze began reaching beyond institutional development to the more complex questions of how early moderns constructed themselves and their society.

Anthropological approaches have demonstrated that ritual and theatre are not fringe elements of early modern political processes, but are central to their meaning and purpose, such that contests over ritual roles, honor, or precedence are expressions of political power and not diversions from it. Social kinship groups are the practical means by which early moderns exercise their belief that the family is God's pattern for political and social relations. Absolutist politics entail negotiations between a baffling variety of parties, including groups whose rituals, rooted in tradition, law, and faith, give them a proprietary responsibility for space and time that translates into more real power than many magistrates held. Religion itself has such a complex range of dimensions and forms that a focus on the formal hierarchy of the Catholic church seems almost quaint, if not peripheral to an understanding of how faith animated local communities. Few historians now would speak of "mere ritual."

As early modern historiography becomes less reductionist in the subjects considered worthy of study and the methods of approaching them, confraternities are being recognized as having more than simply an antiquarian interest or a functionalist social role. Historians encounter confraternities in more and more places as groups which define social and political roles, and mediate changes to a more hierarchical society. Gabriel Le Bras first approached confraternities as a parallel or alternative church, encouraging others to see the brotherhoods as a means of understanding religion as a lived experience centered around social relations rather than as a set of doctrines or institutions. John Bossy expanded on this with the claim that confraternities achieved the "social miracle" of peaceful co-existence by embodying the metaphor of kinship in society, while Ronald Weissman and Richard Trexler saw them as groups by which Florentines steered their way through rites of passage and around antagonistic social relations. Brian Pullan overturned a longstanding historiographical convention when he demonstrated that Catholic states, working through confraternities, developed charitable assistance to the same extent as their Protestant counterparts; Pullan and Edward Muir showed how the ritual and charity of the *Scuole Grandi* were fundamental to Venice's image and operation as a stable society. Contested though they sometimes are, these interpretations have opened a way of understanding confraternities as key agents in the construction of early modern society.

As Christopher Black's essay in this collection demonstrates, the works of Le Bras, Bossy, Pullan, and Weissman were catalysts for the rapid expansion of confraternity studies through the past three decades. Confraternities now constitute one of the most active subjects of research and scholarship in Renaissance and Early Modern European historical studies.

Within the past decade, major monographs have been published dealing with various aspects of confraternal history in Spain, France, the Netherlands, and particularly Italy; scholarly articles have expanded this coverage to areas as diverse as Constantinople and Brazil. Interdisciplinary conferences in Europe and North America have attracted a wide range of historians of politics, art, literature, music, theatre, religion, and ritual to address the topic, and resulted in numerous published essay collections. Within Italian studies, Anglo-American scholars have focused their research largely on the late medieval and Renaissance periods, while Italians have expanded beyond this into the Ancien Régime when the modern state began to take shape. The common theme which all these studies make plain is that confraternities were far more than "purely" devotional groups. Their activity offers insights into the organization and distribution of charity, gender and class relations, the character and uses of civic religion, the shifting dynamics of lay and clerical relations at all levels, and the means by which local elites used religious and charitable institutions to maintain political authority.

This collection aims to demonstrate both some of the common themes which shape recent scholarly approaches to Italian confraternity studies, and the variety of methodological and ideological approaches that characterize the field. Fifteen international scholars, both established and new, demonstrate how the ritual kinship found in confraternities was a significant factor in the social, political, and religious construction of early modern Italy. The collection brings together work on urban centers which have until recently received relatively little attention in English-language scholarship (e.g., Cortona, Ferrara, Bologna, Milan, Naples, Genoa, Turin), with cities which have a longer English-language historiographical tradition (Florence, Venice, Rome), and with rural Piedmont. Each article is based on the author's research in local archives, yet each puts that research into broader comparative context. Together, they address interlocking questions of religion, class, gender, politics, race, and charity that are at the heart of research into early modern history.

Five themes or questions lie at the heart of this collection, and each article addresses one or more of them in distinct ways and with distinct perspectives. These themes are:

1. The prevalence of confraternities in urban centers, and the distinctions of class, gender, and age that characterize them internally and externally.
2. The religious culture of confraternities and their definition of popular/civic religion through ritual, theatre, charity; related to this, the use of confraternal rituals and institutions as a collective means of

defending a group's prerogatives and religiously legitimating its interests.

3. Shifting relations with ecclesiastical authorities (parochial, urban/diocesan, religious orders) before and after the sixteenth-century Catholic/Counter Reformation, with a particular emphasis on confraternities as key agents in the post-Tridentine effort to "Christianize" society.

4. Shifting relations of co-operation, co-optation, and suppression with social hierarchies and political authorities, again with the aim of achieving a more ordered and obedient society.

5. The expanding role of confraternities as agencies directing social welfare and social control of marginal and subordinate groups.

The collection opens with a historiographical review by Christopher Black that surveys the rapid expansion of international scholarship on Italian confraternities over the past thirty years. This review focuses on the five interlocking themes noted above, and highlights the method-ological developments and interpretive disagreements that have marked this scholarship. Fourteen essays follow in roughly chronological order, exploring one or more of these themes as they apply to a particular city or territory over a period of one or two centuries.

Chronologically, the first five of these essays plot key elements in the late medieval and Renaissance development of confraternal rituals, ad-ministration, and social roles, with all their characteristic contradictions (gender, peace-making, civic religion, charity, and politics). The remain-ing nine essays demonstrate the further articulation – and transvaluation – of confraternal models into the early modern period. Thematically, groups of essays pick up individual themes in such a way that readers can make comparisons between times and places. So, for instance, Rondeau, Mackenney, Horowitz, and Torre illustrate the very fluid nature of confraternal organization in the constant adaptation of recognized forms to local or communal needs. The issue of gender in confraternal member-ship and activity is first discussed by Rondeau and Casagrande for late medieval Tuscany and Umbria, and further developed by Esposito and Lazar for fifteenth- and sixteenth-century Rome. The use of confraterni-ties by some authorities to control subordinate groups and by some of these groups to resist authorities is explored by Polizzotto and Terpstra with reference to children, and by Lazar and Horowitz with reference to Jews. Confraternities' contribution to shaping social charity is explored by Bornstein for late medieval Cortona, developed by Esposito, Terpstra, and Lazar for fifteenth- and sixteenth-century Rome and Bologna, and carried on by Lewis for sixteenth- and seventeenth-century Naples. The theme of political manipulation – both of and by confraternities – is explored by Rondeau and Bornstein for late medieval Tuscany; Polizzotto and Terpstra for fifteenth- and sixteenth-century Florence and Bologna; Mackenney, Zardin and Bernardi for sixteenth- and seventeenth-century Venice, Milan, and Genoa, Torre for seventeenth- and eighteenth-century Piedmont, and Eisenbichler for eighteenth-century Florence. The evolving character of popular and civic religion, and its creative/conflictive relationship with the ecclesiastical hierarchy is addressed by Casagrande and Bornstein for late medieval Perugia and Cortona; Lazar and Mackenney for sixteenth-century Rome and Venice, and Zardin, Bernardi, Lewis, and Torre for sixteenth- and seventeenth-century Lombardy, Genoa, Naples, and Piedmont.

These individual studies reveal the contradictory realities that developed as medieval and Renaissance forms metamorphosed through the Ancien Régime. Social change works by incremental steps from the familiar, and as political and religious authorities aimed to develop a more ordered society, confraternities offered a vehicle, a model, and a means of legitimation. Yet they offered the same to the opponents of this process. Confraternities could be the political agencies by which local groups defended their traditional rights and boundaries (Torre), the theatres for the exercise of authority by groups stripped of former political powers (Esposito), or a means "to draw off the political aspirations of the Venetian citizen class" (Mackenney). They could be the agencies through which the moral disciplines of "Christianization" were promoted (Lazar, Bernardi, Torre, Zardin), and also the agencies through which these same disciplines were resisted (Bernardi, Torre).

The transvaluation of tradition is only one of the factors behind the differences these authors demonstrate. Certainly they treat different cities in a peninsula which is notoriously local, and different periods in an era characterized by significant change. More to the point, this collection expresses the variety of ideological and methodological approaches found in confraternity studies today. While all authors see confraternities as agents of social order in an increasingly hierarchical period, they differ in their assessment of whether that order was just, desirable, or successfully imposed. All believe that religion was the indispensable cement which held early modern society together, yet they differ in the way they see religion expressed: some center it in the officers and aims of an institution, others on the rituals of a community, and others in the cohesion of a group. While all base their interpretations in a close reading of archival documents, they differ in the theoretical lenses used to read these documents and interpret their meaning. Some accept the pious intentions voiced in confraternal documents largely on their own terms, while others subject these documents to a hermeneutics of suspicion. Some essays here reflect the hypotheses developed through anthropological and sociological categories, while others maintain the stricter discipline of positivist historiography. By deliberately maintaining these discordant voices, the collection as a whole illustrates the debates which international scholars are engaged in as they seek to recover the role confraternities played in shaping Renaissance and early modern Italian culture and society.

Through the differing interpretations, a common factor in these studies is the central significance of the ritual kinship of *confraternitas* in a society which structured its politics, religious institutions, economic agencies, and social life around family models. Yet these essays also demonstrate that confraternitas itself became more hierarchical through the sixteenth century; this is at the heart of the transvaluation of confraternal kinship referred to above. We need not adopt romantic notions of egalitarian brotherhood in medieval and Renaissance confraternities in order to recognize that both their character and their ideals (however much limited to the realm of rhetoric) begin to shift noticeably. Existing confraternities underwent an ennobling of membership that reflected a more general process of aristocratization in early modern society; this was further reinforced as reforming bishops like Carlo Borromeo and reforming orders like the Jesuits established new and exclusive confraternities on class, occupational, and gender lines in order to draw particular social groups into their reform programs. Networks of parish or peninsular confraternities emerged under the patronage and closer supervision of priests, bishops, or religious orders, with standardized statutes and with their energies directed to very specific social, educational, or devotional purposes; although not always successfully established, these reforms generated further reactions. Parochial and autonomous confraternities alike consolidated their resources and activities in order to protect and increase their traditional prerogatives. Efforts to achieve what Bossy termed the "social miracle" increasingly gave way to concerns of social order, as the ruling paradigm for confraternities became not egalitarian brotherhood, but authoritarian parenthood. Ritual, patronage of shrines, and social charity all became more important as means of maintaining distinctions, not transcending or mediating them. Confraternal stock rose with consolidation of the Ancien Régime, but declined as that regime's values were called into question. The Enlightenment corroded them within and without. Dechristianization rendered confraternal rituals empty for many, while notions of social contract and secular utility became more compelling among the middle and upper classes who had formed the core of confraternal membership. This left confraternities open to charges of being self-indulgent, corrupt, and counter-productive. States under enlightened despots experimented with the suppression, expropriation, and secularization which became the norm once Napoleon crossed the Alps. Ironically, this rejection of Ancien Régime confraternities was not a rejection of traditional confraternitas, or ritual kinship itself. That powerful urge found secularized civic-religious expression in the propagandist evocations of revolutionary brotherhood, in the mutual aid of fraternal lodges, and in the arcane secretive rituals of the Freemasons. Confraternities themselves enjoyed a post-revolutionary restoration, but as little more than parish auxiliaries. They were no longer significant players in the social or political order, and this may be one reason why nineteenth-century political historians found them so easy to ignore. Even though the liberal state took another half-century to expand in Italy, the politics of the Ancien Régime failed to convince, and its traditional ritual bodies failed to impress.

Citizens pledging oaths, planting trees, and donning distinctive red caps as public signs of their commitment to liberty, equality, and fraternity. Men and women gathering to form societies that would carry them through sickness and bury them in death. Professional males adopting secret handshakes and observing ersatz Egyptian rites in nocturnal ceremonies which could be devotional (as members claimed) or politically, economically, or religiously subversive (as critics suspected). Ritual kinship was fundamentally about collectively mediating change, expressing ultimate values, and pursuing socialization; as such, it was inherently political. The earliest confraternities mediated social change during the late medieval expansion of urban society, and early modern confraternities did the same during the rise of commercial and civilized society through the Ancien Régime. Likewise, the political clubs, friendly societies, and lodges of the late-eighteenth and nineteenth centuries gave those experiencing the rapid political, economic, and social change of the early industrial era a collective means of preserving some sense of order and meaning through the flux. In this way, the Enlightenment transvaluation of ritual kinship confirms the fluidity of meanings which confraternal forms could take, and justifies our shifting attention away from any particular religious/devotional context and towards the broader question of how societies accommodate change. Confraternities can certainly help us understand the lay religious culture of medieval and early modern Catholicism, but to leave the investigation there is to be content with a more informed antiquarianism. Confraternal studies offer a means of approaching the much greater question of how spiritual values take secular shape or, in other words, how different forms of ritual kinship shape processes of socialization, adaptation, and legitimation. This collection of essays aims in that direction.

THE DEVELOPMENT OF CONFRATERNITY STUDIES OVER THE PAST THIRTY YEARS

CHRISTOPHER F. BLACK

Since the 1960s lay confraternities in Italy, as elsewhere, have moved from the periphery of medieval religious history to a central place in mainstream studies of social-religious and cultural history up to the eighteenth century. In the early 1960s a student of medieval and Renaissance Italy might have known about confraternities as part of the broader flagellant movement exploding on the scene from 1260; or as contributors to the cultural scene of fourteenth- and fifteenth-century Florence, if they recognized Or San Michele as a confraternity building, or sixteenth century Venice – if it was realized that *Scuola* in the context of, say San Rocco, meant a confraternity and not an educational school. Now it is recognized that confraternities expanded and diversified in Italy through the later medieval, Renaissance, Catholic Reform, and Counter Reformation periods that in this volume are subsumed under the broader term of Early Modern. The Reformation crisis period that saw the collapse of the fraternities or religious guilds (or gilds) in Protestant areas of Germany, in England, and in Scotland, witnessed a major diversification of their roles and activities in Italy, as in Spain and later France.

Confraternities were central to the spiritual life of many urban inhabitants, female as well as male, and more patchily to remoter rural dwellers. They were a key link between the living and the dead. But increasingly we have studied the roles of confraternities in politics, in the structuring

In preparing this chapter I am much indebted to the assistance and encouragement of fellow authors Richard Mackenney, Nicholas Terpstra and Danilo Zardin; of my colleague Sam Cohn, and of my former colleague and *amica simpatica*, Tricia Allerston. For revising this chapter the Editor has opportunely provided me with copies of most other chapters before editing and, in some cases, translation. This has helped me indicate the interpretive context of what my co-authors are analyzing. Archival material has only been cited where supplementary to what can be found in references to my published writings. I have used here: Archivio Storico del Vicariato di Roma (ASVR), Arciconfraternita della Dottrina Cristiana (ADC); Archivio di Stato, Roma (ASR), Camerale II (CII), and Camerale III (CIII).

of social relations and social life, their links with many aspects of social welfare, being involved in hospices and hospitals, prisons and poor houses, in religious education, in the welfare of females from the provision of dowries to secure accommodation to protect vulnerable young girls, battered wives and forsaken widows. The roles of fraternities in cultural life have similarly been much studied since the 1960s; in connection with processions and plays, with religious musical celebrations, as well as with the provision and financing of chapels and church decoration.

This chapter will first highlight the landmark publications, conferences, research projects and institutions that have fostered the expansion of confraternity studies over the past thirty years, and linked them with other developments in historical studies. Subsequently five sections will elaborate on key aspects of confraternity activity and developments, emphasizing what has contributed to broadening our knowledge and understanding. The selectivity of my commentary and examples, governed by my recent research interests, and space limitations, should be compensated for by references in the rich and varied chapters that follow, and in the composite bibliography, so that no major contributor to changing approaches to confraternities through the fifteenth to seventeenth centuries remains unmentioned. Important, but highly specialized studies of local importance, even major contributions to documentary information, may however have been omitted.

Penitential flagellation was one of the significant activities of one type of fraternity. It was renewed interest in medieval flagellation, or discipline (*disciplina*), that most stimulated my generation's interest in early modern confraternities. An anniversary conference in 1960 to celebrate the 1260 flagellant movement produced seminal papers published in 1962, the establishment of a Center in Perugia for the study of discipline confraternities, and the organization of a second conference in 1969 (published in 1972).[1] The conferences and Center set many scholars searching for documentation to establish when and where discipline confraternities existed, and their statutory basis; the pursuit of printed statutes empha-

---

[1] *Movimento dei disciplinati*, in which G. Alberigo's long "Contributi," 156–256, was an important stimulus to research into lay spirituality in the Catholic Reform period; also *Risultati e Prospettive*; the Centro di Documentazione sul Movimento dei Disciplinati, Perugia, has intermittently published a number of studies, printed statutes, and cataloged sources, but suffered from underfunding. For recent comments on the development of different approaches to confraternity studies see: Banker, *Death in Community*, 1–14; Henderson, *Piety and Charity*, 1–8; Terpstra, *Lay Confraternities*, xv–vii; Eisenbichler, "Ricerche nord-americane", and his recent "Italian Scholarship." References below are largely to titles listed in the composite Bibliography. Page references are given only in a few cases for something very precise; and sometimes in the case of my own book *Italian Confraternities* as possibly the easiest way of leading readers to further sources.

sized the importance of post-Tridentine reforms, the continuing and changing roles of fraternities thereafter. This effort coincided with a grandiose project to produce ecclesiastical maps of Italy, with supporting studies. Pioneering work for the atlases expanded the range of sources utilized, and emphasized the expansion of different types of fraternities in the later sixteenth century, and their existence in the south and other places outside the great cities.[2] Gilles Gerard Meersseman in his magisterial collection of studies of Dominican fraternities stressed the geographical range of their existence, and their importance into the Catholic Reform period of the sixteenth century. Brian Pullan pioneered a whole new range of studies of confraternity activities in his *Rich and Poor in Renaissance Venice*. This work revealed the full nature of the *Scuole Grandi*, the small, selective but powerful group of Venetian confraternities, better known to art lovers, and their involvement in a whole range of welfare activities. His work also encouraged some of us to look at more than the statutes to understand activities and members; membership lists, minute books, accounts.[3]

From the 1970s the study of confraternities was broadened by the impact of approaches to, and interpretations of, social history in the early modern period, with the influence of sociology, social anthropology, and quantitative methods; some of this developed older ideas on religious sociology from Gabriel Le Bras.[4] In this context, Richard Trexler's *Public Life in Renaissance Florence* (1980) was seminal in considering social relations, social-political tensions, and rituals in society that threw light on many roles of confraternities. Ronald Weissman in 1982 similarly analyzed the importance of fraternities in Florence's ritual life, in socializing the young and the old; he broke new ground in the analysis of the patterns of membership, of active and passive participation; and gave major insights into what it was like to be a brother in one of these societies. Weissman illustrated how confraternities could change in the transition from republican Renaissance Florence to the Ducal regime leading Counter Reformation changes. A Ph.D. thesis by John Henderson (1983), sought to document and analyze the whole range of Florentine fraternities in the late medieval and Renaissance period; it was widely influential through private consultation, and through articles the author developed from it, until a splendid book appeared in 1994. This combines a major description and analysis of patterns of lay piety through the

---

[2] Rosa, "Geografia"; Rosa (ed.), *Problemi e ricerche*; Black, *Italian Confraternities*, 18–19. Olga Marinelli's massive annotated bibliography, *Confraternite di Perugia*, was an impressive example of what could be accumulated by hunting for relevant printed material from the sixteenth century onwards. [3] Meersseman, *Ordo Fraternitas*; Pullan, *Rich and Poor*.
[4] Le Bras, "Les confréries chrétiennes."

fourteenth and fifteenth centuries, with a heavily documented study of charitable donations and involvement with hospitals and social welfare. It also contextualizes that spectacular artistic monument, the church and tabernacle of Orsanmichele. John Henderson's work, which departs from the eulogistic and complacent approaches of some studies of confraternities, is a good illustration of how studies of urban confraternities developed through the 1970s and 1980s.[5] In juxtaposition, Charles De La Roncière (influenced by Le Bras' religious sociology, but with more understanding of devotional activities), refreshingly focused on the rural context of Tuscan medieval fraternities. Danilo Zardin, specializing on Lombardy, has exemplified how we might look at later rural fraternities, and how they were affected by Catholic reform successes and limitations. In the same period, out of the greater interest of historians on the way death and the afterlife was approached, came important studies that dealt with probably the main concern of confraternities. Here the works of James Banker and Sam Cohn should be emphasized not only for insights into approaches for studying death, memorialization of the dead, or strategies in social welfare, but also for their use of testaments and other notarial records, financial records and artistic evidence, and for their statistical approaches.[6]

Most confraternity studies have been localized, either geographically or by theme and type. Attempts at synthesis, at covering all or large parts of Italy are fraught with difficulty (and are frowned on by some Italian scholars). Gennaro Maria Monti made a brave attempt in 1927 for the medieval period. From the late 1970s there have been new attempts, by Giancarlo Angelozzi (1978), who went into the early modern period; by Roberto Rusconi in a valuable contribution (1986) to the Einaudi *Storia d'Italia* multi-volume work, by Danilo Zardin (1987), who covered northern Italy from the fifteenth to eighteenth century. All these greatly helped in producing my own synthesis in 1989.[7]

In the last decade confraternity studies have become ever more obviously interdisciplinary, and deepened by more research outside the most famous cities. While novelists like David Lodge might satirize the academic conference circuit, and administrators question their costs and

[5] Trexler, *Public Life*; Weissman, *Ritual Brotherhood*; Henderson, *Piety and Charity*, "Charity," "Confraternities" and "Le confraternite."

[6] De La Roncière, "Confréries à Florence," Confréries en Toscane," and "Val d'Elsa"; Zardin, *Confraternite e vita*; Banker, *Death in Community,* and "Death"; Cohn, *Death and Property* and *Cult of Remembrance.*

[7] Angelozzi, *Confraternite laicali*; Monti, *Confraternite medievali*; Rusconi, "Confraternite, compagnie e devozioni"; Zardin, " Italia settentrionale"; Black, *Italian Confraternities,* and *Confraternite Italiane* (with corrections and additional references, but some translation misunderstandings), and "Confraternities" (on wider European scene).

benefits, most authors of this collection would surely laud major American conferences (such as the Congress of Medieval Studies at Kalamazoo, and the Renaissance Studies and Sixteenth Century Studies Conferences), where special sessions on confraternities (linking in with others on art history, drama, and music), have brought scholars together from many lands, dealing with different countries and aspects . These have shown the importance of confraternities as patrons in diverse cultural areas; while paintings, buildings, music, plays, and sacred representations were part of the devotional life, recreation, and propaganda of the fraternities. Several of these conferences have generated collections of papers, whether expansions from papers given or newly commissioned like those here (though the specifically cultural aspects have been omitted from this selection).[8] The sociability of confraternity scholars has suitably stimulated academic co-operation. A conference in Toronto (1989) led to the formation of the Society for Confraternity Studies, a newsletter, *Confraternitas*, and the formation of a special Confraternities Collection housed in the library of the Centre for Reformation and Renaissance Studies at the University of Toronto.[9] Major local Italian celebrations, with conferences and associated exhibitions, such as those for Lorenzo de' Medici in 1992, have generated important new interpretations, written documentation and visual illustrations associated with confraternities.[10] The Centro Ricerche di Storia Religiosa, Puglia, under Liana Bertoldi Lenoci has organized research projects, conferences, publications that have brought much new knowledge of confraternities, religious history and art in a significant part of southern Italy. A 1987 conference in Rome on religious sociability in southern confraternities extended out of the Puglia enterprise, while other Roman conferences contributed to valuable work on Roman confraternities and articles published in the periodical *Ricerche per la Storia Religiosa di Roma*.[11]

The above are highlighted as the landmark developments in the emergence of confraternity studies from a historical backwater into the mainstream. Individual contributions, collaborative efforts and sociabil-

---

[8] Collections of conference papers include: Bertoldi Lenoci (ed.), *Confraternite pugliese*; Eisenbichler (ed.), *Crossing the Boundaries*; Paglia (ed.), *Confraternite e Meridione*; Donnelly and Maher (eds.), *Confraternities and Catholic Reform*.

[9] *Confraternitas*, 1990, ed. William. Bowen and Konrad Eisenbichler, includes listings of confraternity publications, reviews and summaries; as well as information about conferences, research projects and, now, short articles. The 1989 conference papers were published in *Renaissance and Reformation*, vol. 25, no. 1 (Spring 1989), under the title "Ritual and Recreation in Renaissance Confraternities."   [10] See e.g. *Confraternitas* 3, no. 2 (Fall 1992): 29–30, and 6, no. 2 (Fall 1995): 30–31.

[11] *Confraternitas* 1, no. 2 (Fall 1990): 5–8, 23–4, and 4, no. 2, 9 (Fall 1993): 28–9; Bertoldi Lenoci (ed.), *Le confraternite pugliese* and *Confraternite, Chiese*, and her "Sociabilità"; Paglia (ed.), *Confraternite e Meridione*.

ity, and changing trends in historical scholarship generally have produced
major interpretative changes in our view of confraternities, which themselves showed dynamism, diversity and adaptability throughout the early
modern period.

PREVALENCE OF CONFRATERNITIES

Developments since the 1960s have allowed us to know much more
about the numbers and types of confraternities, their membership numbers and profiles, though – as I have outlined elsewhere[12] – the problems
of quantification are enormous, given the vagaries of the survival of
documentation, let alone discrepancies over scholarly interest in different
areas. Pier Luigi Meloni's early attempt at quantification focused on
discipline fraternities, and presented problems through narrow defini-
tions, its reliance on statutes and problematic nomenclature. Subsequent
research has allowed us to obtain a better idea of the growing diversity of
the confraternity scene, as Laudesi companies developed also in the
fifteenth century under the impact of the Bianchi of 1399, and as hospital
and other welfare-orientated societies were added in the fifteenth and
later centuries. Holy Sacrament and other eucharist fraternities, Rosary
and Name of God companies were fostered under Catholic Reform.
Reforming bishops like Gian Matteo Giberti, Carlo Borromeo, and
Gabriele Paleotti promoted various types of parish-based fraternities,
Christian Doctrine societies and so forth, while new or reformed Orders,
notably the Jesuits and Capuchins added many more. In terms of enumer-
ation and typology the important contributions since my summary in
1989 have mainly been those dealing with Puglia and other parts of the
south, previously mentioned. John Henderson's book includes a model
appendix enumerating and classifying the fraternities of one city,
Florence.[13]

Classifying and counting confraternities has proved less simple than
Meloni, for example, perceived. Many "Discipline" fraternities ceased to
have flagellation as a significant devotional activity, and be diversely
active, as with the Venetian Scuole Grandi, whose members paid the
poor to flagellate in processions for them. Other types of fraternities
included flagellation as one of the devotions. Some Jesuit fraternities
encouraged flagellation as a devotion, some as a punishment, others

---

[12] Black, *Italian Confraternities*, ch. 2, 3.

[13] Meloni, "Topografia"; Black, *Italian Confraternities*, 23–32; Henderson, *Piety and Charity*, appendix
for period 1240–1499; Bornstein, *The Bianchi*, is a major recent contribution to the 1399 movement
and its impact; De Sandre Gasparini, "Il Movimento," and Sbriziolo, *Confraternite Veneziane* have
some useful insights into both problems of classification, and evolution of types, in the Veneto.

ignored the practice and concentrated on preparing members for death, or major spiritual and physical welfare in Roman prisons. Mackenney's chapter below raises different problems of confused nomenclature and classification, and demonstrates how fraternities, guilds and welfare societies could change and re-form, while Horowitz' contribution demonstrates that confraternities were not exclusive to the Catholic world, but organized collective life and mutual aid for Jewish communities in Ferrara, Bologna, Rome, Venice, and other centers.[14]

More to be stressed are important developments in our knowledge of the membership of confraternities. That significant numbers of women could be members has finally, if belatedly, been recognized as Giovanna Casagrande says. Serious problems have to be overcome in establishing the numbers, and the degree of their activity and responsibility, as her own and Anna Esposito's chapters below illustrate. Richard Mackenney has recently pointed out that female membership may be significantly disguised if fraternities followed the example of at least two Venetian ones that declared: "we are not naming the *sorelle*, along with the *fratelli*, so as not to multiply the words."[15] If we look hard enough we can find a highly specialized sorority for noble women, like Florence's Compagnia di Santa Caterina da Siena, though details are tantalizingly meager, as they are for Rosary companies (despite some valiant work by Danilo Zardin among others), which were to a greater or lesser extent feminine in membership and orientation. As Jennifer Rondeau has already suggested the presence of women in some Laudesi companies may have significantly affected the complex gender aspects of the Laude as prayers to the Virgin and Christ. One assumes that the admission of women for caring roles in hospital-linked confraternities (as in the Roman scene discussed by Anna Esposito below, and in earlier writings), might similarly have influenced the devotions; but this remains to be clarified.[16]

We now know more about the youth membership of confraternities, and about separate youth confraternities – as often particularly for Florence. Within full adult societies there might be a youth novitiate, from which some passed to full membership. But, as Konrad Eisenbichler

---

[14] Black, *Italian Confraternities*, ch. 4:6 on flagellation, and 23–26 on problems of nomenclature and classification; cf. on latter Henderson, *Piety and Charity*, 1–4; Grendi, "Morfologia"; Torre, "Politics Cloaked," esp. 59–60 on an odd distinction between "company" and "fraternity." My "European Confraternities" will discuss these problems in a wider European context.

[15] Mackenney, "The Guilds of Venice," 40: "in ciaschedun capitoli non siano nominate le sorelle, come li fratelli per non molteplicar troppe parole;" fourteenth century statutes of Scuola di San Zuan Battista, and Scuola di Santi Cosmo e Damiano.

[16] Casagrande, "Women in Confraternities" is useful for more than Umbria; Rondeau, "Prayer and Gender," esp. 228–33; see also: Sebregondi, "Noble Women;" Terpstra, "Women;" Black, *Italian Confraternities*, 34–8, 103–4; Zardin, *Confraternite e vita*.

has shown, Florence particularly had a number of youth confraternities which made major contributions, from the fifteenth to eighteenth centuries, to the cultural life of the city, through plays, sacred representations and musical performances. As he has also recently stressed the Florentine youth confraternities in the fifteenth century not only listened to humanist sermons by leading figures such as Alamanno Rinuccini, Niccolò Machiavelli, Giovanni Nesi and Angelo Poliziano, but had in afternoon sessions sermons regularly given by genuine youths; Nesi is no longer to be seen as unique in this. There can be considerable debate about the roles of these societies, as male bonding organizations, societies that might rescue young males from idleness and a life of sodomy, or encourage it, as training grounds for musicians and composers. Lorenzo Polizzotto's chapter here reinforces Eisenbichler's views of the significant interlinking of patrician and artisan youths in such societies, for political, social, and cultural purposes. Elliott Horowitz has already interestingly contributed to our knowledge about similar Jewish confraternities, especially documenting a youth fraternity started in Asti in 1619 that occupied and educated adolescents and prepared them for marriage.[17]

Diversification came through the new philanthropy (p. 25 below). The widening of philanthropic activity, its extension to society outside the fraternity and immediate family, attracted different kinds of members, either seeking a soul-saving philanthropic role, or preferential treatment as members.

CONFRATERNITIES AND THE REINTERPRETATION OF RENAISSANCE RELIGION AND SOCIETY

Since the 1950s historians have increasingly seen the Burckhardian Renaissance as a great deal more enthusiastically religious, less "individualistic", less pagan. While anti-clericalism might have been both a literary topos and a social reality, it is recognized that Christian devotion could remain strong where it had been before, and might have been enhanced in remoter areas. The nature of the Christian beliefs, the rituals and language changed, under the impact of humanistic scholarship and literature – seen for example in the attitudes to death and the body, the conduct of funerals, the developing of consoling funerals, as studied by Sharon Strocchia for Florence.[18] In major cities at least episcopal and monastic leadership probably declined in favor of more civic and lay centered religious devotion and celebration, as Nicholas Terpstra's study

---

[17] Eisenbichler, *The Boys*, "Angelo Poliziano," "Il ruolo," and "Strutture;" Weissman, "Sacred Eloquence;" cf. Niccoli "Compagnie di bambini," on dangerous children needing saving! Horowitz, "Jewish Youth Confraternity."   [18] Strocchia, *Death and Ritual*.

of Bologna argued. Confraternity studies have contributed to this understanding of changing Christian attitudes and behavior, and an appreciation of corporate behavior; just as they have benefited from the sociological and anthropological trends in general historical interpretation.
Many fifteenth-century Italian cities continued to be riven by factional
strife; corporate bodies such as confraternities – like kinship and neighborhood groups – could both help cohere such factions and be the means
of overcoming conflicts, and be part of peace moves. Jennifer Rondeau's
chapter below on various late medieval cases (mainly in Tuscany), interestingly develops the implications in Giovanna Casagrande's earlier study
of a confraternity protecting the Virgin's Ring as a peace-keeping gesture
in Perugia, which was one of the most faction-ridden cities in the later
fifteenth and early sixteenth centuries.[19]

An appreciation of the complexity and diversity of Florentine fraternity life, and Florentine Christianity, has been and continues to be
fostered by studies of the Medici – Lorenzo de'Medici in particular.
Whether analyzing Medicean political manipulation over neighborhoods
to obtain political support through complex patronage systems, or seeking to unravel the nature of Medicean cultural patronage, confraternities
have come into play – as Polizzotto here further demonstrates. We now
have a better idea of which Medici were members of fraternities (whether
active or not), and their relationship to supporters. Dynamic religious and
social roles for Laudesi confraternities in a "working class," non-
Medicean (possibly anti-Medicean) neighborhood of Florence is (con-
troversially) alleged in a study by Nicholas Eckstein. The attempts to
close down Florentine confraternities, then revive them under new
control and influence reflect the successes and failures of such bodies to
suit certain factions; or to produce some sort of harmony. We know
much more about their relationship to the production of various plays
and the performance of music. Medicean influence might have been a
mixed blessing, as Nerida Newbigin has argued; at times stimulating
artistic and religious creativity, but also undermining fraternal independence and vitality through excessive political manipulation.[20]

The importance of confraternity processions, parading with banners
and emblems, with singers and musicians, candles and torches (whether
in some thanksgiving, or to placate God's apparent wrath), is much better

[19] Terpstra, *Lay Confraternities*; cf. my review in *Journal of Ecclesiastical History* 48 (1997): 359–61;
Casagrande, "Compagnia del S.Anello;" cf. Black, "The Baglioni," and "Perugia".
[20] Black, *Italian Confraternities*, esp. 40–1; Eisenbichler, "Congregazione dei Neri", "Confraternity of
the Blacks", "Plays", and *The Boys*; Trexler, *Public Life*, esp. 407, 411–14, and "Charity;"
Polizotto, "Confraternities, conventicles;" Sebregondi, "Lorenzo de'Medici;" Kent, "The
Buonomini;" Eckstein, *Green Dragon*, and see Trevor Dean's review of it, *English Historical Review*
112 (1997): 727–8; Hatfield, "The Magi;" Newbigin, "Piety and Politics," esp. 24, 37–9.

appreciated. We now have literary historians providing information about plays and sacred representations that were performed in Tuscan and Umbrian cities as well as Rome, and have a better understanding of how confraternities contributed to the religious spectacle that was a major part of Renaissance Christianity, and remained so in altered forms into the Catholic Reform and Baroque periods. Then public plays might have been curtailed, but elaborate Forty Hour (*Quarantore*) devotions, with massive scenic sets, mirrors and light effects were constructed to honor the Host, adored by well-ordered processions of worshippers who came to hear sermons and pray. For the Renaissance period the interlocking of the cultural and social aspects were given prominence in an important collections of essays edited by Timothy Verdon and John Henderson in 1990; much of this focused on Florence.[21]

It is clear from various studies for Florence, Venice and Rome that through the fifteenth and sixteenth centuries the medieval interest in singing and theatricals in confraternities was elaborately developed; the display was affected by moves towards greater ostentation to enhance reputation and fame (whether of the individual or a corporate body), an elaboration of texts by the greater involvement of more literate members of society, and the music by increased promotion of polyphonic music styles brought in from the Netherlands. The musical trends in particular could lead to a tension or division between the professionals and the amateurs, with the "normal" confraternity members having less important participation, as Eisenbichler's recent book shows. The singing of *Laude* had been reinvigorated in Florence by Savonarola and his supporters; as in other areas his martyrdom failed to burn out his influence, and musical reforms in this area were carried forward into the new spirituality in later sixteenth-century Florence, Milan, and Rome, into the Oratorian movement of San Girolamo in Rome, and into the development of religious opera, aided by committed composers like Giovanni Animuccia and Emilio dei Cavalieri.[22]

[21] Verdon and Henderson (eds.), *Christianity and the Renaissance*, esp. Barr, "Music and Spectacle," Newbigin, "Word made Flesh," Ventrone, "Religious Spectacle," Weissman, "Sacred Eloquence;" cf. also for contributions to theatrical and ceremonial aspects through to the Counter Reformation: Eisenbichler, "Nativity," and "Playwright;" Esposito, "Apparati" and "Gonfalone;" Falvey, "Dramatic Traditions" and "Italian Saint Play;" Newbigin, "Piety and politics;" Sensi, "Fraternite disciplinate;" Weil, "Forty Hours;" Wisch, "Passion of Christ", "The Colloseum," and "Roman Church Triumphant;" Hill, "Oratory Music in Florence," esp. no. 3.
[22] Fenlon, "Music and Spirituality;" Wilson, *Music and Merchants*.

THE IMPACT OF CATHOLIC REFORM AND
COUNTER-REFORMATION

Confraternities both helped the promotion of Catholic Reform from the late fifteenth century, through the Tridentine and post-Tridentine periods, and were changed in activity, attitude, organization and patronage by the changing religious mood and procedures. It is now clear that the Oratory of Divine Love promoted by Ettore Vernazza in Rome was central to Catholic Reform from the 1490s, not only leading to the Theatine Order, but to a whole range of fraternities and hospitals, promoting care of syphilitics and other "incurables", and eucharistic devotion. As Edoardo Grendi has indicated, Genoa saw a major cult of the Holy Sacrament in the later fifteenth century, which was taken up by a number of youth fraternities in the early 1500s.[23] Vittorino Meneghin and others have revealed there were similar philanthropic-eucharistic fraternities in cities like Brescia, Feltre, Ferrara and Verona, which also fostered the philanthropic spiritual movements that responded to the social-economic crises of the Italian war period, and the theological struggles of the Reformation.[24] Florentine youth, in and out of fraternities, helped promote the Savonarolan revolution with long-term impacts on the spiritual values of reform movements through the sixteenth century, as Polizzotto has most recently emphasized.[25] In the early 1500s in Venice new spiritual forces provided a launch pad for both Rosary devotion in Italy (to become a major contributor to female spirituality and social role-playing), and Sacrament confraternities that were also to become central to the new religious reform in sixteenth-century Italy. In Venice, as Richard Mackenney indicates below, the initiatives for both Rosary and Sacrament societies were primarily lay, and not subject to official church or state leadership or initial fashioning, while elsewhere the ecclesiastical stimulus was much greater. Reforming bishops like Giberti in Verona and Zanetti in Bologna fostered parochial devotional fraternities ahead of Tridentine legislation and post-Tridentine organization. A study of Matteo Guerra, a saintly reformer in Siena, shows both how clerical congregations and lay confraternities could interlock, and thoughts on the Eucharist, religious education and concern for poor neighbors mingle in the new mid-century reforming mood.[26]

Many Tridentine reformers were suspicious of lay fraternities, and Tridentine legislation sought to impose episcopal control over their

---

[23] Arrizabalaga et al., *The Great Pox*, esp. 145–70; Paschini, *Tre Ricerche*, esp. 11–32; Solfaroli Camillocci, "Divino Amore;" Grendi, "Società dei giovani."

[24] Meneghin "Due Compagnie;" Angelozzi, *Confraternite laicali*, 172–83.

[25] Polizzotto, *The Elect Nation*, esp. 117–23; Polizzotto, "Confraternities, conventicles."

[26] Black, *Italian Confraternities*, 29–30, 190–2; Rosa, "Pietà mariana;" Nardi, "Matteo Guerra."

foundation, their statutes, and their fulfilment of testamentary disposi-
tions. Others saw fraternities as valuable agencies for controlling welfare
for the deserving, and providing a new parochial education for the
populace. Much confraternity scholarship has consolidated our knowledge of the ways post–Tridentine religious and social life was fostered and
monitored through confraternities. As I have recently argued, the evidence is conflicting on the ways parish priests and confraternities interac-
ted. There is no doubt that the new approaches to parish-led reform
fostered numerous confraternities – notably Sacrament, Eucharistic,
Name of God, Rosary, and Christian Doctrine fraternities. Parochial
initiatives could generate enthusiasm in some parishes, but have little
popular following in others. While much impetus for new foundations
came from the reforming bishops and their deputies, lay members of
society – suspicious of the clergy – continued to promote new foundations. Strong local lay feelings could lead to attempts to break away from
the parish church, and clerical domination. Claudio Bernardi's Chapter
below further indicates that the imposition of parochial authority could
generate considerable tension, whether with civic authorities or between
the new fraternities like those of the Holy Sacrament, and traditional
societies still representing medieval and lay spirituality. Angelo Torre's
chapter adds to his earlier work showing the complexity of parochial–fraternity relations, and different kinds of religious communities
in the later post-Tridentine period . It is interesting to note how Pentecostal fraternities (combining an annual feast and some charitable work),
largely associated with French and Swiss fraternal movements, persisted
in Piedmont despite the reform tendencies of post-Tridentine bishops
and Visitors.[27] Evidence from Rome, the Kingdom of Naples, Piedmont,
Umbria, and Tuscany, suggests that after a period of profitable cooper-
ation between reformed parochial systems and confraternities in the
immediate post-tridentine decades, tensions and problems developed
through the seventeenth and eighteenth century, such that fraternities
generally ceased to be puppets or agents of the clergy. This might
undermine good religious practice on the one hand, but forestall excess-
ively conformist social control on the other; fraternities could help pay
for parish churches and their decoration, but also totally disrupt parochial
life and organization.[28]

---

[27] Black, "European Confraternities" (forthcoming), will develop this point.

[28] Black, "Confraternities and the Parish;" see also Black, "Perugia," 443–9; Bertoldi Lenoci,
"Sociabilità;" Casagrande, "Ricerche;" De Sandre Gasparini, *Contadini*; Fiorani, "L'esperienza"
and "Visite;" Prosperi, "Parrocchie;" Russo, "Parrocchie," esp. 234–37, 245–7, 315; Sannino,
"Confraternite potentine," 125, 136; D'Addario, *Aspetti*, 319–20; Torre, *Il comsumo*, and see
Roisin Cossar's review of it in *Confraternitas* 7, 2 (Fall 1996): 14–15; Proietti Pedetta, *Confraternite di
Assisi*; Torre, "Ceremonial Life," and especially his very valuable "Politics" which unfortunately

For reformers like Borromeo, Paleotti and Bellarmine effective reform depended on better religious knowledge, to be imparted through schools of Christian Doctrine, and the dissemination of suitable religious texts, taking advantage of the growth of cheaper printing. Recent research, led among others by Guerrino Pellicia and Paul Grendler has given some insight into the role of confraternities and schools of Christian Doctrine as teaching organizations and improvers of literacy; though my sampling of some Roman records highlighted serious organizational problems that suggest caution about some other optimistic views of the success of such schools.[29]

Also lay confraternities have been increasingly studied for their work in the religious education of both novices and full adult members. As Konrad Eisenbichler has pointed out, youth confraternities earlier had significantly developed the religious education of the youth – independent of the influence of the parish priest. Valuable work – focusing primarily on Borromean Lombardy – is under way on the literature available for confraternity members, what was encouraged and what controlled, and what might be solicited from a printer like Vincenzo Girardone by the confraternity brothers and sisters themselves. As Danilo Zardin stresses, in this region at least this literature and education were part of a campaign to influence all family life and morality through the confraternities. Some of the impetus came from the Jesuits, but initiatives came from within confraternities as well.[30]

The new or reformed religious Orders had rival roles to play in the formation and activity of confraternities from the sixteenth century. Though the massive local study of Callisto Urbanelli has alerted us to the work of Capuchins with confraternities, it is the ongoing work on the many sided contributions of the Jesuits that has been most noticeable, from the works of Pasquale Lopez, Vincenzo Paglia, John O'Malley, Danilo Zardin, and research students in Lombardy and Toronto. Louis Châtellier has emphasized the networking of Jesuit companies and confraternities across Europe, reinforcing their influence. Given the diversity

---

had escaped my attention when writing my talk and chapter on parochial problems.

[29] Pellicia, "Scuole;" Grendler, *Schooling*, esp. ch. 12; cf. ch.10:3 in my *Italian Confraternities*, and *Confraternite Italiane* , and now my "Confraternities and the parish," at note 27; ASVR, ADC, palchetto 168, vol. 417, Congregationi 1599–1608. A new book by Gilberto Aranci, *Formazione religiosa* (which I have not yet seen), on Ippolito Galantini and the Florentine Christian Doctrine teaching seems to be taking important new steps in interpreting post-Tridentine fraternities, under clerical control; see Review by Mary Watt in *Confraternitas* 8, 2 (Fall 1997): 17–18.

[30] Zardin, "Il rilancio;" esp . 110–16, 129; Zardin, "Confraternite e 'congregazioni';" Bottoni, "Libri e lettura;" Stevens, "Vincenzo Girardone," esp. 644–50; Eisenbichler, "Angelo Poliziano," "Il ruolo," and *The Boys*, esp. ch. 10 "The teaching of Christian Doctrine;" Weissman, "Sacred Eloquence;" Rusconi, "Pratica cultuale."

of their attitudes and activities generally they contributed to the diversification of confraternal worship and behavior; from penitential exercises,
Quarantore celebrations, to advocacy of the Seven Acts of Mercy as a
guide to philanthropic activity, which might include running prisons.[31]
Lance Lazar's and Mark Lewis' chapters below develop from this background of Jesuit inspired fraternal activity and devotion.

   Cultural historians have added considerably to our knowledge of the
artistic contributions of confraternities, and the use of the arts as part of
their religious life and propaganda. Graham Dixon and Noel O'Regan
have revealed how important music was for the religious devotion of
Roman confraternity members (as well as sometimes for visiting outsiders, and for the development of musical careers and styles), as Denis
Arnold and now Jonathan Glixon have shown for Venice. For Florence,
Konrad Eisenbichler's book on the Archangel Raphael develops from
John Hill's earlier studies of Florentine oratory music. Music made a
considerable impact on pilgrims to Rome, particularly those coming for
Jubilees, who were welcomed, guided (spiritually and physically) by the
host confraternities of SS. Trinità, the Gonfalone, and Della Morte. Some
of the more spectacular music was linked to the Forty-Hour devotions
(Quarantore), for which leading artists like Gian Lorenzo Bernini and
Pietro della Cortona could provide elaborate scenery and light effects, as
part of Baroque illusionism.[32] In years between much publicized celebrations in San Lorenzo in Damaso, a philanthropic fraternity such as the
Soccorso dei Poveri might organize a Quarantore celebration using lesser
artists and musicians.[33]

   Art historians have paid increasing attention to the role of confraternities as patrons of chapels, altars and altarpieces – as well as the creators of
sometimes architecturally adventurous free-standing Oratories. While

---

[31] Urbanelli, *Cappuccini*; Lopez, "Confraternite laicali;" Paglia, *La Morte Confortata* and "*Pietà dei
Carcerati;*" Châtellier, *The Devout*; O'Malley, *First Jesuits*, esp. ch. 5; Zardin, *Confraternita e Vita*;
Rurale, "L'attività caritativa;" cf. Index of my *Italian Confraternities* under Capuchins and Jesuits;
De Molen (ed.), *Religious Orders*, see ch. 5, O'Malley's "The Society of Jesus," and otherwise the
Index under confraternities.

[32] Arnold, *Giovanni Gabrieli*, 188–210; "Scuola di San Rocco" and "A Venetian confraternity;" Barr,
"Music and Spectacle;" Black, *Italian Confraternities*, esp. 117–21, 272–3; Dixon, "Lenten
Devotions;" Eisenbichler, *The Boys*, esp. ch. 18; Glixon, "Music and Ceremony," "The *Scuole*,"
and "Public ceremony;" Hill, "Oratory Music;" Hammond, *Music and Spectacle*, 148–56, 159–61;
O'Regan, "Palestrina" and *Institutional Patronage*; Weil, "The Devotion;" Weisz,
"*Caritas/Controriforma*," and *Pittura e Misericordia*. An exhibition coinciding with the Edinburgh
International Festival of 1998 ("Effigies and Ecstasies: Roman Baroque Sculpture and Design in the
Age of Bernini"), has highlighted some Quarantore celebrations and surviving designs for them;
see my "'Exceeding Every Expression'."

[33] ASVR, Congregazione del Soccorso dei Poveri in San Lorenzo in Damaso, Congregazione e
Decreti, vol. 4 (1617–29): on 12 March 1629 paid for artists Giulio de Bonis and Giuseppe Buglia,
and *maestro di capella* Giovanni Giacomo for a Quarantore celebration.

their understanding of the artefacts has gained considerably from the work of other historians with less specialized interests, we have benefited from many books, articles and conference papers by art-history specialists who have taken a refreshingly broad approach to their researches and artistic interpretation. So far the interactions have born most fruit in our understanding of the confraternal world of Venice – whether in the Scuole Grandi or in the chapels and altarpieces of the *scuole piccole* – and Rome. Through the sixteenth century and beyond, the artistic environment for confraternity members, at least in the wealthier and better patronized societies, could be important not only for emotional uplift and introspective contemplation, but also for didactic purposes; helping to teach (as in earlier periods) about the Virgin, Christ, and the Saints, but also about the need for charitable works of many kinds. Here especially significant was Paul Hills' study of Tintoretto's paintings for Venetian Sacrament confraternities, emphasizing the links between the Eucharist and helping the poor (whether old men or nursing mothers), in seeking salvation.[34]

CONFRATERNITIES IN RELATION TO THE SOCIAL AND POLITICAL ORDERS

Attitudes of secular as well as religious authorities to confraternities were ambivalent. Such social groupings, bound by rules, often by oaths of secrecy, could be seen as threats to regimes or excluded social groups. They could be potential centers of opposition to the elite or a ruling faction, as frequently alleged in Florence in the fifteenth and sixteenth centuries; if associated with artisan and worker groups they could be suspect as kinds of trade unions against employers; as male bonding societies (discussed below by Jennifer Rondeau in other contexts), they might be accused of fostering the great vice of sodomy, following Michael Rocke's work.[35] It remains to be seen whether the growth of women's sororities were or could be seen as powerful feminist organizations threatening male roles, as well as being undoubtedly important vehicles for female religiosity (discussed below by Giovanna Casagrande).

[34] Hills, "Piety and Patronage;" cf. my *Italian Confraternities*, ch. 11, "Confraternity buildings and their decoration." Other key works in this context to be highlighted: Cope, *Venetian Chapel*; Eisenbichler, *The Boys*, ch. 19, "Art in the Confraternity;" Fortini Brown, "Honor and Necessity;" Henneberg, *L'oratorio*; Humfrey, *The Altarpiece*, and "Competitive Devotions;" Humfrey and Mackenney, "Trade guilds;" *La Liguria delle Casacce*; Sebregondi, *Tre confraternite*; Weisz, "*Caritas/Controriforma*" and *Pittura e Misericordia*; Wisch, "The Passion."

[35] See my *Italian Confraternities*, 38–43, 45–7, 58–62; Rocke, *Forbidden Friendships*, esp. 187–8; Weissman, *Ritual Brotherhood*, esp. 80–105, 128–9; also on fraternities and male bonding, Clawson, "Fraternalism."

Modern research has highlighted different trends in different kinds of fraternities – towards exclusivity and inclusivity. The increased stress on nobility and gentility from the late fifteenth century encouraged the creation of fraternities for the elite only. On the other hand the Catholic reform stress on parochial-based societies fostered the idea that confraternities should co-ordinate people from most levels of society, and both sexes. As the works of Weissman, Terpstra, Olivieri Baldissarri, Zardin, Eisenbichler, and others have shown or suggested, authorities might encourage a compromise whereby confraternities with a socially diverse membership might be supervized and controlled by a social or godly elite, to prevent political, economic or religious subversion.[36] The migration of people into a few large cities, whether from remoter parts of Italy or further afield, saw the expansion of "national" fraternities that provided a social and religious focus for the incomers, fostering job opportunities, and providing a charitable safety net if needed.[37]

A growing emphasis on nobility and honor also encouraged a concern for helping the "poveri vergognosi" or ashamed poor, whether by specialist fraternities or others that felt obliged to give some priority to assisting secretly those too ashamed to seek assistance openly. The Venetian Fraterna Grande of San Antonin, specifically helping the *poveri vergognosi*, debated the issue of shame: "This word shame from which derives shame-faced at times signifies the infamy and dishonour that comes from vice, and from badly done things ... Conversely at times it signifies a sensitivity [*rispetto*] or timidity to do or say or receive something that brings proof or dishonour to us and this sensitivity comes from a modesty and candour [*ingenuità*], and is numbered among the things of praise."[38] We know certainly that the poveri vergognosi included not just poor nobles, but others of "respectability," and therefore capable of shame, further down the social scale; this was certainly true of one of the prototypical fraternities helping the poveri vergognosi, the Florentine Buonomini di San Martino, which initially in the early fifteenth century targeted artisans and respectable workers, as Amleto Spicciani and Dale

---

[36] Eisenbichler, *The Boys*, esp. ch. 8; Fanti, *La Chiesa*, 85–95; Olivieri Baldissarri, *"Poveri Prigioni,"* esp. 103–5, 114–16, 225–6; Terpstra, *Lay Confraternities*, esp. 28–30, 124–5, 139–44, 189, 198; Weissman, *Ritual Brotherhood*, 58; Zardin, "Le confraternite," 88–9. Cf. my *Italian Confraternities*, 88–9.

[37] Black, *Italian Confraternities*, 43–45; Maas, *The German Community* is a major study in this context.

[38] Jonathan Walker, working on his Cambridge University Ph.D. ("Honour and Venetian Nobles, c.1500 – c.1650"), kindly supplied me with this quotation from the Fraterna's *Universal Compendium* of 1529–1653. On *poveri vergognosi* see Black, *Italian Confraternities*, 147–50, 160, 169–74; Kent, "The Buonomini;" Ricci, "Povertà, vergogna;" Pugliese, "Buonomini;" Spicciani, "Poveri vergognosi;" Trexler, "Charity;" Pullan, *Rich and Poor*, 267–8; Henderson, *Piety and Charity*, 389–97; Rurale, "L'attività," esp. 267–72.

Kent have stressed. Given that they had to be helped secretly – and that confraternity brethren were capable of considerable discretion – it is very difficult to discover who specifically was helped and by how much. As Jonathan Walker's thesis will show the Venetian poor nobles could go to considerable lengths in deception to secure assistance – and possibly to exaggerate their degree of poverty and raggedness.

The chief organizing system of urban society in the late medieval and early modern period was the guild (*arte*). While it has been recognized that artisan and trading guilds might have strong religious and charitable aspects, and be in some dimensions also "confraternities", it has only really been in Venice – where there were special legal conditions requiring economic guilds and their members to have religious–charitable fraternities (*scuole*) – that they have been fully studied, notably by Richard Mackenney. Even if from the sixteenth century economic guilds declined in importance, I suggest religious aspects might be worth pursuing further. My brief sampling of late seventeenth- and eighteenth-century Roman guild records suggests that some continued to have a significant religious and welfare dimension, for themselves – and for saving condemned prisoners.[39]

Catholic Reform innovations and enthusiasms could and did lead in various directions; both laity and leading church reformers like Borromeo sought "revolutionary" change in moral and social attitudes and behavior. As Danilo Zardin argues below, the need of the political and social elites, backed by traditional inertia, tended to prevail. Nicholas Terpstra also reminds us in some of his works that government interests might easily encourage the philanthropic enterprises to concentrate on the more restrictive and conservative aspects of welfare. Claudio Bernardi, Dale Kent, and Konrad Eisenbichler have recently stressed how members of ruling families saw the value of sponsoring confraternities, if well controlled, for regulated philanthropy, patronage control, and glorification of their family image.[40]

SOCIAL WELFARE AND SOCIAL CONTROL

Much exciting work in recent decades has exemplified how early modern fraternities expanded the scope of philanthropic activity, for members

---

[39] Mackenney, "Continuity and Change," *Tradesmen and Traders*, and "The Guilds of Venice;" Pullan, "The *Scuole;*" ASR CII, Arti e Mestieri: Busta 6 , *Bombardieri di Castello* and *Caffetieri* (foglio 12); Busta 25, *Muratori, Stoccatori, Imbiancatori,* and *Musicanti* (foglio 56); Busta 19, *Lanari.*

[40] Robert Buranello's Review of Bernardi, *Carnevale* (which I have not yet consulted), in *Confraternitas* 7/2 (Fall 1996): 10–11; Kent, "The Buonomini;" Eisenbichler, *The Boys,* esp. ch.20 on the obsequies of Cosimo II Medici.

and their relatives, but also for outsiders, as Italy faced crises in the social order, notably occasioned by war, dearth and disease from 1494. Brian Pullan's studies of the Venetian Scuole Grandi awakened interest in philanthropic activities, as did the wider debates about poverty, and conflicting attitudes to the poor and remedies under the "new philanthropy". Pullan sees the confraternities as "the most adaptable organization for dispensing charity" in the period.[41] Some later medieval fraternities did exercise charity beyond the provision of suitable funerals for members and immediate relatives; in providing dowries; in running small hospices or hospitals for sick travelers and pilgrims, unsupported pregnant women, the old and destitute; in issuing alms in food or money; in (by the fifteenth century) escorting prisoners to their execution in a comforting manner. By the sixteenth century the care of prisoners, whether condemned to death or not, was a major activity for some confraternities, as various important specialist studies have shown. As Nicholas Terpstra and Giovanni Romeo have argued, not only did the comforting of the condemned (securing a contrite confession and penitence) become a specialist activity of elite fraternity members, as in Bologna or Naples, but their work could be seen as enhancing elitist social control and discipline, and Inquisitorial-led morality, as much as charitably helping poor prisoners and their families.[42] A wide range of confraternities, at least in the Papal State, gained the privilege of securing the release of prisoners from execution or the galleys (with some possible financial gain to the fraternity's finances from the lucky "saved"); surviving petitions can throw interesting light on attitudes to crime and punishment, as my own samplings for Rome revealed.[43]

Much research has been done on confraternity involvement in hospitals, hospices, orphanages, conservatories for vulnerable children and women, and in helping the poor in their homes or at oratory and church doors, and in providing dowries for marriage or nunnery entrance. We face many frustrations in not knowing the amount of input from frater-

[41] Pullan, *Rich and Poor*, and *Poverty and Charity*, which usefully reprints his major articles, including "Support and Redeem" (no. 5), from which I quote, 183. Cf. my *Italian Confraternities*, chs. 7–10; Cavallo, *Charity and Power*, "Patterns" and "Conceptions;" Zardin (ed.), *Città e Poveri*, which includes Pullan's "Povertà, Carità;" Grendi "Pauperismo" and "Ideologia;" Weissman, "Brothers and Strangers."

[42] Black, *Italian Confraternities*, 217–23; Edgerton, *Pictures and Punishment*; Fanti, "La conforteria;" Olivieri Baldissarri, "*Poveri Prigioni*"; Paglia, *La morte confortata*, "*Pietà dei Carcerati*," and "Le confraternite;" Prosperi, "Il sangue;" Romeo, *Aspettando il boia*; Scarabello, "La fraterna;" Terpstra, "Piety and Punishment;" Pullan, "Charity;" Weisz, *Pittura e Misericordia*; Mascia, *Confraternita dei Bianchi*.

[43] ASR, CIII, Confraternite, Buste 1968, 1971, 1973. I discussed some of this material in a paper, "Welfare and the Enclosed," to the Twenty-Seventh International Congress of Medieval Studies, Kalamazoo 1992.

nity members, whether in visiting or directly assisting the needy, sick and wounded, or in raising money – as opposed to appointing and intermittently supervising paid officials. Whether in evidence from the period, or in modern analyses, it is often difficult to isolate confraternal contributions to institutions dealing with the poor. We also need to know more about who was helped by different institutions; who received dowries or money; who were taken into institutions; whether help was primarily for local networks of neighbors or kinship groups. There have been some significant local studies seeking various solutions to such problems.[44]

Among the most interesting and controversial investigations of early modern confraternity activity have been those concerned with vulnerable girls and women – dealing with repentant prostitutes and their daughters, abandoned children, battered wives, and so forth. Debates concern the extent to which institutions shifted attention from the really poor and vulnerable, to those less needy (and potentially less troublesome); and the extent to which such institutions were more concerned with strict male control and morality, than with loving care for one's neighbor. But as some of us detect, there could be variations between those institutions preoccupied with rigid control, and those more concerned with easing the path of the innocent or sinful, the vulnerable or the temptress, back into family society.[45]

Various works have emphasized that fraternal assistance to the poor and needy was discriminatory, favoring "deserving" (very young, old, female) over "undeserving" (idle able-bodied, the morally vicious and criminal); fraternities have been shown to be involved in "social control" by institutionalizing and disciplining the undeserving in "hospitals" or conservatories that might be prison-like or strict convents.[46] Confraternity brothers and sisters, who seldom came from the poorest sectors of society (unless they were in a fraternity for licensed beggars), might not want to sully themselves with contact with the most dangerous and disgusting orders of society. Some voluntarily followed Jesuits or Capuchins in dealing with the messiest sick in hospitals, and the gentlemanly brethren of a Compagnia di San Michele in Florence were chosen to visit the poor during the great plague of 1630; they were responsible

---

[44] My *Italian Confraternities*, ch. 7:3 ("The preferred poor"), and Ch. 9 faced such issues, and indicated major and minor studies. See now also Zardin "Carità;" Gazzini, "Solidarietà vicinale;" D'Amelia, Grendi, "Ideologia;" D'Amelia, "Economia familiare;" Henderson, *Piety and Charity*, part 2 "Charity;" Navarrini and Belfanti, "Problema della povertà;" Terpstra. *Lay Confraternities*, 193–205, and his "Apprenticeship;" see note 45 below.

[45] Cavallo, *Charity and power*, ch. 4; Ciammitti, "Fanciulle" and "Quanto costa;" Cohen, *Women's Asylums*; my *Italian Confraternities*, 206–13.

[46] A key specific study was Calori, *Una iniziativa*; Terpstra, *Lay Confraternities*, 203–5; cf. Erba, "Pauperismo;" Grendi, "Pauperismo;" Fatica, "Reclusione."

for a report revealing "a degree and diffusion of poverty absolutely unimaginable," and they organized the supply of new clean mattresses for thousands of poor.[47]

The shift of a confraternity to involvement in philanthropic activities could change its complexion; the receipt of a legacy to offer a mere two dowries a year was enough to change the Urbino Corpus Domini confraternity from one primarily for gentlemen and citizens (and the budding painter Federico Barocci), to one including the poor, miserable and begging. This suggests that further thought is needed on motivations for joining fraternities, and for offering philanthropy; join to do something for one's soul and for "neighbours", or to receive?[48]

Since the modern expansion of confraternity studies started with consideration of the 1260 events it is hardly surprising that the last decades of the early modern period have often been neglected. However the work of historians dealing with southern Italy in particular has emphasized that fraternities continued to be founded into the eighteenth century. But also, as Mackenney's chapter on Venice shows, a northern city seemingly replete with medieval and early Catholic Reform scuole could find room for more in the eighteenth century. Other scholars like Bottoni, Eisenbichler, Hill, and Zardin have thrown light on northern fraternities. They emphasize the ambivalent position that fraternities continued to be founded or relaunched, yet came under attack (as Eisenbichler's Chapter here partly shows) from "enlightened" thinkers, rulers and ministers for perpetuating "superstitious" rites and cults, for wasting legacies, for encouraging the idle through charity, and for undermining the leadership and control of the parish priest (as Peter Leopold of Tuscany argued). Confraternity funds might also be tempting for ministers wanting to improve education.[49]

From thirty years of research we have realized more obviously that confraternities were very diverse in membership, motivation, and activity; they generated opposition and enthusiasm, and they adapted to wider political, social, and religious changes. They still leave many puzzles to be

---

[47] Cipolla, *Fighting the Plague,* 15

[48] Moranti, *Corpus Domini,* 36, 227. Sandra Cavallo, though not particularly concerned with fraternities has some valuable reflections on attitudes to charity, and how historians have (mis)handled interpretations, in her "Motivations of Benefactors".

[49] Bertoldi Lenoci (ed.) *Confraternite Pugliese* has many relevant articles; Black, "Confraternities and the Parish," at n. 43 and 44; Bottoni, "Confraternite milanesi;" Eisenbichler, *The Boys,* esp. ch. 21 "The Final Years;" Hill, "Oratory Music," esp. 3: "The Confraternities;" Nardi, "Matteo Guerra," which also deals with eighteenth century; Sannino, "Confraternite potentine" and others in Paglia (ed.), *Confraternite e Meridione*; Torre, "Politics Cloaked" and "Village Ceremonial;" Zardin, "Confraternite e 'congregationi'," and "Italia settentrionale."

investigated, and new areas to be researched. In all periods we need much more detail about who where members, how active they really were, and when. To understand the socio-political importance of confraternities it would help to identify the normal active members (not just a few elite noble men and women), and study what else they did in their community. We might better understand then how far they were agencies of political, godly, and moral control. While some papers here are furthering our knowledge about women and confraternities, there is a great more to be done in discovering the nature and degree of female participation.

Catholic Reform saw expansion, a shift of activities and devotions, and supposedly more outside control. It would be helpful to know how much lay voluntarism remained, how much parish priests and other clergy took control. Southern Italy saw a major expansion of devotional fraternities under Catholic Reform leadership and pressures, at least as far as names, altars, and dedications tell us, but much needs to be learned about the extent of activity that followed; and the extent of philanthropic work conducted in a largely poverty-stricken society. As I was asked at a recent seminar in London, were or are southerners reluctant to join corporate groups like guilds and confraternities voluntarily, and if so, why? Is the southern expansion from the late sixteenth century almost entirely due to leadership and imposition from above, by bishops and Jesuits?

This general chapter should help to contextualize the way my co-authors are building on past approaches and breaking new ground, even if still more for the north and centre, than for the southern Italy.

2

HOMOSOCIALITY AND CIVIC (DIS)ORDER IN LATE MEDIEVAL ITALIAN CONFRATERNITIES

JENNIFER FISK RONDEAU

Civic and spiritual peace were goals explicitly sought by the people of late medieval urban Italy, yet in spite of enormous efforts by secular and ecclesiastical authorities alike, and the expenditure of enormous amounts of creative energy on the establishment of new political structures and new laws, and the proscription of old forms of vendetta-provoking behavior, peace continued to elude its pursuers during the thirteenth and fourteenth centuries.[1] This essay examines some of the roles late medieval confraternities played in promoting peace in Italian cities, as they co-operated with communal authorities in their mutual concern for civic order; it also reveals that precisely in the kinds of co-operation they maintained with structures of communal power confraternities ultimately posed as much of a challenge to peace as they did a guarantee of its promotion. This ambivalent relationship between confraternal and communal peacemaking reflected similar tensions between other public groups, all of them ultimately grounded in the inevitable strains of a fundamentally homosocial society.

In 1216, an anonymous Florentine chronicler tells us, a dispute arose, initially between two men, but ultimately between two family factions.

The following archival abbreviations will be used in the notes that follow: *Archivio di Stato di Firenze* (*ASF*); *Compagnie Religiose Soppresse* (*CRS*); Biblioteca Nazionale di Firenze, Fondo Magliabechiano (Mgˡ); Bibliotheque de l'Arsenal de Paris, ms. 8521 (Ars); Biblioteca Comunale di Cortona, ms. 91 (Cort); Biblioteca Comunale di Arezzo, Fraternita dei Laici ms. 180 (Aret); Biblioteca Trivulziana di Milano, ms. 535 (Triv). These last five references are to conventional abbreviations for some of the major Italian lauda collections.

[1] So, for example, Dante's *De Monarchia*, or the *Defensor Pacis* of Marsilius of Padua; Giordano da Pisa, discussed in Del Corno, *Giordano da Pisa*, or Remigio de' Girolami, in Rupp, *Ordo Caritatis* and Davis, "An Early Florentine Political Theorist" are examples of early preachers involved in peace-making. See also Thompson, *Revival Preachers and Politics*; Bornstein, *The Bianchi*, esp. 162–212; Vauchez, "Une campagne de pacification"; Starn, *Contrary Commonwealth*; *Violence and Civil Disorder*, ed. Martines; Jones, "Communes and Despots".

The original parties to the dispute were Oddo Arrighi and Buondelmonte de' Buondelmonti, and their initial disagreement arose over a
point of dinner-table etiquette on the occasion of the knighting of a
member of a third family, the Mazzinghi. Peace between the two original
antagonists was initially sought, and it was agreed that Buondelmonte
should marry a niece of Oddo Arrighi, a daughter of the Amidei family.
At the urging of the wife of a member of another family, the Donati,
however, he "went to pledge troth with the girl of the Donati family; and
her of the Amidei he left waiting at the church door." Particularly given
the already strained relations between Buondelmonte and Arrighi, such a
slight could not go unchallenged. After taking counsel with friends and
relatives at the church of Santa Maria sopra Porta, Arrighi and his allies
met Buondelmonte, accompanied by his bride, on Easter morning at the
statue of Mars, and killed him. "The ambush had been in the houses of
the Amidei . . . On this day . . . for the first time new names were heard, to
wit, Guelph party and Ghibelline party."[2]

This is, in other words, a story, one of the most famous stories, about
the origins of the political dispute that was to loom so large in the next
two centuries of Italian history. As such, it is told and retold, then and
now, in an ongoing effort to understand not just this particular, albeit
influential, instance of factionalism in medieval and Renaissance urban
Italy, but also the problem of factionalism and civic disorder more
generally.[3] Yet one significant aspect of the story is often noted, but given
little substantial attention. The cause of the vendetta – the central figures
around whom were arranged both the repudiation of the marriage and
the eventual murder – was a pair of (one should perhaps say three)
women, and more precisely the marriage alliances they either negotiated
or of whose negotiations they were a part. The failed marriage negotiations – indeed the fact that they were ever undertaken at all – and the
repudiation of the Amidei girl (we never learn her name), I would like to
suggest represent an important aspect of Florentine, and Italian, society
and politics that has significant bearing on our understanding of the
invariably, although not necessarily obviously, gendered social and spiritual relations in which members of communes and confraternities alike
participated.

The important relations between historical actors in the story of the

---

[2] "Pseudo-Brunetto Latini," anonymous chronicle, in *I primi due secoli*, ed. Villari, 2, 233; Villari tr.,
The First Two Centuries of Florentine History, 173–4; *Quellen und Forschungen*, ed. Hartwig, 2, 221ff.,
English tr. repr. in Latini, *Medieval and Renaissance Florence*, 1, 106–7.

[3] Compagni, *Cronica* (I.2), ed. Del Lungo, in *RRIISS*, p. 8–12. Bornstein tr., *Dino Compagni's
Chronicle*, 7–8. Villani, *Cronica*, ed. Dragomanni, 5. 38; Dante, *Inferno* 38.106–8 and *Paradiso*,
16.136–47; Lansing, *The Florentine Magnates*, 125–6.

Buondelmonte murder are clearly marked, and replicated in successive historical accounts, as those "between men," as Eve Sedgwick has put it.[4] As such, they would appear simply to replicate what we know to have been the almost exclusively masculine quality of public life in urban Italy in the age of the communes. This masculine quality, however – these primary relations between men – are invariably mediated or triangulated at key moments by men's relations with women. Marriage negotiations were particularly important in structuring both alliances and feuds among groups of men, as well as between the individual actors – really more representatives of their clans, as we see in the case of Oddo Arrighi, who always takes counsel and acts with the assistance of his "friends and relatives" – whose quarrel sparks the Buondelmonte-Arrighi vendetta. It is the fact of this silent presence of women between men that I want to call attention to here, together with the fact that although women are always necessary to social and political relations between men, they are almost invariably silent, and often invisible (an important exception in the Buondelmonte story is the one woman who is also named, Madonna Gualdrada, wife of Messer Forese Donati, for whose daughter Buondelmonte repudiates the daughter of the Amidei – but even she is not given the power to name her daughter). The significant social relations in this story are, to borrow Sedgwick's term, homosocial. That is to say, men's strongest social ties are invariably among themselves, but those ties must ultimately be represented by, deflected onto, or negotiated by means of, ties with women. According to Sedgwick, such deflection or negotiation is compelled by the homoerotic potential of homosocial relations, a potential whose realization must be forestalled by means of the mediating figures of women.

Leaving aside only momentarily the question of a repressed homo-erotics, primary social, political, and personal bonds between men can certainly be viewed as typical of urban Italy in the late middle ages. Although the story of the Buondelmonte story is a story about the Florentine aristocracy, the homosocial relations it depicts and reproduces are to be found everywhere in the social and political history of Italy in the following three centuries. The crucial role of marriage negotiations in cementing alliances between men of all social and political classes is attested from well before the thirteenth century and down through the fifteenth century and beyond, and the dominance in public life of other mediated relations between men is even better documented, once we bother to look for it.[5] In the case of nuptial rituals, not only were most of

[4] Kosofsky Sedgwick, *Between Men*.

[5] Klapisch-Zuber, *Women, Family, and Ritual*; eadem, *La maison et le nom*; Kuehn, *Law, Family, and Women*; Klapisch and David Herlihy, *Tuscans and their Families* (additional source material and notes

the financial arrangements associated with marriage made between the male members of the bride's family (her father or a brother or brothers) and the groom, or the groom's family, but frequently the rituals surrounding betrothal and the marriage itself were enacted between the men as well, in one case including even the betrothal kiss signifying the promise of future marriage.[6] In this last case at least we do not have to look too far for a perhaps overly obvious expression of the (thinly) repressed erotic that is also an important element of Sedgwick's homosocial dynamic, but such a simplistic appropriation is not, in fact, my primary intention here. Marriage is, after all, an institution fundamentally circumscribed by the demands of power, of property and of sex – or, put another way, a fundamental institutionalization of human desire. As such, it was also an institution whose control medieval people hotly contested, whether the contest was waged between clergy and laity, men and women, people of unequal social or political status, or parents and children. And while modern scholars have rightly focused a great deal of attention on the fact that men (especially fathers) sought to control the bodies of women (especially their daughters) through marriage negotiations, the important fact that what seems to have mattered most to the men in question was what such control could do for their relations with one another has quietly been set to one side. An important corollary of that goal, however, has continued to be emphasized, and that is the fact that the concern with control was bound up with a deep-seated anxiety about its potential instability, either to be realized in practice (daughters and wives and mothers did refuse to co-operate on occasion), or to produce the desired effect (peace, stable alliances) once it was realized.

The family, then, would appear at this particular historical moment to be the primary locus for the formation of homosocial bonds and for the playing out of the necessary repression of the homoerotic desire those bonds simultaneously represent and threaten. The family was also, we must recall, viewed both theoretically and practically as the fundamental unit of society and of what we might call public order – in ways both recognizable to modern political ideology and in ways very strange to it. Families and family alliances were the groups first and most commonly associated with political factionalism; their organization and structure formed common models for other groups, such as military societies, guilds, communes, and confraternities themselves. Traditional practice and the new Aristotelian political theory grounded public association in

---

in French original, *Les toscans et leurs familles*); Molho, *Marriage Alliance*; *The Family in Italy*, ed. Kertzer and Saller; Hughes, "Representing the Family" and "Invisible Madonnas?"; Herlihy, "The Towns of Northern Italy."

[6] Hall, *The Arnolfini Betrothal*, 54 (citing Brandileone, *Saggi*), 67; Altieri, *Li nuptiali*.

the initial joining of man and wife, and as ideology such views gained currency throughout the late middle ages. Dante, so bitterly familiar with the fruits of factionalism, associated the learning of language and the good old times of peace and tranquillity with mothers rocking their children's cradles – as he also, more ambiguously, associated the recognition of common citizenship with the recognition of common language, albeit this time between members of two opposing Florentine factions.[7]

Confraternities, too, understood themselves, as the name we now give them suggests, to be structured according to family relations. They often called themselves brotherhoods, and explicitly elaborated on the meaning of ties between brothers as models for their members' relations.[8] The 1262 statutes of the *fraternitas* of Santa Maria della Misericordia in Arezzo, for example, contain a lengthy exposition of the meaning of brotherly ties between members, inflected also with the language of political association:

> People may surely claim to be gathered together in the Saviour's name when they come together at set times to carry out his will and commandment concerning mercy, and when they oblige themselves freely and unanimously to abide by certain common salutary laws for this purpose. This brotherhood of mercy, I say, derives the origin and vigour of its laws from our patriarch, the teacher of the gentiles, the apostle Paul... This brotherhood is also eagerly recommended by the prince of the apostles... The merciful works of this brotherhood are expressed and commanded by the Lord through Moses in the Old Law... How glorious and pleasing such brotherhood is, which is enlightened by such teaching and adorned with such examples![9]

The theoretical authority of the structure and the work (specifically, the works of mercy) of this brotherhood derive from the explicitly "patriarchal vigor" of Paul, Peter, and Moses; the maternal figure is supplied by Mary in her role as Mother of Mercy, the avowed patron of the brotherhood.

This particular brotherhood, interestingly and relatively unusually, in fact included "sisters," although they are not called such in the statutes. But women were permitted to join the confraternity, although their role, as in other confraternities they were permitted to join, was a truncated one. They were not required to pay the same dues, nor to attend meetings, nor were they allowed to perform any of

---

[7] *Paradiso*, 15.97–150; *Inferno* 10.   [8] See especially Chenu, "'Fraternitas'," *passim*.
[9] Meersseman, *Ordo Fraternitatis* 2, 1019; Tugwell tr., *Early Dominicans*, 438.

the confraternity's public functions, such as ritual begging or public processions. Indeed, their role seems to replicate the statutes' preoccupation with the familial model, permitting and even requiring their presence since the confraternity claims to represent and to serve the entire city and diocese of Arezzo, but making certain that their voices and roles are contained and limited within safely private, male-controlled bounds.[10]

Another example of the necessary marginalization of women in confraternity membership, one that expresses a sense of the threat of disorder (as well as order) women could also represent to the masculine order (and potential disorder) of confraternal life, is to be found a little over a century later in Florence, during the papal interdict. In 1377, the confraternity of Santa Reparata, or San Zenobi, was persuaded to admit a group of women who had petitioned the men to be allowed to join in order to be provided with spiritual guidance, which they were otherwise lacking. The men demurred at first, but finally agreed on the grounds that spiritual and social disorder would otherwise ensue, adding the proviso, however, that the women would be permitted to pray on behalf of all members of the confraternity, and to contribute money and candles to the company; the confraternity's spiritual benefits in the afterlife (most notably its rich treasury of indulgences) would accrue to them, but they would not be allowed to join in the public or social life of the confraternity. All members of the confraternity, men and women alike, were obliged to pray privately for the souls of all deceased members, men and women, but participation in its elaborate ritual devotions, public burial in its habit, material assistance in time of need, remained exclusively the prerogative of the men.[11] The simultaneous admission and marginalization of women in this company marks the men's recognition of the necessity for relations with women, and the threat an excess of those relations could pose to the primary bonds of the group, those between men. It is the telling homosocial irony of this story that the disorder created by the interdict in the first place, and represented by the women, had its origins in political disputes by the fourteenth-century heirs to precisely those Guelph and Ghibelline factions begun by the Buondelmonte murder. And it may well have been increasing pressure from other political bodies that pushed Santa Reparata into dealing with the women as it did, since its connections to the communal government, as reflected in numbers of company officers who were also members

---

[10] Meersseman, *Ordo Fraternitatis* 2, 1022; Tugwell, *Early Dominicans*, 444.
[11] *ASF, CRS* Z.1.2170 ff. 17r ff.

of Florence's chief magistracy, the priorate, were becoming greater by
the late 1370s.[12]

Class as well as gender distinctions marked patterns of confraternity
membership as well. Only a very few companies claimed the kind of
broad-based membership that the Arezzo Misericordia did in theory –
and even there in practice the company came to be run, not too
surprisingly, by the city's social and political elites. These class distinctions were invariably reinscriptions of larger social and political divisions as well. We can discern them at work most readily in Florence,
where the officers of the city's largest, wealthiest, and most prominent
confraternity, that of the Madonna of Or San Michele, were more
frequently than any other confraternity members to be found sitting
on the city's priorate, and where, apparently as a not too surprising
result, plentiful legislation was passed promoting the company's activities, assigning communal revenues for the construction of a new
palace and granary to be run by the company, and designating the
company as distributor of public alms to hospitals and individuals.[13]
Similarly, in San Sepolcro, in Siena, in Pisa, communal governments
promoted the interests of a few confraternities whose members included large numbers of city office-holders[14] – although only in Pisa
did the commune go so far, in 1286, as expressly to forbid the
establishment of any "fraternity" in the city save that of Santa Lucia de
Ricucchi. This particular company was founded by a group of the
city's prominent merchants, who, according to one account, thought
that since other trades and crafts in the city enjoyed the pious protection of association with particular churches, they also would form such
an association. (Interestingly, in spite of this confraternity's political
and social centrality, the parish church with which it was associated
stood outside the city gate, where newer guilds were more prominent
in the quarter's economy, and where relatively less prosperous and
politically prominent Pisans lived.)[15]

The problem of creating unity out of faction that Santa Lucia in Pisa
attempted to address, however, in spite of its unusually favored status
in official eyes, was one that often united confraternities and communes in pursuit of the common goal of peace. In Bologna the
company known in its early years simply as the *devoti* was granted

---

[12] Based on a comparison of lists of officers appearing in fourteenth-century statutes and accounts
     books (ASF, CRS Z.1.2170, Z.1.2176, Z.1.2182, Z.1.2186 – partially printed in Orioli, *Le
     confraternite medievali*) with lists of priors in Stefani, *Cronaca fiorentina*.
[13] Legislation and officers' lists published in La Sorsa, *La Compagnia d'Or San Michele*, passim.
[14] Banker, *Death in the Community*, 51–9, 71–4, 105–7; Bowsky, *A Medieval Italian Commune*, 264–6.
[15] Bonaini, *Breve Populi*, 1, 632–4, 703–10; Herlihy, *Pisa in the Early Renaissance*, 139.

communal protection in the 1260s and 1270s, and its statutes explicitly state its commitment to the twinned goals of spiritual and civic peace.[16] This group may have been the product of peace-making efforts led by the mendicants in the wake of the 1233 revivalist preaching movement known as the Alleluia; by the middle of the thirteenth century it had certainly become involved in efforts at city-wide pacification. The devoti attempted in different ways at different times also to address the problem of multiple and conflicting allegiances, of overlapping bonds between men, by laying out varying hierarchies of corporate allegiance in successive redactions of their statutes, so that at times the *arti* or *armi* (guilds or military companies that formed the basis of Bologna's communal government) were to take precedence over the confraternity in times of strife, while at other times the confraternity claimed its members' primary allegiance.

Most early confraternity statutes – from Arezzo, Cortona, Florence, Bologna, Siena, Pisa, San Sepolcro – repeat a standard formula to the effect that the confraternity was established at least in part to promote the peace and order of the city. Most companies did not go as far as the Bologna devoti in attempting to articulate mechanisms for intervening in times of disorder, but it is clear that they and the communal governments with which they so frequently intersected understood their central role in maintaining good order in the city. The 1312 reformed statutes of the company of Santa Katerina in Pisa, for example, state that laude are to be sung "to the honor and good condition of our city of Pisa and to the health and salvation of all faithful Christians and especially of the brothers of the said fraternity."[17] A roughly contemporary collection of the company's laude reflects this concern with public order, including as it does laude to the local *beati* Giordano da Pisa and Ranerius, in which they are praised both for their promotion of the company and for their roles in city-wide preaching and peace-making.[18] The 1364 statutes of the company of Santa Croce in Borgo San Sepolcro begin with a dedication to Father, Son, and Holy Spirit, to all the saints, to the Holy Cross, to the Roman Church, and to "the good and peaceful condition of the Commune and people of the region of Borgo San Sepolcro."[19] Companies whose tasks included provision of alms to the city's needy as a whole (not just to their own members), such as the Arezzo Misericordia, or Or San Michele in Florence, understood, and

---

[16] Gaudenzi, *Statuti*, 425; Frati, *Statuti*, 1, 268; Fanti, "La confraternita" and "Gli inizi"; Maragi, "Gli antichi statuti."   [17] Meersseman, *Ordo Fraternitatis*, 2, 1056.

[18] Staaff, *Le laudario de Pise*, 226 (on Giordano), 255 (on Ranerius).

[19] Banker, *Death in the Community*, 210.

were understood by their cities' governments, to be assisting in the larger goal of maintaining civic order, in addition to providing particularly for the spiritual health of the companies' members. So, for example, Florence assigned communal revenues for the construction of the new palace and granary of Or San Michele in the 1330s, because civic order writ large depended on the company's proper distribution of the city's grain supply. A decade later, public celebration of the cult of Saint Anne was also entrusted to Or San Michele after the expulsion of Walter of Brienne on Anne's feast day in 1343 and the subsequent establishment of a more popular regime, with whose liberation from the "yoke of pernicious tyranny" Saint Anne (and by extension the confraternity) thus came to be associated.[20]

The laude that all these companies sang were also performed publicly, and their efficacy was understood to extend to all who heard them, not just those selected *confratelli* who sang them, according to contemporary indulgences.[21] Initially, early chronicles and statutes suggest, laude were sung by an entire company, most often during its private devotions, but quite rapidly instructors of lauda-singing came to be established as regular officers of most companies, and by the 1330s at least part-time professional lauda-singers were being employed by major confraternities.[22] This concern for the quality of public performance also argues strongly for a larger cultural belief in the importance of listening to as well as singing the laude. The texts of these songs often connect spiritual and sociopolitical goals, explicitly praying to God, Mary, Christ, or the saints that they send peace to the city or specially protect it, as in the following typical example, which appears (with appropriately altered city names) in several manuscripts:

> Blessed virgin mother,
> May Florence be placed in your care;
> through you may peace be ordained,
> for you have power over it.
>
> Virgin, without sin
> you carried the blessed one in your womb;
> to you may the state
> of Florence be commended.[23]

---

[20] La Sorsa, *La Compagnia d'Or San Michele*, 213–14, 219–20; Henderson, *Piety and Charity*, 236; Crum and Wilkins, "In the Defense of Florentine Republicanism."

[21] Meersseman, *Ordo Fraternitatis*, 2, 1047–8.

[22] Wilson, *Music and Merchants, passim*; D'Accone, "Alcune note" and "Le compagnie dei laudesi."

[23] "Vergine madre beata,/ Firence vi sia raccomandata;/ per voi vi sia la pace ordinata,/ c'avete di cio la balia.// Vergine, sanca peccato/ portasti nel ventre beato;/ ad voi raccomando lo stato:/ Firence con voi sempre sia." *Laude fiorentine* 1, 179–80 (Mgl2); also in Mgl1 and Ars.

Another typical early lauda from Cortona, on the cult of Corpus Christ, closes with the following line, linking the collective salvation embodied in the host to peace and political order:

> "Sanctus, sanctus," we sing
> to the king of all the world,
> "Dominus, Deus," we say,
> for he is the true God in whom we rejoice;
> devoutly we pray to him
> that he send peace to the world
> and maintain the city of Cortona
> in good condition [stato].[24]

The peace of individual cities was also linked to devotion to local saints or beati. The cult of the holy Sienese maker of wool combs, Pier Pettinaio, whose intercessory powers were commemorated in Dante's *Purgatorio*, was promoted by the commune of Siena, taken up by the city's confraternities, and commemorated in locally sung laude.[25] The Franciscan Guido Vagnotelli, who according to legend was converted by a sermon preached in Cortona by Francis himself, was specially addressed in collections of local laude spanning three centuries.[26] And in Pisa, the laude to Giordano da Pisa and to Ranerius mentioned above associate not only these figures themselves but the singing of laude in their honor with political order; one goes so far as to define as a Pisan citizen anyone who sings it to the honor of Ranerius.[27]

No matter how strongly confraternities sought to promote civic peace, however – no matter how thorough-going their ritual activities or their engagement in what we might call public assistance programs, no matter how strong their support from their cities' governments – as groups competing for certain kinds of public recognition and engaged in certain kinds of organized activity, they were also viewed with hostility and suspicion by communal authorities and by other corporate bodies within the communes, especially the guilds. We have already seen that as early as the late thirteenth century, Pisa had officially prohibited all confraternities save for a single one with strong links to the city's socioeconomic and political oligarchy. This prohibition on the one hand appears to be the

---

[24] "'Sanctus, sanctus,' si cantiamo,/ a lo re de tucto el mondo,/ 'Dominus, Deus,' diciamo,/ che egli e vero Dio giocondo;/ devotamente lo preghiamo/ ch'elli mandi pace al mondo/ e la cita de Cortona/ si mantenga in buo' stato." (*Laude cortonesi* 2, 62 [Aret]; also in Cort and Triv.) See also Rubin, *Corpus Christi*.

[25] Vauchez, "La commune de Sienne," 758 and refs. in n. 4; Dante, *Purgatorio*, 13:124–9; Meersseman, *Ordo Fraternitatis*, 2, 954–68.

[26] Cort, *Laude cortonesi*, 1.2, 457–8; Triv (*Laude cortonesi*, 3, 39–40).

[27] Staaff, *Le laudario de Pise*, 226 and 255.

most extreme example of communal efforts to regulate, promote, and suppress confraternity activity; on the other hand, however, its evident incoherence and ineffectuality are typical of official efforts at repression and control of these groups. In spite of the fact that the apparent reason for promotion of Santa Lucia de Ricucchi was the establishment and maintenance of civic order grounded in good and fair commercial practice, there were no political penalties assigned for infraction; rather, offenders were levied relatively minor money fines. Furthermore, the ban on other companies seems to have been honored more in the breach than in the observance, since only a few years after the first promulgation of the communal statute, in 1312, several related confraternities reformed their statutes and were evidently engaged in considerable public ritual activity, including both flagellation and lauda-singing.[28] Just a year later, in 1313, and again in 1323, the commune repromulgated the ban on all companies save Santa Lucia – and public lauda-singing by confraternities continued unchecked, with active promotion by ecclesiastical and civic authorities alike.[29]

We can only infer the Pisan commune's reasons for such feeble attempts at confraternity regulation, from a sermon preached by Archbishop Visconti on the origins and purpose of the company of Santa Lucia. Unwittingly Visconti suggests that competition may have lain at the heart of the motives of the company's original founders, the city's merchants. Since other trades and crafts had their confraternities, and enjoyed the spiritual guidance of specific religious orders associated with individual churches, why should the merchants not have their own company? And unlike those other groups, the merchants possessed significant economic and political power, to the point where they evidently sought to eliminate the competition altogether. Visconti's vision of mercantile obligation, discussed below, is rather different from this more cynical one – but the two are not necessarily incompatible. His sermon reminds Pisa's merchant oligarchy of their particular obligation to uphold the peace through the practice of both good commerce and proper piety, organized most effectively through the confraternity. One could just as easily read the commune's granting of exclusive "fraternal" privileges to Santa Lucia as the promotion of peace through confraternal unity, as opposed to the plurality represented by a multitude of trade- and craft-based confraternities.[30]

In Florence at about the same time, it appears that economic competition did in fact bring some of the city's leading confraternities into

---

[28] Meersseman, *Ordo Fraternitatis*, 2, 1056 ff.

[29] Bonaini, *Breve Populi*, 2, 501; Meersseman, *Ordo Fraternitatis*, 2, 1058–63; Staaff, "Le laudario," xvii–xxv.   [30] Bonaini, *Breve Populi*, 1, 633

conflict with other groups and with individuals over the disposition of wills. So popular had legacies to confraternities become – and evidently not just from confraternity members but from other pious citizens as well – that other expectant beneficiaries began to contest such legacies. The commune of Florence intervened in the matter in 1329, granting twelve of the city's leading companies the right to be represented in court by procurators – in other words, granting them a very particular kind of juridical status they had previously lacked.[31] What is particularly interesting about this legislation for the present argument is the fact that on the one hand we have the city stepping in to protect the claims of confraternities, while on the other hand we have citizens, acting both individually and collectively, to contest those claims. At a time when control over the government itself was being contested by various individuals and collectivities, communal concern for confraternal interests represented both the political and pious interdependence of commune and confraternities, and the inevitable entanglement of confraternities in webs of public conflict once they emerged as publicly recognized institutions – however much their publicly stated goals might include that of public peace.[32]

Guilds in particular formed loci of such collective conflict, with the commune sometimes attempting to regulate their relations with confraternities as well. In 1317, just twelve years before rights of procuratorship were granted by the commune, the wool guild banned sottoposti, or dependent wool workers (especially the combers and beaters, whom the legislation singles out, as opposed to the lanifices, the big owners and operators of wool shops) from joining the confraternity of San Marco.[33] The rationale was explicitly class-based: "wise and good merchants" governed the confraternity, and so (presumably) they would not want, nor would it be appropriate for them, to associate with their social and political inferiors. Moreover, confraternity membership would give the sottoposti the opportunity to plot against the wool guild ("faciant conventiculas"), presumably in order to form their own, independent, guild or guilds. More generally, the wool guild required all sottoposti to swear to the guild consuls that they had not joined any other corporation, including confraternities. Robert Davidsohn has argued that the larger concern of Florence's leading guildsmen about workers forming confraternities represents their anxieties about potential demands for higher wages and better working conditions, but my reading of the evidence, particularly viewed in light of larger political debates and what we have

---

[31] Morini, *Documenti inediti*, 2–6; ASF, *Diplomatico di Santa Maria Nuova*, 31 March, 1329; ASF, Archivio del Bigallo, vol. 1669, f. 6r.

[32] On contested government participation, Becker, *Florence in Transition*, 1; Najemy, *Corporatism and Consensus*; Starn, *Contrary Commonwealth*.   [33] *Statuto dell'arte della Lana*, 1, 203.

seen of communal and confraternal relations elsewhere, suggests that
major guild worries were far more about the possibilities – realized in
1378 with the Ciompi revolt – of demands for political rights, or, to put it
another way, about potential political competition. The 1325 statutes of
the podesta of Florence regulated the leadership of what were evidently
seen as workers' confraternities, and "festive associations" comprising
more than twelve members, whose purpose was to celebrate the major
liturgical feasts, were also forbidden.[34] Such legislation would appear to
represent an extension from one guild's intervention in confraternity
organization into the larger realm of the city's religious companies as a
whole.

   In other words, by the first quarter of the fourteenth century, there is
some evidence to suggest that confraternities were among the various
groups competing for public power within the Italian communes, in
addition to working toward reduction or elimination of such competition. That class, at least – class based primarily although not exclusively on
possession of political rights rather than socioeconomic status – was an
important issue, although not necessarily always a conscious one, for
confraternities, is quite clear, as is the fact that it carried the potential to
become a matter of public contention.

   The problem was not simply one of class, however (and in practice the
class issues could cut in very different ways). Nor was it really one of
confraternity contestation of power, whether economic or political.
Rather, the problem lay precisely in the closeness of confraternity goals
and, especially, organization and structure, to those of the communes and
of the guilds or military societies or residential units or family clans (to a
lesser degree) upon which communal government was based. It was the
access of the disenfranchised to the basic structures of power that authorities feared the most. The threat of insurrection by dependent workers or
disenfranchised groups loomed large in communal Italy from the time of
the "popular" revolts of the thirteenth century onward – and nowhere
was this threat more pressing than in Florence, where public fears were
realized in the Ciompi revolt of 1378, and were foreshadowed by continual electoral debates from the 1290s onward. There is a fundamental
incoherence, of course, to the fears expressed by the wool guild in 1317,
since a confraternity in which the powerful members of the guild functioned as officers might just as easily have been viewed as providing an
opportunity for close supervision of sottoposti, rather than as giving them
the opportunity for independent political action. But it is precisely the
incoherence of the fear – here, or in the efforts of the Pisan commune to

---

[34] Davidsohn, *Storia di Firenze*, 6, 212.

suppress all but a single confraternity – that demonstrates the connection people tended to make between confraternal organization and the precise opposite of many confraternities' stated goal of peace, namely political dissent. The language of all guild and communal legislation regarding confraternities in the first century or so of their established involvement in Italian city life suggests that it was exactly the opportunity to organize, around whatever pretext, that most threatened the established order. The making of statutes and the election of officers are the two activities invariably characterized as subversive by communal statutes repressing or promoting confraternities – activities that were necessary in order to speak and act effectively in the public realm. Such organization might promote communal goals, but its very presence potentially subverted them as well.

I would like to suggest that this kind of class-based anxiety about the political threat represented by confraternities represents a kind of variation on Sedgwick's homosocial dynamic – a variation in which class rather than gender relations dominate the field of attraction and repression. It is that recognition of similar desires in other groups that drives guilds and communes to repress such desires where they carry the possibility of spilling over from the necessary tasks of guaranteeing social and spiritual order into the realm of unsettling that order. Other scholars have argued that confraternities served to suspend temporarily the social and political divisions characterized by the other forms of association characteristic of Italian urban life, permitting men of different backgrounds and interests to come together momentarily to enjoy relief from the agonistic relations that ordinarily structured their encounters with one another, in jockeying for political, economic, and social position.[35] According to this line of thinking, the preoccupation of the guilds in particular with political status (especially in the thirteenth and fourteenth centuries), guaranteed that they would resist the tendency toward what we might call temporary democratization represented by confraternity meetings and organization. I want to argue for a refinement of this perspective, one which acknowledges the potential of confraternities to act as solvents of social tension, but which also recognizes that in the organization that they shared with other politically concerned groups, and in all these groups' mutual but conflicted concern with goals both political and spiritual, there were bound to be grave tensions reflected in confraternities' public lives as well. Furthermore, the invariably homosocial quality of all these associations, which replicated bonds not just between men, but construed along principles of exclusion and

---

[35] Weissman, *Ritual Brotherhood*; Trexler, *Public Life*; see also Rubin, "Small Groups."

repression based on gender and class, meant inevitable tension – one is tempted to call it the return of the repressed – as well.

Ecclesiastical as well as civic authorities shared these concerns, too, especially as time wore on. Or San Michele, that bastion of civic pride and privilege in Florence, was always carefully scrutinized and regulated by the communal magistracy; not too surprisingly, it came under increasing suspicion in the late fourteenth and fifteenth centuries, together with the city's other major confraternities dedicated to public assistance, the Misericordia and the Bigallo. The commune indeed went so far as to suppress these companies in 1419, and to repromulgate their suppression periodically thereafter – and such suspicion and suppression continued to characterize official response to confraternities down until the nineteenth century. In the fifteenth century, too, that great promoter of civic and spiritual reform, Archbishop Antoninus, voiced frequent concern over the seditious impact confraternities could have on social and religious life in the city.[36]

Archbishop Visconti's sermon that includes the story of the origins of the Pisan confraternity of Santa Lucia dei Ricucchi was preached in the church of Saint Francis in that city, and elaborates an ideology of commercial society that further illustrates some of the structural tensions I have been describing, as well as a vision of how confraternities might represent resolution of those tensions. He reminds his audience that it ought to be attractive (delectabile) to be a merchant, since the blessed Francis himself was both merchant and saint "in tempore nostro." Not only ought merchants to be particularly devoted to Francis and to the Franciscans, but they had founded the fraternity of Santa Lucia so that more of the city's notables might be able to come together. The vintners met in the church of Saint John the Baptist, Visconti tells us, the bakers in San Marco, and others at the Carmine, or with the Sacchites. So why should the merchants not have their own fraternity, which would encourage them both in piety and in the practice of good, peaceable, and loving commerce?[37]

Visconti's vision sounds terrific in theory, but in practice, of course, things were not so easy. Although he does not seem to have envisioned an official stranglehold of merchants on confraternity life in Pisa, the commune came to do so, as we have seen, for reasons no doubt much like those of the wool guild or the commune of Florence. In the next generation of public preachers, Giordano da Pisa, while sharing Visconti's sense of the spiritual potential of a commercially based society, also recognized more clearly the failures of commercial practice, especially as

---

[36] Henderson, *Piety and Charity*, 49–50, 419–21.   [37] Bonaini, *Breve populi*, 633.

represented by guild activity and organization. In a sermon preached in the church of Santa Maria Novella in Florence – at a place and time where many confraternity as well as guild members would have been members of his audience – Giordano, in good mendicant fashion, articulated a vision of commerce as the ultimate means to Christian salvation. The proper end of crafts and manufacture (*arti* – which also means guilds) and commerce (*mercatantie*), he says, is mutual assistance, congregation, and love. We make for and buy from one another because we cannot supply all our own needs or wants (*difatti*), and so the fundamental activities of the marketplace bring us together to help one another.

> This then is the order and the purpose of commerce, that is assistance and love. If all crafts and commerce were carried out in this order and with this purpose, we would all be saints.[38]

Giordano's larger point, however, is that this ideal is not realized in practice. The guilds (he plays on *arte* as manufacture and arti as guilds) in practice have so corrupted the marketplace that even innocent citizens who are not guild members are contaminated by contact with deceitful selling practices and the dread sin of usury. The entire city, which might have been saved through commerce, is undone through its perversion.

Giordano's ideal is a world much like that articulated in confraternity statutes and to a certain extent realized in their activities. But it is also a highly rarefied vision of the perfect urban community, and in addition to the particular structural problems faced by late medieval Italian cities, we must also remember that generally notions of community tend notoriously to mask tension and conflict between groups.[39] The problem Giordano points to is the one with which this paper began, and the one discussed by many recent scholars of confraternities as well, namely the failure of urban groups to bring themselves together, to transcend their group particularity in order to achieve a larger harmonious ideal. Not only guilds but also confraternities were part of this problem. The mendicants were jealous of their spiritual success: Giovanni Villani's account of the foundation of Or San Michele in Florence includes the comment that the Dominicans and Franciscans were bitterly envious of the confraternity's success, seeing in it a threat to their perceived monopoly on popular spiritual

---

[38] "Questo e dunque l'ordine e il fine de la mercatantia, cioe subventione e amore. Se a questo ordine e a questo fine si facessero l'arti e le mercatantie, tutti saremmo santi, tutte sarabber sante." Delcorno, *La predicazione*, 98–104.

[39] Rubin, "Small Groups;" *Urban Life*, ed. Zimmerman and Weissman.

guidance.[40] Visconti's sermon on Santa Lucia in Pisa contains the suggestion that part of that confraternity's foundation had to do with competition among churches, especially mendicant churches, for the patronage of socially powerful groups in the city. And many confraternities themselves went to great lengths to distinguish themselves and their members through entrance or membership requirements, secret rituals, the wearing of special robes, reservation of prerogatives, and the like. These marks of exclusivity have both a spiritual and a social significance. On the one hand they remind us that confraternities were, *pace* Visconti and Giordano, struggling to reconcile daily engagement in urban commerce with a set of Christian values in many respects fundamentally at odds with their new urban milieu; on the other, they also replicate the tendency toward group solidarity, exclusivity, and conflict, grounded in fundamentally homosocial relations, that were found everywhere in late medieval urban Italy.

The search for peace in Italy's cities in the fourteenth century would thus appear to have been doomed from the start, no matter how many or how pious the spiritually oriented groups that participated in it. It was doomed both in the sense that the specific structures of group organization in this milieu invariably replicated one another and competed with one another, and in the larger sense that the mechanisms of repression and exclusion on which those structures rested inevitably guaranteed instability and the repetition of precisely that instability repression was supposed to combat. When it comes to confraternity participation in this unstable order of things, Giordano is right on both counts. Confraternities did indeed sometimes serve to remind their cities of the possibilities for mutual assistance and love – and just as often they reminded them of how impossible such goals were.

It is, moreover, the specifically homosocial character of corporate association, especially as embodied in confraternities, that helped to create this bitterly ironic situation. Political power, just as much as sex, has its own erotic dynamic that was nowhere played out more explicitly than in the urban setting of the confraternities. I have argued that power can depend on a mechanics of repression predicated on class as well as gender relations, and in confraternities' replication and refusal of class distinctions the homosociality they shared with other urban groups was both reaffirmed and challenged – truly a threatening as well as a consoling vision.

Confraternal hopes for peace persisted long after the great days of

---

[40] Villani, *Cronaca*, 479.

the communes had passed, however. Well into the fifteenth century laude claiming the political efficacy not only of divine intervention but of confraternity singing continued to be publicly performed, in a world in which a different kind of internal urban peace had been precariously achieved, based on very different notions of political authority – and at the cost of nearly continual external violations of peace. For all those violations, however, the belief persisted, in groups we would call primarily secular as well as in those we would call spiritually oriented, that temporal and eternal peace were inextricably linked, that all had to work together toward peace as a common goal in this world and the next – however much that belief failed to be realized in practice, owing to social structures whose manipulation tended only to reproduce the problems they were designed to address.

3

CONFRATERNITIES AND LAY FEMALE RELIGIOSITY IN LATE MEDIEVAL AND RENAISSANCE UMBRIA

GIOVANNA CASAGRANDE

Many scholars have noted women's participation in late medieval and early modern fraternal associations. Yet this presence rarely constitutes the specific topic of research.[1] While women are undoubtedly found within at least certain types of confraternities, it is difficult to determine how their presence should be qualified. To adopt the terminology used by Angela Groppi in her discussion of women's participation in the late medieval workplace, we must determine what their *esserci* (presence) is in terms of *valere* (worth).[2]

In his magisterial work, *Ordo Fraternitatis*, G. G. Meersseman recorded women's involvement in Italian and European fraternities from at least the tenth and eleventh centuries. Between the thirteenth and fifteenth centuries the Dominican order oversaw an extensive diffusion of mixed Marian fraternities. The statute of the fraternity of the Virgin in Arezzo (1262) establishes the admission of women "because God does not make any discrimination between men and women in order to perform the works of salvation."[3] In practice, however, women could only carry out certain duties of a religious-devotional character such as prayers and attendance at monthly meetings and the feast-days of the Virgin. They were excluded from the administration of the fraternity itself. The Dominicans also provided scope for the recruitment of women to later devotional confraternities such as those of the Rosary and, from

---

Abbreviations: Assisi, Archivio Capitolare di S. Rufino (AACSR); Perugia, Archivio della Cattedrale (ACPg); Perugia, Archivio Diocesano (ADPg); Perugia, Archivio di Stato (ASP); Perugia, Archivio di Stato, Corporazioni religiose soppresse (ASP, CRS); Perugia, Biblioteca Comunale Augusta (BAP); Gubbio, Archivio Vescovile (GAV). Translated by Rodney Lokaj, University of Edinburgh.

[1] Casagrande, "Women in Confraternities." Terpstra, "Women in the Brotherhood."
[2] Groppi, *Il lavoro delle donne*.   [3] Meersseman, *Ordo fraternitatis*, 2, 1022.

the fifteenth century on, to confraternities of St. Peter Martyr which undertook the defence of the faith.[4]

Various studies have given us an idea of how female participation in fraternal groups could change from one urban setting to an other. De La Roncière noted that Florence, for example, seems to have had few women in its fraternities, while in the outlying countryside a much higher number of women appear in both separate and mixed confraternities.[5] In the fourteenth century, Florence's company of S. Frediano enrolled women and allowed them to participate in spiritual benefits and in certain fraternal initiatives, such as the procession of the first Sunday of every month. Statutes of 1323 exclude these same women from the hierarchical confraternal administration.[6] As Weissman showed, similar limits were placed on female participation in the Florentine parish confraternities at the beginning of the sixteenth century.[7]

In the Veneto, De Sandre Gasparini noticed an increase in female participation between the fourteenth and fifteenth centuries when the confraternities expanded and included entire family groups. Statutes of 1478 for the confraternity of San Rocco in Villa del Bosco outside Padua reveal the co-existence of men and women with the same religious-devotional rights and duties such as prayers, processions, and the rite of the focaccia (flat-cake), the involvement of family groups within the confraternity, and the exclusion of women from positions of authority and management within the fraternity.[8]

For Bologna, Terpstra noticed a declining trend in the female presence throughout the fifteenth century. This negative trend was likely due to several factors, particularly women's exclusion from the administrative responsibilities peculiar to the male component; the predominance of the flagellant penitential model among new and reformed confraternities; and a revival of misogynistic themes emphasizing the dangerousness of women.[9]

In Sansepolcro, in the upper Tiber River valley, statutes of 1269 for the confraternity of San Bartolomeo allowed for men and women provided they were registered separately. The *rectores* were exclusively male. Between the thirteenth and fourteenth centuries the fraternity, whose main aim was to provide charity for the needy and burial, requiems, and prayers for the dead, accepted hundreds of women of various social

[4] *Ibid.*, 754–920. Casagrande, "Women in Confraternities," 5.
[5] De La Roncière, "Les confréries à Florence", 303–4.
[6] Papi, "Le confraternite fiorentine", 126–7, 129.   [7] Weissman, *Ritual Brotherhood*, 212–13.
[8] De Sandre Gasparini, "Il movimento delle confraternite," 385–6, and *Contadini, chiesa, confraternita*.
[9] Terpstra, *Lay Confraternities*, 120–3.

backgrounds whether married or widowed. According to Banker, women came more and more to set the character of the fraternity as the men moved on to the newer flagellant fraternities by the first decades of the fourteenth century.[10]

In Bergamo, of ten medieval confraternal statutes published by Little, only three include openings for women. Even here, however, women were not allowed to participate in confraternal administration. The statutes of 1265 for the *Consortium seu congregatio* of Misericordia allow women on the condition that they be morally sound. These women must be registered in a special book so that something may be known about them and so that alms might occasionally be asked of them.[11] Women partook of the spiritual benefits of the fraternity and, like the men, had to make confession twice a year. Evidence of female membership is found in the confraternity's *Liber fraternitatis*. This matriculation list, begun in 1295 and added to until at least 1339, listed membership by neighborhood both within and outside the city walls. It recorded 1,717 women through that time period, including the wives of illustrious citizens, lay sisters, and nuns. In the opinion of Brolis, this high number of entrants demonstrates the Misericordia's continuing popularity in Bergamo at this time.[12] Statutes of 1326 for the Misericordia confraternity of the outlying communities of Nembro and Alzano Superiore also allow admission of women.[13]

As for the flagellant confraternities in and around the city of Bergamo, the bishop himself granted the privilege of female aggregation in 1336. Women were accepted by the prior and enrolled in the *matricula*. Married women required their husbands' consent, and single women that of their fathers or brothers. Women's duties consisted in prayers, alms and participating in burial services. They had the right to be accompanied in their own burial by the other members of the fraternity.[14] The vernacular statutes written over a century later in 1459 reiterate that women were to be accepted upon consent from the husband, father, brother, or mother, and that they were bound, like the men, to all other obligations, were actively involved in every spiritual benefit and were granted equal rights to funerary services. These statutes add, however, that women were utterly excluded from "*far disciplina*."[15]

Across late-medieval Italy, then, the space available to women in confraternities was limited by an ever-changing array of openings, limits, and preclusions. Some had no women, others were exclusively female,

---

[10] Banker, *Death in the Community*, 38–74, 143–73, 188–90.

[11] Little, *Libertà, carità, fraternità*, 112, 117.

[12] Brolis, "Confraternite bergamasche", 338, 340–2.

[13] Little, *Libertà. carità, fraternità*, 184.   [14] *Ibid.*, 204.

[15] Alberigo, "Contributi alla storia," 243–4. Meersseman, *Ordo fraternitatis*, I, 500–1, 503.

and yet others were apparently the female auxiliaries of male fraternities. Many mixed confraternities included women in the membership while excluding them from the administrative hierarchy, not to mention from particular religious-devotional practices.

Female presence does not guarantee meaningful participation. This is due to the fact that these women were present (esserci) without the fullness of worth (valere) which instead characterized the male universe. Angela Groppi's terminology is particularly appropriate here since the worlds of guilds and the confraternities are parallel. While women were present in various facets of the medieval world of work, it is more problematic to determine how much they really counted both socially and in the context of organized work in guilds.[16] In this sense, women's role in the guilds, especially from the point of view of corporate organization, is well reflected in the varying, complex world of confraternities.

Research on women in confraternities is complicated by the type of documentation. Matriculation lists are often rich in female names, but what does this prove? There is no doubt that women were definitely admitted into the particular fraternity in question. The statutes may provide for their admission and deem necessary the writing out of separate *matriculae*. Yet chapters on the administrative practices and religious-charitable-devotional duties fail to mention these women. It is as if they had been swept away by the statutory rules, the council deliberations and by whatever else left them no space or role whatsoever in the operative and decisional organs of the association. Esserci, therefore, but not valere!

The limits placed on these relegated women are not peculiar to this field, but form what we may call the "circle of exclusions." Women could not gain access to any priestly office; a military career was precluded to them; they were excluded from civil, political and administrative power, not to mention from university and, therefore, from intellectual work. What was left was family life with its limitations and conditions. When they could work outside the home they were often not given their full due; women did not or could not gain access to every sphere of artisanal or professional work. They did, however, have a greater range of choice on the religious front. Beyond monastic-cloistered life, they could become recluses, lay sisters, or penitent-tertiaries.

Confraternities were associations with religious objectives regarding worship, devotion, charity, penance, the search for salvation, and moral and spiritual edification. This does not imply, however, that those adhering necessarily took on a canonical-juridical status as *religiosæ personæ*, that

[16] Groppi, "Il lavoro delle donne," 145. Shahar, "Regulation and Presentation," 501–22. Greci, "Donne e corporazioni," 71–91 and Guerra Medici, *L'aria di città*, 124–33.

is, a clerical status or similar. In their perfectly lay nature, confraternities reflected the female lay condition with all the limits and exclusions to which late medieval and early modern women were subject.

Before turning to the distinct approaches taken by those confraternities emphasizing flagellant discipline on the one hand, and those emphasizing praise to the Virgin on the other, we should briefly note another form of confraternity: that is, congregations of clergy who enrolled lay members for specific spiritual benefits. A fourteenth-century manuscript concerning the *congregatio* of the clergy in Perugia but held in the Chapter library of the Cathedral of Toledo (Spain) gives lists of names of both men and women. One can distinguish 6 married couples plus 34 women and 27 men registered individually. It would seem to be a mixed matriculation list, but is more likely a list of deceased members for whom the congregatio was obliged to say mass. After the first folio with its lists, there is a calendar which notes the main daily and monthly feasts, and gives numerous names of clerics and lay men with at times the specification "*de nostra congregatione.*" The registration of couples is rare. It is common, however, to find the women registered with either the simple name, or with the patronymic or the name of the husband, brother or son, or with the place name.[17] In certain cases the specification *de nostra congregatione* is expressed. Seeing that it is indeed a calendar, the entries obviously refer to deceased members for whom masses must be said. It is not clear whether all the lay men and women listed were actually part of the congregation, or only those listed "de nostra congregatione". We may, however, be absolutely sure that lay women were allowed into the congregation and did in fact enjoy the spiritual benefits. This "congregatio" in Perugia is probably an example of an earlier type of association which included lay men or women as auxiliaries without granting them any administrative power. Their participation was linked to the search for salvation of their souls.[18] Although technically termed "confraternities," they should be distinguished from the groups discussed below which met regularly for worship and had a demonstrable corporate life.

THE CASE OF FLAGELLANT CONFRATERNITIES

As Meersseman noted, women were excluded from flagellation, and in only a few cases were they allowed to participate in spiritual benefits, prayers and suffrages. Angelozzi, De Sandre Gasparini, and Terpstra have further explored this exclusion of women from the practice of self-

---

[17] Eg., *Ciacus de nostra congregatione* (c. 4r); *Criscembene de nostra congregatione* (c. 4r). *Ugolinus et mater sua domina Beatrice de nostra congregatione* (c. 4v); *obiit Suppolinus et uxor eius domina Bonadomane* (c. 5r).

[18] Mezzanotte, "Le vicende del capitolo," 109–10, 121–5. Rigon, *Clero e città,* 169–70.

flagellation, whether public or privately within the confraternal oratory, not to mention the other limits placed on their participation in corporate life. My own research, in Perugia particularly but also in other towns in Umbria, confirms this picture.[19]

The rare documentary signs concerning women in flagellant confraternities in Umbria between the fourteenth and fifteenth centuries do not substantially contradict the groups' decidedly and/or prevalently masculine character. In some cases women's exclusion is clearly expressed, as in the statutes (ante 1347) of the *disciplinati* of S. Rufino in Assisi which read: "Let anyone avoid long conversations and gatherings of women like deadly plague, in that they bring about lust and moral disorder."[20] Such inveterate misogyny viewing women as dangerous temptresses was commonplace. The regulations of 1339 regarding the *disciplinati del Crocifisso di S. Agostino* in Gubbio state that: "women are absolutely forbidden to enter into the fraternity and that entrance is forbidden them for whatever reasons, and this clause must be respected forever."[21] The appearance of a woman as *rectrix* and governess of this confraternity's *Ospedale Nuovo* in 1427 does not necessarily imply that women were admitted into the fraternity itself.[22]

Perugia is the city where the movement of the disciplinati began in 1260 and at least twelve penitential fraternities could be found in the first half of the fourteenth century.[23] Yet for a number of reasons, women played no part in these associations. Beyond the sense of shame emphasized by Meersseman, one must consider both the penitential spirit which aims to avoid temptation, particularly sexual temptation, and also the meaning and practice of flagellation.[24] Flagellation was an appropriation of the figure of Christ, an act of imitative piety and identification with God the Man which contemporaries considered unseemly for women.[25] Chiara da Rimini's desire to stage a mystery play one Good Friday with public flagellation was seen as a violation of the religious, social, and mental order.[26]

Yet we must also recognize public and political motivations for women's exclusion from flagellation.[27] Men's greater public role translated into a greater profile and standing within the confraternities. In the

---

[19] Meersseman, *Ordo fraternitatis*, 1, 498–504. Angelozzi, *Confraternite laicali*, 52. De Sandre Gasparini, *Statuti di confraternite*, 43. Terpstra, *Lay Confraternities*, 123. Casagrande, *Religiosità penitenziale*, 436–8.

[20] AACSR, ms. 75, c. 3r. Nicolini, "Statuto della fraternita," 313. Casagrande, *Religiosità penitenziale*, 437.   [21] GAV, II.C.14, c. 16v.   [22] Menichetti, *I 50 ospedali*, 143.

[23] Casagrande, *Religiosità penitenziale*, 395–6.

[24] Meersseman, *Ordo fraternitatis*, 1, 499, cf. note 21. De Sandre Gasparini, *Statuti di confraternite*, 12.

[25] Terpstra, *Lay Confraternities*, 123. Casagrande, *Religiosità penitenziale*, 438.

[26] Dalarun, "*Lapsus linguae*" 40–1, 307–9.   [27] Meersseman, *Ordo fraternitatis*, 1, 499.

specific case of Perugia, the city underwent constitutional upheaval in the early fourteenth century by which power was vested in the guilds; only those belonging to guilds could gain access to the priorate. As a result, the guilds increasingly became the social platform from which the public role of men and the power of the city emanated. They monopolized the institutional expression of the world of work. There is no doubt that Perugian women worked at least in certain capacities as bakers, inn-keepers, pork-butchers, and greengrocers, but there is equally no doubt that their role within the guilds was marginalized.[28] Even in those rare cases when they might have the opportunity to belong to one, they could not gain access to public offices. The flourishing of flagellant confraternities in the very same time period is not co-incidental, from the point of view of women or men. Excluded from office in guilds and in the popular government, women did not succeed in finding a place within those strong, demanding, disciplinati confraternities which were then growing so rapidly. Once established, this exclusion remained and spread. Soon we see women being excluded from confraternities strongly dedicated to charitable work, such as the *Fraternita dell'Ospedale di S. Maria della Misericordia*.[29]

THE CASE OF MARIAN CONFRATERNITIES, LAUDESI AND RACCOMANDATI

There remained a group of confraternities to which women were admitted. These were mixed fraternities of a Marian or laud singing nature, or the so-called confraternities of *Raccomandati* (the Recommended of the Virgin). These fraternities spread throughout Umbria during the thirteenth century, encouraged and organized both by the Mendicant orders and by the ecclesiastical authorities. In Orvieto, for example, there were at least two such confraternities, one linked to the Dominicans, the other to the Franciscans.[30] One of the most famous medieval *laudarios*, or books of praise songs, was produced for the Franciscan confraternity. On c. 4r a matriculation list dated 1313 is headed: "The under-mentioned are the men and women of the fraternity of the Holy Virgin Mary, which is established in Orvieto in the church of the Friars Minor of the Order of St. Francis."[31] Unfortunately, the extant list bears only its first page concerning the men. This Marian confraternity admitted women, but at the same time, the codex contains a matriculation list of the living and dead members of a related flagellant confraternity dedicated to Saint

[28] Casagrande-Ottaviani, "Donne negli statuti comunali", 32–4.
[29] Valeri, *La fraternita dell'Ospedale*.
[30] Meersseman, *Ordo fraternitatis*, 2, 1041–2. Casagrande, *Religiosità penitenziale*, 392.
[31] Lazzarini, "Il codice Vitt. Em. 528," 485 n. 12. Scentoni (ed.), *Laudario orvietano*, 36 n. 63.

Francis without, however, any mention of women! This is a tangible demonstration of the distinctions between Marian and flagellant confraternities, with the former open to female presence while the latter are exclusively male.

A similar pattern is repeated elsewhere in Umbria. In Montefalco, near Spoleto, a confraternity established in 1257 and dedicated to the Virgin and Saint Francis enrolled both men and women.[32] Similarly in Perugia the fraternity of Saint Mary, already active around the middle of the thirteenth century, was closely linked to the church of Saint Dominic whose well-known, published statutes dating back to 1312 reveal the full admission of women; these are, however, excluded from the management of the fraternity. In the sixteenth century the fraternity was to be superseded by a fraternity of the Rosary which remained open to both men and women.[33]

The Dominicans of Perugia must have been responsible for the diffusion of Marian fraternities in the area surrounding Lake Trasimeno. The convent chronicle mentions a certain friar Andrea di Giovanni "who also was particularly devoted to the Mother of God; in fact with his care and zeal he started a fraternity of men and women dedicated to the Holy Virgin in Isola Polvese and in neighboring places; he gave those fraternities a rule and a *modus vivendi* in praise and glory of God, our Savior".[34] In the thirteenth and fourteenth centuries, Isola Polvese in Lake Trasimeno hosted a temporary settlement of Dominicans.[35] The friars influenced the *cura animarum* of lay people in the area immediately in and around the lake, and by the first half of the fourteenth century several confraternities dedicated to Saint Mary are to be found in such hamlets as Pian di Carpine, Montecolognola, S. Feliciano, Zocco, Monte del Lago, Isola Polvese and Isola Maggiore.[36] Extant documents suggest that in most cases there was one confraternity which was articulated into male and female branches.[37]

In Perugia itself, we can document the existence of a mixed-gender confraternity dedicated to Saint Mary and Saint Anthony from 1297, the year bishop Bulgaro Montemelini grants the group an indulgence.[38] Well into the fourteenth century this confraternity seems to distinguish itself into two parallel entities: the *fraternita della Madonna* and the *fraternita di S.*

[32] Nessi, "Storia e arte," 310–11.

[33] Meersseman, *Ordo fraternitatis*, 2, 1012–23; 1063–66; 3, 1190–92. Casagrande, *Religiosità penitenziale*, 391, 393, 435.

[34] Maiarelli (ed.), *Cronaca di S. Domenico*, 54. Meersseman, *Ordo fraternitatis*, 2, 1066.

[35] ASP, CRS, S. Domenico, *Pergamene*, 19; Casagrande, *Religiosità penitenziale*, 435–6.

[36] ASP, Ospedale della Misericordia, *Bastardelli*, 5, cc. 2r–3r, 46r–7r; 6, c. 15v; 9, cc. 1v–6r, 7v, 8v, 9r, 12v–14r, 21r; 10, cc. 72r, 78r, 161r. ASP, CRS, Monte Morcino, *Pergamene*, 436. ASP, Fondo Gardone, busta 80, 19 luglio, 1341.   [37] Casagrande, *Religiosità penitenziale*, 436.

[38] ASP, CRS, Monte Morcino, *Pergamene*, 13.

Antonio Abate. Whereas only this second one is clearly a flagellant group, both are under the parish church of Saint Anthony Abbot in the *rione* of Porta Sole.[39] Most likely, an original fraternal nucleus divided into flagellant male and Marian-devotional female groups, an option likely preferred by the male disciplinati.[40] In this case, the women's confraternity seems to have lasted an extraordinarily long time and to have taken on increasing responsibility for the administration of the local church. It is certain that a *societas mulierum Madonne* at the parish church of Saint Anthony is autonomously active in the sixteenth century. Sale contracts for 1507–8 identify two women qualified both as *ministre et procuratrices capelle dominarum* and as *abbatisse seu ministre rerum et bonorum fraternitatis Virginis Marie.*[41] Between 1561 and 1570 the societas mulierum Madonne was in charge of the chapel of the Virgin, with all the relevant managerial responsibilities.[42] A Visitation report of 1594 notes that "the fraternity owns some real estate which yield three *salmae* of wheat every year and one *mediolenum* of olive oil every second year and accounts are kept by the prioress."[43] The report further noted that the chapel altar was well kept, the *societas* usually accompanied the Sacrament when it was carried to the ill, and that members carried the figure of the Virgin in procession on Ascension Day.[44] The *Capitoli et Costitutioni* of 1616 provide a clear picture of the devotional duties which this female association carried out with a fair amount of autonomy. These statutes were written when a canon from Perugia, Timoteo Timotei, was prior of Saint Anthony's and decided to correct some abuses within this female fraternity. His efforts were not entirely successful, since the prioress was accused of fraudulent dealing in the fraternity's property only a year later.[45] At the same time, the 1616 statutes give us an idea of the administrative structures and spiritual exercises typical of female confraternities. The confraternity was governed by an abbess and a prioress appointed for a year (ch. 7). The prioress was charged with such administrative work as checking the income and the *robbe* of the fraternity (ch. 15). Expenses, sales and purchases were decided by majority rule (ch. 11), but soon such decisional power was given to the abbess and prioress provided they acted on behalf of the entire company. The sisters met every Sunday of the month to discuss matters pertaining to the good of the company (ch. 9). Two women were designated to visit their fellow sisters who were ill (ch. 10).

---

[39] ASP, Notarile, *Protocolli*, 2, c. 56rv; cf. *Chiese e conventi . . . I protocolli notarili di Perugia*, 2.19.

[40] Casagrande, "Women in Confraternities", 10 and *Religiosità penitenziale*, 393, 437.

[41] ASP, Notarile, *Bastardelli*, 1015, cc. 270v–1v, 301v–2v.

[42] ADPg, *Visitationes*, 1, cc. 48v–9r.   [43] ADPg, *Visitationes*, 10, cc. 320v–1r.

[44] ADPg, *Visitationes*, 10, cc. 320v–1r. Siepi, "Descrizione", 129–30

[45] ADPg, *Litterae DD Superiorum*, b. II, ad annum 1617; *Hospitalia et confraternitates*, folio without date. The fraternity was abolished in 1697 (Siepi, "Descrizione," 130).

As regards collective worship, the confraternity managed the chapel with a female sacristan (ch. 14); the sisters were required to take confession and communion three times a year (Easter, Christmas, Assumption of the Virgin) (ch. 3); every Saturday they were to have a mass celebrated in honour of the Holy Virgin and every Monday for the Dead (ch. 5). For private devotions, they were to recite the *Pater Noster* and *Ave Maria* twenty-five times each on Saturdays and Mondays (ch. 4).[46] The women's autonomy was only limited by the common post-Tridentine practice of having the bishop or vicar check their accounts.

The groups designated *Raccomandati della Vergine* began in Rome, and shared a *forma vitae* first written out between 1260 and 1270; their aim was to pursue a pious Catholic life following the Church's prescriptions on behaviour, sacramental practices, prayer.[47] Women were clearly included; amongst the fraternities of Raccomandati in Umbria, the one in Assisi has a matriculation list recording 85 women and 284 men.[48] But familiar patterns appear. The normative-statutory texts produced between the thirteenth and fourteenth centuries mention the possibility of female participation, but also indicate a low level of involvement of women in fraternal life.[49] In the church of Saint Rufinus, for example, both women and men are obliged to participate in the celebration of mass, however, it is not at all clear whether the same women were involved in the other particularly significant moments of public confraternal life such as laud singing or "carrying the panel portraying our Lady the Holy Virgin or the lanterns on feast days and solemn Sundays, when our fraternity meets."[50] Women were excluded from every office and charge; the matriculation list concerning the women is not as precise and detailed as the one regarding the men; the prior decided upon the admission of women into the fraternity; and there was no solemn admission ceremony provided for these women as there was with men.[51] A confraternity of raccomandati in Todi enrolled women but did not offer them the image of the Virgin which male members received from the company's rector.[52]

Finally, the confraternity of S. Maria del Mercato in Gubbio constitutes an interesting case which a larger number of documents allows us to study in greater depth.[53] This confraternity had been of a Marian-laud

[46] BAP, ms. 1471/IV.
[47] AACSR, fasc. III, n. 121. Cf. Casagrande, "Lettere d'indulgenza," 189–98.
[48] AACSR, ms.77, cc. 21v–3v; cf. Casagrande, "Statuto e matricola," 225–8 and "La fraternita dei raccomandati," 39.   [49] AACSR, ms. 77, c. 3v; Casagrande, "Statuto e matricola," 205.
[50] AACSR, ms. 77, cc. 2r, 8r, 12v, 14v, 15v. Casagrande, "Statuto e matricola," 204, 209, 211–13.
[51] AACSR ms. 77, c. 7r. Casagrande, "Statuto e matricola," 207–08.
[52] Mancini, "I disciplinati di Porta Fratta," 274–5.
[53] GAV, C. II.C.13. Fiorucci, "S. Maria del Mercato."

singing type ever since its inception at the end of the thirteenth-century.[54] In the first decades of the fourteenth century the group was renewed and membership increased with the judicial, religious, and spiritual support of the bishop Francesco Gabrielli. The Mendicant orders do not seem to have exerted any role in this fraternity which, judging by an early fourteenth century set of statutes, was under the direct authority of the bishop. The statutes open with the prescription that a *liber fraternitatis* be established in which all the names of those belonging to the fraternity might be included, *seorsum masculi et seorsum femine*.[55] No explicit role is set out for the female members in the balance of the document. When referring, however, to *omnes et singule persone fraternitatis*, or simply to *omnes* who must congregate in church for mass or for other specific celebrations, the statutes very probably imply women as well. Similarly it is likely that general regulations concerning the recitation of prayer also apply to women. The female component is, however, excluded from every involvement in fraternal offices and from the most significant and public events such as following the cross in procession, singing lauds, flagellation (on Fridays) and the gathering and distribution of alms.

Despite the limits placed on women, the matriculation list reveals a significant female presence. The list extends over the course of the fourteenth century, during which period the female component became almost twice as large as the male membership (see table A).

The only contemporary matriculation list noting female membership is that of the raccomandati in Assisi, but there the gender ratio was decidedly different, with 85 women to 284 men. In Gubbio the registration of women is more precise, and is recorded according to city quarter. In some cases these women are the wives of fraternal members, in others, the mothers and daughters. Nine women belonging to Gubbio's first family in the first half of the fourteenth century, the Gabrielli, are among the names listed. They were the wives, daughters and sisters of the male members of the family who were also enrolled in the fraternity. The honorific of *dominae* precedes some of these female names and would seem to denote women of greater social-economic status. In this regard it is interesting to note that while the absolute number of these women of higher status is roughly equivalent for each of the quarters (with the exception of S. Pietro), their presence as a percentage of female membership varies widely from one quarter to the next (see table B).

This fraternity in Gubbio recruited many members from the religious orders, and here too the female preponderance is overwhelming. Out of a

---

[54] GAV, *Sezione Pergamene della Curia Vescovile*, 1, 2, 3, 5. Fiorucci, "S. Maria del Mercato," 115–24.
[55] GAV, C.II.13, c. 5v.

Table A. *Recruitment to the confraternity of S. Maria del Mercato of Gubbio in the fourteenth century.*

City quarters	Lay men	Lay women
S. Andrea	158	279
S. Giuliano	175	371
S. Martino	318	581
S. Pietro	441	929
Total	1092	2160

GAV, C.II.13, cc. 19r–41r. Fiorucci, *S. Maria del Mercato*, 69–89.

Table B. *Gentlewomen in the confraternity of S. Maria del Mercato of Gubbio in the fourteenth century*

City Quarters	Women	Dominae	
S. Andrea	279	47	(16.84%)
S. Giuliano	371	43	(11.59%)
S. Martino	579	45	(7.77%)
S. Pietro	929	35	(3.77%)

total of 444 religious noted in the list, 60 are men and 384 are women. In very few cases is the monastery identified. Among these *sorores* there might also have been recluses and/or tertiaries.

Slightly more than one hundred years after its inception, this old fraternity in Gubbio was renewed under the impact of the popular movement of the *Bianchi* in 1399. Devotion to the Virgin played a central role in the devotions of these white-robed penitents, while the practice of discipline was not necessarily present right from the beginning. As a result, women are found actively participating in the processions of the Bianchi.[56] Gubbio's S. Maria del Mercato would in time take on the qualification "dei Bianchi" in its title, and though predominantly female in the fourteenth century, had a very reduced component of women according to a rough copy of a fifteenth-century matriculation list.[57] There is no clear explanation for this change, which is borne out more clearly in some of the other documents. A set of vernacular statutes produced in 1463–4 clearly point out the dominant role of men: the managerial-administrative chapters make no reference to women whatsoever. By this period, the Commune had put the fraternity in full charge of a hospital which had been instituted under communal auspices in the fourteenth century. Since this involved the confraternity in tasks which

---

[56] Tognetti, "Sul moto dei Bianchi," 209, 211, 213, 217, 244–6, 303, 317, 339; Bornstein, *Bianchi of 1399*. Fiorucci, "S. Maria del Mercato," 173–81.   [57] GAV, C.II.13, c. 63r.

Table C. *Mixed Confraternities in Perugian Visitation Reports of 1592–5*

Place	Church	Dedicatory Title
Mantignana	S. Maria	società della Vergine
Antria	—	SS. Rocco e Sebastiano
Compignano	S. Cristoforo	Rosario
Pieve Caina	S. Maria	Rosario
Spina	S. Nicolò	Madonna
Perugia	S. Simone	società del SS.Sacramento e della Madonna
Perugia	S. Donato	SS. Sacramento
Perugia	S. Angelo	SS. Sacramento
Perugia	S. Cristoforo	SS. Sacramento e Vergine
Perugia	S. Elisabetta	SS. Sacramento e Vergine
Perugia	S. Andrea	SS. Sacramento
Perugia	S. Savino	SS. Sacramento
Perugia	S. Maria dei Servi	Crocifisso
Perugia	—	Madonna del Pianto
Perugia	—	SS. Annunziata
Perugia	S. Domenico	Rosario

were both public and civil and also economic and administrative, only men could take on positions of authority within the fraternity and the hospital.

LONGER TRENDS: THE PASTORAL VISITATION OF 1592–5

Elsewhere I have discussed the activities of mixed or exclusively female aggregations in the dioceses of Spoleto and Perugia based on the reports of apostolic and pastoral visitors.[58] Examining the pastoral visit which Napoleone Comitoli carried out in the years 1592–5 will allow us to check such female presence in the diocese of Perugia. Comitoli was bishop of Perugia from 1591 to 1624, and a proponent of the Tridentine program for spiritual and administrative diocesan reform.[59] Although his first visit was carried out exhaustively and systematically, the information it offers concerning women in confraternities is rather scanty.[60] While the visitor usually takes great care in noting down every single corporate or associative group, place by place and church by church, the specific composition of *societates*, *fraternitates* and *confraternitates* is seldom mentioned. The diocese of Perugia in both its city and territory appears to hold 147 societates and confraternities, 16 of which are mixed aggrega-

---

[58] Casagrande, "Ricerche."

[59] Gabrijelcic, "Vescovi e cattedrale," 521. Chiacchella, "Città della Controriforma," 14–16.

[60] ADPg, *Visitationes*, 10.

Table D. *Female confraternities in Perugian visitation reports of 1592–5*

Place	Church	Dedicatory title
S. Giovanni di Pian di Capine		società della Vergine (altar)
Montecolognola	S. Maria	società delle donne (altar of the Virgin)
Monte Fontignano (Monte del Lago)	S. Andrea	società della donne (Rosary and Conception altars)
S. Savino	S. Maria Maddalena	società del SS. Sacramento
Passignano		società delle donne (altar)
Gaiche	S. Lorenzo	donne dell'Annunziata (altar)
Castel Rigone	Madonna dei Miracoli	altar of the Virgin kept by women
Ponte Pattoli	S. Maria	Madonna (altar)
Perugia	S. Antonio	Madonna

tions and 9 exclusively female groups.[61] The mixed groups are listed in table C, and the female groups in table D.

These tables convey the information given in Comitoli's reports, but the reports themselves probably under-estimate the spread of women in confraternities, for at least three reasons. First, the reports specify the composition of societates and fraternities only in certain instances. Second, parallel reports generated from earlier apostolic and pastoral visits demonstrate that some confraternities which Comitoli's reports imply were male-only, must indeed have been mixed. There is a significant number of such groups, including a confraternity of disciplinati in Oro, a Marian confraternity in Cenerente (for which Comitoli speaks only of *confratres*), groups in Prepo and Casalina, a Rosary confraternity in S. Agnese/S. Enea, a fraternity of the Sacrament in Deruta, and a fraternity of the Name of Jesus in Solomeo. By the same token, Comitoli's report fails to note other confraternities which, according to previous apostolic and pastoral visits, were exclusively female, such as a fraternity of the Madonna del Serraglio in Corciano, fraternities of the Madonna in Tuoro, Agello and Cerqueto, the fraternity of the Madonna della Quercia on Isola Polvese, fraternities of the Rosary in Badiola and Passignano, and the fraternity of the Conception in Castiglione Ugolino.[62]

Third, documentation from other sources beyond the apostolic and pastoral visitations provides corroborative evidence of female confraternities. In the Church of Pieve Petroia, at the foot of Monte Tezio, for

[61] This corrects an earlier study in which I counted 138 fraternities. "Ricerche", 39. For Perugian confraternities, see Marinelli, *Le confraternite di Perugia*; Black, *Italian Confraternities*; Casagrande, "Monasteri, nuovi ordini," 102; Proietti Pedetta, "Culto, devozione", 39–46.
[62] Casagrande, "Ricerche".

example, there was a fraternity of the Madonna with statutes dating from 1589. This devotional group had celebrations at the feast of the Annunciation, and aimed to lead its members into lives of good manners, customs, piety, and charity. Both brothers and sisters were to set perfect examples and not be blasphemous; a certain internal support system was provided for in case of death or infirmity of both brothers and sisters; the confraternity was governed by male priors who were charged with the overall administration. The women, for their part, were provided with two *priore* who must have a house where they might keep the garments of the Madonna, "and clothe her at the appropriate times" ("*e rivestirla à suoi tempi*") – clearly a significant ritual requiring respect for the Virgin's modesty and so deemed more appropriately the task of female as opposed to male members. Women were required to give only half of the amount of admission fees and alms deemed necessary for the men. This was a modest company in a rural area where cases of extreme poverty were not unknown. Hence "delinquent" brothers had to pay their own pecuniary fines unless too poor to do so. Comitoli makes no mention of this company at all. He does note, however, an altar of the Virgin connected to the society of the Sacrament.[63]

Returning to Comitoli's reports, we can extract data from both his reports and parallel documentation which allow us to develop a picture, albeit sketchy, of the nature of some of the female confraternities which he found in his Visitations. In Ponte Pattoli, a female confraternity Comitoli identified had at least thirty members. Their names are given in a contemporary extant matriculation list. The first woman on the list is *Madonna Eusepia della Penna delli Aregucci,* and it is safe to assume that she was probably also the most prestigious female member, since the others lack her honorific term of address and family name, and are registered more simply by their marriage ties, such as *La Giulia de Andreano, la Clementia moglie di Renzo.*[64]

In the church of Madonna dei Miracoli in Castel Rigone, Comitoli points out that the altar dedicated to the Virgin is kept by a confraternity of women. According to a visitation report almost two decades earlier, this *societas mulierum* was instituted in 1496 with written regulations and the explicit obligation to manage the altar dedicated to the Virgin.[65] The lay sisters visited other female members who were ill, providing help with alms and accompanying their deceased sisters to the grave. They celebrated masses and anniversaries but did not have any property. They did,

[63] ADPg, *Statuti delle confraternite, Capitoli da osservarsi da quelli della Compagnia della Madonna della Pieve di Petroia* (1589). ADPg, *Visitationes*, 10, c. 196v. Casagrande, "Ricerche", 43, 60 n. 90.
[64] ADPg, *Visitationes*, 10, c. 227rv. ADPg, *Hospitalia et confraternitates, Donne della Compagnia della Madonna del Ponte di Pattole.*   [65] ADPg, *Visitationes*, 10, c. 163v. ADPg, *Visite*, 7/5, year 1577.

however, accept offerings from members, and collected alms publicly. A *Libro de la fraternita de le donne di Castel Rigone 1559–1687* gives us a fuller picture of the arrangements at this church-cum-sanctuary of the Madonna dei Miracoli. While the Virgin's altar was in the care of an exclusively female fraternity under the governance of three *priore*, there was also a hospital associated with the shrine which was under the administration of an exclusively male fraternity.[66]

The co-existence of separate male and female confraternities in a single church, each entrusted with a distinct function, must have been relatively common. In the same hamlet of Castel Rigone at the church of S. Bartolomeo there was a male confraternity of Corpus Christi, but in the same church the parish priest instituted a *societas mulierum viduarum* which had no rules beyond taking communion the first Sunday of every month.[67]

As to the mixed confraternities identified in Comitoli's first visitation reports, we can find additional information on a few of the groups in the city of Perugia itself. The company of the Most Holy Sacrament in the church of S. Angelo had statutes dictated by the Dominican bishop Vincenzo Ercolani (1579–86). The presence of women in this group may be due to the fact that a pre-existing female company of the Madonna di Monte Cardello had been integrated into it.[68] The mixed society in the church of S. Cristoforo managed the altars of the Virgin and of the Sacrament, with the women taking care of the Virgin, and the men taking care of the Sacrament. An analogous society in the church of S. Elisabetta solemnized the feast of the Visitation and celebrated "several masses for the sisters the day after."[69]

Whereas the mixed composition of the fraternity of the Rosary in S. Domenico seems normal, the female presence in the flagellant fraternity of the Annunziata is far more unusual, for the general reasons discussed above.[70] It certainly is the only case in Perugia of women being accepted into a flagellant confraternity[71]. An answer may lie in a charitable role undertaken by the confraternity in 1558. From that year until 1645, the group took in *convertite*, or those prostitutes seeking to leave the profession. This no doubt made it necessary to recruit some "honest" or respectable women into the confraternity for a number of purely practical

[66] *L'archivio della confraternita*, 39–40. Cf. also *Costituzioni e capitoli della confraternita della Madonna de' Miracoli*.   [67] ADPg, *Visite*, 7/5, year 1577.

[68] *Raccolta di orazioni*. Siepi, "Descrizione," 68–9.   [69] ADPg, *Visitationes*, 10, c. 325r–v.

[70] Meersseman, *Ordo fraternitatis*, 2, 996; 3, 1191. Casagrande, *Religiosità penitenziale*, 396; Pizzoni, "Confraternita dell'Annunziata."

[71] S. Agostino, S. Domenico and S. Francesco in 1472 declare "che femine non possano entrare nelle nostre case" (Perugia, *Archivio Braccio Fortebracci*, A VI 513, c. 10r; Casagrande, "Women in Confraternities", 9–10).

reasons relating to direct care of the convertite. Indeed, Comitoli in his visitation report notes, "in this fraternity there are also women who used to receive those prostitutes who decided to change their lives."[72] Having said this, however, the revised statutes of 1587 make no reference whatsoever to women, which is a clear sign of their subordinate role in the male organization of the confraternity.

Between 1542 and 1627, a massive influx of women swelled the company of S. Anello/S. Giuseppe in Perugia. The matriculation list counts for more than 1800 women divided according to city quarter.[73] The names of those who belonged to the families of the oligarchy certainly stood out: Alfani, Armanni, Baldeschi, Baglioni, Benincasa, Bontempi, Cavaceppi, Coppoli, della Corgna, della Penna, Graziani, Montemelini, Montesperelli, Oddi, Paolucci, Perinelli, Sciri, Signorelli, Sozi. Yet these are joined by the wives and daughters of such tradesmen as bakers, wool-workers, barbers, druggists, cobblers, haberdashers, shoe-makers, masons, carpenters, glaziers, and weavers. Some servant women had followed their masters into the company, but indications of other types of female trades are quite rare; for example there are only two "*spizocharelle*" (pork-butchers). Numerous women belonging to monastic communities join the company from the monasteries of the Beata Colomba, S. Tommaso, S. Giuliana, and S. Lucia. There are also some Franciscan tertiary sisters and a group of Florentine Dominican sisters amongst whom we may find Caterina de' Ricci. Twenty-four other women come from the territory surrounding Perugia such as Castiglione della Valle. This massive female presence suited the company's orientation to public worship and devotion since its founding by the Franciscan Observant Bernardino da Feltre in 1487.[74] Around the presumed relic of the Virgin's nuptial ring, the company presented itself as a *summa* of devotion focused on Mary, Joseph, and Christ (in the form of the Holy Sacrament). This devotional circuit of Virgin-Mother, model husband, and Son-Redeemer underscored the sacralization of marriage and the family. Such a company by its very nature included both men and women. Significantly, the oldest statutes, dating from the late fifteenth century, do not distinguish between male and female roles.[75] But times changed, and the revised statutes of 1584 required that male and female members be registered separately. The women had the same obligations as the men in the devotion to the Holy Sacrament (daily prayers, masses, procession of Corpus Domini, etc.) and were allowed to choose those

[72] ADPg, *Visitationes*, 10, cc. 359r–360r. Black, *Italian confraternities*, 211. Pizzoni, "Confraternita dell'Annunziata," 150.

[73] ACPg, Compagnia del SS. Sacramento/S. Giuseppe (S. Anello), *Matricola* n. 3.

[74] BAP, ms. 3106, c. 1r; Casagrande, "Devozione e municipalità," 163.

[75] BAP, ms. 3106, c. 65v; Casagrande, "Devozione e municipalità," 183.

amongst them who should visit their ill sisters. The management of the company remained, however, completely male.[76]

By the seventeenth century other associations included women. The company of the Nome di Dio/ di Gesù instituted in the church of S. Domenico accepted married women, sisters and nuns. Its female branch was governed by two priore and a female sacristan. The *priore* appear to be of elevated social background, inasmuch as they belonged to families of the oligarchy such as Alfani, Baldeschi, Baglioni, della Penna, Perinelli, Pontani, Armanni, Beccuti, Graziani, etc. [77] Another group, Confraternita del Suffragio in S. Maria di Colle reveals an opening for women in its statutes of 1628. [78] Finally, undated statutes of the late sixteenth or early seventeenth centuries show that the confraternity administering the Misericordia hospital, which as we saw earlier had refused to enroll women, establishes a subordinate group entitled *la nova compagnia delle Donne in aiuto al buon governo dell'Hospitale della Misericordia*. This company was to number fifty women (ten from each quarter) who were charged with checking the female wards of the large city hospital for any problems or needs.[79]

GENERAL CONSIDERATIONS

This survey of women's participation in Umbrian confraternities allows us to make some general observations. In certain medieval fraternities women appear in great numbers but their presence is suspended between esserci and valere, between mere presence and real worth. Their level of involvement is limited and must be placed in a larger context. Recent studies point out that the space available for religious female action throughout the thirteenth, fourteenth and fifteenth centuries was expanding, with a blossoming of forms of religious life no longer and not only linked to traditional monastic expressions. A universe of recluses, *conversae*, oblates, and penitent tertiaries animates these centuries.[80] The tertiary penitential solution was perhaps most common in the period from the fourteenth century to the early sixteenth century. This was the most open, practicable and, at the same time, the safest form which could guarantee links with the relevant orders, possess its own rules and therefore offer the certain canonic-juridical status of *religiosae personae*. Throughout the fifteenth century cities such as Perugia, Assisi, Città di

---

[76] ACPg, Compagnia del SS. Sacramento/S. Giuseppe (S. Anello), *Matricola* n. 4, cc. 97r–9v.

[77] ASP, CRS, S. Domenico, Misc. 77; Black, *Italian Confraternities*, 37; Casagrande, "Women in Confraternities," 12.

[78] BAP, ms. 1386, cc. 419–20; Casagrande, "Women in Confraternities," 12–3.

[79] ADPg, *Hospitalia et confraternitates*.

[80] Benvenuti Papi, "*In castro poenitentiae*", and "*Regularis familia*". Casagrande, *Religiosità penitenziale*.

Castello, and Foligno saw a significant expansion of houses and monasteries of tertiaries (most of them Franciscan). Here a "universe in the feminine" associated itself with and organized itself around leader figures who were widows or unmarried women of good economic and property-owning backgrounds, whether of the aristocracy/nobility or not. Foligno with the congregation of the B. Angelina da Montegiove, and Perugia with the congregation formed around the community of S. Agnese became, if only for a short period of time, centers promoting new, open (non cloistering) communitary-monastic realities.[81] The world of tertiaries appears to me as having offered late medieval women the fullest possibility of female religious action, and one which might have occupied more of the attention of lay women who were seeking some communal outlet for their religious and devotional impulses. If this were the case, women would have been less hindered by their marginalization in confraternities.

The situation changes somewhat at the beginning of the early modern period, as women's membership in confraternities and societates, both mixed or exclusively female, increases. Women joined both traditional Marian associations and the newer confraternities which focused their devotions on the Sacrament and the Rosary. Two factors are particularly important in explaining this. First, the cloistering of tertiary communities reduced their appeal to women who wished to remain lay. Second, the desire on the part of the hierarchy for greater control and stricter arrangement of the faithful via a diffusion of networked and interrelated fraternal associations increased the drive to recruit women into fraternities, companies and societies.[82]

I have only given an overview of a broad network of possible forms of aggregation. Women were not excluded from all forms of confraternal sociability, but extant documents do not put much significance on their roles and duties (whether administrative or anything else). This reflects the broader contemporary marginalization of women through a "circle of exclusions." As we move into the early modern period, the space left open to women is effectively an extension of the sphere of domestic life. Women could escape such a life only through the various forms of religious life, but that also meant having to give up their lay-secular status. For those wanting to keep such lay-secular status, confraternal space offered a margin of possible and necessary – albeit limited – acceptance.

---

[81] *Le terziarie francescane della beata Angelina; Biografie antiche della beata Angelina.* Casagrande, *Religiosità penitenziale,* 234–50.

[82] Pazzelli, *La vita claustrale,* 15. Zardin, "Il rilancio delle confraternite." Black, *Italian Confraternities,* 38.

4

THE BOUNDS OF COMMUNITY: COMMUNE, PARISH, CONFRATERNITY, AND CHARITY AT THE DAWN OF A NEW ERA IN CORTONA

DANIEL BORNSTEIN

The statutes of the fraternity of Santa Maria in the church of San Vincenzo, redacted in 1481 "for the honor and greatness of the Holy Mother Church and the entire Christian faith," are much like those of any other pious confraternity in late medieval Italy.[1] Their fourteen clauses establish the procedures for electing the fraternity's prior, stipulate that he will be assisted by a treasurer and five counselors, regulate the expenditure of the fraternity's funds, and specify that each prior and treasurer promptly consign to their successors the financial records of their term in office. They require that all the men and women of the fraternity assemble on the first Sunday of each month, the major Marian feasts and all the *pasque* (Christmas, Epiphany, Easter, and Pentecost), and any other time the prior orders a procession. They insist that all the men of the fraternity make and maintain peace with one another. They instruct the prior to visit any sick member, look to his physical needs, and urge him to see to his spiritual condition by making a proper confession; and they remind dying members to leave to the fraternity half of the candles that are carried to their burial. They order every man and woman belonging to the fraternity to say an Our Father and a Hail Mary when they sit down to eat, and then make the sign of the cross over their food;

Research for this essay was supported by a grant-in-aid from the American Philosophical Society, a Special Opportunities in Archival Research grant from the National Endowment for the Humanities, and an International Research Travel Grant, and a grant from the Program to Enhance Scholarly and Creative Activities of Texas A&M University. I am grateful to all of those institutions for their generous support and to Dott. Bruno Gialluca for facilitating my research in innumerable ways.

[1] Archivio storico del comune di Cortona [henceforth ACC], Z 63, ff. 1r–2r. For an excellent overview of modern scholarship on Italian confraternities, see Rusconi, "Confraternite, compagnie e devozioni."

to say fifteen Our Fathers and Hail Marys for the souls of any deceased
members as soon as possible after their death; and to say an Our Father
and a Hail Mary every time they pass the entrance of the cemetery as they
go to church, for the remission of sins of all those who have passed from
this life. They oblige all the men of the fraternity to accompany the prior
when the office is recited and to remain for the entire mass; and instruct
those who are unable to do so to recite twenty-five Our Fathers and Hail
Marys with the Requiem Eternam for the souls of the deceased. And they
enjoin the prior and treasurer to read the statutes (or have them read) at
the monthly meeting, or at least at the start of the year when the prior and
treasurer are elected, so that all the men and women of the fraternity may
observe them for the good of their souls and the honor of God and the
Virgin Mary.[2] A final clause, added in the time of Domenico di Niccolò,
prior, and Francesco di Giovanni, treasurer, with the approval of the
syndic and of sixteen men of the fraternity, provides for the creation of a
confraternal supply of grain, to be ready in case of need.[3]

These utterly undistinguished statutes could have been redacted any-
where in the Italian peninsula, at any time in the fourteenth and fifteenth
centuries. Even the carefully archaizing hand in which they were written,
intended to lend greater dignity and antiquity to the institution, could as
easily be dated to 1381 as 1481. The piety they propound is as common
and as constant as the institutional form they define. It is a simple piety,
based on recitation of the most basic prayers and attendance at the most
essential rite of Christian worship, on the chief feasts of the liturgical year.
It is a practical piety, offering sustenance in times of dearth, comfort and
care in times of illness, and reassurance at the moment of death.[4] And it is
a corporate piety, urging reciprocal peace and mutual assistance among
the brethren of the fraternity, and extending this community of the living
beyond the grave, to assure the dead of the fraternity an honorable burial
and help them to find eternal rest.[5] Such are the obvious conclusions to
which a reading of the statutes will lead, conclusions that are in harmony
with those of any number of other studies of Italian confraternities, based
on the more or less sensitive reading of countless numbingly similar
confraternal statutes.[6]

---

[2] On the potential of this regular reading of the confraternal statutes to shape lay piety, see
Meersseman, "La riforma delle confraternite laicali," 27–8, and Bornstein, *The Bianchi of 1399*, 32–5.

[3] A list of nineteen men (and five women, all related to one or another of the men), in the same
handwriting as the statutes and presumably representing the persons who assented to this addition, is
found on ACC, Z 63, f. 3r.

[4] On confraternal charity, see Henderson, *Piety and Charity*, and Terpstra, *Lay Confraternities and Civic
Religion*.

[5] On confraternities as vehicles of social harmony, see Weissman, *Ritual Brotherhood*; on memorialization, see Banker, *Death in the Community*.

[6] Agostino Paravicini Bagliani has noted that Italian scholarship in this field has been characterized by

But these statutes were not redacted just anytime or any place. They are from the small city of Cortona, in southern Tuscany, and belong to the fraternity associated with Cortona's cathedral church; and in the century leading up to 1481, Cortona gradually but irrevocably lost its political and ecclesiastical independence. Cortona had acquired a distinct juridical identity early in the fourteenth century, with the erection of Cortona as a separate diocese in 1325 and the almost simultaneous establishment of the Casali family as *signori* of Cortona.[7] Cortona managed to maintain its precarious independence throughout the Trecento, thanks in no small part to its location at the intersection of the Perugian, Aretine, and Sienese spheres of influence. But as Florence extended its Tuscan hegemony around 1400, Cortona's position proved untenable. No longer able to balance one powerful neighbor against another, the last of the Casali signori lost Cortona in 1409 to King Ladislao of Naples, who two years later sold his prize to the Florentines for 60,000 florins. The civic councils of Cortona pleaded – with considerable success – to retain their local weights and measures and currency, their local jurisdiction over civil and criminal cases, and their local officials. But Florence supplied a captain to exercise supreme authority in its name, with a staff of notaries to assist him in his administration and a garrison to enforce his decisions and orders; and when the long-lived Cortonese bishop Enoch Cioncolari finally passed away in 1426, his successor, Matteo Ughi, was just the first in a long series of Florentines to occupy the see of Cortona.[8] In ecclesiastical as in civic affairs, Cortona had fallen under Florentine sway.

THE FRATERNITY AND ITS BOOK

The statutes of 1481 represent at most a refoundation or reform of the confraternity, since a fraternity of San Vincenzo existed as early as 13 June 1363, when Mone olim Brandini de Cortona left it a candle worth £4 to be lit on the feast of Corpus Christi.[9] But that fraternity may have passed out of existence, to be refounded in 1381. Starting in that year, and continuing for four decades, we have the record of income and expendi-

an almost exclusive reliance on statutes and other normative texts: "Présentation," *Le mouvement confraternel*, 5. For some notably sensitive readings of confraternal statutes, see *Statuti di confraternite religiose*, ed. De Sandre Gasparini, and Brufani, "La fraternita di S. Stefano." In Italian scholarship, even studies of the economic aspects of devotional confraternities tend to be based exclusively on the statutes, rather than on financial records: see, for instance, Mira, "Primi sondaggi." For a precious exception to this rule, see Varanini, "Spunti per una indagine."

[7] Mancini, *Cortona nel Medio Evo*, 97–102.   [8] Mirri, *I vescovi di Cortona*.

[9] Biblioteca Comunale e dell'Accademia Etrusca di Cortona [henceforth BCC], ms. 415, Imbreviaturae ser Rinaldi Toti, nempe filii Christophori, notarii Cortonensis ab anno 1358 ad annum 1374, part II, f. 23r–v.

tures kept by the prior and treasurer of the fraternity.[10] Whether the
fraternity, too, began a new existence in 1381 remains unclear.[11] The
declaration of the prior Francesco di Naldo Fantozo that "these are the
expenditures of our first year" (f. 3r) certainly suggests that the confraternity itself began in that year; and Viva di Naldo, who succeeded
Francesco di Naldo Fantozo in office, is later referred to as the "second
prior of our fraternity" (96r). However, the registration in 1381 of cash
received from the previous treasurer (2r) is puzzling; and "our first year"
could refer instead to the first year that Francesco di Naldo Fantozo was
prior and Donato di Pucciarello his treasurer – and in fact they did
continue in office for the following year.

It was rare indeed for the prior to serve two years in a row; the only
other time it happened in these forty years was 1412–13, when Renzo di
Uccio was prior (with unfortunate results, to which we shall return). The
office of treasurer, on the other hand, tended to be dominated by a few
persons whose names recur frequently: in the fifteen years from 1401 to
1415, for instance, it was held twice by Pietro di Pucciarello, three times
by Niccolò di Francesco del Bretto, and fully nine times by Mamigliano
dei Santi. Evidently the statutes did not require the regular circulation of
offices, and as a result leadership of the fraternity tended to be dominated
by a handful of men who were more respected, more socially prominent,
or simply more trusted by their brethren. While 37 different people
occupied the chief offices of the fraternity of San Vincenzo in the 37 years
for which we know the names of the prior and treasurer (information for
1385–8 is lacking), more than half the time those offices were held by one
of only seven people.[12]

Whether they held office ten times or only once, all of the office-
holders of the fraternity of San Vincenzo were men. It is possible that
membership in the fraternity was initially restricted to men, though
without statutes or a matriculation list it is impossible to be entirely sure.
By 1400, at any rate, women were being admitted as members: the
fraternity's income for that summer includes 6 *soldi* from "three women

---

[10] ACC, Z 3, pezzo 9: fraternita di San Vincenzo, entrata e uscita (1381–1422). The volume consists
of 152 folios in six groupings (of ff. 28 + 25 + 26 + 23 + 26 + 24); the last folio is torn and partially
missing, and water damage has rendered the top center of some folios illegible.

[11] If its statutes had survived, we would know exactly when the fraternity of San Vincenzo was
founded and for what declared purpose. But the original statutes have vanished, perhaps discarded
when the new ones – or new copy of the old ones – were drawn up in 1481. On the problem of
distinguishing foundations from reforms, see Meersseman, "La riforma delle confraternite laicali."

[12] Donato di Pucciarello was prior or treasurer on five occasions and his brother Pietro di Pucciarello
on four, Francesco di Giovanni di Niccolò in five years, Francesco di Naldo Fantozo in four,
Giovanni di Pietro also in four, Niccolò di Francesco del Bretto in six, and the ever-present
Mamigliano dei Santi was one of the chief officers of the fraternity in ten different years.

who inscribed themselves in the fraternity of San Vincenzo" and another s. 2 d. 6 from the wife of Bambigliano for the same reason (f. 65r). Membership fees were not usually registered in the book, so no conclusive case can be made on the basis of previous silence; but the sheer novelty of having women join the fraternity may explain why the fees were recorded this year – and not in later ones, when it was no longer a novelty. If this was indeed a new development, the reasons behind it seem many and complex. One was probably the menace of epidemic mortality, which threatened men and women alike in the plague year of 1400: the plague's capacity to disrupt normal funeral and mourning customs was notorious, and women surely wished to share in the promise of decent burial and proper memorialization, guaranteed by membership in a religious institution. That institution itself needed to consider the costs that faced it: a single page (f. 68r) registers expenditures for the burials of seventeen people in October 1400, sixteen of whom seem to be children of members of the fraternity or of persons close to them. Given the pressure of these expenses, the men of the fraternity may have been impressed by the potential financial contribution that could come from women – a potential that had recently been demonstrated most effectively, when the donations received on 25 January 1400 from "the men of the church" amounted to only 4 soldi, while those gathered a week later, on the first Sunday of February, "from the men and the women" totalled s. 18 d. 6, better than four times as much (f. 65r). Finally, there was the close personal connection with one of the officers of the fraternity: "Bambigliano" (whose wife paid s. 2 d. 6 to join the fraternity) is a variant spelling of "Mamigliano," and Mamigliano dei Santi was prior of the fraternity of San Vincenzo in 1400 – the first of the many times in which he appears among the leaders of the fraternity. In any case, a reference to the "men and women" of the fraternity of San Vincenzo turns up in 1419 (135r); and the unusually elaborate preamble to the record of income for 1421 confirms that the fraternity then included both men and women, though it seems that only men took part in electing the officials.[13] That itself may explain why all its officers were men.[14]

---

[13] "Al nome de Dio e dela sua madre vergene Maria e del beato santo Vincentio e del beato santo Lorenzo e del beato santo Stefano e del beato santo Nicholo e de tutti li santi e le sante dela corte del paradiso, a honore e stato e mantenemento degli uomini e donne ['donne" written a second time by mistake, and cancelled] dela fraternita del beato misser santo Vincentio, qui de socto scrivaremo tucte l'entrate pervenarà [changed from pervenute] ale mane de Bartolomeo de Giovanni de Bienasaie [inserted: priore] e de Giovanni de Bartolomeo d'Antonio suo camarlengo del detto priore nella detta fraternita, electi per gli uomini dela detta fratenita con tutte le sollenità e modi che contano li capitoli dela detta fraternita per uno anno proximo che dia venire." ACC, Z 3, pezzo 9, f. 142r.

[14] I have found no clear evidence of female officers in any of the confraternities of Cortona during the

These officers, unsurprisingly, were persons of some substance. Their assessments in the Cortonese *catasto* of 1402 show that most of them held property valued between £400 and £1,000, though several declared holdings of less than £100 and a few held more than £1,000 worth of real estate; one, Francesco di Naldo Fantozo, owned 22 pieces of property, worth over £3,000.[15] We may guess – though in the absence of matriculation lists it can be no more than a reasonable guess – that the officials of San Vincenzo were, on average, wealthier than their non-office holding brethren. There is no doubt, however, that the wealth of even the richest of them paled beside that of Cortona's patriciate, people like Tomasso di ser Francesco di ser Ranieri di Guido Boscie of the Tomassi family, whose declaration lists hundreds of properties and covers eleven large folios, recto and verso.[16] Though far from impoverished, the officials of San Vincenzo were at best moderately well off.

In large part, this reflects the character of the neighborhood where San Vincenzo was located. The area within the city walls was already built up by the time Cortona was elevated to the dignity of an episcopal seat in 1325, forcing the new bishop to locate his cathedral church outside the walls. Pope John XXII assigned him San Vincenzo, in the sparsely inhabited *borgo* on the southern edge of the city.[17] This eccentric location (and perhaps the steep climb from San Vincenzo to the center of town) proved inconvenient to the bishops, who preferred to reside by the old *pieve* of Santa Maria, which became in 1508, and remains to this day, the cathedral church of Cortona. San Vincenzo thus functioned less as the bishop's cathedral than as the parish church of Borgo San Vincenzo, and it belonged in practice, if not in canon law, to the faithful it served. If the addresses of its officials accurately reflect those of the membership at large, the fraternity of San Vincenzo engaged the participation primarily of residents of the *terziere* and *borgo* of San Vincenzo, just inside and outside the city gate. Such neighborhoods typically received recent immigrants to the city, persons who were often poorer and always less deeply rooted

---

fourteenth and fifteenth centuries. The mention of "la bella prioressa" in the records of the fraternity of San Michelangelo in November 1375 probably refers to the wife of Cristofano di Ceccolo di Marco, who on 7 October 1375 was elected prior for six months. See ACC, Z 3, pezzo 11, f. 10r: "Ancho ebe da sere Francescho che l'ebe da la bella prioressa dela detta frateneta, adì XIII de novenbre [1375], £IIII." In the sixteenth century, however, chapter 12 of the statutes of the Compagnia della Santa Croce that met in San Francesco states quite explicitly that even if men should someday be admitted to this female association, leadership was reserved to the women: "Ultimam, intendiamo che se mai questa Compagnia moltiplicassi in numero di huomini et di donne, solamente le donne habbino il governo, sì di Priora come anco di Camarlinga." BCC, ms. 411, f. 12r.

[15] ACC, C 6: catasto of 1402, ter. San Vincenzo; the declaration of Franciscus Gnaldi Fantozi is on f. 250r.   [16] ACC, C 4: catasto of 1402, ter. San Marco, ff. 197r–207v.

[17] The text of the bull is published in Mirri, *I vescovi di Cortona*, 21–5.

than the better established Cortonese families, and hence eager for the sort of fellowship and support – spiritual, social, and economic – offered by associations like the fraternity of San Vincenzo.

CHARITY AND PIETY

Fraternities like that of San Vincenzo in Cortona helped to bind together the social fabric in innumerable small but crucial ways. They fed the hungry, clothed the naked, comforted those in prison, visited the sick, and buried the dead. In 1381, the year that its record of income and expenditures opens, the fraternity of San Vincenzo gave 5 soldi to lame Biagio the tailor when he was sick, and the same sum to the wife of Giovanni from La Fratta when she was in labor, for wine (f. 4v). Another 5 soldi were given to two pilgrims on their way home from Jerusalem (3r), while 20 soldi went to Maddalena del Techia to help get her son-in-law out of prison (3v) and a gold florin (worth five Cortonese lire) to a leading member of the fraternity, Serra, to help marry off the daughter of Ladovitia (4v). On October 28 the fraternity gave 5 soldi to Govino when he fell ill (4v); and a week later, on November 5, it spent nearly three times as much to bury him.[18]

The fraternity of San Vincenzo did not function simply as a society for mutual assistance, as its statutes would seem to suggest. All those in need, whether or not they were affiliated with the fraternity, could hope to receive something from its helping hands. While most of its aid went to its neighbors in Cortona, complete strangers, like those pilgrims returning from Jerusalem, could also be objects of its charity. The brethren of San Vincenzo gave 5 soldi to a sick man from the contado of Arezzo on 7 January 1382, and in 1390 they buried two pilgrims who died while passing through Cortona and a soldier who died at the inn of Paolo d'Arezzo (ff. 28v and 30v). Such works of mercy did not come cheap; the burial of the two pilgrims cost San Vincenzo £1, and that of the soldier another 15 soldi. But they could count on the spiritual merit they earned by performing their works of mercy – and recoup their costs by selling the personal belongings of these unfortunate wayfarers. The mantle of one of the pilgrims reaped them £2 s. 10, while the cloak and mantle that had belonged to the soldier (who evidently dressed with considerably greater flair and ostentation) brought in £6 (25r-v).

With these sums, and with donations, bequests, payments for honorable burials, and so on, they kept the roof over their church, plastered it and stopped its leaks – and they were very clear about calling San

---

[18] ACC, Z 3, pezzo 9, f. 5r. The page is torn, but one can still see that the sum spent on Govino's funeral was at least s. 14 d. 5.

Vincenzo, which was the cathedral church of the bishop of Cortona, *their* church.[19] Every month, they handed their chaplains 4 soldi for reciting mass and litanies on the first Sunday of the month; and every thirty years or so, they put new antiphonals in the hands of their priests (in 1382 [9r] and 1413 [110v]), or helped them redeem a pawned book (84r, in 1405). In spring, on the feast of Corpus Christi, they gave the priests candles, wine, cheese, and cherries, both sweet and tart (4r, 7v); in August, on the feast of the invention of the body of St. Stephen, they regaled them with white wine and melons; and on 26 December, the main feast of St. Stephen, their expenditures included the purchase not only of wine, bread, cheese, and loin of pork (or sometimes fish), but also wood to build a fire for the priests. Their piety, in short, was a practical piety that responded quite sensibly to the seasons.

In some cases, the fraternity maintained a long-standing relationship with these recipients of charity, to whom they provided support over the course of years. The lame tailor Biagio who received 5 soldi in 1381, when he was sick (4v), was helped out two years later with a gift of twice that sum in the dead of winter, on 15 January 1383 (9v). In August 1383, the fraternity paid 10 soldi to the priests and clerics who attended the burial of Biagio's daughter and to the man who dug her grave.[20] And in 1390, the fraternity's payment of 10 soldi to Biagio on 15 September was followed immediately by the expenditure of another 10 soldi "for the burial of the said Biagio" (30v). But even Biagio's death did not bring an end to this charitable relationship, since a year later Biagio's widow received a series of small sums "for the love of God."[21]

In 1392, the fraternity of San Vincenzo formalized its relationship with Biagio's surviving daughter, Paola del Vagliente, who left her belongings to the fraternity and became its *"raccomandata"* (40r). For the next quarter-century, the fraternity paid the taxes on Paola's house and helped her out with occasional small sums of money, rarely amounting to as much as an entire lira in any one year. When crops failed, they gave her a little grain and olive oil; when she fell sick, they paid for her treatment; and in her last illness, they showered her with attention, spending £2 s. 15 d. 5 on wine, meat, and sugar for their elderly raccomandata. When Paola del Vagliente finally died, in the summer of 1416, she received a far more elaborate funeral than that usually provided by the fraternity: £3 s.

---

[19] In 1390, a series of payments for work on the roof culminates with £7 to "maiestro Ventura che tolse a rischo ad aconciare la nostra ghiesa" (29v).

[20] ACC, Z 3, pezzo 9, f. 15r: "s. 10 per l'amore de dio a doi preti e a cherci che forono a sepellire la figluola de Biasgio sartore sciancato e a custuoie che fece la fossa."

[21] She received 5 soldi on 8 June 1391, another 5 soldi a week later, on 15 June (35r), and s. 5 d. 6 in the fall (35v).

7 were lavished on her burial, while another woman was interred that summer for a mere 10 soldi – the same sum spent to bury Paola's sister back in 1383 and their father in 1390.[22]

The following January, the fraternity paid a small fee to have Paola del Vagliente's listing canceled from the catasto and added to the fraternity's list of landholdings.[23] At that time, the fraternity of San Vincenzo finally came into possession of the property that Paola had promised it back in 1392, twenty-five years earlier, and there may have been some in the fraternity who thought that it was hardly worth the wait: the total estate they inherited consisted of a house in the terziere of San Vincenzo valued at £70 and some farmland in Rio Loreto, in the locality known as Pratella, worth half that amount. But caring for "Paola del Vagliente nostra raccomandata" represented more than just a legal obligation entered into when Paola left her land to the fraternity of San Vincenzo: it was a moral commitment extending over several decades and at least two generations.

The brethren of San Vincenzo took their charitable obligations seriously – so much so that the confraternity typically ran a deficit. But lest they seem too constantly pious, we should note that in May 1390 they had to pay 5 soldi to get their songbook out of hock: their boys had pawned it on their way back from the procession, when they wanted to drink at the fraternity's expense.[24] The clergy they assisted were not without their own little flaws. When a certain fra Antonio landed in prison, the fraternity of San Vincenzo deemed his need sufficiently great (and his unspecified transgression sufficiently innocuous) as to merit a charitable *staio* of grain (111v). The financial shenanigans uncovered in 1416, however, were something else entirely: a gross misappropriation of confraternal monies, and falsification of records in an attempt to conceal this peculation.

---

[22] ACC, Z 3, pezzo 9, f. 125r. The undated entry recording Paola's funeral expenses appears between others dated 18 June and 1 August.

[23] ACC, C 6: catasto of 1402, ter. San Vincenzo, f. 206r; ACC, C 7: Catasto dei beni ecclesiastici, 1402, f. 181r; and ACC, Z 3, pezzo 9, f. 126r. It is only in the catasto record that Paola's name is given as "Paula Blaxii zoppi"; the confraternal account book never mentions that she was the daughter of the lame tailor Biagio. Since the transfer was recorded in the catasto on "MCCCCXVI die VIIII januarii," it is clear that the public documents of the city of Cortona had already shifted to the Florentine system of starting the year on 25 March, while the private records of the confraternity continued to follow the Cortonese tradition of starting the new year on 1 January.

[24] ACC, Z 3, pezzo 9, f. 29r: "E più spesi per recolgliare el libro dele laude che l'onpegniaro e' nostri garzoni quando revenemmo dala priccesione: volsaro bere ale spese dela fraterneta."

THE AUDIT OF 1416

On 11 January 1416, the chancellor of Cortona charged three citizens
with the task of auditing the city's religious institutions.[25] The three
"*ragionieri de' luoghi piatosi*" – Bettino di Bartolomeo di Bettino, Battista
di Niccolò di Guglielmuccio, and Folco di Giovanni di Goro – immediately set to work: a worn and faded note on the front of the account book
of the fraternity of San Vincenzo indicates that the book was consigned
on 13 January 1416, just two days after the auditors took office.[26] And less
than two weeks later, having completed their work with admirable
efficiency, the auditors returned the account book of the fraternity of San
Vincenzo to its owners.

This audit does not look like an ordinary review. The auditors asked
for the books of San Vincenzo as soon as they took office, and they seem
to have examined them with a particular quarry in mind. Rather than
check the entire book, they looked at the three years leading up to their
appointment, marking slight corrections and signing the balance for each
year as they went.[27] They apparently worked backward from the present,
since their note recording the completion of the audit on 24 January 1416
is found under the earliest year checked, 1413.[28] And it was in the
accounts for that year that they uncovered a major irregularity in the
fraternity's bookkeeping.

On 14 January 1414, the prior for 1413 (and for 1412), Renzo di
Uccio, turned over to his successor, Donato di Pucciarello, the records of
his administration. (The treasurer remained Mamigliano dei Santi, who
filled that office almost continually: between 1409 and 1415, the only year
Mamigliano was *not* treasurer was 1411.) According to Renzo di Uccio,
the expenditures for 1413 totalled £57 s. 17 d. 2, while the income
amounted to only £43 s. 2 d. 9; the deficit of £14 s. 14 d. 5, well within
the normal range, still allowed him to hand over to the new administra-

---

25 The audit of the records of the fraternity of San Vincenzo includes a declaration of the official basis
   of the auditors' authority: "Reveduta et calcolata la detta ragione per noi, Folco di Giovanni e
   Battista de Nicholo di Guglielmuccio e per Bettino di Bartolomeo di Bettino, ragionieri de luoghi
   piatosi, chiamati ello consiglio del comuno di Cortona a dì 11 de genaio 1416; fo la nostra tratta del
   oficio per mano di ser Yachomo cancellieri del detto comuno ello sopradetto anno e dì
   soprascritto." ACC, Z 3, pezzo 9, f. 117v.
26 "Prodotto fo el detto libro per Pietro de Ceccho presente priore de la fraterneta de Santo Vincenzo;
   fo prodotto a dì 13 de gienaio 1416." ACC, Z 3, pezzo 9, f. 1r. In recording the consignment of the
   account book, the auditors inverted the prior's name: Francesco di Pietro (not Pietro di Cecco) di
   Puccio was the prior whose year in office was just then coming to an end (f. 118r).
27 Their *saldo* for 1413 is found on f. 112r, for 1414 on f. 117v (where a correction in different ink, and
   in the hand of Bettino di Bartolomeo di Bettino, revises downward the amount by which income
   exceeded expenditures, from £1 s. 14 d. 6 to only s. 18 d. 6), and for 1415 on f. 121v.
28 "Fo reveduta a dì 24 de gienaio 1416 per noi Batissta de Nicholo de Ghoglielmuccio e per Bettino
   de Bartolomeio de Bettino e per me Folcho de Giovanni de Ghoro." ACC, Z 3, pezzo 9, f. 112r.

tion £9 s. 14 d. 6 in cash on hand.[29] But two years later, in January 1416, the auditors discovered that Renzo's accounting had been incomplete. As they declared:

> We find that there came into the hands of Renzo di Uccio, the aforesaid prior of the said fraternity in the said year of 1413, goods from the inheritance that had belonged to Tofano, known as Santamora, the which income appears in a notebook written by the said Renzo's hand in the aforesaid year. The said income derived from household goods sold by the said Renzo, and pigs sold by the said Renzo, and pigs sold by Meio del Serra, and a heifer that had belonged to Santamora which the said Meio kept, and wine that the said Meio also received. We find that the said income amounts to 44 florins, 640 lire, 11 soldi, and 9 denari, including in this total 109 lire and 2 soldi entered as money owed for stuff from the shop given to Niccolò del Serra, as appears in the said Renzo's notebook. In all, 44 florins, £640 s. 11 d. 9.[30]

Since the florin was worth five Cortonese lire, the income from this inheritance which Renzo di Uccio had recorded in his notebook but somehow forgotten to transfer into the fraternity's account book amounted to slightly over 860 lire – twenty times the income of £43 s. 2 d. 9 that he *had* reported for the year. But there were also substantial expenses – 20 florins, £592 s. 10 d. 6 – recorded in Renzo's notebook but not reported in the fraternity's, so that in the end the unreported income exceeded expenses by only the still considerable sum of 24 florins, £101 s. 18 d. 5, or just shy of £222.

It might barely be possible (and certainly charitable) to ascribe Renzo's sloppy accounting to lack of experience: after all, he had never held office in the fraternity before his election as prior in 1412. But his treasurer, Mamigliano dei Santi, had virtually monopolized the office of treasurer in the decade leading up to the audit of 1416, making ignorance of proper accounting procedures a most implausible excuse. The greed of an eager social climber seems far more likely an explanation. Renzo lived with his brother Liberatore at the

---

[29] ACC, Z 3, pezzo 9, f. 112r.

[30] "Trovamo che sono pervenute ale mani de Renco d'Uccio priore predetto de la detta frateneta in lo detto anno de 1413 de bieni de eredetà che fo de Tofano detto Santamora, la quale entrata apare a uno basstardello scritto per mano del detto Renco del anno predetto, e de usuta la detta entrata de masaritie de chasa vendute per lo detto Renço e de porci venduti per lo detto Renço e de porci venduti per Meio del Serra e d'una gioencia che se retene el detto Meio che fo de Santamora e de vino che ebe ancho el detto Meio. Trovamamo che sono la detta entrata [cancelled: £] fiorini quarantaquattro e £ seicentoquaranta e s. undecie d. nuove, chomputato in quessta entrata £ centonuove [cancelled: li qua] e s. doi li quali apare avere datone chose de botiga a Nicholo del Serra si cho' apare al basstardello del detto Renço; sonno in tutto fiorini 44, £640 s. 11 d. 9." ACC, Z 3, pezzo 9, f. 109r.

time of the catasto of 1402, when their property was estimated at a respectable £560; their next-door neighbors were the far wealthier Meio and Niccolò del Serra, who would be Renzo's partners in this affair.³¹ Liberatore was the more successful brother, the one who increased their holdings through marriage and through purchase. In contrast, when Renzo di Uccio entered the tax rolls on his own in 1405, it was with a single piece of farmland valued £24. He sought to make his way by attaching himself to powerful patrons, men like Giovanni Passerini, with whom he acquired joint ownership of a house in 1415. Not that Renzo ever amounted to very much: at their peak, his landholdings were valued at only £289 – and all of them, strikingly, were listed as owned conjointly with much richer partners. These, presumably, were the hidden backers who helped him to office. They were also, one suspects, the true beneficiaries of Renzo's shady dealings, and the people who helped him make restitution when he got caught. For on 16 February 1416, barely three weeks after the completion of the audit that had uncovered his lapse, Renzo di Uccio turned over the missing funds to the new officials of the fraternity, without liquidating any of his property.³²

That is the last we see of Renzo di Uccio in the accounts of the fraternity of San Vincenzo. Mamigliano dei Santi, who had been so prominent in the affairs of the fraternity for so many years, likewise vanishes from their records. After the audit of 1416, his name never again figures among the officers of the fraternity of San Vincenzo – though he irritatingly held his former brethren to a punctilious accounting of money owed him, receiving from them late in 1416 the petty sum of s. 2 d. 1 for the gabella on the olives (f. 125v). With that settled, they wrote him out of their books – and he them: not one bit of Mamigliano dei Santi's property passed to the fraternity of San Vincenzo upon his death.³³ Nor, of course, did any of Renzo di Uccio's, when his entry in the catasto was cancelled on 17 July 1439.

Such failure to remember the confraternity in one's will was most exceptional. Both the confraternal statutes and established practice

---

³¹ ACC, C 6: catasto of 1402, ter. San Vincenzo, f. 214v.

³² "E più recevette fiorini vintiquattro £ centouna s. diciotto d. cinque, ei quali ebbe da Renzo d'Uccio detto Bracha, ei quali denari avanzaro al suo tempo che fo priore sicome apare al saldo dela sua ragione per mano dei rasgionieri del comuno in questo libro." ACC, Z 3, pezzo 9, f. 122r.

³³ ACC, C 6: catasto of 1402, ter. San Vincenzo, f. 264r. It is not clear exactly when Mamigliano died. By far his most valuable bit of property passed to his wife, Margarita, on 9 July 1418, as restitution of her dowry; but his share of the house he owned jointly with his brother Matteo was not transferred to Matteo until 12 September 1434. Could it be that Mamigliano's marriage did not survive his disgrace, and that the earlier of these transfers of property reflects his social death and the latter his physical death?

required that brethren leave something to the fraternity; if Renzo di Uccio and Mamigliano dei Santi did not, it was because their membership in the fraternity of San Vincenzo had come to a jagged and unpleasant end in 1416. Others, however, fulfilled their obligation, and San Vincenzo's endowment grew steadily as a result. The bequest from Santamora that threw temptation in Renzo's way is a case in point: when a catasto of ecclesiastical property was prepared at the start of the fifteenth century, the fraternity of San Vincenzo's total worth was £453; the inheritance from Santamora, valued at £632, more than doubled that.[34] By the end of the century, the value of San Vincenzo's property had grown nearly fivefold, to £2,180; and since the fraternity normally operated at a deficit because of its charitable activities, that growth must be ascribed to bequests from its brethen. One might say that the fraternity of San Vincenzo survived as an institution because of the deaths of the individual members.[35]

THE NEW REGIME

Audits of Cortona's charitable institutions seem to have become standard practice in the early fifteenth century. They may have begun in 1402, in conjunction with the tighter civic controls over ecclesiastical property that generated in that year a *Catasto dei beni ecclesiastici* comparable in every respect to the massive volumes that registered and assessed lay property. As early as 8 January 1402 someone reviewed the income of the fraternity of San Vincenzo for the previous year, though this cryptic and unsigned note does not clarify whether this was an internal or external audit.[36] Within a few years, the nomination of civic officials charged with auditing religious institutions – the "ragionieri de' luoghi piatosi" – was a regular feature of communal administration, and traces of their inspections, recorded in standard formulae, can be found in the financial records

---

[34] ACC, C 7: Catasto dei beni ecclesiastici, f. 181r.

[35] Bornstein, "Corporazioni spirituali," 85–6.

[36] ACC, Z 3, pezzo 9, f. 72v: "Reveduta la rasgione del'entrata del camalengho al tempo di Matheio di Bonanuccio priore di la detta frateneta et Mamigliano di Santi suvo camalengho, Mᵒıııırᶜdoie adì vııı di gienaio; monta l'etrata del detto ano £xxvıııı s. dodece d. vı." The audit was performed *during* the time of Matteo and Mamigliano, who held office in 1402, but *of* the income for 1401 – which did indeed total the sum given. It was probably the work of outside auditors, since the handwriting of this note differs from that which records income and expenditures during Matteo and Mamigliano's term in office, and the terms "reveduta" and "rasgione" – standard in the audits performed by the town officials – were not normally used by the confraternity's bookkeepers. I suspect that the public audits were just getting started at this point, and the auditors had yet to standardize the formula of their attestation.

of a number of churches, fraternities, and hospitals.[37] On 15 January 1405, the accounts of the church of Santa Margherita of Cortona for 1404 were reviewed by Niccolò di Angelo di maestro Vanni, Biagio di ser Angelo di Zaffarino, and Francesco di ser Nino di Cecco, "auditors elected in the council of the people of the city of Cortona to review the accounts of pious institutions."[38] Three other commissioners – Francesco di Venturuccio di Goro, Antonio di Franceschino di Pace, and Bartolomeo di Pietro di Pace, prior of the fraternity of Santa Maria della Misericordia – checked the books of the church of Santa Margherita for 1405 on 21 March 1406 and those of the hospital of Santa Margherita on 10 May.[39] The books of Santa Margherita for 1408 were checked by the auditors Biagio di ser Angelo di Zaffarino, Stefano di Bonuccio, and Bartolomeo di maestro Pietro di ser Meo dei Boni, who found that the very impressive income (£951 s. 14 d. 2) recorded by the church was surpassed (slightly) by expenditures of £982 s. 5 d. 2, most of which were dedicated to ongoing construction projects.[40] The first folio of the volume in which the *soprastanti* of Santa Margherita of Cortona registered that church's substantial property holdings (as distinguished from current income and expenditures) bears a note similar in content and format to that found on the front of the account book of San Vincenzo, but dated a year earlier, 8 January 1415.[41] And four and a half years later, in the second half of 1419, the accounts of the hospital of Santa Margherita were scrutinized by the three "ragionieri dei luoghi pii," who specified that they were then serving their six month term in office.[42]

This six-month term (rather than the annual term in office implied by the auditors' *saldi* for the first decade of the fifteenth century) may have been an administrative innovation, introduced by Florence when it

---

[37] One notable exception is the fraternity of San Michelangelo, which met in the church of San Cristofano. Its three surviving account books cover the span of 120 years almost without interruption, and show no sign of ever having been subjected to an outside audit: ACC, Z 3, pezzo 11 (1373–1401); Z 2, pezzo 6 (1403–1478), and Z 3, pezzo 4 (1468–1494). This fraternity was the poorest in Cortona, and its income and expenditures may have been deemed too insignificant to merit official review.

[38] ACC, Z 2, pezzo 1: Santa Margherita da Cortona, entrata e uscita, 1403–1408; f. 11r: "Reveduta salda e fatta la detta rasgione per Nicholo d'Angelo de maestro Vanni priore de la fraternita de Santa Maria Magiure dela Misericordia e per Biasgio de ser Angelo de Zaffarino e per Francesscho de ser Nino de Ceccho, rasgioneri eletti nel consilglio de li homini dela cità de Cortona sopra a revedere le rasgione dei luoghi pii; veduta dì xv de genaio 1405."

[39] ACC, Z 2, pezzo 1, f. 110v; ACC, Z 3, pezzo 1: ospedale di Santa Margherita, entrata e uscita, 1405, 1419–20; f. 28r.   [40] ACC, Z 2, pezzo 1, ff. 40v (income) and 139v (expenditures).

[41] "Prodotto el libro di Santa Margarita da Felipo di Framcesscho di ser Lipo adì VIII di genaio 1415 a noi rasgioneri." ACC, Z 9, pezzo 1: Libro de la libra di Santa Margharita de Chortona, f. 1r.

[42] "Noi Cristofano de Tomasso, Bartolomeio de Staso, Giovanni di Chola, rasgionieri dei luoghi pii, eletti e chiamati per li priori e conselglio del comuno di Cortona per sei mesi prossimi che degono venire comenzando del mese de lulglio." ACC, Z 3, pezzo 1, f. 11r.

acquired Cortona in 1411. Certainly, the tighter fiscal control exercised by the *città dominante* and the ravenous appetite of the Florentine fisc are evident in the records of San Vincenzo, which after 1411 are sprinkled ever more thickly with payments of taxes on grain and olives and the land that produced them, on houses and their inhabitants. In 1417 and 1418, the fraternity was paying its share of an enormous levy of 80,000 florins.[43] By 1419, the harmful effects of this drain of capital were evident even to Cortona's Florentine masters, who were debating "how to alleviate the crushing economic burden imposed by the mother city on its subjects."[44]

Florence did not originate the practice of auditing religious institutions, nor did it create the officials responsible for conducting those audits. As we have seen, the "ragionieri de' luoghi piatosi" existed from the start of the century. But the Florentine presence changed the rules by which the game of politics was played in Cortona. This little provincial town, with its population of less than 5,000, had a ruling class that was comparably tiny, and the same few people inevitably circulated through the offices of the civic government and pious foundations. Niccolò di Angelo di maestro Vanni was prior of the fraternity of Santa Maria della Misericordia, by far the largest charitable institution in Cortona, when he audited the books of Santa Margherita for 1404. And he had a very direct and personal interest in the finances of Santa Margherita, since he had been one of the three soprastanti of that church for the year 1403. When he held that post once again, in 1408, one of his fellow soprastanti was Giovanni di ser Nino di Cecco – whose brother Francesco had helped Niccolò di Angelo audit the church of Santa Margherita in 1405.[45] The persons who managed the property of Cortona's ecclesiastical foundations and the auditors who checked their books enjoyed an all too cozy relationship. The advent of Florentine rule threatened to disrupt that relationship, as it forced the leading families of Cortona to play a more complicated political game, jockeying for social position and cultural esteem under the eye of a foreign power. That eye could be, erratically and unpredictably, either watchful or inattentive, greedy or disinterested, piercing or glazed. But it was there, and little lapses like that of Renzo di Uccio could no longer be winked at or glossed over. A stricter accounting was required.

---

[43] ACC, Z 3, pezzo 9, ff. 130v and 134r.
[44] Molho, *Florentine Public Finances*, 42.   [45] ACC, Z 2, pezzo 1, ff. 2r, 5v, 11r, and 34r.

5

MEN AND WOMEN IN ROMAN CONFRATERNITIES IN THE FIFTEENTH AND SIXTEENTH CENTURIES: ROLES, FUNCTIONS, EXPECTATIONS

ANNA ESPOSITO

Men and women joining Rome's Gonfalone confraternity in the late fifteenth century swore a membership oath which expressed the religious attitudes common to a large part of the devout laity.[1] The venerable brotherhood's statutes, revised in 1495, lay out a program of private devotions and collective activities necessary to obtain the soul's salvation.[2] Brothers and sisters had to "perform deeds which were pleasing" to God, to the Virgin Mary, and to the patron saints, in accordance with the instructions laid down by the confraternity's administering bodies regarding two general areas of collective life. First, regarding the economic management of the confraternity, applicants pledged to "procure the honor, use and enhancement of the places, buildings and property of the said company," and accept the attendant social duties, carry them out conscientiously, and give an account of them at the end of the mandate. Second, regarding devotional practices, members agreed both to participate in public events, marching in processions and attending funerals, memorial services, and anniversaries organized for deceased fellow-members and benefactors, and to offer up private prayers for these *defunti* on the occasion of their funeral and on the anniversaries of their death.

---

[1] See the wide-ranging survey in Miccoli's "La storia religiosa," 793–875. Archival abbreviations employed in the notes which follow: Archivio di Stato di Roma (ASR); Archivio Segreto Vaticano (ASV); Archivio Storico del Vicariato di Roma (ASVR); Archivio di S. Giovanni dei Fiorentini di Roma (AFR); Arciconfraternita della SS. Annunziata in S. Maria sopra Minerva (SS. Annunziata); Arciconfraternita di S. Giovanni Battista della Pietà dei Fiorentini (Pietà); Arciconfraternita della SS. Concezione in S. Lorenzo in Damaso (SS. Concezione); Ospedale di S. Maria della Consolazione (Consolazione); Ospedale del S. Salvatore ad Sancta Sanctorum (Salvatore).

[2] The statutes of the Gonfalone confraternity have been edited by Esposito: "Le 'confraternite' del Gonfalone." Part VI of the statutes contains the form of the oath.

The "program" which the new member of the Gonfalone confraternity undertook to follow is laid out in great detail in the seventy-four
articles of the statutes and resembles those drawn up by other religious lay
associations of the time. In the closing decades of the fifteenth century
and the beginning of the sixteenth, the confraternities carried out far-
reaching reforms of their rules in line with contemporary changes in
religious practice and social life. In Rome the devout layman had a wide
choice of devotional associations which he could join.[3] All were open to
citizens of every social class, with the exception of the confraternities
which had been formed for specific purposes, such as those for the
compatriots from a particular city or for the members of certain guilds.

All the statutes of the leading confraternities[4] required a commission to
investigate the "reputation, way of life and morals" of a new applicant in
order to find out, in the words of a 1452 document relating to the
Salvatore confraternity, "whether he is of upright life and behaves as a
Christian should, confessing his sins and attending church."[5] Those
proven to be "of scandalous reputation, living in fear of neither God nor
the Virgin Mary,"[6] or more explicitly, "practicing usury or living in sin,"
could easily be excluded.[7] Once an applicant's good reputation had been
established, it was advantageous in some confraternities if a relative was
already a member. As early as 1331 the statutes of the Salvatore confraternity (in which the number of both lay and clerical members who
could belong was restricted) allow for the possibility that "a son or
brother of the deceased ... can be admitted to the society."[8] This is an
early indication of the Salvatore's tendency "to exploit social connections
as a basis for unity and integration in its membership." In its 1474 reform
it introduced the further requirement that its members belong to no other
confraternities,[9] a unique restriction and one characteristic of this highly
elitist association, which from its beginnings attracted many members
from Rome's newly prominent citizenry. Very different motives led the
Società della Consolazione to establish in its new statutes of 1505 a
privileged application procedure for "persons of distinguished family,
reputation and standing," whereby these were admitted into the com-

---

[3] Maroni Lumbroso and Martini, *Le confraternite romane.*

[4] Statutes from the fourteenth and fifteenth centuries survive for the following confraternities: the
Raccomandati del Salvatore, the Grazie e Consolazione, the Gonfalone, the SS. Annunziata and the
SS. Concezione.

[5] Pavan, "Gli statuti," 48. The procedure was common among Italian confraternities. For Paduan
confraternities: De Sandre Gasparini, *Confraternite padovane,* xxxvi–xl.

[6] See Esposito, "Le confraternite e gli ospedali", article 14. Article 4 of the Gonfalone statutes is
similar (Esposito, "Le 'confraternite' del Gonfalone," 108–9).

[7] Pavan, "Gli statuti," 66 (article 16). Article 4 from the 1444 statutes of S. Maria delle Grazie is similar
(Pelaez, "S. Maria delle Grazie," 83).   [8] Pavan, "Gli statuti," 66 (article 19).   [9] *Ibid.,* 47, 49.

pany "without further discussion or examination," unlike applicants from different social classes.[10] Such privileged access was certainly introduced with the purpose of increasing the number of wealthy members in the new organization, formed from the amalgamation of three small confraternities, but the provision also reveals that those who were responsible for drawing up the new statutes[11] were aware of the new social values prevailing in the city.[12] Throughout the fifteenth century, society in Rome and in the whole of Italy was centered increasingly and irreversibly on the aristocracy. Just as a gradually growing number of Roman middle-class citizens abandoned trade for the prospect of employment in the Papal Curia, so a sharper consciousness of class differences and a defensive awareness of one's own social status were emerging.[13]

If we turn from the confraternities' statutes to their matriculation lists and minute books, we can see that by the end of the fifteenth century different confraternities drew on different social classes for their membership. The members of some, like the Raccomandati del Salvatore or the Company of the SS. Annunziata alla Minerva, came very largely from the newly rich and influential citizenry and from the families of the traditional Roman nobility. From the mid fifteenth century onwards in particular, a considerable proportion of their membership was constituted by "barones, militares, nobiles" and members of the higher clergy,[14] who brought prestige and financial support. In others, like S. Maria della Consolazione or the Gonfalone, both formed from the union of small Marian confraternities dating back to the fourteenth century,[15] the membership remained largely made up of merchants and artisans whose wealth was more restricted or more recently acquired. It is clear that a large number of the city's *homines novi* who acquired prominent fortunes and social status in the course of the century preferred to join and lend their support to organizations which were administered more openly and in which their influence could carry more weight, although it was always possible for them to belong to other confraternities (multiple membership was common practice both in Italy and other countries[16]) or to enroll their own relatives in them.

---

[10] Esposito, "Le confraternite e gli ospedali," 163. The nobility also received privileged treatment in the Paduan confraternities (see De Sandre Gasparini, *Confraternite padovane*, xlv–xlviii) and in the Venetian flagellant "scuole" (see Sbriziolo, "Confraternite veneziane', 734–6.

[11] Those who were responsible for drawing up the statutes were members of the confraternity.

[12] Esposito, "Le confraternite e gli ospedali," 155.

[13] Rusconi, "Confraternite, compagnie e devozioni," 478. Jones, "Economia e società,".355–7.

[14] ASR, SS. Annunziata, b. 3, nr. 201 (papal bull with the granting of indulgences issued by Sixtus IV in 1473). Esposito, "Ad dotandum puellas."

[15] Esposito, "Le confraternite e gli ospedali" and "Le 'confraternite' del Gonfalone."

[16] Vauchez, *I laici*, 131–3.

A further important element must be borne in mind in seeking to trace the transformations in the social composition of the city's confraternities. At the end of the fifteenth century, these were notable for the social diversity of their membership. This was true to a greater degree in the more recently founded confraternities, such as the SS. Annunziata, but it was also the case in the older and more prestigious foundations such as the Salvatore. However, the popes, who were by now in undisputed control of the city, which had become the home of an international court and the capital of a separate state,[17] were intent on weakening urban associations like the devotional confraternities, which served to bring together different social classes, by encouraging the enrollment and participation of "outsiders" from the staff employed in the Papal Curia or in the higher echelons of the Church hierarchy.[18] Their aim was to build up a closer connection with the confraternities by dismantling the social and municipal framework within which they had traditionally worked and thus reinforce their control over the city through the channel of its charitable organizations.[19] From the point of view of the confraternities, the presence among their number of members who enjoyed access to the Pope and who could therefore solicit and obtain with comparative ease a variety of favors ranging from the concession of indulgences to the granting of tax exemptions – such requests grew in number throughout the century – was found to be increasingly advantageous.[20]

Other motives could lie behind the application to join a particular confraternity: the wish to maintain one's own family traditions and contacts with other families who belonged to the confraternity in the shared interests of social alliances and partnerships, or a desire on the part of individuals or groups who had not yet been accepted into established society or who had only recently settled in the city to acquire social recognition and respectability: in such cases, to become a member of a confraternity meant "acquiring an acknowledged social role."[21]

---

[17] On this question see *Roma capitale (1447–1527)*. Prodi analyses the political and institutional transformation of Rome from the mid fifteenth century onwards in *The Papal Prince*, particularly ch. 1–3. [18] Hurtubise, "La présence des étrangers," 57–80. [19] Piccialuti, *La carità*.

[20] Such requests were common practice among all the Roman confraternities at the end of the fifteenth century, but it was only in the society of SS. Concezione that a special clause in the 1494 statutes explicitly stated that the priors were responsible for obtaining "plenariam indulgentiam a Summo Pontifice, qua habita, apponantur cedule per Urbem ... et hoc idem per tubicines manifestius nuntietur" (article 104), ASVR, SS. Concezione, ms. 1, ff. 33v–34r.

[21] Vauchez, *I laici*, 130. Alberigo, "Contributo alla storia," 180–1. Morghen, "Le confraternite dei Disciplinati," 321. On political use of the confraternities in Florence, Weissman, *Ritual Brotherhood*, 164–73; Henderson, "Le confraternite religiose."

"IURO DE . . . OBEDIRE LI SIGNORI GUARDIANI . . . ET
ACCEPTARE ET EXERCITARE OGNE OFFICIO."

Almost all the Roman confraternities of the fifteenth century were
organized in a similar way: a collegiate structure headed by two or three
exclusively lay members. They were called guardians or priors and were
supported by one secretary, who was always a notary, one treasurer, two
syndics, and thirteen officers, each representing a different "rione" or
area of the city. All held their posts for a year, with the exception of the
secretary, whose tenure in certain confraternities was *perpetuo*.[22] Individual guardians were called the "ruler, head and leader of the whole
company . . . from whom arises all the good and all the evil experienced in
this venerable company"[23] and they enjoyed wide powers. There was
hardly a single aspect of the confraternity's activities which did not come
under their control, from the election of the other officers to the choice
of the confraternity's own priests, from the management of the "ospedali" and their revenues to the organization of religious ceremonies
and processions. Only when it was a question of selling off the confraternity's real estate were the guardians obliged to consult their fellow
officers. However, the guardians' ample powers were balanced by their
onerous duties, which required an unfailing commitment and sense of
responsibility: besides having to preside over all the meetings of the
confraternity and carry out its business, they had to pay weekly or
monthly visits to the ospedali and preside at feasts and ceremonies.[24] The
office of guardian, at least in those confraternities where there were three
guardians at the head, also reflected the changes in membership when a
reform at the end of the fifteenth century introduced a rule that the
triumvirate was henceforth to be made up of two Roman citizens and a
forensis or non-Roman[25]. This ensured that the non-Roman members,
who by now formed a large part of the membership in some confraternities, had their own representative among those who directed the organisation, as was already the case with the trade guilds.[26]

---

[22] This was the case in the Consolazione and in the SS. Annunziata. Ordained priests and auxiliary
staff of various kinds who were responsible for managing the ospedali or the confraternity's funds
could also take part in the administrative bodies.

[23] Esposito, "Le 'confraternite' del Gonfalone," article 10 and article 8.

[24] On the role of the guardians in the Salvatore confraternity, see Pavan, "Gli statuti," 51–2.

[25] See article 11 of the SS. Annunziata statutes: Esposito, "Le confraternite del matrimonio," 32.
Article 6 from the statutes of SS. Concezione gives more detail and shows even more clearly how
diverse the populace of Rome had now become: of the three priors, two had to be Romans "unus
verus et nobilis, alius dummodo sit Rome coniugatus vel longo tempore ipsam habitatus vel
pontifici aut Romane Curie offitialis. Tertius vero exterus" (see ASVR, SS. Concezione, c. 5r).

[26] On the "forenses'" participation in late medieval Roman corporations and confraternities,
Esposito, *Un'altra Roma*, 85–90.

In theory all who belonged to the confraternity could be elected to any post; in practice the most prestigious offices in Roman confraternities were the appanage of a restricted number of families. These came to control all the confraternity's business and administered its assets, which, thanks to bequests and donations of property and land, were often considerable. Recent historical studies of confraternities in other Italian cities[27] have shown how such continuity and unity helped to ensure "the prosperity and survival of the confraternity."[28]

The best known example of this phenomenon in Rome is the guardianship of the Salvatore confraternity, a position of great power since the guardian was responsible for the vast estates of the Lateran ospedale. As such, the post was a stronghold of the most prominent families in the city, those who in the fourteenth century had participated in Roman government and who had been magistrates in the city administration in the fifteenth century.[29] An examination of the names of the officers in the administrative records of the company reveals that in the years from 1428 to 1500 the two important and apparently interchangeable posts of guardian and treasurer were held by confratelli from fewer than twenty families. An individual who had held the post of guardian had to wait three years before he could be re-elected; this was not the case with the office of treasurer, which could be held for several years at a time. On occasion a guardian was nominated treasurer at the end of his tenure or the treasurer took over the guardianship. In this way some individuals succeeded in keeping control of the company's affairs for several consecutive years; frequently the names of the same men or of those who belonged to their families or their factions reappear, after a certain interval of time, in the same offices or in the list of the Consiglio dei Tredici. Other names appear at regular intervals as guardian, as often as five times in the course of twenty years.[30]

We find the same alternation of the leading offices among the members of the most prominent families in fifteenth-century Rome in the more recently established confraternity of SS. Annunziata, for which the administrative records from 1476 have survived. Some of these families also belonged to the Salvatore confraternity, at least until 1474 when it decreed that its members could not belong to any other company. A typical example is the Massimi family. They had made their fortune in the spice trade and later established themselves as prominent entrepreneurs and merchants. One of the leading members of the family, Paolo, had been excluded in 1476 from the Salvatore confraternity "because he

---

[27] Weissman, *Ritual brotherhood*. Vincent, *Des charités bien ordonnées*, 234–5. Black, *Italian Confraternities*, 80–1.   [28] Rusconi, "Confraternite, compagnie e devozioni," 476.
[29] Pavan, "La confraternita del Salvatore," 87–9.   [30] Fiori, "I necrologi del Salvatore."

refused to swear that he would not join other confraternities"[31] and had been admitted to the SS. Annunziata, where he can be found holding the office of prior in the very same year. We can similarly find the names of his son Francesco and nephew Pietro as priors within the first ten years for which we have documentation for the company (1476–86).[32]

Further examples could be adduced. What they reveal above all is that the families of late fifteenth-century Rome, who were excluded from participation in significant political and economic activity (since both were controlled by the Curia and external financial interests), sought by way of compensation to "assert their identity and function within the shrinking possibilities offered by civic life" by taking part in the city's confraternities and other charitable organizations.[33] To play a leading role in the financial administration and social responsibilities of these associations was evidently important for those citizens whose political interests were restricted by the concentration of the city's political life in the hands of the Curia, and whose commercial initiative was curtailed by the limited productive capacity of Rome. This was a widespread phenomenon: throughout the sixteenth century and in the whole of Italy, the consolidation of larger states reduced the number of small independent governments. As a result, "fewer people were involved in politically or administratively responsible roles (even if there was a growth in bureaucracies)."[34]

"ET SIMILMENTE IURO ANDARE AD TUTTE ET SINGULE PROCESSIONI, OBSEQUI DI MORTI, CONGREGAZIONI, ANNIVERSARI ET MESSE."

In the course of the fifteenth century, important changes took place in the spiritual attitudes and devotional practices of the individual members of the Roman confraternities. The religious life of the fourteenth-century confraternities had revolved round daily prayers, especially the Paternoster and Ave Maria, assiduous frequentation of the sacraments, especially confession, and penitential practices. These were now supplanted in importance by liturgical ceremonies, processions, and, as far as the Gonfalone confraternity was concerned, the performance of *sacre rappresentazioni*.

We can see these changes most clearly in the Gonfalone confraternity. It was created from the union of small brotherhoods, some of them

---

[31] Egidi, *Necrologi e libri affini*, 2, 485.
[32] On Paolo Massimi, Modigliani, "Li nobili huomini di Roma," 359; Ait, *Tra scienza e mercato*. 58–9. On Francesco and Pietro, Modigliani, *I Porcari*, 74.
[33] Pavan, "La confraternita del Salvatore," 89.   [34] Black, *Italian Confraternities*, p. 80.

flagellants, dating back to the fourteenth century; at the end of the fifteenth century it introduced radical changes to its original devotional requirements, especially penitential practices. Flagellation remained as a symbol linked to the penitential robes worn by the confratello, but its practice was now restricted to Good Friday or special ceremonies. All interest now focused on external display: there was a proliferation of public events, especially the enactment of the Passion. The preparation and mounting of this performance was considered to be the "origin and foundation of this venerable company." The commitment demanded was considerable: each year the Gonfalone organised at least twelve public ceremonies in addition to the *recita* at the Colosseum, comprising celebrations and processions which were all provided for and regulated by the statutes. This leaves out of account the non-statutory public events which could be organized by the confraternity whenever they saw fit.[35] Within the Consolazione confraternity a similar shift took place from a more inward spirituality towards a greater emphasis on social good works and the liturgical ceremonies associated with the miraculous images of the Virgin Mary in the company's possession. An active role in such ceremonies was reserved for the *guardiani* and other *particulari personi* ("special persons"); the ordinary confratelli played no part except that of spectators.[36]

All the members, on the other hand, in Rome and elsewhere, were always involved in the processions, especially those held in honor of the confraternity's patron saint and those directly connected to the city's religious life, when the presence of the confraternity in the civic community could be affirmed. Such occasions were important "especially when we consider how scarce and neglected the opportunities were for such civic gatherings in the late fifteenth century."[37] The sheer proliferation of

[35] Esposito, "Le 'confraternite' del Gonfalone." On the Gonfalone's performance of the "sacre rappresentazioni," Vattasso, *Per la storia del dramma sacro in Italia*, 38–101. The practice of flagellation on Good Friday is not mentioned in the 1495 statutes; however, the purchase of "mazzolli de corda trafilata per fare le discipline per li desciplinati de lo venerdi sancto" ("coils of rope for the Good Friday flagellants") is itemized as expenditure in the confraternity's account books (ASV, Gonfalone, reg. 159, c. 51r) as are the laundry charges for washing the bloodstained white sackcloth robes worn by the flagellants ("che furono insanguinati da li battuti": ASV, Gonfalone, reg. 162, c. 63v).

[36] Esposito, "Le confraternite e gli ospedali," 156. The reference is to article 32 of the statutes on p. 169.

[37] Rusconi, "Confraternite, compagnie e devozioni," 479. In Rome public banquets were apparently still popular; most of the statutes which have been studied mention them in connection with the confraternity's feast day. They were open to all on payment of a contribution. In some confraternities it was the custom of the officials to dine together when they had their monthly meetings to discuss the confraternity's business "ut predicta habilius et commodius fieri possint, sumptibus societatis" in the words of article 53 of the SS. Annunziata statutes (Esposito, "Le confraternite del matrimonio," 43–4). The account books also show that members took part in

confraternal festivals and processions must undoubtedly have meant that such civic rituals were increasingly confined to local neighborhoods; one exception was the feast of the Assumption of the Virgin Mary, which retained its significance for the entire city. It has been rightly described as "the great religious feast of the Roman populace" in which the two guiding spirits of the city, the Roman municipality and the Papal Curia, normally estranged and antagonistic, came together in a rare moment of unity. A great procession was organized for the occasion. It wound its way through a large part of the city and was an opportunity for the *Comune*, represented by its leading magistrates and guild members, to assert its unity and identity. It was also a public moment of glory for the Salvatore confraternity, which was responsible for organising the procession.[38]

Together with processions, the other dominant aspect of confraternal devotion in this period were funerary rites. It has rightly been observed that in the late middle ages "religious feeling became increasingly focused on the thought of death." It was a thought closely linked to the awareness of sin and of the need for atonement as well as to "an assessment of how much merit could be accumulated in indulgences, in the charitable munificence of almsgiving and bequests, in acts of penitence."[39] Such fears and the need for reassurance and hope were shared by all the confratelli; they responded by giving each other mutual aid during illness or need, but especially at the moment of death or after death. This was a fundamental rule from the beginning of the confraternal movement, and it took principal effect on two particular occasions which every member swore on oath to attend: the funeral of a member, for which each confratello had to recite prayers (eg., the five Paternosters and five Ave Marias laid down in the Gonfalone's statutes), and the anniversaries of his death, which were commemorated annually in the church where the member was buried. These observances were also to be held for all those "who have left something to our company"[40] or who had paid a sum which varied between 25 and 50 florins according to confraternity.

---

these banquets: in 1482, for example, no fewer than eighty confratelli were present (see ASR, SS. Annunziata, reg. 548, c. 37v). On confraternal banquets, see De Sandre Gasparini, *Confraternite padovane*, lxx–xvii–xci; Black, *Italian Confraternities*, 91–2.

[38] On the procession for the Assumption of the Virgin Mary, see Pavan, "Gli statuti," 38; Esposito, "Le 'confraternite' del Gonfalone," 104. The processions for the "maritagio" organized either by the Gonfalone or by the Annunziata were little more than local neighborhood events (Esposito, "Apparati e suggestioni," 316–8). On the importance of the processions organized by a confraternity for the feast day of its patron saint, see De Sandre Gasparini, *Confraternite padovane*, xci–xciii; Rusconi, "Confraternite, compagnie, e devozioni," 478–9.

[39] Frugoni, "Bianchi del 1399", 237. Miccoli, "La storia religiosa", 859.

[40] Esposito, "Le 'confraternite' del Gonfalone," 128 (article 44), 127 (article 43).

Memorialization was the most frequently requested "service" provided by the Roman confraternities as the high number of legacies in fifteenth-century testaments shows,[41] especially for the associations which were able to give guarantees of stability and continuity. The concern to lighten the pains of Purgatory and to ensure eternal life, closely related to the desire to perpetuate the memory of oneself in society – a desire felt all the more keenly in circumstances which increased people's sense of precariousness and solitude – found numerous channels of expression in confraternal activity. By means of legacies and donations the individual member could strengthen his ties to the confraternity and participate more inwardly in its spiritual benefits. At the same time he could ensure his survival in the memory of his fellow-members and fellow-citizens either by commissioning works of art to embellish the places where the confraternity met to worship or to carry out its charitable works, or by giving a painting or object which could be used for devotional purposes. On occasion the confraternity itself provided for this need by commissioning work for the decoration of its centres of worship, including the less important ones.[42]

"IURO . . . DE FARE COSA A LORO GRATA, SALUTIFERA DELLA MIA ANIMA."

Until the second half of the fifteenth century few confraternities in Rome failed to heed the call to comfort and assist the poor and sick and to put as much effort as possible into establishing and equipping their own ospedale. This was a common development among the confraternities, one which made these lay organizations the principal if not the sole providers of such aid.[43] The Raccomandati del Salvatore were among the most active; they had begun the trend by setting up an 'ospedale' within the Lateran in 1333. At first these charitable institutions appeared to be for the benefit of the confraternity's members only. Soon, however, help was

---

[41] A thorough study of wills in late medieval Rome has not yet been carried out; at present only the results of partial research are available to us: for the Parione neighborhood during the reign of Sixtus IV (Barbalarga, "Gli atteggiamenti devozionali"); for the whole of Rome but only under the pontificate of Martin V (Sanfilippo, "Morire a Roma"); and for a particular section of the populace (Lombardo and Morelli, "Donne e testamenti"). On the importance of marking the anniversaries of deaths, which became a special function of the confraternities, Chiffoleau, *La comptabilité de l'au-delà*. 206–10; Rusconi, "Confraternite, compagnie, e devozioni", 480.

[42] Esposito, "Le confraternite romane." The administrative records of the confraternities are a particularly interesting source in this connection: those of the S. Maria della Consolazione (ASR, Consolazione, reg. 746) and of the Raccomandati del Salvatore (ASR, Salvatore, vol. 1006 and reg. 373), for example, are rich in information. On particular aspects of the confraternities' commissioning activities, see the articles in Eisenbichler (ed.), *Crossing the Boundaries*.

[43] Mollat, "En guise de préface," 29.

available not only to all the city's *pauperes et infirmi* but also to pilgrims.
Both their physical and spiritual well-being were attended to. Assistance
was prompted not only by "a sense of the importance of charitable works,
but also as a pragmatic response on the part of the merchants, landowners
and entrepreneurs who made up most of the membership of the Raccomandati to the widely felt need to maintain public order."[44] Many of
the lay confraternities which emerged in the course of the fourteenth and
fifteenth centuries felt impelled in the same way as the Raccomandati to
comfort and help the neediest and most distressed among their fellow-
citizens by setting up ospedali in the most central and densely populated
areas of the city. They were initially seen as places where such people
could find lodging and shelter, but there are also early indications of the
medical assistance which later came to define their function.[45] For the
men who belonged to the confraternities, the setting up of such ospedali
was a paramount act of charity. The concern for the weak, infirm, and
abandoned, especially for those who were no longer able to support
themselves financially or who had no family to sustain them, was widespread in late medieval urban society: various solutions to the problem
were adopted, such as the establishment of the *domus pauperum* for the
neediest. These were set up by private individuals, and frequently
managed and controlled by confraternities; nearly ten such institutions
were administered by the Raccomandati del Salvatore.[46] For persons of
higher social standing who had fallen on hard times special houses were
set up, reserved for those confraternity members who wished to be taken
into care, together with their belongings. Such a practice is documented
in the Gonfalone, for example, whose 1495 statutes provide for the
accommodation of women in the *ospizio* of S. Maria Maddalena and of
men in S. XL Martiri, where they were to be "carefully looked after using
their own resources, supplementing these, where they do not suffice,
with our [the confraternity's] own funds."[47] The setting up of ospedali,
however, was certainly not the confraternities' only way of providing
charity; there is evidence for the distribution of money, food – especially
bread and beans – and clothes.[48] Furthermore, towards the end of the

[44] Pavan, "La confraternita del Salvatore," 85.

[45] Pastore, "Strutture assistenziali." Cosmacini, *Storia della medicina*. Esposito, "Gli ospedali romani".

[46] ASR, Salvatore, reg. 373, c. 4r; cass. 413, n. 9; cass. 418, n. 14.

[47] Esposito, "Le 'confraternite' del Gonfalone," 129 (article 47); see also Pavan, "Gli statuti," 60.

[48] The Salvatore distributed bread to the inmates of the Campidoglio prison as well as to various
churches in the city (ASR, Salvatore, reg. 374, c. 8r); during Lent it also handed out bread and
boiled beans to the poor who came to the "ospedale" (ASR, Salvatore, vol. 1009, c.2r). The
Gonfalone did the same on the feast day of the Forty Martyrs, giving out beans and bread "infra
povere persone," while during the festival at the sanctuary of the Annunziata in via Oratoria on the
first Sunday in May, wine, fish, and oil were also provided (Esposito, "Le 'confraternite' del

fifteenth century new forms of assistance began to emerge which were aimed at succouring new categories of sufferers who had hitherto been disregarded by the city's charitable organizations: prisoners, condemned men, the shame-faced poor, and women.

"DE LE DONNE DE LA COMPAGNIA"

The inclusion of women as members of the Roman confraternities was not new; all the confraternities mentioned so far included men, women, and clerics, with the sole exception of the Raccomandati del Salvatore which did not admit women until 1452.[49] As early as the end of the thirteenth century, women were members of the Raccomandati della Vergine; they also subsequently belonged to the various flagellant groups which made up the *Compagnia della Frusta*.[50] As in the rest of Italy, until the early fifteenth century Roman women who belonged to a confraternity were either restricted to receiving the spiritual benefits and indulgences, as in the S. Spirito confraternity,[51] or engaged for the most part in devotional activity, such as private daily prayers or more regular attendance for confession and communion. When a woman sought admission, the men in the confraternity usually followed the familiar procedure of gathering information on the candidate and reporting back to the assembled company so that her application could be put to the vote; this, for example, was the practice in the Gonfalone.[52] Other companies, such as the Pietà dei Fiorentini, enrolled without investigation women whose husbands were already members on payment of a fee of "10 soldi." Such privileged access was extended to all widows aged

Gonfalone," 124 (articles 36, 37). On the clothes which were given to the poor, see ASVR, SS. Concezione, ms. 1, cap. 103, c. 33v.   [49] Egidi, *Necrologi e libri affini*, 2, 451.

[50] Barone, "Il movimento francescano," 76; Barone and Piazzoni, "Le più antiche carte," 28–9; Esposito, "Le 'confraternite' del Gonfalone," 92–3. On the women who belonged to the flagellant confraternities, Meersseman, *Ordo fraternitatis*, 498–504.

[51] The S. Spirito confraternity was supported and managed by the hospitaller order of the same name; its members, even proxy members, could only share in the spiritual grace conferred. However, we can find many autograph subscriptions in the *Liber fraternitatis*, which has been fortunately preserved, and some of these are by women. The only Roman women among them are Palozza wife of Ieronimo di Renzo Altieri and Lucrezia daughter of Renzo Altieri (Egidi, *Necrologi e libri affini*, 2, 378 [a. 1480]). The subscription of a Florentine noblewoman is particularly interesting: "I, Lauretta wife of Carlo Martelli, in order to receive the indulgences conceded to the confraternity of the 'ospedale' of Santo Spirito, have been admitted into this company together with my mother Donna Nanina, widow of Giovanni de Medici, on the eighth day of May 1482, in testimony of which event I have written the above in my own hand, both my own name and that of the said Donna Nanina, who was present, and by her own command, because she does not know how to write" (Egidi, *Necrologi e libri affini*, 2, 325–6). On literacy among Tuscan women, Miglio, "Leggere e scrivere il volgare" and Miglio, "Scrivere al femminile."

[52] Esposito, "Le 'confraternite' del Gonfalone," 129 (article 48).

fifty on condition that they had been virtuous and chaste ("honeste nel corpo suo"). Applications from women who were younger than fifty had to be voted upon and were successful only if three-quarters of the male members approved.[53] An analysis of the matriculation lists of the "sisters" in Roman confraternities[54] reveals that the majority not only were related to men who were already members of the same association – a common enough phenomenon throughout Italy – but are identified in the lists by their relationship as wife, daughter or sister, unless they belonged to a religious order.[55] Once she had been admitted, the new woman member, like her male counterpart, swore to be "good and useful . . . and to do all things which befitted a woman" – at least according to the 1495 statutes of the Gonfalone. For members of that confraternity, for example, this included participating in all the confraternity's "processions, masses, anniversaries and feasts" (particularly the feast of S. Lucia when young virgins were given dowries), and attending the confraternity's monthly service and sermon in the church of S. Apostoli. The women gathered annually at the same church to elect a prioress.[56] The gathering in S. Apostoli on the first Sunday of each month had a social as well as devotional purpose and was marked by a certain degree of ceremonious-ness. The "fattori" of the confraternity (a kind of factotum) had to unfurl the company's banner or gonfalon in front of the church ("fare extendere lo confallone") once the women had finished dining together ("da poi pranso per le donne") which they did after listening to the sermon, an unusual practice among the female members of Italian confraternities.[57]

In the late fifteenth-century statutes of the SS. Annunziata alla Minerva, we can similarly find rules which applied specifically to its women members. The administrative organization of the confraternity included, alongside the male officers and elected by them, two prioresses and fourteen consiliariae[58] with specifically designated responsibilities. On the feast day of the Annunciation, each of the prioresses and the "consiliariae" were expected to attend one of the young girls who were to receive gifts of money for their dowries.[59] Normally they had different

[53] AFR, Pietà, "Statuti," ms. 1 (a. 1456), cap. 4.
[54] Matriculation listings of women are known for the confraternities of S. Maria in Portico (which merged with the Consolazione in 1505), S. Maria dell'Anima dei Tedeschi (both of these, together with S. Spirito, are published in Egidi, *Necrologi e libri affini*), and, from 1526 onwards, SS. Annunziata. See AFR, SS. Annunziata, reg. 734.
[55] Terpstra, "Women in the Brotherhood," 202–3; Lombardo and Morelli, "Donne e testamenti," 44–6. Vincent, *Des charités bien ordonnées*, 204–7.
[56] Esposito, "Le 'confraternite' del Gonfalone," 129–30 (articles 48, 49, 50).
[57] De Sandre Gasperini, *Confraternite padovane*, xl–xliii; Black, *Italian Confraternities*, 34–8; Terpstra, "Women in the Brotherhood;" Casagrande, "Women in confraternities."
[58] Esposito, "Le confraternite del matrimonio," 32 (article 11).   [59] *Ibid.*, article 33.

duties to perform, although these too were related in some way to the specific charitable act of the distribution of dowries. The "consiliariae" had a duty to "visit sick women and persuade them to leave something to the confraternity" and to check "whether any married women members had died childless" in order to recover their dowries. It was the prioresses' responsibility to examine the reports of the "consiliariae" and then report in their turn to the priors and to the secretary.[60] The sixteenth-century reforms of the statutes also reveal that the prioresses, "nobiles et etatis mature," were entrusted with the task of inviting other noble matrons to attend the "maritagio" and act as chaperones for the young girls who were to receive dowries, thus lending greater dignity to the ceremony.[61] The charitable work of distributing dowries was carried out by the confraternity of SS. Concezione in S. Lorenzo in Damaso, in which similar arrangements were made in 1494 for its women members, and from 1494 onwards, by the Raccomandati del Salvatore,[62] where, on 6 May 1497, the congregation accepted the proposal put forward by some officers that two female guardians should be appointed alongside their male counterparts. The women were to be the guardians' wives or be otherwise related to them; failing that, they could be two matrons who belonged to the confraternity.[63] There is no evidence that this decision was ever acted upon. It is nevertheless an important indication that, towards the end of the fifteenth century, even an elitist confraternity such as the Salvatore began to feel the need for female representation, if only of a nominal kind, as the result perhaps of pressure from its own female members.

Thus, although the women of Rome were never able to exercise the real responsibilities which their male relatives held in the city's confraternities they succeeded, unlike their counterparts in the rest of Italy, in acquiring a distinct if marginal role within these institutions. Their success in this was helped by the change which we have already noted in the kind of devotional activity practiced by the confraternities, which increasingly took the form of ritual display − processions, feasts and ceremonies − and by the new kind of charitable work which they undertook with the distribution of dowries and the maintenance of ospedali. However, another factor should also be taken into consideration: the growing success enjoyed in Rome by the Tertiaries and by the practice of *bizzocaggio* which enabled women to follow a way of life based on the Gospel "obeying rules and wearing habits stipulated by the Church authorities" while remaining in their own houses or sharing the

---

[60] *Ibid.*, article 16.   [61] *Ibid.*, article 72.
[62] Pavan, "Gli statuti," cap. 72.   [63] ASR, Salvatore, reg. 29, c. 97v.

so-called *case sante* with a small group of like-minded women.[64] Such
women were for the most part widowed or unmarried. The fact that they
were not obliged to lead a conventual life meant that they could combine
practical charitable work among their neighbors with the intense spiritual
activity characteristic of the "true religious who were the models of
Christian perfection,"[65] exemplified most famously by S. Francesca
Romana and the oblates of Tor de' Specchi.[66] The tertiaries or *bizzoche*
came from every social class and every locality in the city. Their devotional and charitable activities may have provided a model and encouragement to those Roman women who, while unwilling or unable to
follow a religious rule of life, nevertheless wished to play a greater role, as
far as the men would allow them to, in the social and devotional life of the
confraternities. Significantly, increasing numbers of women were employed as *hospitalarie* to look after the inmates in the ospedali or to
manage, on behalf of the confratelli, the wards reserved for women.[67]
They also helped in such crises as plague epidemics by visiting the houses
of other women members of the confraternity, accompanying and tend-
ing those who had been left on their own and attending their funeral
when they died.[68] Roman women played an even more notable role as
benefactresses of the city's welfare institutions, either by leaving legacies
after their death to fund works *pro fabrica*, or by making specific donations
to hospitals to enable them to buy grain, food and medicine. A wide-
ranging register of such gifts compiled by Marco Antonio Altieri in 1525
shows the importance of such gifts to the work of the Salvatore confraternity.[69]

   In addition to these activities, towards the end of the fifteenth century
the majority of wills left by Roman noblewomen almost invariably leave
legacies to "bizzoche" and female tertiaries. The wish to establish a *domus
pauperum mulierum* in the testatrix's house or the legacy of dowry money
to be managed by the confraternity to which she belonged are also not
infrequently found. Women left without family or financial support
received special attention, not only from other women but from the
entire society, and not only in Rome but throughout Italy; great importance was given to the safeguarding of female honor, which was seen "as

[64] On the 'bizocali' or tertiary groups of women living in what in Rome were known as "case sante,"
   Esposito, "S. Francesca."
[65] Barone, "Società e religiosità femminile," 87. Zarri, "Dalla profezia," 185–6.
[66] Esposito, "S. Francesca." Picasso (ed.), *Una santa tutta romana*. Bartolomei Romagnoli, "Santa
   Francesca Romana."
[67] Esposito, "Gli ospedali romani," 246–7. On the Spanish "ospedali" for women, Piñeiro,
   "L'ospedale della nazione castigliana," 59–61. On the German "ospedali," Barbée, "Von
   deutscher Nationalgeschichte," 23–52.
[68] Esposito, "Le 'confraternite' del Gonfalone," 129 (article 46).   [69] ASR, Salvatore, reg. 373.

an essential component of family and municipal honour."[70] It was essentially this thinking which lay behind the gift of dowries to poor girls, considered to be especially at risk of being dishonored, the establishment of *ospedalia mulierum* and hostels for women left alone and without means of support, precursors of the convents for the city's prostitutes or women's boarding schools which were so numerous in sixteenth-century Rome.

[70] Zarri, "Dalla profezia," 193–6.

6

THE MEDICI AND THE YOUTH CONFRATERNITY OF THE PURIFICATION OF THE VIRGIN, 1434–1506

LORENZO POLIZZOTTO

Much has been written on the manipulation of Florentine confraternities and of the whole Florentine confraternal structure by interest groups, families, and individuals since the appearance of the pioneering articles of Rab Hatfield on the Compagnia dei Magi and of Richard Trexler on adolescent confraternities in 1970 and 1974 respectively.[1] Most subsequent studies on Florentine confraternities have broached the subject and have provided valuable if restricted information on it.[2] Notwithstanding their usefulness, we still lack specific analyses of the changes wrought by these manipulations on the internal lives and activities of the affected confraternities. We also do not have a clear understanding of the reasons which prompted such interest groups to seek to control confraternities; nor, finally, are we fully conversant with the means they employed to do so. This paper addresses some of these issues by analyzing the youth confraternity of the Purification of the Virgin both before and after its takeover by the Medici. It concentrates on the first eighty years of the confraternity's life and on two only of its five incarnations.

In the process, it also considers, albeit indirectly, two larger, related issues. These are, first, the nature of patronage; patronage understood as a carefully calculated exchange between patron and client, in this case the

Archives, archival series and manuscript libraries used are here listed together with their acronyms employed in the essay; Archivio di Stato di Firenze (ASF); Compagnie religiose soppresse da Pietro Leopoldo (CRSPL); Archivio del Convento di S. Marco (ACSM); Biblioteca Nazionale Centrale di Firenze: (BNF); Magliabechiano (Magl.); British Library (BL); Biblioteca Medicea Laurenziana di Firenze (BMLF).   [1] Hatfield, "The Compagnia de' Magi;" Trexler, "Ritual in Florence."

[2] Particularly important here are the works of Weissman, especially his *Ritual Brotherhood*, Henderson, *Piety and Charity*, and Eisenbichler, whose series of important articles and monograph, *Boys of the Archangel Raphael* expanded the field of Florentine youth confraternities. I should like to thank professors K. Eisenbichler, N. Newbigin, J. Henderson, and C. Turrill for their generous assistance in the research and composition of this essay.

Medici and the confraternity of the Purification. Secondly, the reasons for Florence's preoccupation with youths. This preoccupation, which could be defined as a youth culture, meant that children and juveniles, in the words of Robert Davidsohn, the great German historian of Florence, played a very important role in all Florentine religious and political movements of popular significance.[3] Whereas Davidsohn dismissed this youthful participation in matters elsewhere reserved to adults merely as evidence of a congenital failing in the Italian character, I think it is of great historical significance and thus requires careful assessment.

Now to the confraternity itself and to its pre-Medicean history. The Purification was founded on 8 September 1427 in the church of S. Maria dei Servi, known as the Annunziata, by members of the confraternity of the Archangel Gabriel, another youth confraternity founded in 1410. It appears that the confraternity of the Archangel Gabriel had proved so popular that it had become too unwieldy, hence the decision to split it into two. After the division, the two confraternities went their separate ways. The Purification's early years were fairly precarious. It did not have its own meeting-place and for a while met in the Annunziata, moving later to the hospital of S. Matteo where it could rely on the protection of the adult confraternity of Santa Maria della Pietà, known also as the Buca of S. Girolamo. Cosimo de' Medici, shortly after his return from exile in 1434, placed the Purification under his protection and had premises built for it within the convent of S. Marco, which at the time Cosimo and his brother Lorenzo were extending and refurbishing for the newly installed Observant Dominicans. The Purification moved to the new premises in 1444.[4]

To this early period, to be more exact to the years between 1431 and 1434, there belongs the first, surviving, book of statutes of the Purification.[5] It predates Cosimo's takeover of the confraternity and its move to

[3] Davidsohn, *Storia di Firenze*, 2, part 2, 49.

[4] "Capitoli ... della schuola di purificatione della Vergine Maria e di Santo Zenobi," BNF Magl. VIII, 1500, Inserto 11, f. 83v (I am using the foliation in pencil on the bottom, left-hand side of the folio; hereafter this MS is cited as "Capitoli ... della schuola di purificatione"); ASF CRSPL 1654, Inserto 29, ff. 178r–v and *passim*. See also Eisenbichler "Strutture amministrative," 952–3.

[5] MS BMLF Acquisti e doni, 336, *incipit* "Questi sono li statuti e ordinatione de la compagnia over fraternitade de la purificatione de la vergine maria" (hereafter cited as "Statuti ... de la purificatione"). The library catalogue mistakenly dates the manuscript to the fourteenth century, as does also Wilson, *Music and Merchants*, 20, n. 66. Internal evidence, that is a reference to a bull of indulgence conferred to the company by Pope Eugenius IV (1431–47) gives us the *terminus a quo*. The discrepancies between some of the regulations in the statutes and the way these regulations were put into practice by the confraternity after September/October 1434 – the date on which its administrative documentation begins – provide the *terminus ad quem*. The document presents a number of problems, some of which will be mentioned in the course of this paper. A full discussion of the manuscript is provided in the monograph on the Purification which I am in the process of completing.

S. Marco; it predates also the bull of 1442 issued by Eugenius IV, then in exile in Florence, which sought to regulate youth confraternities by placing them under the jurisdiction of a commission of overseers comprising the guardians of the four existing confraternities, the Prior of S. Marco and the Abbot of the Badia. The bull of 1442 led to the compilation of new statutes for existing youth confraternities.[6] The chance survival of the early statutes of the Purification is thus most fortunate in that they allow us to see the factors which had led to the institution of the Purification and the original aims it had set itself, as well as the structure it had adopted before the heavy-handed intervention by Cosimo, the Dominicans of S. Marco, and the Pope himself.

The document reveals that the confraternity, even at this early stage, was structurally very complex. In its method of election, tenure of office and syndication of office-holders, the Purification followed closely the practices of the Florentine government. Most interesting, in the light of later developments, is the fact that the position of confessor/corrector of the confraternity was exercised exclusively by Servites. Indeed, the statutes themselves had been drawn up by a Servite of northern, Venetian origin. The confessor/corrector had almost total power over the members and officials of the confraternity; he had last say in the induction of new members, in the election of lay officials and in the expulsion of both ordinary members and officials. Membership was restricted to youths of no less than twelve but no more than eighteen years of age. Upon turning nineteen years of age, they had to leave the Purification and join, if they wished, the adult confraternity of S. Maria della Pietà.[7]

The choice of twelve years as the age of induction is easily explained. Twelve was the generally recognized onset of maturity; the age of transition from childhood to adolescence.[8] It was also the earliest age at which youths, after elementary schooling, began formal education either in grammar, in *scuole di grammatica*, or in commercial arithmetic (*abaco*) in their place of employment, or more rarely in specialized schools.[9] It was, finally, the age at which the larger proportion of youths began their

---

[6] The post-1434 statutes of the Purification, the Nativity, and S. Niccolò del Ceppo have survived and have been consulted. For S. Giovanni Evangelista only the 1427 statutes have been consulted. The present location of the post-1434 statutes, once in the library of Major J. R. Abbey, is not known. A description of them and a reproduction of the miniated first page are to be found in Alexander and De La Mare, *The Italian Manuscripts*, 32–5.

[7] "Statuti . . . de la purificatione," ff. 2v–7v. The adult confraternity is here called "Sancta Maria de passione," one of the many "off-key" terms that reveal the writer's non-Florentine origins.

[8] Giannarelli, "Nota sui dodici anni," 132.

[9] There was not, of course, a statutory age for beginning this "secondary" stage of education. Available evidence suggests that 12 was the more common age of entry, especially in the *scuole d'abaco* and in conjunction with the beginning of apprenticeship. On education see Klapisch-Zuber, *Women, Family, and Ritual*, 108–9; Grendler, *Books and Schools*, 6, 185–205.

apprenticeship in the numerous small *botteghe* scattered throughout the city of Florence.[10] The reasons for the choice of eighteen as the age at which members were obliged to leave the confraternity are similarly clear-cut. In Florence, but also elsewhere in Europe, eighteen was the statutory age of majority.[11] Eighteen was an important legal threshold, though it did not in itself confer juridical independence nor even political enfranchizement which, for members of politically qualified families, took place when they turned twenty-five years of age. Eighteen was also significant for other reasons: it was the age at which the majority of apprenticeships were completed and at which independence but also new responsibilities were acquired.[12] By restricting membership to youths in the twelve to eighteen age group, the founders of the Purification must have been aware that they were primarily targeting apprentices, the most numerous but also the most vulnerable segment of the youthful population. It should not be forgotten, moreover, that youths in this age bracket were deemed to be at both the most vulnerable and most troublesome stage of their development: vulnerable in that, while still immature, they were removed from close family supervision and could either be easily exploited or led astray by new masters and companions; troublesome because these were the very years in which, apart from contending with sexual awakening, initiation and experimentation, they had the need to assert themselves and were likely to adopt rebellious attitudes and even to engage in aggressive and violent behavior.[13]

Membership lists for this early period have not survived. What has come down to us are the annual records of the induction of new members, which, useful as they undoubtedly are, fail to provide information on the total number of members for any given year. The lack of documentation prior to 1434 makes it impossible even to estimate the numbers of members the confraternity was able to attract during these years. Once the records begin, at the end of October 1434, we witness a veritable rush to join the Purification. In the five months to the end of the Florentine year, on 24 March, twenty-five new members joined the Purification. In the following year, eighty-eight new members joined; in 1436, seventy-nine new members; in 1437, forty-five; in 1438, fifty-

[10]   Though Klapisch-Zuber has correctly noted that 14 was the legal age for starting an apprenticeship, *Women, Family, and Ritual*, 108, the average age for beginning an appprenticeship in the *arte della lana* in the sixteenth century was 12: Marcello, "Andare a bottega," 242. This was the case also in fifteenth-century Cologne and France: Mitterauer, *A History of Youth*, 70.

[11]   Kuehn, *Emancipation in Late Medieval Florence*, 46,87.

[12]   Mitterauer, *A History of Youth*, 66. At eighteen all the young men in the Innocenti had to leave the hospital and fend for themselves : Marcello, "Andare a bottega," 246.

[13]   Youths became juridically accountable for their actions between twelve and fourteen years of age: Niccoli, *Il seme della violenza*, 10.

three; in 1439, one hundred and twenty-six; and in 1440, one hundred and thirty-nine.[14] In the following three years there was a gradual decline in enrollments: eighty-three for 1441; sixty-seven for 1442; and fifty-seven for 1443, the last year before the Purification moved to new premises in S. Marco.[15] In the first nine and a half years of its documented history, therefore, the Purification attracted seven hundred and sixty-two new members.

It cannot be assumed that these rates of yearly enrollments were normal. Indeed, the fact that their recording begins in the very month of Cosimo de' Medici's return from his Venetian exile, suggests the opposite: that the resolution of the political crisis which the return of Cosimo signified led to an abnormal increase in enrollments.[16] It could well be also that the Medici, upon their return, had signaled their interest in the confraternity, thus causing the influx of new members. Be that as it may, it would be quite safe to estimate that, by the end of the decade, even accounting for the yearly departure of members who had reached the upper age limit, the Purification had no fewer and perhaps considerably more than six hundred members. Once it is remembered that in 1427 it had begun operating with a core of twelve members drawn from the Nativity,[17] then the progress it had made was nothing short of prodigious. While on the subject, it is instructive to consider that, numerically, the Purification's membership constituted approximately 14 percent of all the youths of Florence in the relevant age bracket.[18] The Purification's success in attracting so many members, notwithstanding the political factors which may also have applied, demonstrates that youth confraternities filled a perceived religious and social need.

Equally instructive is the membership profile. As expected, the majority of newly enrolling members were either recently qualified artisans or apprentices and *garzoni* still learning a trade. All trades were represented, with a slight preponderance of workers in the textile industry, as was to be expected in a confraternity whose meeting place was in an area with a

---

[14] ASF CRSPL 1654, Inserto 29, ff. 2r–34v.   [15] *Ibid.*, ff. 34v–53v.

[16] It could well be, of course, that confraternities, even including youth confraternities, had been forbidden to meet during the crisis and that, as a consequence, there was a rush to join them once they were permitted to re-open. I have not come across any document confirming that confraternities were closed in these years. It should be remembered, however, that such decrees were seldom incorporated in the deliberations of the Signori and Collegi since they were promulgated by means of public bans by the Otto di Guardia e Balia, the committee of public safety; and for these years, the records of the Otto di Guardia are not complete.

[17] "Capitoli … della schuola di purificatione," f. 4v.

[18] This figure, which I must stress, is very approximate, is based on the statistics provided in Klapisch-Zuber, and Herlihy, *Les Toscans*, appx. v, table 2, 660–1.

high concentration of botteghe and workshops, many of them connected with the wool and silk trades.[19] A substantial number of members were attending commercial school (*abaco*), suggesting that they too were destined for a career in trade or commerce. Only a handful of the youths is described as still attending school (*scuola*): a term which, in the context, clearly denoted a scuola di grammatica and indicated, therefore, that these youths were destined for a professional career. For a number of youths, most of them belonging to eminent Florentine families, no qualifying information is provided, since their name alone revealed their status and calling. Members from eminent, politically qualified families were outnumbered 4:1 by members from the *popolo minuto*.[20] Provenance of the members is not specifically recorded. It is possible, however, to determine the provenance of individual, eminent, members of the confraternity, by turning to *prioristi* and other contemporary sources listing the geographical distribution of politically qualified families.[21] From this we find that the eminent members came from all quarters (*quartieri*) and districts (*gonfaloni*) of the city, and, excepting the Oltrarno area which was poorly represented, were distributed fairly evenly across the remaining three districts of the city. Most of the eminent family names in Florence are represented, such as the Acciaiuoli, Buondelmonti, Davanzati, Guicciardini, Salviati, Tornabuoni and even the Medici, though not from the Giovanni di Bicci line, but from cadet branches of the family.[22] The political orientation of the eminent families represented in the Purification was equally diverse. All factions involved in the struggle for control of the Florentine state were represented; Mediceans and anti-Mediceans, as well as a substantial proportion of neutrals, families, that is, which had sought safety and survival in non-alignment.[23]

It is far more difficult to determine the provenance of members from the popolo minuto. Here one has to be guided by the scribes' recording of the details, especially occupational details, of the enrolling members. I have assumed that a precise statement by the scribe of where the youths' pursued their trade or occupation, invariably expressed with the definite article in an articulated preposition, reveals his familiarity with these firms

---

[19] For descriptions of the mixed nature of the area see Elam, "Lorenzo de' Medici," esp. 49–51, and "Il palazzo nel contesto della città," 44–5; Sodini, *Il gonfalone del Leon d'oro, passim*.

[20] These figures have been derived from an examination of the members enrolling for the years 1434–9: ASF CRSPL 1654, Inserto 29, ff. 2r–34r.

[21] Particularly useful here have been: Priorista Gaddi, BL Egerton MS 3764, and Giovanni Cambi, "Il libro degli abili al consiglio," MS BNF Passerini 39.

[22] ASF CRSPL 1654, Inserto 29, ff. 2r–53v.

[23] For political alignments, I have relied on Kent, *The Rise of the Medici* and Rubinstein, *The Government of Florence*.

and hence their local character.[24] Since the records were compiled in the Hospital of San Matteo, it would be safe to assume that these places lay in its vicinity, in the S. Giovanni quarter of the city. An examination of the scribes' entries with these assumption in mind suggests that the over-whelming majority of the youths from the popolo minuto worked or went to school in the S. Giovanni quarter, and most probably in the districts of Drago and Lion d'oro.

The statutes decreed that members were to meet every Sunday and every holy day of obligation. Devotions would begin with the reading, by one of the boys, of a devout text, followed by an act of reconciliation and then the correction of all those members who had transgressed against the rules. Devotions were to continue with the recitation of the Office of the Virgin and end with general prayers for absent members of the confraternity and for those who had entered holy orders, for its officials, for the souls of the departed, and for the city's as well as all Christian rulers.[25]

Judging by the statutes, the confraternity set itself two main tasks. It sought, first, to check the youths' natural unruliness, which had greatly troubled Florence in the recent past, by attempting to remove them from moral danger and temptation. To this end, members were forbidden to gamble, to joust, to engage in horseracing, to hunt or trap birds, and either to engage or to be spectators in musical, dancing and carnival spectacles or performances. They were not to frequent taverns or other immoral places, or to pursue illicit trades. They were always to dress neatly and modestly, refrain from rowdiness in the streets, remain at home during the night hours and live chastely. The confraternity also sought to prepare them for adulthood by instituting an educational and spiritual programme which was mandatory. Members not only received instruction in behavior, but were trained to assume the responsibilities of adult life through their involvement in the running of the confraternity's affairs. In addition, they were to learn by heart the Ten Commandments and the articles of faith as well as the sacramental and theological precepts of the Church. They were required to engage in daily religious and devotional practices; to attend Mass, recite a set number of prayers at different times and occasions of the day, and venerate holy images. They also had to fast every Saturday and on every major feast day of the Virgin, confess every month and take Communion three times per year.[26] The

---

[24] This point is best expressed, perhaps, by transcribing a couple of typical entries : "Giovanni di Giuliano ista al setaiuolo" is an example of what I take to be a statement revealing the scribe's familiarity with the bottega which is thus assumed to lie in the vicinity of the Hospital of S. Matteo; whereas an entry of the type: "Simone d'Antonio ista a righattiere" is taken to convey the scribe's unfamiliarity with it and consequently it is assumed that it does not lie in the vicinity of the hospital. Both examples are from ASF CRSPL 1654, Inserto 29, f. 5v.

[25] "Statuti ... de la purificatione," ff.12r–15v.   [26] Ibid., ff. 8v–11r.

primacy of this educational and catechetical role was freely acknowledged by the officials who invariably referred to their confraternity as a "scuola."[27]

The control and acculturation of youths, however, were merely means to an end. These youths were, in fact, invested with the responsibility of leading Florence to its pre-ordained destiny, to the temporal and spiritual inheritance long promised to the city by God. Amongst the Florentines there existed a cherished belief that their city was especially favored by God, destined to play a leading role in Christendom and even to lead it to a new age of wisdom and prosperity.[28] The Ciompi revolt and, later, the reverses suffered during the war against Milan had severely shaken but not destroyed the Florentines' belief in their destiny. This belief sustained them during the long and disastrous war against Giangaleazzo Visconti. The miraculous delivery from the Milanese threat could not but confirm them in their conviction. Victory against "tyranny" was accompanied by even stronger official statements of Florentine primacy in the political, religious, and cultural fields.[29] This vision of future leadership contrasted markedly with existing conditions, characterized by recurrent crises and vulnerability to internal and external threats. Divisions amongst the inhabitants, factionalism among the members of the governing elite and the general disregard for the common good were seen as the factors which prevented Florence from fulfilling its destiny.

Much of the frustration felt by the Florentines was directed against adult confraternities. They were accused of having become instruments of individual or factional ambitions, of contributing to the disintegration of the Florentine polity and hence of preventing Florence from receiving the promised blessings. Attempts were made in 1415, 1419, and again in 1426 to regulate them, to limit their influence and even to suppress them.[30] And yet, in the very midst of this official campaign against adult confraternities, civil and ecclesiastical authorities lent their support to the establishment of youth confraternities. There was nothing illogical in their stand. Youth confraternities, unlike their corrupt adult counterparts, through their educational and catechetical programs, were entrusted with the mission of raising a new generation of civic minded Florentines who would lead Florence to its inheritance. That the officials of these confraternities knew what was expected of them is clearly revealed by an analysis of the ritual of investiture instituted to receive new

---

[27] Indeed, even to the extent of scribes scoring out the word *confraternita* and replacing it with *scuola*, see, for example ASF CRSPL 1654, Inserto 29, ff.1r, 172v, 179v.

[28] Weinstein, "The Myth of Florence," 15–44.

[29] On all this, see Baron, *The Crisis of the Early Italian Renaissance* and the literature spawned by the conflict.

[30] Monti, *Le confraternite medievali*, vol.i, p. 181; Polizzotto, "Confraternities, Conventicles and Political Dissent," 237–44.

members. In the Purification, once the postulant had answered a set of questions posed by the governor, he was dressed in a white surplice with the injunction to renew himself and to become a new man, by assuming the new habits of justice, charity, and sanctity.[31] A girdle was then fastened around his body as a symbol of chastity, which he was enjoined to keep for the love of the Virgin.[32] After which, the governor and the members together sang the *Magnificat* [33]and the *Nunc dimittis*,[34] and exchanged the sign of peace with the newly accepted novice.

The two canticles chosen to celebrate the investiture are highly significant. They were not only expressions of thanksgiving to God for deigning to bestow His grace on humble creatures, but also hymns of messianic faith in Christ's imminent redemption of mankind and in the glory which the nation of Israel would derive from it. Particularly striking was the parallel established between the presentation of Christ to the temple and the presentation of the newly inducted novice to the assembled confraternity. Simeon's prophecy regarding Christ's redemptive mission was seen to apply, by inference, to the newly received novice. He, too, was invested with a redemptive mission akin to that entrusted to Christ, and so, of course, were all other members of the Purification who had undergone the same ceremony of investiture. In the way it was staged, the ceremony of investiture was endowed with quasi-sacramental significance. It consecrated the youths to God, and made them an instrument of His grace by conferring upon them a messianic role. Implicit in all this was also the identification of Florence with Israel: Through these youths, Florence was to acquire glory as Israel had acquired it through the coming of the Messiah. So varied and important were the meanings attached to it that it is not surprising that the ceremony of investiture was the most important event in the confraternity's calendar. Its pivotal importance was appreciated also by the illuminator of the statutes, who chose to illustrate the initial letter of the manuscript with the presentation of Christ to the temple and consecration of His life to God, rather than with the Purification of the Virgin.[35] All these elements help to explain why it should have long been thought that the Purification was founded to encourage and to prepare boys to consecrate their lives to God by undertaking an ecclesiastical career.[36] The possibility that some of the boys would choose to do so was contemplated by the statutes.[37] It was not, however, expected of them.

The acquisition of Cosimo de' Medici as patron, the move to S.

---

[31] "Statuti ... de la purificatione" f. 17v.   [32] *Ibid.*   [33] Luke 1: 46–55.

[34] Luke 3: 29–35.   [35] "Statuti ... de la purificatione," f. 1r.

[36] del Migliore, "Zibaldone," MS BNF Magl. XXV, 418, f. 37r; Loddi, "Notizie del convento di S. Marco," MS ACSM (no location number), f. 32r; Monti, *Le confraternite medievali*, 1, 184.

[37] "Statuti ... de la purificatione," f. 10r.

Marco, and Eugenius IV's intervention with the bull of 1442 wrought some important changes upon the confraternity. These changes were incorporated into its new statutes, adopted on 29 June 1444, the day in which it took possession of its new premises.[38] The new statutes reveal that the confraternity had acquired, since the earlier draft of 1431–4, a new titular saint, S. Zanobi – one of the patron saints of Florence – becoming the "Schuola di Purificatione della Vergine Maria e di Sancto Zenobio."[39] It was soon to adopt, moreover, two new patron saints: Saints Cosmas and Damian – or rather, as the confraternity's documents invariably refer to them, Saints Cosimo and Damiano – the martyred physicians who were Cosimo de' Medici's patron saints. The chapel in the new meeting-place was dedicated not to the Virgin and S. Zanobi, as one would expect, but to Saints Cosmas and Damian. An altarpiece depicting the two saints was provided by Cosimo. This chapel was invariably referred to in the confraternity's documents solely as San Cosimo. The new statutes decreed that, in thanksgiving, at every meeting of the confraternity members should pray for Cosimo in the chapel of S. Cosimo, before the altar dedicated to Saints Cosimo and Damiano and embellished by the altarpiece depicting the two saints.[40] The distinction between praying for and praying to was thus blurred; earthly and heavenly patrons merged into one. Here we can detect the beginnings of the process of exaltation not only of Cosimo but also of his descendants which by the end of the century was to turn them, in some circles at least, into figures of worship.[41]

The move to S. Marco and the new statutes signaled also major changes to the confraternity's life, to its devotional practices, its spiritual aims and, in particular, its public role. The ages of induction into and departure from the confraternity were modified and extended. Before being accepted into the confraternity, youths had to have completed their twelfth year of age. They could join until they had turned twenty-one; and they were required to make their departure once they had turned

[38] Despite a lengthy search and the kind assistance of many people, I have not been able to find the present location of this manuscript which was sold by Sotheby to Martin Breslauer in 1958 and by the latter to Lathrop C. Harper of New York in 1960. I have used a later copy, dated 1478, in BNF MS Magl. VIII. 1500. Inserto 11(see above, n.4). I wish here to thank Dr. Charles E. Pierce, jr., Director of the Pierpont Morgan Library of New York, Mr. B. H. Breslauer, Mr. Felix de Marez Oyens of Christie's France, and Mr. Christopher de Hamel of Sotheby for their courteous replies to my queries regarding the present whereabouts of the 1444 statutes.

[39] This is the title given to it in the 1444 statutes and in the 1478 copy of them; see *ibid.*, f. 82r and Martin Breslauer sale *Catalogue 91* (London, 1959), 59. It should be pointed out, however, that already in the years after 1434 S. Zanobi had become a patron of the company. The exact year in which he was adopted as a titular saint is not known.

[40] "Capitoli ... della schuola di purificatione," f. 82r-v.

[41] Trexler, "Lorenzo de' Medici," esp. 293–4, 307–8; Polizzotto, "Prophecy, Politics and History," 115–17.

twenty-four.[42] The new regulations enabled youth confraternities to exercise their influence over members to the age at which, if eligible, they qualified for public office. This in turn provided greater scope for political indoctrination, especially in confraternities like the Purification, which had allowed themselves to become utterly dependent on a powerful and politically ambitious patron. Ultimately, this had the effect of politicizing the Purification and turning it into an instrument of personal ambition: the very outcome which it, and other youth confraternities, had been created to combat.

While the timing and the frequency of meetings did not change dramatically, far more precise instructions were given in the new statutes on how to conduct prayers and devotions. The previous regulations regarding behavior and deportment were restated, but with one innovation: greater stress was placed on virginity and chastity, accompanied by injunctions to keep boys of different age groups separate, so as to minimize the possibilities of older boys corrupting younger ones and of both groups engaging in homosexual acts. In the new statutes, far less emphasis was placed on catechetical activities, which had been so central before.[43] Still present in the new statutes, but similarly more subdued, was the theme of the youths' redemptive mission.[44] All in all, while it cannot be maintained that the original aims of the Purification had been abandoned, it is undeniable that they had been modified, the better to conform to the new political reality and to the role which the confraternity was expected to play in it. A tangible proof of this change in orientation is provided by the miniature in the initial letter of the 1444 statutes which no longer depicts the presentation of Jesus to the Temple, but rather the Virgin and Child with S. Zanobi.[45]

Totally new in the 1444 statutes is the public, ceremonial and ritual role which the youths of the Purification were asked to play. Its members, attired in white surplices, were required to take part in a number of ecclesiastical and civic processions. In addition, they were also expected to prepare and perform publicly in their meeting-place an annual Purification play, on the day of the Purification. Finally, on the feast days of S. Zanobi and of Saints Cosmas and Damian, the confraternity was thrown open to the public. On those days, the youths had to decorate the oratory and chapel; they had to ensure that visitors were properly received and given the opportunity to attend divine services and to venerate the holy images there displayed.[46]

---

[42] "Capitoli ... della schuola di purificatione," ff. 93r, 94v.   [43] Ibid., ff. 89v–92v.

[44] This change of emphasis is best seen in the investiture ceremony which no longer required the singing of the Magnificat and of the Nunc dimittis: ibid., f. 93v.

[45] Reproduced in Sotheby's Sale catalogue, December 1958, part I, lot 18.

[46] "Capitoli ... della schuola di purificatione," ff. 98r–9r.

To understand the full significance of these changes, Cosimo's patron-age of the Purification must be viewed in its proper context: that is, as a component of his patronage of S. Marco. It is my contention that the patronage of the S. Marco complex was central to the formulation of the Medici's visual language of power. If it is remembered that S. Marco was the first large-scale project patronized by Cosimo upon his return from exile in 1434, one can begin to understand its importance in his scheme. Once he persuaded Pope Eugenius to transfer the convent to the Observ-ant Dominicans, Cosimo proceeded to rebuild S. Marco in such a way as to reflect his conception of the position he held in Florence.[47] His primacy in the city was emphasized throughout the S. Marco complex by the placement of Medici arms in the most prominent positions. He acquired sole rights over the high altar and had it dedicated to S. Mark and to Saints Cosmas and Damian. Fra Angelico was commissioned to paint a new altarpiece – *Madonna Enthroned with Eight Saints and Angels* – which, with the *predella* in nine panels illustrating the lives and martyrdom of Saints Cosmas and Damian, glorified the Medici and praised the power they exercised by God's will. The altar was consecrated on 6 January 1443 in the presence of Eugenius IV. It became a focus of civic and popular devotion partly because Eugenius IV granted an indulgence of seven years to those who visited it on the anniversary of its consecration, and partly because the government decreed that all members of the Signoria should also visit it yearly on the same day.[48]

The meeting-place of the confraternity of the Purification received much the same treatment. It too was meant to play an identical role in reinforcing, sanctioning and legitimizing Medici power in Florence. An illustration of how closely linked the convent and the confraternity were in Medicean designs and how aware members of the Purification were of what was expected of them, is provided by the commissioning in 1461 of another altarpiece, this time for the oratory attached to the chapel. The painter "chosen" by the Purification for the task was Benozzo Gozzoli, the Medici's favorite artist, who had painted their palace chapel and also Cosimo's cells in S. Marco. No painter was better acquainted with Medici aims and with the means by which they could best be conveyed to the viewer. Even so, nothing was left to chance. Gozzoli's contract stipulated that he should place "in the middle of the said panel the figure of Our Lady with her seat in the manner and form and with decorations of the kind and in the likeness of the altarpiece on the high altar of S. Marco."[49]

[47] "Annalia conventus S. Marci," MS BMLF San Marco 370, ff. 4v–7r. Rubinstein, "Lay Patronage and Observant Reform," 66.   [48] On all this see Polizzotto, "Lorenzo il Magnifico," 335–7.

[49] That is, of course, Fra Angelico's *Madonna Enthroned with Eight Saints and Angels*. The text of the contract is now available in Cole Ahl, *Benozzo Gozzoli*, 277–8; translation taken from Chambers, *Patrons and Artists*, 53–5.

The Purification was conscious of its obligations to its patrons, and eager to fulfil them. The occasion to do so was provided by the numerous public activities centered on S. Marco in which the confraternity engaged, such as the open days which the Purification had instituted, the yearly staging of the Purification play, and even on the occasion of the visits made by the Signoria to the high altar of the church of S. Marco on the day of the Epiphany. The members of the Purification repaid their debt to the Medici also in a more direct way. Every time the youths appeared in public (no fewer than two-hundred strong,[50] dressed in white with the insignia of their company on their shoulders, marching behind a banner painted by Fra Angelico), they reflected their patrons' concern for them and for their city's moral well-being. They also exemplified the Medici's generosity in ensuring that they received a proper religious and civic upbringing, in order to strengthen the bond between God and Florence. At the same time, however, Cosimo and the Medici were associated with the Purification's messianic mission, thus legitimizing Cosimo's rule over Florence and conveying the message that he was the founder of a divinely sanctioned dynasty.[51] The confraternity's banner with the image of Saint Zanobi, moreover, was evidence of the patriotism of the Purification and of its Medici patrons. Finally, the annual Purification plays – with their optimistic message of future happiness and their praise for a well-ordered polity ruled by just and generous rulers who punished sinners, rewarded the virtuous and healed discord – helped to propagate the Medici's notions of their rule and of the contribution they made to Florence.[52]

Why the S. Marco complex – that is, the convent and the confraternity of the Purification – should have been given such a role in the Medici's consolidation of their hegemony is easily explained. The complex was, in fact, at the very heart of the Medici's source of local, popular support. The Medici's popular, as opposed to their socially and politically eminent, supporters came mainly from the two contiguous districts of Lion d'oro and Drago whose principal parish churches were S. Lorenzo and S. Marco. The Medici houses and eventually their palace lay at the boundary of the two parishes. Other Medici possessions, such as the Medici

50 The number is suggested by the fact that the Purification kept two hundred and twenty processional surplices in store, but since the members had to supply their own surplices the numbers could be much higher; ASF CRSPL 1646, Inserto 7, f. CCXIIr.

51 For the currency of this notion almost a century later see Polizzotto, "Prophecy, Politics and History," passim.

52 Two of these plays have been published by Newbigin in Nuovo Corpus di sacre rappresentazioni, pp. 29–55, 79–106. Though as Newbigin points out no documents links the second of these two plays to the confraternity of the Purification, there are no doubts in my mind that it issued from it. On these plays see also Newbigin, "The Word Made Flesh," esp. 362–8.

gardens and stables, surrounded S. Marco and were situated within its parish. Much of the real estate investment of the Medici, moreover, was centered on the neighborhood of S. Marco, the Hospital of S. Matteo and the SS. Annunziata, in a still underdeveloped area, devoid of entrenched eminent families, which was gradually being settled by small shopkeepers, tradesmen, and members of the popolo minuto.[53]

Even before the Medicean takeover, membership of the Purification was predominantly drawn from this geographic area and from this class of people. These were undoubtedly factors which attracted Cosimo's interest and which induced him to extend his patronage over the Purification. In so doing, Cosimo was acknowledging the importance of his local basis of support and demonstrating his gratitude in a tangible and highly visible way. He was also, at the same time, showing his commitment to the future of Florence: not only to its political and religious destiny but also to its industrial primacy and educational leadership. One should not forget, finally, another important, if less exalted, reason for Cosimo's interest in the Purification. An examination of the records of the confraternity shows that it was a large, financial institution in its own right and that it played a very important role in the economic life of the districts of Drago and Lion d'oro. Patronage of such an institution could not but enhance Cosimo's reputation as a benefactor in districts which were feeling the effects of a recession in the wool trade and were already committed to him politically because of the promise of an economic recovery he represented.

The Medici connection and the move to S. Marco had immediate effects on the Purification's enrollments. Numbers began to climb once again, making the Purification one of the largest sodalities in Florence. Enrollment in the Purification, moreover, became a way of demonstrating Medicean sympathies on the part of members of politically qualified families. As a consequence there ensued a gradual "aristocratization" of membership, which by the end of the century was to reduce to 2:1 the proportion of members from the popolo minuto as against those drawn from eminent families.[54] The creation, in 1452, of an associated adult confraternity dedicated to the Holy Trinity, whose task was to oversee the youths' activities, seems to have been a strategy intended to ensure the continued Medicean character of the Purification at a time of opposition to the regime. So politically trustworthy did the Purification become that it was no longer thought necessary to have representatives of the Medici family as members, as had been the case immediately after Cosimo's return from exile.

---

[53] Indeed, S. Marco was surrounded by Medici properties; on all this see the works cited in n. 19 above.   [54] Based on lists in ASF CRSPL 1650, Inserto 18, ff. CLXXXXVIIr–CCXIVr.

While there is no clear-cut evidence that the youths of the Purification acted in concert to defend the Medici in their hours of need, there are indications that they may have done so, or certainly that they were expected to. In 1983, professors D. and F. W. Kent published a letter to Lorenzo de' Medici from a group of "giovani et garzoni" from the "canto della macina," a street corner about halfway between the Medici palace and the convent of S. Marco and in the catchment area of the confraternity of the Purification. In this letter – unfortunately unsigned – the "giovani et garzoni" relate that on the day of Giuliano de' Medici's murder, they had armed themselves, rushed to defend the Medici palace, and hunted down conspirators.[55] We cannot know whether these "giovani et garzoni" belonged to the Purification, but it was from youths like them, and from the same area, that the confraternity drew the greater proportion of its members. We know, moreover, that the Medici faction was wont to meet in S. Marco and that it was in the Medicean gardens, directly opposite the main entrance to the meeting-place of the Purification, that Piero di Lorenzo de' Medici rallied his supporters on the night of 7 November 1494 in an attempt to put down the revolt against him.[56]

Relations between the Purification and the convent of S. Marco during Savonarola's heyday and after the expulsion of the Medici in 1494 are also very revealing as to the confraternity's political loyalties. The convent was determined to evict the Purification from its rightful place in order, ostensibly, to build a dormitory for its novices. The confraternity refused to budge and appealed to the exiled Cardinal Giovanni de' Medici to intervene in its favor; which he did in a most threatening manner. For eight years the Purification held out and, while the acrimonious dispute lasted, eschewed participation in Savonarolan reforming initiatives. Indeed, it even managed to avoid the reorganization of the youth confraternities undertaken by Savonarola and his followers to cleanse them of Medicean influence and fit them to lead Florence to its promised blessings. The convent was finally able to convince the confraternity to move, but on the latter's terms, and at considerable cost. It undertook to build identical premises for the Purification in the Medici gardens, on land confiscated from the Medici and purchased from the Signoria for the purpose.[57] On 1 May 1506, at the height of republican ascendancy, the whole of Florence witnessed the curious spectacle of the Savonarolan friars of S. Marco escorting the youths of the Purification to their newly completed premises. The assembled youths walked in pro-

---

[55] Kent and Kent, "Two Vignettes," 252–60.
[56] Hatfield, "The Compagnia de' Magi," 137, n.144.
[57] ASF CRSPL 1646, Inserto 7, ff. CCXLr–CCXLIV where a detailed summary of the controversy and of its resolution is given.

cession behind their banner. They took possession of their new meeting-hall which, as they had insisted, displayed all the symbols of Medici power and was decorated with draperies carrying the Medici arms.[58] It was a show of loyalty and defiance not lost on the friars of S. Marco.

[58] *Ibid.*, ff. CCXLIIIv–CCXLIVr.

7

IN LOCO PARENTIS: CONFRATERNITIES AND ABANDONED CHILDREN IN FLORENCE AND BOLOGNA

NICHOLAS TERPSTRA

The conservatory and the orphanage were institutions largely new to the sixteenth century. These lay-directed hostels surrounded orphaned and abandoned girls and boys with the kind of protection, discipline and care associated with the convents and monasteries on which they were so obviously based and of which, some historians would argue, they were so obviously an extension. Such children had traditionally found shelter in the extended family, religious houses, and multi-purpose *ospedali*, but the conservatory and orphanage as specialized institutions spread only from the sixteenth century.[1] While far more children found shelter in foundling homes and workhouse orphanages, the more restrictive conservatories and orphanages tell more about the role of class and social kinship in the construction of social order. This article will review the origins of conservatories and orphanages in Florence and Bologna, discuss entrance requirements and life in the homes, and consider whether administration of these homes by confraternities had any particular significance. On a purely practical level, confraternities provided a traditional institutional format for lay charitable administration. The Catholic Reform movement broadly promoted both confraternities and charitable institutions for marginal groups, and the new orders of the reform found the quasi-confraternal lay congregations an adaptable and more controllable vehicle for the kind of lay charitable work that extended the efforts of the regular clergy. But practical considerations alone offer insufficient explanation, particularly for a time not ruled by bottom lines, quality management

Archival abbreviations: Archivio Arcivescovile di Bologna (AAB); Archivio di Stato di Bologna (ASB); Pii Istituti Educativi (PIE); Archivio di Stato di Firenze (ASF); Biblioteca Comunale di Bologna (BCB); Biblioteca Moreniana Firenze (BMF); Fondo Demaniale (Dem).
[1] Black, *Italian Confraternities*, 200–13.

strategies, or any of the other nostrums of modern business administration. Confraternities structured their internal life and social outreach around the model of kinship, and their heavy involvement in shelters for children was not co-incidental or insignificant; it underscored the fundamental purpose of conservatories and orphanages as acting *in loco parentis* at a time when the metaphor of the family was reshaping political relations and redefining the rights and duties of citizens. In recent years there have been many studies which examined how secular urban and territorial governments employed religious symbols, ceremonies, and myths. Yet few studies have examined how confraternities functioned politically. This case study of conservatories and orphanages illustrates how confraternal charitable institutions helped transfer the religious rhetoric of kinship into the political realm, and thereby helped legitimate the assertion by ruling groups that their political authority was "paternal."

Bologna gained five conservatories through the sixteenth and early seventeenth centuries. The first emerged during the famine of 1505 when many traditional hospitals were pressed to take on orphans and abandoned children. According to the chronicler Ghirardacci, citizens concerned with the honor of a group of young *fanciulle* who had been driven into public begging by the famine led the girls first to the syphilitics' hospital of S. Giobbe, then to a series of homes and convents before settling on a home and the name of *Santa Marta*. No one knew quite what to make of the girls or their situation. In 1526 a few joined the convent of S. Bernardino della Pugliola and in 1554 the conservatory came under the supervision of the confraternal *Opera dei Poveri Vergognosi*, which devised a set of statutes and appointed a group of twelve gentlewomen to oversee daily administration together with a group of resident nuns. Its new confraternal patrons restricted admission to girls aged eleven to fifteen, of wealthy merchant or gentle families which had fallen on hard times. Frequent statute revisions and clarifications over the following century demonstrate that they had as much difficulty defining these so-called "shame-faced poor" as do modern historians. Various records of the later sixteenth and seventeenth century record twenty-three to twenty-nine girls in the home, governed and served by a shifting number of nuns and lay matrons or servants for a total *famiglia* of thirty to forty.[2] The *Conservatorio di S. Croce* was established in 1583 by a merchant Bonifazio dalle Balle to maintain, educate, train, and dower the daughters of prostitutes.

---

[2] Statute revisions of 1558, 1580, and 1641 dealt exclusively with defining the "veri Vergognosi": BCB ms. 3633, 135–8; 172–80. AAB, S. Marta, Busta 621, 33D. Ghirardacci, *Historia di Bologna*, 338. Guidicini, *Cose notabili*, 5, 251–2. Fanti, *Gli archivi*, 62–3. S. Marta was initially also known as S. Maria de Castitate.

Governance was informal until a protracted fight with some Franciscan tertiaries who had offered their quarters and later demanded control turned so messy that Archbishop Alfonso Paleotti ordered statutes written in 1609. These acknowledged the tertiaries' control of the quarters, but left administration in the hands of a congregation of twenty citizens representing noble, professional, artisanal, and clerical interests. The 1609 statutes projected a parallel congregation of gentlewomen providing daily oversight; while they figure in contemporary administrative records as Visitors, they disappear in later statute revisions. Entrance requirements broadened to include any legitimate Bolognese girls aged ten to thirteen of threatened honor, with the result that few were the daughters of prostitutes; possibly 20 percent were subsidized by their families or guardians. As with S. Marta, a resident community of roughly ten nuns and lay staff supervised the life and education of the girls, and also their piecework in the city's dominant silk industry. In August 1610 the confraternity limited the the entire famiglia to thirty "mouths," but records from before and after this date suggest that its normal size ranged from forty to forty-five, with a deliberate effort made to recruit from across the city.[3] Bologna's *Conservatorio di S. Giuseppe* emerged in 1606 at the encouragement of Jesuit Giorgio Giustiniani to give prompt and short-term help to girls aged fourteen to eighteen; these it channeled into domestic service rather than marriage or the convent. Twelve gentlewomen comprised its earliest governing congregation, joined in 1631 by seven male Conservators who handled finance and administration. Its rules reflected local experience, Jesuit efficiency, and a wariness of fraud: no dowries were available, fee-paying girls were accepted, "graduates" of other conservatories or orphanages were refused, and all girls required sponsors who had to offer security that the girl would be taken back after a fixed period. With many girls staying only a few weeks or months, S. Giuseppe's size fluctuated wildly. While its Congregation decided in 1630 to feed no more than eight mouths, through the century its famiglia usually numbered nine to fourteen girls and three or four guardians and servants.[4] These three conservatories began as private initiatives and were later entrusted to confraternities; they were overshadowed by a fourth

---

[3] ASB PIE, S. Croce, "Congregazioni 1609–1637," ms. 3, c.8r; "Ammissioni e Dotazioni, 1619–1711," Busta 83, [folios for 1663, 1676, 1691]; "Statuti 1609–1818," Cartone I, ms. 2, cap I, 2, 10, 19; Camillo Faggioli, "Origine ed appunti storici del Conservatorio delle zitelle di S. Croce..." [1876 mss. history], Cart. I, 3–16. Vittori, "Bonifacio dalle Balle," 305, 331–2, 336–42. Fanti, *Gli archivi*, 76–78. Giacomelli, "Conservazione," 211–13.

[4] AAB 619, fasc. 31, 31 c [reports of 1646, 1660, 1667, 1690]. ASB PIE, S. Giuseppe, "Ingresso e Ussita delle Putte," Cart. I, cc. 5v–7v; "Atti della Congregatione, 1631–1656," Cart. 19, ms. 1a, [21–IV–1630]; "Regole," Cart I, Libro +, 1–5, 22–5, 35. Fanti, *Gli archivi*, 82–3. Giacomelli, "Conservazione," 213–16.

Bolognese institution S. *Maria del Baraccano*, which began as a confraternal hostel in 1439 and developed into a conservatory only in 1527–8. This was at once the largest and the most exclusive of the Bolognese conservatories, taking in girls aged ten to twelve of "honest condition" and Bolognese parentage, who had neither begged nor been in service. In 1553 it absorbed the conservatory of S. *Gregorio* located outside the city walls, of whose previous history little is known. Statutes of that year set a limit of seventy-five girls overseen by a resident matron and priest and an unspecified number of servants; actual enrollment fluctuated by about a dozen above and below this mean until the 1640s, when it dropped to approximately fifty. Fee-paying girls were welcome, and while they joined the others in school, lace-making piecework, and worship, they could not access the dowries guaranteed by the confraternity to daughters of Bolognese citizens. A congregation of twelve confratelli and an unspecified number of gentlewomen oversaw daily administration.[5]

Bolognese boys were entrusted to one of three institutions, each of which emerged in years of demographic crisis brought on by famine or plague. Orphanage officials maintained enrollment records less diligently than their conservatory counterparts, so determining the size of these institutions can be difficult. S. *Bartolomeo di Reno* was the companion institution to the conservatory of S. Maria del Baraccano, undergoing a similar transformation from pilgrim's hostel to orphanage in the late 1520s. Its sponsoring confraternity of artisans was divided on the shift, but naysayers were outvoted by a steady influx of patrician members into a separate branch of the brotherhood. It was Bologna's largest orphanage, sheltering over one hundred boys during the famine of 1590. Legitimate sons of Bolognese fathers, these boys were accepted between ages seven and eleven, given a basic education, and then channeled into apprenticeships in the city. Most left the orphanage by age 16. Able boys were given an advanced education in preparation for the priesthood or monastery.[6] When famine hit again in the late 1550s, the confraternity of S. *Maria Maddalena* engineered a similar transformation in its pilgrims' hostel of S. *Onofrio*. The brothers received permission to enroll orphans and abandoned boys in 1557, and rebuilt or expanded their dormitory in 1574. It appears that initially two boys slept in each of the fifteen beds: in 1595, after failing to record a single recruit for nine years, the confraternity

---

[5] ASB PIE, S. Maria del Baraccano, "Capitoli [1553]," Cart. 1, ms. 2, cc. 3r, 5v–6v, 10r–11r; "Campione delle Donzel," ms. 7, "Instrumenti," Busta 43, 41/2 [1535]. Ciammitti, "Quanto costa." Fanti, *Gli archivi*, 68–72. Giacomelli, "Conservazione," 208–11. Terpstra, *Lay Confraternities*, 190–6.

[6] ASB PIE, S. Bartolomeo di Reno, Busta 7, ms. 1, cc 1v, 50r; busta 7, ms. 2, cc. 5r–v, 9r–10v, 23v. Giacomelli, "Conservazione," 203–205. Terpstra, "Ospedali e bambini", 218–229.

reprimanded the resident guardian for bypassing proper entrance procedures and then hurriedly approved twenty-eight boys. A century later
there were only sixteen to eighteen boys, overseen by a married couple, a
priest, and two servants for a total of twenty-one to twenty-four
"mouths." Boys aged seven to twelve could apply to enter, providing
both a baptismal certificate and their father's death certificate before
being considered. They received education and apprenticeship opportunities, and were to be on their way by age eighteen.[7] By 1590 an
accelerating cycle of famines so strained the capacity of Bologna's main
poorhouse, the *Ospedale dei Mendicanti*, that Archbishop Paleotti and the
Senate asked the confraternity of S. *Giacomo* to shelter some boys in their
pilgrims' hostel. Later accounts claim that they took in 30 *putti* the
following year and, having decided to make this a permanent shift in
function, followed the lead of S. Bartolomeo and S. Maria Maddalena in
establishing a separate branch of the brotherhood to accommodate patrician members. Mid-seventeenth century pastoral visits show that the
number of boys had fallen to ten to twelve, overseen by a guardian
couple, a priest, three servants, and a confraternity of over thirty men.[8]

The situation for abandoned girls in Florence was roughly similar in
that the four conservatories established in the sixteenth century began as
the work of individuals or small groups and gradually worked into the
hands of a confraternity or congregation; a fifth opened in the early
seventeenth century as the work of a confraternity-cum-magistracy.
Leonarda Barducci Ginori established the first distinct home, initially
called the *Ospedale delle Povere Fanciulle Abbandonate* in 1541; this private
effort paralleled the emergence of a state *Ospedale degli Abbandonati* for
boys the following year. Administrators of the orphanage gave financial
and administrative assistance to the conservatory until Ginori's death in
1550. Cosimo I then ordered it closed, but it came instead under the
administration of a newly created confraternity, the *Compagnia di S. Maria
Vergine*, and under the protection of Cosimo's wife Eleonora di Toledo;
since it retained both its original name and quarters on Piazza San Felice,
it is unlikely that its residents were turned out by Cosimo's closure.
Sometimes officially called the *Casa di S. Maria Vergine* after its confraternal sponsors, it was more commonly known as the *Ceppo* from the
monastery which became its home in 1564. In that same year, it took over

---

[7] ASB PIE, S. Onofrio, Busta 2, ms. 3, cap. 18; Busta 5, ms. 9, [np]; ms. 78, cc. 1r–4v. AAB,
Miscellanea vecchie, 622 [1672, 1690].

[8] ASB Dem, S. Giacomo, 12/6470, vol. 2, cc. 1r–v, and loose sheet: "Obligo degl'Uomini della
Compagnia larga di S. Giacomo Maggiore, eretta l'Anno 1604"; vol. 3, "Memoriale all' E/mo e
Rev. Princ. Il Sig.re Card.le Arcivesco di Bologna Per li confratelli della Compagnia stretta di S.
Giacomo" [n.p.]. AAB, Miscellanee vecchie, cart. 619, Item G, "Visite Pastorali" 1662, 1672 [n.p.].
Fanti, *Gli archivi*, 79. Giacomelli, "Conservazione," 205.

the conservatory of S. *Niccolò* which had been founded in 1556 when Cosimo I urged the magistracy of the *Otto di guardia e balia* to offer some shelter to those girls who, without parents and guardians were *"violate"* in Florence's streets, shops, and stalls. The Otto di guardia e balia entrusted administration to Francesco Rosati, a member of the Compagnia di S. Maria Vergine, under whose care it grew to house eighty to ninety girls. Rosati appealed at least twice to Cosimo to let the confraternity take over both houses, and when the Duke finally relented, the brothers established a separate five-member congregation to oversee S. Niccolò. Though now under the care of a single confraternity, the two homes maintained distinct quarters until 1620. They also served distinct groups, the Ceppo gathering girls of higher status and less "experience" than S. Niccolò. Both set a minimum age of ten, though in practice S. Niccolò took in girls as young as three. The Ceppo seems to have been smaller, beginning in 1552 with eighteen girls, and enrolling eighty-eight through the following four years. By the 1570s, S. Niccolò had been trimmed to fifty-three inmates, and kept roughly to this figure until 1620. After their physical union in that year, the Ceppo and S. Niccolò counted ninety-seven bocche, dropping to seventy-two in 1646 and to forty-seven in 1689.[9] A third *Conservatorio della Pietà* emerged in 1554 as the work of a group of pious women headed by Margherita di Carlo Borromei and assisted by two religious, including an Antonio da Milano who may have been the priest of the Compagnia di S. Maria Vergine. Sixty young girls entered this new conservatory, by some accounts rising to 160 within a few years. The nuns of S. Maria degli Angeli offered care and instruction, while a supporting body of 200 gentlewomen offered financial and administrative support. After 1557, a Dominican friar, Alessandro Capocchi, became the *padre spirituale* of the work and convinced its supporters to vest governing authority in a congregation of 17 gentlewomen; Capocchi was a major figure in late sixteenth-century charitable relief and took on the spiritual direction of the Ceppo in 1580.[10] The famine of 1590–1 led to the opening of Florence's fourth conservatory. Giovan Battista Botti was the prime mover behind *S. Caterina*. He enlisted the help of two others including Girolamo Michelozzi, a confratello of the Compagnia di S. Maria Vergine, and received from Grand Duke Ferdinand I the Ospedale Broccardi in Via San Gallo which had until

---

[9] ASF, S. Maria e S. Niccolò del Ceppo, "Capitoli ed ordini [1598]", ms. 69, cc. 1r–3r, 12r–14r, 17r–19v.; "Fanciulle Accettate, 1558–1621," ms. 59, cc. 105v–18v; 129v–35r. Manno Tolu, "Abbandonate fiorentine," 1007–15; 1017–18. Lombardi, "Poveri a Firenze," 167–70.

[10] BMF, Bigazzi, ms. 61, "Capitoli, o costitutioni [1570]," c. 1v. BMF, Acquisti diversi 93, "Cronica, overo Istoria della Pietà di Firenze," 1–4, 13. Manno Tolu, "Abbandonate fiorentine," 1009. Lombardi, "Poveri a Firenze," 167. D'Addario, "Religiosità e carità," 100–1.

then been the quarters of Florence's orphanage, the Ospedale degli Abbandonati. Here they sheltered approximately 80 girls aged 6 and over.[11] Finally, in 1615 the confraternity-magistracy of the Bigallo, further discussed below, built a *Convento per le Povere Fanciulle Derelitte* housing 40 girls adjacent to the convent of S. Caterina.[12]

Florentine boys were the subjects of an ambitious expansion of charitable enclosure under Cosimo I. An Ospedale degli Abbandonati opened in 1542 as the first dedicated orphanage in the city, supplementing the work of a range of other confraternal, guild, and private ospedali which had included abandoned boys among their charitable charges. Chief among these had been the shelter of the *Compagnia di S. Maria del Bigallo*, a confraternity dating to 1244. In March 1542 Cosimo I launched a far-reaching consolidation of poor relief which made the Ospedale degli Abbandonati the main charge and beneficiary of a magistracy empowered to inventory the possessions, reform the administrations, and appropriate the excess revenues of over 200 charitable ospedali in the dominion. Politics, finances, and shifting ambitions curbed this plan, but not before Cosimo I had moved to secure its finances by suppressing the Bigallo confraternity and transferring its assets, testamentary responsibilities, and name over to the magistracy. He thereby created a hybrid of mixed purpose, identity, and resources – an institution which was part government magistracy and part religious confraternity; partly charged with macromanagement of the Florentine state's social services, and partly charged with micromanagement of a particular orphanage. It was, in other words, the classic early modern bureaucracy. Although it retained its prominent public building on Piazza S. Giovanni, under whose loggia Florentines continued abandoning their children, over succeeding decades it housed its boys in a variety of dormitories in different parts of the city. Its administrators kept no consistent records of enrollments, but a 1562 Florentine census records 95 bocche.[13]

Like contemporary foundling homes and workhouses, conservatories and orphanages used the metaphor of the family to describe internal relations. Differing circumstances, in particular the age, tenure, and training of children, determined the extent to which they could translate this rhetoric into practice. In both cities, orphanages tended to accept boys from ages 3 to 10, while conservatories accepted girls from ages 10

---

[11] ASF, S. Caterina, ms. 7, "Capitoli ed ordini [1591+]," Cap. I/1–3, 5–7. Manno Tolu, "Abbandonate fiorentine," 1012. Lombardi, "Poveri a Firenze" 167–168.

[12] ASF Bigallo, 1669/IV "Statuti, privilegi, bolle suppliche, 1318–1733," cc. 46r–v. D'Addario, "Religiosità e carità," 131–2.

[13] For a broader discussion and archival references, see: Terpstra, "Confraternities and Public Charity." Lombardi, "Poveri a Firenze," 165–72. Trexler, "Orbatello," 444.

through 16 (though in practice younger girls entered as well). As they became older, boys were more often sent to apprenticeships outside the home, while most girls did piecework for the textile trades in workshops within the tight enclosure of the conservatory. By late adolescence, boys were turned out of the homes whether there was any permanent place for them or not. By contrast, most girls had to wait for a spouse, an employer, a family member, or a mother superior to provide their ticket of leave, and in the absence of this could remain resident into their twenties, thirties or beyond. Age and gender combined to create significant differences in institutional climate, and not surprisingly the notion of the home as a surrogate family became more developed among the young women of the conservatories (predominantly older, resident, and longer-term) than among the boys in the orphanages (predominantly younger, mobile, short-term). Conservatory inmates were encouraged to consider each other siblings; older girls who had been given a greater role in the day-to-day running of the home were like older sisters; and the mature woman hired as the resident *guardiana* with direct responsibility for maintenance, security, and deportment was the mother; one of the "mothers" at S. Niccolò was a girl who had first entered the conservatory as an orphan, and statutes for both S. Caterina and the Pietà stipulated that its teachers and staff all be older inmates. Orphanages used the metaphor of family less frequently, and like contemporary foundling homes and workhouses applied it more often to the staff and confraternal supervisors than to the residents themselves; few of these latter seem to have been drawn into the management of their homes.

While conservatories and orphanages differed from each other in the degree to which they adapted the rhetoric of kinship to the reality of daily administration, they shared a characteristic which distinguished them from other charitable institutions that used the family metaphor. Unlike foundling homes and workhouses, conservatories and orphanages were far more deliberate about the family that was created internally. Age, residency, and parentage requirements ensured that only a small proportion of the girls and boys who were orphaned and abandoned in these cities would actually find a home in the conservatory or orphanage. Between them, the Bolognese homes could shelter between 125 and 180 girls and 130 to 160 boys; their Florentine counterparts could shelter from 250 to 300 girls and perhaps 100 boys. No such restrictions operated in the cases of foundling homes and workhouses. In the mid-sixteenth century, over 500 foundlings were entering Florence's Innocenti annually; by 1579 there were 968 females in residence, 733 of them old enough to be married. Bologna's Ospedale dei Mendicanti enrolled 800 when it opened in 1563, and its numbers rose to over 1400 during the worst of the famine of 1590; the bulk of these were women and children, including orphans.[14] Foundling homes might seek to set out conditions and qualifications in their statutes, but these were pretty much wiped off the page with every turn of the wheel, that discrete entryway that preserved the anonymity of those abandoning infants. And they were rendered null by the fact that infants abandoned in other places of the city and surrounding countryside were funneled into the foundling home as well. Workhouses were somewhat more successful in enforcing entry qualifications, but only slightly so. As quasi-disciplinary institutions that functioned as a refuge of last resort for those poor whose formal and informal support networks had given way, and who could not on any pretext be given a one-way ticket out of town, workhouses were seldom in a position to exercise fully those entry qualifications that they may have written into their statutes. What were the results? Across Italy, both foundling homes and workhouses struggled to find places for the poor who flowed through their gates in normal circumstances, and whose numbers mounted to a veritable flood when disasters like the plagues and famines of the 1520s, the 1550s, and the 1590s struck. Their struggle to offer short-term shelter to these crisis poor was compounded by the fact that these same institutions were simultaneously forced to provide long-term shelter to those of their charges who could not be reintegrated into society. Boys could simply be turned out when they had reached their mid-teens, whether any permanent position had been found for them or not, but not so girls. And so both foundling homes and workhouses found themselves saddled with a permanent population of adult women who, usually due to some infirmity or impediment, could not be reintegrated into society.

This was the concrete result for those institutions which could not discriminate among their entrants. Seeing other ospedali with, as Brian Pullan puts it, "increasing numbers of aging women, highly institutionalized and equipped with a special jargon of their own, fit to live nowhere but in the hospital itself" conservatory and orphanage governors readily adopted specific and selective entry requirements.[15] Most stipulated that admissions be entertained only if there was a bed free. Knowing that it was difficult to find permanent homes for girls or boys who were infirm, physically, or mentally disabled, foreign, born into the ranks of the *sottoposti*, or in the case of girls specifically, sexually experienced, these governors simplified their own futures by refusing admittance to such children. Knowing that the lure of a dowry could overcome at least some of these impediments, they demonstrated some flexibility with those girls

14 Gavitt, "Charity and State Building," 238–41. Calori, *L'Opera dei Mendicanti*, 23–4.
15 Pullan, "Orphans and foundlings," 14. Fubini Leuzzi, "Fanciulle degli Innocenti," 863–99.

whose guardians offered the requisite cash or promises. Whoever said you can't choose your family? Each of the homes under study had strict procedures for assessing applicants. Among conservatories, Bologna's S. Maria del Baraccano had a committee of three governesses appointed from among the membership of the patrician sponsoring confraternity review applicants and make recommendations to the confraternal corporale, which then voted on the application. Florence's Ceppo had its Madre Priora weed out those clearly unworthy applicants, and then subjected all who remained to a detailed examination by a five member panel; two of these would check on her parentage and on how she had survived since being orphaned or abandoned. These would report to the other three, and the girl's nomination would have to be supported by four of the five panel members before she could be admitted.[16] Florence's S. Caterina originally allowed the girls themselves to vote on an entrant after a two-month trial period, but scratched this and left the decision to the six *Signori operai* who supervised the conservatory's affairs, and who had a more direct interest in its viability.[17] In their statutes, these governors blandly noted that girls who were blind, deaf, mute, hunchbacked, or crippled would "weigh down the place" (*gravare il luogo*) and so shouldn't be accepted; other dead-weights included those who had begged, who had been servants, or who were the daughters or nieces of prostitutes. Boys had to pass a similar, if less searching, examination before admission. Florence's Ospedale degli Abbandonati began by requiring only a *pro forma* vote of its 12 governing captains, reflecting the fact that it originated as a comprehensive shelter. Within a matter of decades, the captains required written applications whose truth was sworn to by worthy citizens of the abandoned child's neighborhood or town. They were however continually frustrated by the abandonment of children under their loggia on Piazza S. Giovanni, and may for that reason have given up keeping accurate records of their enrollment.[18] In Bologna, the minute books for S. Bartolomeo di Reno and S. Onofrio show that both required written nominations whose veracity was checked by pairs of confraternal *Visitatori* who visited the nominees, their promoters, and any relatives. Only boys who had passed a preliminary vote in the confraternal *corporale* were so reviewed, and they were accepted only after a discussion and vote on the confraternal visitors' report.[19]

The active participation of confraternal overseers in screening or-

---

[16] ASB PIE, S. Maria del Baraccano, Cart 1, ms. 2, cc. 6v–7v. ASF, S. Maria e S. Niccolò del Ceppo, ms. 69, cc. 12r–13v.   [17] ASF, S. Caterina, ms. 7, cap. I/2, 5, 6, 7.

[18] ASF, Bigallo,mss. 1459, 1460, "Fede per Bambini" ms. 1669/II, cc. 9r–11r.; 1669/IV, c. 44v.

[19] ASB PIE, S. Bartolomeo di Reno, 7/1, 7/2; S. Onofrio, Busta 4, ms. 7; Busta 5, ms. 9.

phaned and abandoned boys and girls underscores the fact that the confraternities who sponsored these homes saw themselves as far more than simply fund-raisers or managerial advisors. Lay brothers and sisters took an active and direct interest in the day-to-day management of conservatories and orphanages. In an extreme instance, Signora Margherita Angiosoli Fantuzzi, one of the twelve gentlewomen who oversaw Bologna's Conservatory of S. Giuseppe, moved into the home to take up duties as Governess when the existing employee left suddenly in October, 1639.[20] Bonifacio dalle Balle, founder of the Conservatory of S. Croce in the same city gave it his entire fortune and eventually moved into a small apartment on the premises – though not without raising some eyebrows in the brotherhood and in the city.[21] Yet even when they stopped short of such an immediate identification with their metaphorical children, confraternal overseers had close and consistent contact with their charges, particularly when taking their turns as officers deputed to investigate applicants, to make periodic checks of conditions in the home, or to find masters, spouses, or convents for their charges. No child could leave the orphanage or conservatory without approval of the confratelli and consorelle.

If confratelli and consorelle were actively involved in day-to-day management of the conservatories and orphanages, the question then rises: what kind of home were they aiming to create, for whom, and why? The many conditions and qualifications which applicants had to meet demonstrate that they were not exclusive by practical necessity, but by deliberate intent: the legitimate children of legitimately born citizen fathers; boys and girls who had never begged, nor been in service, nor been in a workhouse orphanage. In her study of early modern Amsterdam's *Burgerweeshuis* orphanage, Anne McCants notes that it aimed "to protect the social status of burgher children" by adopting similar entrance qualifications and by ensuring that the children received the diet (relatively generous in meat, animal products, and sugar), education and, upon leavetaking, the clothes (most notably a hat) which would prepare them to participate socially with members of their peer group. The home's governing regents, commonly addressed as "fathers" of the institution, spent 50 percent more per child than their counterparts at the orphanage for the poor, even though both were state institutions whose accounts were reviewed by civic authorities.[22] Similar concerns shaped Florentine and Bolognese conservatories and orphanages. These were not overcrowded Dickensian hell-holes like contemporary foundling homes and workhouse orphanages, but schools for citizens: S. Bar-

---

[20] ASB PIE, S. Giuseppe, Cart. 23, ms. 1, c. c.52r–v.   [21] ASB PIE, S. Croce, ms. 3, c. 16r.
[22] McCants, "Meeting Needs," 198, 200–7.

tolomeo and later S. Onofrio ensured that there was a separate bed for each boy. All homes educated their charges in basic literacy and numeracy, in Christian Doctrine, and in good manners and customs. Those of higher standing went further: S. Bartolomeo had a music master, while the Bigallo had three masters designated, in that creative way the Florentines had with numbers, *lettore primo, lettore secondo, lettore tertio* teaching not only the three Rs of religion, reading, and writing, but also the liberal arts. Able Bolognese orphans were eligible for scholarships that would pay their way through university. In matters of clothing, homes aimed to cut costs by encouraging relatives or charities to clothe the children, but then faced the jealousies and fights which came when some dressed more elaborately than others. Concerns about extravagance and jealously led to dress codes stipulating clothes which were modest in cut, color, and fabric at Bologna's conservatories of S. Marta, S. Giuseppe, and S. Croce and uniforms at that city's S. Maria del Baraccano, S. Onofrio, and S. Bartolomeo di Reno, and at Florence's Bigallo and S. Caterina. S. Onofrio went a step further and required a 20 lire entry deposit which was given back at "graduation" in order to provide all boys with a new set of clothes upon their return to "normal" society; this same orphanage was careful to provide hats, handkerchiefs, and silk items of clothing to its charges.[23] At a time when, as Ottavia Niccoli has shown, the youth culture of the streets was considered a real and present danger to polite, urban middle-class society, these homes aimed to isolate, preserve, and nurture not just individuals, but a way of life which books of manners were beginning to spell out, and which particular segments of urban society were beginning to consider normative.[24] Here is where the enclosure of the workhouse and foundling home differed from that of the conservatories and orphanages: while the former aimed to keep a potentially unruly population off the streets, the latter aimed to preserve the moral, mental, and physical purity of those inside from contagion. Their discipline was more formative than punitive, and in light of frequent complaints of laxity we should not assume that the rules were followed literally. Conservatories were more tightly enclosed and strictly run than orphanages both because confraternal guardians knew that a lapse in moral reputation would effect marriage prospects for all their charges, and because nuns and priests more often served as resident guardians, and modeled the conservatories on convents.

---

[23] ASB PIE, S. Bartolomeo di Reno, 7, ms. 1a, cc. 1r, 4v, 10r, 11r–v. ASB PIE, S. Croce, 2, fasc. 20 ASB PIE, S. Giuseppe, 1, ms. +, p. 18. ASB PIE, S. Maria del Baraccano, 1, ms. 2, cc. 6r, 9v–10r. ASB PIE, S. Onfrio, 2, ms. 3, cap. 18; ms. 78, cc. 4v, 5v, 48v, 49r, 51r. ASF, S. Caterina, 7, III/10. ASF, Ceppo, 69, 12r–14v. BCB ms. B3633, 145–7. Toniolo, "Gli esposti in collegio," 99–116.

[24] Niccoli, *Il seme della violenza*, 24–39, 89–139. See also many of the valuable contributions to Prodi, *Disciplina dell'anima*.

When assessing the importance of administration by confratelli and consorelle, it is important to recognize that different confraternal models existed. For our analysis, we can distinguish at least two: the collegiate and the congregational. In the collegiate model, a confraternity open to all comers and ranging from a few dozen to a few hundred members would entrust distinct charitable or devotional functions to semi-autonomous subordinate groups, allowing each group to elect or appoint executive boards of overseers headed by a Rector to administer its designated work: we find this in Bologna's S. Marta, S. Maria del Baraccano, S. Bartolomeo di Reno, S. Maria Maddalena (sponsor of S. Onofrio), and S. Giacomo. In the congregational model a restricted, far smaller, and often self-perpetuating body focused its energies on one work only: we see this in Bologna's S. Croce and S. Giuseppe, and in Florence's Bigallo, S. Caterina, Pietà, and to some degree, Ceppo and S. Niccolò. Bolognese charitable confraternities adopting the collegiate model usually divided into two groups: a devotional *stretta* cell whose artisan members practiced flagellant discipline and were less immediately concerned with charitable institutions; and an administrative *larga* cell which oversaw daily management of the homes by means of a board of about twelve members drawn in annual or semi-annual rotation from among its membership of merchants, guild masters, professionals, and nobles. The S. Bartolomeo di Reno, S. Maria Maddalena, and S. Giacomo larga cells were deliberately created after establishment of the orphanage precisely to accommodate those higher-born Bolognese who had the capacities and connections for administration but who were less interested in flagellating with artisans; the high-born brothers and sisters of S. Maria del Baraccano practiced a similar distinction. Tensions over control of property, legacies, and the brotherhood itself usually grew out of these distinctions, in part because in all cases the high-born charitable administrators of the larga soon made moves to control the whole confraternity and appropriate its revenues. After constitutional changes in Bologna in the 1550s which divided the city's Senate into committees of *Assunti* to oversee distinct areas of civic administration, we also see that senators served exclusively as the Rectors overseeing the major homes organized on the traditional model, very likely since their large open memberships made them semi-public institutions. To win their co-operation, these senators sometimes received the power to place girls or boys in the homes during their term. The S. Marta conservatory adopted the more secretive administration of its sponsoring Compagnia dei Poveri Vergognosi, while the S. Croce and S. Giuseppe conservatories were run by closed congregations.

All the Florentine institutions adopted some version of the congregational model. The Bigallo offers the clearest example: Cosimo I's suppression did away with the broader membership of the confraternity and left its twelve Captains serving at the appointment and pleasure of the Duke; yet these twelve Captains had still to fulfill the testamentary obligations of the confraternity. The Pietà and S. Caterina conservatories were similarly run by appointed or self-perpetuating congregations which arose with the specific and limited purpose of administering a home; the former moved quite deliberately to a congregational model with no clear accountability of its seventeen female governors to its larger body of supporting gentlewomen. Florence's Compagnia di S. Maria Vergine was a hybrid of the two confraternal models. It emerged with the specific purpose of assuming administration of the Ospedale delle Povere Abbandonate after the death of Lionarda Ginori, and its members were instrumental in the three conservatories founded through the end of the sixteenth century – most closely with S. Niccolò, which it effectively absorbed. Yet the confraternity's thirty members (forty after 1584) were recruited by nomination, served life-terms, and undertook no other corporate activities beyond the conservatory.[25] As such, it more closely resembled the administrative congregations than it did the open, multi-faceted Bolognese confraternities; we might almost consider it a voluntary equivalent of the Bigallo.

The congregational model was a far cry from the traditional, medieval confraternity, and some might argue that it should not be considered with the other lay brotherhoods considered here. Yet that would be drawing the analysis too narrowly. Across early modern Italy, the conjuncture of ennobling and Catholic reform introduced new forms under the confraternal rubric. As John O'Malley has pointed out, the congregations were continuous with, albeit distinct from, earlier lay confraternities; for the Jesuits, Tridentine bishops, and some laity they represented a reformed model of the traditional confraternity.[26] In this volume, Richard MacKenney analyzes the variety of names and forms adopted by early modern Venetian brotherhoods, and Mark Lewis the evolution of Neapolitan Jesuit confraternities from the collegial to the congregational model. In many cities, single confraternities took dominant roles in the local cult and local charity by absorbing other brotherhoods and by limiting the number and *qualità* of their own members. I have argued elsewhere that we could describe these as *confraternite maggiori* since they attain a local dominance similar to that of the consolidated *ospedale maggiori* of fifteenth-century towns, and become quasi-governmental

---

[25] ASF, Ceppo, 69, cc. 3r–4v.   [26] O'Malley, *First Jesuits*, 197–9.

charitable agencies. As such they are the characteristic early modern compromises on the continuum from the ecclesiastical charities of the middle ages to the state bureaucracies of the industrial period.[27] In short, early modern social and political realities brought considerable change to confraternities' internal administration and external reach. What is significant for our purposes here is that despite their different forms, the groups overseeing conservatories and orphanages in Bologna and Florence considered themselves confraternities (with the possible exception of the Bigallo, whose Captains frequently and not always successfully petitioned the Grand Dukes for the full powers and privileges of a state magistracy).[28]

The collegiate and congregational models adopted in the two cities reflected local charitable traditions and the political culture of the sixteenth century. Florence's local traditions were shaped by the fact that most of its hospitals were in some way proprietary, and the families or guilds who had established and maintained them jealously guarded their rights and property by concentrating power in small, appointed boards operating with a high degree of secrecy. Bologna's hospitals, by contrast, had almost all grown out of the large *laudesi* confraternities of the thirteenth and fourteenth centuries, and even when patricians began infiltrating and co-opting them in the later fifteenth and early sixteenth centuries, the tradition of a broad membership electing an executive board remained strong; the only institutions to adopt the congregational model were founded by individuals late in the sixteenth century. Moreover, both traditions were adaptable to new political realities. Lorenzo Polizzotto has shown how Savonarolan *piagnoni* sought through the first decades of the sixteenth century to build an institutional base and a following for their cause by infiltrating Florence's charitable institutions.[29] This may have been a factor in Cosimo I's attempt to put all such charities under the control of a single confraternity-magistracy whose members were appointed by him, though it leaves unresolved the question of why orphanages were subsumed under the Bigallo, while conservatories were not. While he himself seems soon to have realized how quixotic and counter-productive the project was, Cosimo I's initial action marked a deliberate effort to centralize poor relief. On first reading, the effort fit well with other actions by which he built a state bureaucracy whose supervisory reach and territorial officials circumvented the Florentine patricians who had placed Cosimo in power on the expectation that he would be their puppet. On closer examination, it appears that Cosimo soon realized that the Bigallo could aggrandize those

---

[27] Terpstra, "Kinship Translated."   [28] ASF Bigallo, 1669/IV, cc. 45r–v.
[29] Polizzotto, *Elect Nation*, 208–10, 289–90.

patricians while aggravating the dominion, and so he deliberately undermined its efforts to develop into a state magistracy and aimed instead to reinforce its duties and identity as a confraternity – albeit a large and powerful one.[30]

Bologna's political dynamic developed differently after Pope Leo X's constitution divided power between the Papal Legate and a Senate appointed by the pope. The early decades of this new political order were critical, since the Senate was working to preserve local autonomy while papal governors like Francesco Guicciardini sought to establish strong papal authority. Patricians moved into confraternal charitable institutions in part to enhance their local authority by becoming publicly identified with charity and by gaining access to confraternal financial resources and patronage. They maintained solidarity in relations vis à vis the papacy, but factionalism continued as families vied within and between each other for papal appointment to the Senate. Confraternal organization of charities divided power and so allowed for participation by broad elements within the oligarchy. The tradition of drawing executive administrations from broadly based membership bodies further ensured that mutually suspicious patricians could spread power and keep an eye on each other as they kept an eye on the city. This in part explains why groups numbering dozens of patricians periodically joined S. Bartolomeo (98 in 1593) and S. Maria Maddalena (62 in 1580; 80 in 1595; 48 in 1600).[31]

The ruling groups in both cities were clearly hard-nosed and quite inventive in their ability to adapt existing confraternal structures and traditions to the new political realities of the sixteenth century. But why stick with confraternities at all? Would it not make more sense to push the logic of Cosimo I's consolidation all the way to an overhaul of relief which would put all conservatories and orphanages under a state magistracy? From the vantage point of the children themselves, it made little difference whether the hand of the confraternal brother or the hand of the magistrate lay on their shoulders. From the vantage point of their overseers the distinction was significant. Politically, confraternal organization ensured that power would be shared, and offered a forum for pursuing the kind of negotiation necessary in an oligarchic society; this was arguably of greater concern in Bologna than Florence. Socially, it associated patricians with charity in the eyes of the populace. Financially, it brought in alms, dues, and legacies which, as the account books consistently demonstrate, were still vital to running the home. Beyond this, it is doubtful whether early moderns could even think of relief of

---

[30] Terpstra, "Confraternities and Public Charity."
[31] ASB, PIE, S. Bartolomeo di Reno, 7/2, cc. 35r–36r. ASB, PIE, S. Maria Maddalena, 4/VII [25–III–1580]; 5/9 [29–X–1595; 19–XI–1600].

children – or any other marginal groups – in purely secular terms; confraternities were particularly appropriate vehicles of social welfare because they bridged state and private, lay and ecclesiastical, family and public.

Having noted the practical benefits of confraternal administration of charitable institutions, is it naive to assume that the rhetoric of kinship meant anything to confratelli and consorelle? I would argue that its meaning intensified as social kinship was transvalued. Kinship had signified horizontal relations among a socially heterogeneous group of confraternal brothers. As family metaphors came to dominate political discourse and ennobling changed the social composition of the brotherhoods, confraternal kinship moved toward signifying vertical relations between rulers and ruled. In both Florence and Bologna, the confraternities in question were all dominated by lay brothers and sisters drawn from the upper ranks of the land-owning or commercial elite. In these institutions, this civic patriciate faced most directly the consequences of its assertion of paternal (or parental, since some of these institutions are run by men and women together) authority over the civic community: it had to provide young women and men with both immediate subsistence and a future. The former translated into the kind of food, clothing, and shelter found in contemporary infirmaries, hostels, workhouses, and ospedali, but the latter required discipline, education, work opportunities, and dowries, that is, care that went far beyond traditional charity and came closer to the kind of duties which the patriciate had towards their own blood kin. Through these institutions, it provided for those young girls and boys who had no relatives to plan a future, *or* acted as the temporary extended family for those children and adolescents whose blood brothers, sisters, or uncles needed time to establish themselves before they could re-assume their expected roles as guardians, *or* acted as the permanent guardians for those women who had no other means of support. This paternal care was made public with every procession in which abandoned children marched with their confraternal protectors, and at every wedding where a conservatory girl was presented to her groom by her confraternal parents (as was the custom for S. Maria del Baraccano). The rhetoric of social kinship – which I would take to incorporate both the fact of confraternal involvement and the writing about it – was not a pious smokescreen used to mask some of the political advantages which access to this kind of charity and patronage offered to the conservatories' confraternal patrons. Rather it expressed what they believed to be their God-given duty to act as the nurturing, directing mothers and fathers who could mitigate family breakdowns in a society challenged by famine, plague, wars, and the rest. Their concept of kinship was far from egalitarian: it was hierarchical, exclusive, paternalistic, disciplinary, and in many ways self-serving. Their exclusions and exceptions framed their concept of which of these victims really counted in the social family – a concept which was contemporaneously finding fuller expression in the concepts and laws of citizenship. Confraternal robes cloaked these patricians and their actions with religious – and hence political – legitimacy. By assuming through the confraternity the duties traditionally undertaken by kin, the urban elites substantiated and thereby legitimated their claims to parental authority over the civic/territorial community, and particularly over its marginal groups.

8

THE FIRST JESUIT CONFRATERNITIES
AND MARGINALIZED GROUPS IN
SIXTEENTH-CENTURY ROME

LANCE LAZAR

This article explores the ideological sources of Jesuit missionary activity by focusing on three of the first Jesuit confraternities founded in the 1540s in Rome. These confraternities administered houses for reformed prostitutes, daughters of prostitutes, and newly converted Jews and Muslims, and became the models for similar institutions throughout Italy. They illustrate a central feature of the Jesuit urban apostolate: to enlist elites in the reform of the most "public" sinners living on the margins of society. Focusing on these institutions also helps to recover women's roles in Catholic reform, to measure attitudes toward subcultures perceived as threatening, and to provide a clearer picture of the Jesuits and their relations with the laity generally.

Prostitutes, Jews, and Muslims stood out as symbols of the need for conversion because they were highly visible figures considered to be outside God's grace. By 1542, Ignatius Loyola established a new kind of institution, the *Casa di Santa Marta,* as a shelter where former prostitutes and battered women could stay before deciding whether to become a nun, to be reconciled with their husbands, or to get married; its administration was entrusted to a confraternity, the *Compagnia della grazia.*[1] Almost simultaneously, a second confraternal shelter, the *Conservatorio di Santa Caterina delle vergini miserabili,* was established for the daughters of prostitutes and other young women who were thought to be in danger of turning to prostitution. While the Casa di Santa Marta eventually re-

---

This article employs materials located in the Archivio Segreto Vaticano (ASV: Monastero di S. Marta), the Archivio di stato di Roma (ASR: S. Caterina della rosa), the Archivio storico del vicariato di Roma (ASVR: Casa dei catecumeni), the Archivio Capitolino (ACAP), the Archivum romanum societatis Iesu (ARSI), and the Monumenta Historica Societatis Iesu (MI).

[1] O'Malley, *First Jesuits,* 165–99.

verted to a more traditional conventual format, it and S. Caterina provided models which the Jesuits transplanted to at least seventeen other
cities along the Italian peninsula, in most cases preserving the original
formula. Also in 1542, Ignatius influenced Pope Paul III to remove the
requirement for Jews and Muslims to forfeit all property upon conversion.[2] Shortly thereafter, he founded a house where new converts could
live while learning the new faith, and placed it under the administration
of the *Confraternita di S. Giuseppe dei catecumeni*. As with the women's
shelters, the Jesuits relied heavily on support from noble women and their
aristocratic Spanish connections to get this institution off the ground.

Their organization of these institutions places the Jesuits squarely in the
midst of the new experiments in poor relief occurring throughout
Europe in the sixteenth century. Recent studies on poor relief emphasize
that welfare policy cut across confessional lines and needed to be flexible
in order to adjust to local circumstances.[3] Within Italy, ruling groups vied
with prelates to gain control of confraternities, which remained the
predominant model for charitable activity through the sixteenth century,
but whose devotional role became ever more linked to communal goals.[4]
Scholars such as Brian Pullan have argued that the most telling legacy of
sixteenth-century schemes for the poor was the expansion in the scope of
organized charity: not only to support the poor, but actively to redeem
them as well. The new institutions sought to amend the character and
behavior of the outcast poor in order to integrate them within a highly
disciplined Christian society.[5]

Research on Jesuit confraternal activity has often focused on the
Marian congregations, beginning with the *Prima primaria* founded by Jan
Leunis in the Roman College in 1563. These sodalities, which could
count among their members emperors, popes, kings, and cardinals,
sought not only the conversion of the individual soul, but also the reform
of the whole of society.[6] The Jesuits characteristically targeted the elites,
but by the end of the sixteenth century (when they frequently had
multiple congregations attached to each house), they expanded the
formula to include professionals, merchants, and artisans. Nevertheless,
their congregations were always segregated by class to promote affinity,
decorum, and social stability.[7] While limiting their membership to strictly

---

[2] Simonsohn, *Apostolic See*, #2119.   [3] Black, *Italian Confraternities*, 130–50.
[4] Terpstra, *Lay Confraternities*, 179–216; Weissman, *Ritual Brotherhood*, 195–235; Rusconi, "Con-
    fraternite," 471–506; Zardin, "Carità," 11–15.
[5] Pullan, "Support and Redeem," 180–1; Prodi (ed.), *Disciplina, passim.*
[6] Chatellier, *Europe*, xi, 16, 89–108. By the suppression of the Jesuits in 1773, there were roughly
    2,500 congregations. Then they were dispersed on the diocesan level and multiplied geometrically;
    by the 1950s there were over 80,000 aggregated congregations: Stierli, "Devotion to Mary," 19–20.
[7] Chatellier, *Europe*, 49–66, 113–29.

segregated social classes, the affiliated congregations from the outset directed much of their charitable activity toward the poor. In this regard, the Marian congregations were following the patterns established by the earliest Jesuit confraternities, which in turn took their shape from Ignatius' direction of charitable works in Rome.

Shortly after Ignatius and two of his companions arrived in Rome in the fall of 1537, they began preaching, teaching, administering the sacraments (especially confession and communion), directing the *Spiritual Exercises*, and visiting hospitals and prisons. These ministries coincided with the period of deliberation on how the companions should proceed: whether to join another order, or to start their own.[8] Yet Ignatius' return to his home town of Azpeitia for three months in 1535 provides an equally important key to understanding his attitudes toward social justice for the poor, and the place of women in the reform of society.

Ignatius had made the vow to go to Jerusalem (or Rome) with the six other original companions at Montmartre in 1534, and in many ways had taken the first steps toward a new order.[9] Since he returned to the land where the Loyolas were the principal family, he was able to exercise considerable influence in shaping a more pious community. His activity in Azpeitia already represents in germinal form the model for the later Jesuit apostolate.[10] When he arrived, he did not stay with his brother in the family castle, but instead chose to live in the poor Magdalen hospital. Besides caring for the sick in the hospital, he began teaching Christian doctrine (catechism) to children, and soon afterward to adults. Although not yet a priest, he preached so fervently against fornication that five women leading wayward lives repented. He engaged in peacemaking within his own family as well as between rival town factions, and resolved disputes between the clergy and laity, including abuses of benefices. He endorsed confraternal charity, especially the new Confraternity of the Most Holy Sacrament, which he later encouraged to affiliate with the Archconfraternity in the Dominican church of the Minerva in Rome.[11]

In all these activities, Ignatius anticipated the future missionary practices of the Jesuits. Moreover, regarding the reform of society, Ignatius launched four initiatives in Azpeitia, all aimed at the laity.[12] First, he instituted the noontime ringing of church bells as a reminder for the citizens to recite prayers for those in mortal sin; he designated the remainder of his own inheritance in order to endow the bell-ringers' salaries in perpetuity. Second, he procured through town officials a ban on cardplaying and selling cards. Third, he arranged statutes with tough

[8] Demoustier, "First Companions", 9–17.   [9] Dudon, *St. Ignatius*: 154–74.
[10] Olin (ed.), *Autobiography*, 82–4.   [11] MI Font. Doc., 655–7.
[12] Young (ed.), *Letters*, 42–5; Brieskorn, "Ignatius in Azpeitia," 95–112.

penalties for single women who illicitly wore the hats reserved for married women. Here Ignatius was targeting priestly concubinage (not just sumptuary laws), and the clerics and women who openly flaunted sexual mores and ecclesiastical law through public affiliation.

Fourth, and most importantly, Ignatius had the town council draw up Ordinances prohibiting begging from door to door, and providing public relief co-ordinated by the stewards of the poor.[13] Travelers and even pilgrims on the way to Compostela were not permitted to beg, and were instead directed to a suburban hospital designated to aid them with shelter and food. The Ordinances discriminated among the local poor as well: on pain of fines, citizens were required to inform the stewards of all beggars who were able to work but refused to do so, the latter being subject to six days in prison and a hundred lashes. The town council was charged with investigating and cataloging all the needy, and only those listed would have a right to assistance. The Ordinances also foresaw the needs of the shame-faced poor with two additional stewards (one chosen from the laity and one from the clergy). Besides collecting alms on Sundays and feast days, the stewards administered and distributed public revenues allocated for poor relief.

These provisions are remarkably similar to the tough new poor laws of humanist inspiration erected in Protestant Germany and the Catholic Low Countries in the 1520s and promulgated throughout the lands of Charles V and in France and England in the 1530s.[14] Ignatius' program thus placed little Azpeitia on the map of European-wide reforms of poor relief. It is highly likely that Ignatius came in contact with the new approaches during his summer excursions in 1528, 29, and 30 to visit the Spanish communities in Flanders (and once in England) in order to beg support for his university studies in Paris. Ignatius would have had ample first-hand experience of the laws implemented in 1525 and 26 in Ypres and Bruges, and on one such excursion (probably in 1529), he enjoyed the hospitality of Juan Luis Vives.[15] Vives' ideas on poor relief gained dubious notoriety when the Franciscan vicar of the bishop of Tournai sniffed the odor of Lutheran heresy (for the prohibition of begging), but the *De subventione pauperum* (1526) soon reached a broad European audience in several Latin and vernacular editions. Whether or not Ignatius immediately warmed to Vives' ideas, he was still in Paris pursuing his studies in 1531 when the Sorbonne pronounced that the poor-relief reform of Ypres was indeed in concordance with the Scriptures, the

---

[13] MI Font Doc., 439–62.

[14] Jütte, *Poverty and Deviance*, 100–42; Geremek, *History of Poverty*, 6–13, 120–77.

[15] Olin, "Erasmus and Loyola," 123–7.

teachings of the Apostles, and the laws of the Church – so Ignatius knew that his reforms had already passed the test.

Ignatius' initiatives in Azpeitia resemble more closely the Flemish model rather than the more radical programs pursued in Protestant Germany. The Flemings employed and embellished existing institutions, and while emphasizing lay involvement, they did not impede clerical prerogatives. Highlighting their accretive rather than abortive character-istics, the Flemish reforms have been characterized as a gradual process of "municipalization," in contrast to the outright "secularization" found in Germany.[16] Underlying all of Ignatius' reforms, however, are two guid-ing principles: first, that the community as a whole is responsible for the moral well-being of all of its members, including those at the margins[17]; and second, that the best way to shepherd the strays back to communal norms is through pragmatic lay initiatives. Thus, one finds in this brief stay in Azpeitia the kernel of the Jesuit urban mission.

It is in Rome, however, where these guiding principles received their greatest elaboration, and where the distinctively Jesuit model of mobile missionary activity was forged.[18] Indeed, Rome provided the most im-portant model for the *Constitutions,* which codified the Jesuits' "way of proceeding." Regarding poor relief, Ignatius realized that (while the Jesuits' mission might be mobile) the needs of the recipient of the aid were usually best met over an extended time:

> when there are some spiritual works which continue longer and are of more lasting value, such as certain pious foundations for the aid of our fellowmen, and other works less durable which give help on a few occasions and only for a short while, then it is certain that the first ought to be preferred to the second.[19]

It was precisely to solve this conundrum – how to build stable, self-sustaining institutions when the members of the order were constantly on the move – that confraternal charity presented the ideal medium. It also helps to explain the ubiquitous involvement of Jesuits in confraternal charity throughout Italy, and especially in Rome.

Besides founding the three confraternities governing S. Marta, S. Caterina, and the Catechumens, Ignatius also organized in the 1540s the *Arciconfraternita de' Santissimi Dodici Apostoli.* Comprised of twelve noble members who canvased each of the twelve neighborhoods of Rome, they provided aid to the shame-faced poor and in the seven-

---

16 Italian parallels: Henderson, *Piety,* 351; Terpstra, "Apprenticeship," 101–20.
17 Alves, "Christian Social Organism," 4–7.
18 Prosperi, "Missionary," 164–6; O'Malley, "Mission," 5–9.
19 Ganss (ed.), *Constitutions,* 262–84, esp. 276.

teenth century administered Rome's largest free pharmacy.[20] Though not the founder, Ignatius also gave much early support to the *Arciconfraternita di S. Maria della Visitazione degli Orfani,* the largest orphanage for boys and girls approved by Paul III in 1540.[21] Diego Lainez, the second general, continued regularly to support the Ignatian initiatives, and provided the first buildings for the *Confraternita* and *Spedale di S. Maria della Pietà dei Pazzerelli,* Rome's first insane asylum (and Europe's oldest in continuous existence) founded by Ferrante Ruiz (a former chaplain for S. Caterina) in 1548.

The *Prima primaria* sodality, founded in the *Collegio Romano* in 1563, proved so popular that it split into four separate congregations (in addition to another three for students in the *Collegio Germanico* and four for future priests in the Roman Seminary) by the end of the century.[22] Usually the Marian congregations practiced a variety of works, rather than any one principal charity, but they became especially known for visiting prisons and hospitals. Meeting in the Casa Professa by the church of the Gesù, the Jesuit headquarters, were another five congregations for adults: the *Assunta,* for nobles (1593); the *Natività* for merchants (1594); the *Annuntiata* for artisans (1595); the *Concettione* also for artisans (1597); and the *Immacolata* for priests (1611). In 1648, General Carafa added another confraternity there, the *Buona Morte.*[23] In the nearby Oratory of Francis Xavier, Padre Caravita organized general communions which attracted as many as 30,000 communicants a day with the *Congregazione della Madonna della Pietà e di San Francesco Saverio* in the second and third decades of the seventeenth century. The *Arciconfraternità della Pietà dei Carcerati,* founded by the French Jesuit Jean Tellier in 1575, rounded out the lot:[24] in total, over two-dozen confraternities to which the Jesuits lent their talents in the eternal city.[25]

Yet S. Marta (*della grazia*), S. Caterina, and S. Giuseppe stood apart from the rest of the Jesuit confraternities. This was in part because they were the first founded by Ignatius, and in part because they were the most frequently imitated models before the Marian congregations became the virtually exclusive outlet of Jesuit confraternal affiliation.

---

[20] Pecchiai, *Barbarini*, 158; Tacchi-Venturi, *Storia*, 2, 2: 147–209.

[21] Jesuits, Barnabites, and Somascans all later tried to claim this institution as their own, though it remained in lay control through the seventeenth century: Romani, "Vicende archivistiche," 787–8.

[22] Delplace, *Histoire*, 11–14; Mullan, *Prima Primaria*, 53–5; Castellini, *Congregazione dei nobili*, 20–32.

[23] De' Rossi, (ed.), *Ritratto:* 395; Maroni-Lumbroso, et al., *Le confraternite romane;* Fiorani (ed.), *Ricerche,* esp. vols. 5–6; Piccialuti, *Carità.*   [24] Paglia, *Morte confortata, passim,* and *Pietà, passim.*

[25] Naples by the 1600s had at least 15 Jesuit confraternities, and Brussels at least 19: Delplace, *Histoire,* 78, 99; Genoa counted nearly 30 by the 1700s: Grendi, "Morfologia," 280–4.

But these three confraternities are especially worthy of note because they best illustrate a central feature of Jesuit confraternal activity: the purposeful, selective application of resources to produce the greatest calculated effect – specifically, the reform of the most public sinners on the margins.

JESUITS AND PROSTITUTES: THE *CASA DI S. MARTA*

Because prostitutes (and Jews) had been in Rome since before there were Christians, the new urgency to bring them into the fold is another tell-tale indication of the change in culture under Paul III. Given the high ratio of men and the transient population, the city's prostitutes found their clientele among the members of the pontifical court and the diplomatic corps. Alongside a few elite courtesans were legions of women who plied their trade in miserable conditions. Limited employment opportunities and the high cost of wedding dowries forced most into prostitution as a means of self-support. While the number of prostitutes remains disputable, it is clear that prostitution was of widespread concern in sixteenth-century Roman society, and reform-minded prelates began to take notice.

By 1520, Cardinal Giulio de Medici established the new Monastery of S. Maria Maddalena of the "Reformed Prostitutes" (*convertite*). That same year, Giulio secured official approval from his cousin Leo X, and had his own recently founded Compagnia della Carità placed in charge of the monastery's administration.[26] Gregory Martin, an English priest living in Rome from 1576 –8, summed up the repentance of these "convertites" for his English audience: "These be therefore so called bycause they are converted from their naughty life, and of common whores and harlots made good christian wemen."[27]

The model of the penitent convert as an alternative to prostitution was not new, and by the fourteenth century Magdalene houses for prostitutes as well as virgins could be found throughout Europe.[28] But while some women chose – either freely or out of desperation – the life of the convertite with its imposed practices of severe penance and cloister, clearly, it was not an attractive alternative for every prostitute who felt the compunction to reform. Moreover, for those prostitutes who were already married and estranged from their husbands, taking the monastic vow was usually not an option at all.

In order to provide alternatives, Ignatius established the *Casa di Santa Marta* in 1541 –2, with a confraternity, the *Compagnia della grazia*, in

---

[26] Paschini, *Tre ricerche*, 3–88.   [27] Martin, *Roma Sancta*, 143. Cohen, *Womens' Asylums*, 13–81.
[28] Haskins, *Mary Magdalen*, 170–87, 276–91.

charge of its administration.[29] The important innovation was in providing a place for women to stay for a limited period before deciding whether to become a nun, to be reconciled with their husbands, to get married, or in a few cases, to be placed as domestic servants for aristocratic women.

The free choice accorded these marginalized women and the psychological penetration of the resources made available to them are particularly striking. A confraternity member asked each woman who came to live in the house a set of thirteen questions in order to discern the circumstances of her past life, and her reasons for seeking refuge. The confraternity inquired about all the details that connected her to the Christian community: her age, origin, family, children, current marital status, and possible previous affiliation with a religious order, as well as her health, finances, and possible crimes outstanding. Her motivations were also sought: did she have any intent to marry or enter the religious life, did she come to the house out of passion or desperation? Through the questions, she learned what to expect of the life inside: she was asked to consent to obey the prioress and officers; she was advised that she could not leave or have contact with the outside without the permission of the confraternity; if she did depart without consent, she would forfeit her belongings, and might face public punishment. Finally, she would have to make a general confession and receive communion.[30]

The statutes outline the vital need of the Christian republic for a stable homelife and honesty between spouses. Thus, the stage is set for the return of these women (both married and single, living in fornication) to civil society. Yet that return is to be paved not through coercion, but through their own free election, guaranteed and "helped as much as possible for the greater praise and glory of God." By furnishing these women a haven and the disciplined life inside the House, Ignatius effectively prepared them for the choice of a way of life which occurs at the end of the second week in the *Spiritual Exercises*.[31] In principle, the House served as a retreat, and through the formation of their Jesuit confessors, the women were encouraged to make the "right" choice for themselves. While they would not actually be making the *Spiritual Exercises,* and of course were bound by the limits and obligations of the House, nevertheless, the opportunities for self-reflection made available to these women – mostly from the lowest rungs of society – would have approached those available only to elites.

To put this new plan in action, Ignatius collected around himself pious

---

[29] Chauvin, "Ignace et courtisans"; Matteucci, "'Se è mossa". Scaduto, *Azione*, 639–44.
[30] The original statutes, entrance questionnaire, and membership list are published in Tacchi Venturi, *Storia*, 1, 2: 284–313.   [31] Ignatius of Loyola, *Spiritual Exercises*, paragraphs 169–89.

men and noble ladies interested in giving these women a new start. Pedro
de Ribadeneira later recalled:

> [Ignatius] went with [the prostitutes] either to the newly established
> convent or to the house of some highborn lady, in which the girls were to
> be at first accustomed to domestic tasks and then, spurred by the example
> and admonitions of other girls, to a life of virtue."[32]

The list of original members of the Compagnia della grazia is a virtual
Who's Who list of mid-sixteenth-century Rome: besides Rodolfo Pio
da Carpi, the first Cardinal Protector, there were another fourteen
cardinals and seven bishops and archbishops. Eleven women represented such Roman noble families as the Colonna, Orsini, della Rovere
and Farnese, and highly placed Spanish supporters, especially Eleonora
Osorio, wife of the Imperial Ambassador. Thus in this earliest of the
Jesuits' Roman initiatives, we find already the model of co-opting the
social elites for the service of those at the margin.

Its innovatory character as a refuge for women without a vow
meant that contemporaries were skeptical and suspicious, and soon the
Jesuits were accused of keeping a private seraglio.[33] But after a rough
start, S. Marta expanded until it became a victim of its own success.
Once inside the refuge, many of the former prostitutes chose not to
leave. Instead, they took a monastic vow, so soon the original building
needed to be divided to accommodate a convent.[34] Later, a nearby
property was purchased and named *S. Maria felice* in order to house just
the *malmaritate* – those women, often battered, who were married but
could not live with their husbands. By 1563, the divided S. Marta
convent had been completely absorbed by the professed nuns, and
since S. Marta no longer served its original purpose, a new institution
sprang up to fill the need: the *Casa Pia,* initiated by Pius IV and
Charles Borromeo (who soon thereafter became the Cardinal Protector of S. Marta).[35] S. Marta then began to accept chaste women, so that
by 1578, Gregory XIII made it a convent exclusively for virgins, and it
soon became reserved for only the most noble families of Italy.[36]

What is distinctive about S. Marta is not only the dramatic change
in its character and the status of the women that it served, but the
network of noble women who, as the most active members of the
Compagnia della grazia, were responsible for its foundation. As is clear
from Ignatius' correspondence, the circle of noble Spaniard and Roman matrons contributed not only their money (and that of their

---

[32] Rahner (ed.), *Letters*, 436.   [33] MI Epp. VI, I, 663–6, and MI Font. Doc. 689–96.
[34] ASV, S. Marta, vol. 1, 2r–5v.   [35] ASV, S. Marta, vol. 212. Tomo XIII, n. X.
[36] Dunn, "Nuns as Patrons," 452–5.

wealthy husbands), but also their efforts securing lodging for the convertite and malmaritate in the first years. They took these women into their own houses, found other aristocratic ladies who would accept them, and oversaw the day-to-day needs of the refuge as its Prioress, as Isabella Roser did before 1545; these female members of the confraternity took an active role in the administration of the *Casa*, though their participation seems to have ebbed once S. Marta became a convent.[37] Thus, S. Marta represents not only the reform of women, but also reform by women, which was to become a recurring feature of Jesuit-inspired charitable activity. Indeed, in many ways S. Marta stands at the beginning of a wave of institutions founded for and by women in early modern Rome.[38]

The Jesuits transplanted this formula to other cities where they traveled on missions. Precisely because it was in Rome and had the special attention of Ignatius, S. Marta became the most copied confraternal charity before the Marian congregations. By 1547, similar houses under confraternal direction had been founded in Bologna, Agrigento, and Palermo (once again through the good offices of Eleonora Osorio). By 1551, another four houses were functioning in Trapani, Messina, Casola in Lunigiana, and Modena. Florence, Padua, and Venice would have their refuges by 1577, and as late as 1628, S. Marta still served as the model for a house in Naples.[39]

JESUITS AND THE DAUGHTERS OF PROSTITUTES: THE *CONSERVATORIO DI S. CATERINA*

Experience and contact with prostitutes through the Casa di Santa Marta alerted Ignatius to a related social concern: the initiation of young girls, often the daughters of prostitutes, into the business. Some mothers counted on their daughters as their own form of pension plan, serving as their daughter's procuress once their own age removed them from the market. In 1589 for example, confraternity officers recorded the reluctance of one prostitute to have her daughter placed in S. Caterina saying "that she would see to it that her daughter always had bread to eat." Yet other women, who had too many mouths to feed, and no other means of support, became prostitutes themselves, or initiated their older daughters.[40]

[37] Rahner (ed.), *Letters, passim*.
[38] Gemini, "Interventi di politica"; Groppi, *Conservatori*, 15–67; Valone, "Quirinal Hill," and "Piety and Patronage." On womens' networks: Ferrante, (ed.), *Ragnatelle, passim*.
[39] Tacchi Venturi, *Storia*, 2, 2: 299–304; Lopez, *Riforma cattolica*, 86–7.
[40] Ciammitti, "La dote," 116–23.

Almost simultaneously with the founding of S. Marta's *Compagnia della grazia*, Ignatius promoted the *Compagnia delle vergini miserabili di Santa Caterina* specifically to curtail this cycle of prostitution; the same elite women who had supported S. Marta became involved with this new venture.[41] As with S. Marta, the first girls were placed informally in houses of noble ladies. Yet, with the purchase of a house by 1544 and the selection of an active Cardinal Protector (Federico Cesi), it stabilized more quickly under its confraternal administration and the Jesuits more quickly stepped to the side.[42]

A high-ranking cleric (not a Jesuit) presided over all the meetings, yet the various other offices, particularly the visitors and deputies, were almost exclusively held by laymen, at least into the early seventeenth century (for which the most regular minutes are preserved).[43] As one might expect, although the confraternity was officially opened to both sexes, and included such aristocratic female members as Margherita d'Austria, no female ever appears as an officer in the weekly meetings, although some occasionally attended. When women do appear in the archives as members of the confraternity, it is usually as benefactors. Thus, while women could belong, and could certainly contribute to the pious work of the confraternity – indeed they were instrumental in the earliest years – they did not exercise a formal role in its administration.

An outside observer of the confraternity described its members in 1558 as "Prelates and gentlemen, either officials or good merchants, with the protection of a cardinal."[44] Because Rome was dominated by clerics, it is not surprising that they received precedence, and since no membership lists survive, we may never know how many of the confraternity's members came from the artisanal classes. S. Caterina's *Constitutions,* first published in 1582, prohibited members who were in debt to the confraternity by more than 25 *scudi* from voting and speaking during the weekly meetings. While it would have been difficult for poorer members to keep up with the expected monthly contribution, but they were not removed from the confraternity.[45] The confraternity nonetheless targeted "more important and public persons," particularly during the hardest years.[46]

The members' own pious donations were from the outset the confraternity's most important source of income. The most conspicuous early donation came from Cardinal Federico Cesi, who built the church which stands today,[47] and also remembered in his will the best-known

---

[41] Vasaio-Zambonini, "Tessuto", Sabatine, "S. Caterina," Lazar, "E faucibus daemonis."
[42] ASR, *S. Caterina*, b. 22.   [43] ASR, *S. Caterina*, registro 1, *Decreti.*
[44] Armellini (ed.), "Origine d'alcuni," 155–60.
[45] *Constitutioni*, ch. 24. 50 scudi was considered an attractive dowry for an artisan until the 1600s.
[46] Ganss (ed.), *Constitutions*, 274–5.   [47] Quattrone, *S. Caterina*, 14–67.

Ignatius-inspired institutions in Rome (the Orphans, St. Catherine, Catechumens, and St. Martha). For the next three generations, the Cesi family continued the tradition of supporting the *Compagnia delle vergini miserabili* and the Jesuits.[48]

Donors to the Conservatory included prostitutes. Isabella de Luna, a famous courtesan from Spain, left in 1573 enough income to dower four *zitelle* a year starting in 1584.[49] Another telling contribution came from Lucrezia Albini, an alumna of the conservatory, who in 1585 contributed all her possessions.[50] Dowries supplied by the confraternity to those alumnae who later died without children were to be restored to the confraternity. Such restitution was often not possible in practice because the husband disappeared or did not have enough money to repay.[51]

Admission to the Conservatory was restricted to girls between the ages of ten and twelve, who were healthy, nice-looking, and without physical impairment.[52] The confraternity would accept only those girls who were in an urgent state of moral jeopardy, and who, if not removed from their present environment would surely succumb to prostitution. Thus, girls under ten were deemed not at risk, whereas girls over twelve were believed already to be corrupted.[53]

Despite the great variety of sources of income, it is clear from the weekly meeting minutes and "List of the Maids" (*Alfabeto delle zitelle*) that the great majority of the admitted girls had insufficient money to pay for her dowry. Every effort was made at the moment of entrance to secure the 50 scudi (by the seventeenth century, increased to 80 scudi) for marriage or the 150 or more scudi needed to enter a monastery.[54] Confraternal visitors solicited contributions from relatives, friends, or neighbors of the girl. They also sought a donation from the clerical and lay members of the *Compagnia delle vergini miserabili* itself, and from other confraternities – notably the *Annunziata* in the Minerva. Every year the Annunziata dowered upwards of 200 women in a highly ritualized ceremony over which the Pope presided.[55] A sizable number of dowries were also guaranteed by the Confraternity of St. James of the Spanish, testimony to a lingering Spanish influence at St. Catherine's.[56] By the mid-seventeenth century, S. Caterina had received so many endowments

---

[48] ACAP, *Fondo notarile*, sez. V, vol. I, and VI.   [49] ASR, *S. Caterina*, b. 21 (1573), b. 2 (1584).

[50] ASR, *S. Caterina*, b. 52, and b. 53 for others.   [51] Camerano, "Assistenza," 250–9.

[52] *Constitutioni*, ch. 19: "non abbino manco di dieci anni, nè più di dodici compiti, e siano vistose, e sane, non zoppe, no guercie, o altra sorte d'indisposizioni cattive, e siano figliole di Cortigiane, ò donne di mala vita, overo d'estrema povertà ... e ... non accettandole siano per capitar male ..."

[53] Fanucci, "Trattato," 166–8.   [54] ASR, *S. Caterina*, b. 53.   [55] Esposito, *Ad dotandum*, 5–18.

[56] ASR, *S. Caterina*, b. 79. Sometimes several institutions pooled their resources to provide a larger dowry: one *zitella* who entered a convent received a dowry of 265 scudi from eight confraternities. ASR, *S. Caterina*, vol. 21 and b. 53.

that the institution became a boarding school for the daughters of the elite, and, as with S. Marta, the original purpose had completely disappeared.

The Jesuits were quick to utilize the original model of S. Caterina in other cities where they preached. Already by 1548, Jerome Nadal had set up a *Compagnia delle vergini periclitanti* in Trapani. By 1557, the *Fanciulle della pietà,* undertaken by Marietta Gondi with Jesuit support, were functioning in Florence. One of the most successful of Jesuit preachers, Benedetto Palmio, started before 1559 the best known and most studied of all these institutions, the *Conservatorio di S. Maria della Presentazione delle Zitelle* in Venice and another in Padua. By 1564 in Naples, the Jesuits had established the *Santa casa dello spirito santo.* While Brescia's began in 1570, Carlo Borromeo approved the Jesuits' work on the *Casa pia di S. Sofia* in Milan in 1574. By 1576, Princess Maria of Portugal, wife of Alessandro Farnese had established a *Casa delle vergini preservate* in Parma on the recommendation of her Jesuit confessor Sebastiano Morales. Bologna and Siena were to follow by 1586. In all, ten institutions within forty years had followed S. Caterina's lead.[57]

JESUITS AND NEW CONVERTS: THE *CASA DEI CATECUMENI*

Christians had long sought conversion of the Jews. Under Gregory the Great, Jews gained papal protection which in theory, if not in practice, prohibited forced baptisms. Nevertheless, canon law always dictated a separate and inferior status for the Jews and Innocent III introduced in the Fourth Lateran Council the first sumptuary requirements. By the later fifteenth century, the balance between toleration and coercion, though always precarious, tilted decidedly toward the latter.[58]

It is important to emphasize that Ignatius' vision for the Catechumen House did not target Jews exclusively, but rather sought the conversion of the whole world, including Islam, and any other infidels that might come along.[59] The Catechumen houses founded by the Jesuits in Venice (1557) and Naples (1601) often supported majorities of Muslim converts.[60] Muslim slaves in Italy (usually either domestic servants or oarsmen

[57] Trapani: Villaret, *Congregations mariales,* 27. Venice: Puppi (ed.), *Le Zitelle,* 9–96; Ellero (ed.), *L'archivio IRE,* 215–22. Parma, Florence, Naples, Milan, Brescia, Siena, Bologna: Tacchi-Venturi, *Storia:* 2, 2: 189–90.

[58] Parente, "Confronto ideologico;" Stow, "Church and the Jews." Friedman, "Jews"; Pakter, *Canon Law,* 263–304.

[59] Rudt de Collenberg, "Baptème des Juifs;" Rodocanachi, *Saint-Siège;* Milano, *Il ghetto* and "Battesimi di Ebrei."

[60] Pullan, *Jews,* 255–312, esp. 256; Aikema, (ed.), *Regno dei poveri,* 215–25. Selwyn, "Procur[ing]," 25–6.

on galleys) were generally not coerced to accept Christianity.[61] The presence of an equal number of Christian slaves in Muslim hands guaranteed this uneasy détente. Since confraternities (along with municipal and diplomatic bureaucracies) came to mediate slave exchanges and ransoms, it is not surprising that the Jesuits entrusted the administration of the Houses for Catechumens to confraternal care as well.[62]

As with the prostitutes, any group representing dissenting beliefs or practices in the midst of the *Corpus Christianum* was considered problematic. Within the first year of arrival in Rome, and before they had a stable residence of their own, the Jesuits began taking into their rented home young Jews who expressed an interest in baptism. Unlike the prostitutes, the (male) Jews could stay in the Jesuits' house without scandal. The same noble women who supported S. Marta, such as Margherita d'Austria and Cardinal Alessandro Farnese's mother Girolama Orsini, were among the earliest supporters of the Catechumens. The first specific mention of a Jewish convert (reported in a letter of Ignatius of 1541) involves a 31-year-old whose love for a Christian prostitute was doubly forbidden. Only a double ceremony could solve this "doomed" affair: his baptism by the Jesuit Salmeron was followed immediately by their marriage.[63]

A common inspiration guided both S. Marta and the Catechumen House: provide room and board for the period of formation leading up to the free choice of a new state in life.[64] Rather than the usual array of high-ranking prelates, Ignatius placed the confraternity's administration in the hands of a secular priest named Giovanni de Torano. Just three days after the canonical erection of the Casa di S. Marta, the Pope issued the bull *Illius qui pro dominici,* which created the confraternity of S. Giuseppe to be made up of twelve priests with de Torano as the leader (and assigned to them the small church of S. Giovanni in Mercatello, later flattened to make the square in front of the Victor Emmanuel monument). Within a year Paul III intervened again, this time to make the confraternity open to laymen, and to elevate it to an archconfraternity able to aggregate affiliated houses.[65]

Two signs from 1546 that Ignatius was considering expansion of this work outside Rome include an attempt to found a similar organization in Padua, apparently without a long success, and the establishment of the first extern college of the Society in Gandía for students including Moorish children.[66] But the relationship between de Torano and the

[61] Bono, *Corsari,* 202–35.

[62] Lucchini, *La merce umana.* Pagano (ed.), *L'archivio del Gonfalone, passim.*

[63] Hoffmann, *Ursprung,* 2–4.

[64] *Regole delle neofite della casa de catecumme.* Biblioteca Nazionale di Roma, Misc.B. 1303.19., #2.

[65] Simonsohn, *Apostolic See,* v. 5: #2119, 2221, 2361.   [66] MHSI Epist. Mixt. II: 299–301.

Jesuits soon soured. By 1547, he had accused them of heresy, revealing the secrets of the confessional, sodomy, and more.[67] The Jesuits were cleared of all charges and de Torano banished from Rome in 1551. As with S. Marta and S. Caterina, Ignatius limited his own involvement once some stability had been achieved, yet continued to send Jesuit catechetical instructors. Other instructors and some confraternal members were recruited from the graduated neophytes (indeed, some became Jesuits, or members of other orders, and frequently became unwelcome proselytizers among their former co-religionists).[68] The example of the *Casa dei catecumeni* was not lost on Ignatius' followers. In virtually all the Italian cities with a sizable Jewish or Muslim population, the Jesuits became involved in planting similar houses: Venice (1557); Ferrara (1561); Milan (1565); Bologna (1568); Ancona (1573); Naples (1601); Reggio Emilia (1630); and Modena (1631).[69]

Besides providing a temporary home for the individual interested in conversion, a primary responsibility of the confraternity was to arrange a suitable Godfather – not infrequently a high-ranking cleric or nobleman.[70] The Godfather's responsibility was to shepherd financially the transition to Christianity, so that in theory the spiritual "liberation" was matched by material security. This could mean providing a woman with a dowry for marriage or to enter a convent, or ensuring a man's ability to support himself and his family; in inheritance disputes, the confraternity also became a litigant.[71] The convert assumed the Godfather's name upon baptism – usually in a public ceremony orchestrated to provide the edifying spectacle of the worldwide advancement of the faith.[72] Regrettably, it also served as a foil for the tragic spectacle of the execution on the gallows or on the stake of the occasional convicted recidivist, or the even more rare Christian convert to Judaism. Since baptism was considered an indelible step, return to one's former faith was an act of heresy, though this did not stop some individuals from drifting back and forth between the two faiths.[73]

After the baptism, the confraternity oversaw the continued education of the neophyte, which might extend to material support as well. Giulia

[67] Tamburini (ed.), *Santi e Peccatori*, 61–4.

[68] Sola, "Juan Bautisto Eliano."

[69] Marzola: *Chiesa Ferrarese*: 1, 620–3. Milan and Modena: Stow, *Catholic Thought*, 200–10. Ancona: Hoffmann, *Ursprung*, 123. Work with catechumens in Naples began as early as 1573: Lopez, *Clero magia*, 57–114. Reggio Emilia, *Capitoli ed ordini*, 7. In Genoa and Mantua, catechumens were housed along with other groups: Pullan, *Jews*, 273; Florence eventually had a house as well: Browe, *Die Judenmission*, 177. Livorno is the conspicuous exception, but its Jewish population was shielded by the Medici Dukes.   [70] Sermoneta, "Il Mestiere" and Stow, "A Tale of Uncertainties."

[71] Simonsohn, *Apostolic*, #1870, 2155, etc., and Stow, *Jews, passim*.

[72] Martin, *Roma Sancta*, 75–83.   [73] Pullan, "Old Catholicism," 13–22, and "Ship," 25–58.

Colonna provided conspicuous early support for the Catechumens by donating some houses near piazza Margana which provided the first convent for female neophytes who decided to take the veil. She revoked a previous donation of the houses to the Archconfraternity of the Annunziata in the Dominican church of the Minerva, so as to give them to the Catechumens in 1562.[74] When this monastery proved too small, Pius V in 1566 provided the church and convent of S. Basilio. The men (both catechumens and neophytes) remained at S. Giovanni until 1577 when Gregory XIII established the *Collegio dei Neofiti,* and entrusted their education to the Jesuits of the Roman College. After the enormous and lucrative devotion to a miraculous image of the Virgin, Gregory helped Cardinal Sirleto build the church of S. Maria dei Monti on the site in 1582, and transferred the confraternity chapel there. In 1634, the Confraternity's Cardinal Protector, the Cappuchin Antonio Barberini (brother of Urban VIII), constructed the enormous Collegio dei Neofiti next door, and had the last Catechumens from S. Giovanni transferred there. Unlike S. Marta and S. Caterina, the House of the Catechumens never swayed from its original purpose. Linked to ever-increasing proselytizing efforts (Popes imposed on the Jews heavier taxation and obligatory weekly attendance of conversionary sermons, among other coercive measures), it remained fixed in its role as a primary portal to the Christian world right up to the nineteenth century.[75]

CONCLUSIONS

All three institutions served as the primary models for Jesuit confraternal activity before the better-known Marian congregations became the norm. By the 1550s and 1560s, when the Jesuits were making regular missionary progress throughout Italy, establishing confraternities wherever they preached had become a standard practice, codified in manuals and rulebooks.[76] The practice had become so diffuse that General Acquaviva even had to prohibit Jesuits on missions after 1582 from making new rules for confraternities.[77] According to a Jesuit from the Neapolitan province, the founding of congregations in every town and village "was the greatest good that could be achieved, because with their partaking of the sacrament, their exhortations and disciplines, all the good done during the mission is maintained."[78] We will only understand the Jesuit

---

[74] Moroni, *Dizionario,* vol. 47, 271.

[75] Martano, "Missione inutile," 93–110; Simonsohn, "Jewish Converts."

[76] "Istruzione" in ARSI, Inst. 50, fols. 150–69; Guidetti, *Missioni,* 5–19, 56–60.

[77] Mullan, *Studied,* doc. #4. In 1584 Gregory XIII elevated the *Prima primaria* to an archconfraternity, thus providing a standardized set of statutes.   [78] Gentilcore, "Adapt yourselves," 281.

ideal of mission in practice by recognizing the role of their confraternities in spreading new forms of interventive charity.[79]

While not imputing characteristics from the Marian Congregations back onto these earlier institutions, let us briefly retrace the patterns and methodologies that grew into the distinctively Jesuit model for confraternal activity. The most important shared feature is the emphasis on bringing marginalized groups to center stage. Once these groups were identified, then a lay organization (preferably uniting the most influential members of the community) would be established to organize charitable relief. Because the needs could and did vary from town to town, the Jesuits' first confraternities did not become associated with any one kind of institution, but rather assumed the whole gamut of charitable activity. Frequently, "high profile" charities were their targets.

Significantly, in the early years, while still following closely the ideal of temporary and itinerant missionary activity, the Jesuits pursued an uncharacteristically "hands-off" approach to organizational control. The goal was to place the confraternity on a stable foundation, and then move on: to provide the inspiration (often by drafting the statutes) without committing to the later administration. The confraternal membership of these earliest institutions, similar to their three Roman models, was exclusively adult, and preferably elite. The membership reflected those individuals whom the Jesuits most frequently orbited when arriving in a new city, often the Spanish aristocracy, and frequently women, to whom they directed the *Spiritual Exercises*.

Once the Jesuits themselves became more tied down by teaching in the schools, their confraternal activity changed as well.[80] They began for the first time to focus on the devotional formation of students through confraternities.[81] The longer sojourn of the Jesuits at a school allowed for a more structured paternal model to develop. The *Padre,* always appointed by the Rector of a college, had final say in all activities of the congregation, and was a long-term director for the extensive devotional activities that became so characteristic of the Marian congregations.[82]

Partly because the devotional works loomed so large, the charitable works undertaken by the student confraternities, both before and after the Prima primaria, were more limited. They were intermittent in nature and provided through service rather than payment (hospital or prison visiting for instance). Even a student confraternity composed of nobles,

---

[79] On confraternal use in Jesuit missions: Rinaldi, "Gesuiti in Campania," 243–57; Lopez, "Confraternite laicali," 193–205; Di Molfetta, "Confraternite parrocchiali," 355–74. Novi Chavarria, "L'attività," 159–85.

[80] O'Malley, "Jesuits Changed," 30–2.   [81] Trexler, *Dependence,* 171–343.

[82] Mullan, *Prima primaria,* 325–40.

for instance, would not take on the ultimate financial responsibility for a conservatory or refuge. Yet this student-born model of charity as service, rather than fiscal responsibility, could also be turned around for use in the rural missions. After preaching for a week in a village, a Jesuit could easily leave in his wake a Name of God confraternity, or Holy Sacrament Confraternity, which would require no capital outlay by the members and no further supervision by the Jesuit. Only if there were a Jesuit anchor in the town, such as a school or professed house, then perhaps a Marian congregation might be organized, with more exacting devotional requirements.

With the Marian congregations, then, the Jesuits too had their third order, held tightly by their side and nestled securely under their protective gaze. Yet their earliest institutions did not follow this pattern, and indeed in the 1540s and 50s, the Jesuits took directed action so as not to be responsible for their on-going administration. The example the Jesuits drew from S. Marta, S. Caterina, S. Giuseppe, and the many institutions they spawned, was not of organizational structure, but of outreach and apostolic activity. By co-opting the elites to work for the poor and marginalized groups, the Jesuits were advancing their plan for the reform of the whole of society. Their innovation and rapid imitation alert us to the centrality of confraternal charity for Jesuit missionary activity, as well as the power and flexibility of the confraternal model for poor relief in the Mediterranean world.

9

JEWISH CONFRATERNAL PIETY IN SIXTEENTH-CENTURY FERRARA: CONTINUITY AND CHANGE

ELLIOTT HOROWITZ

Shortly before the Jewish New Year of 1515, fifty-seven men and fourteen women gathered together in the synagogue of Ferrara's then still modest Jewish community in order to form, with the consent of the latter's leadership, a pious confraternity which was evidently the first of its kind among Italian Jewry. The synagogue in which they met had been established in the 1480s in a building which had been given to the community for that purpose by Ser Samuel Melli of Rome, who had purchased it from a member of the Norzi family, Ferrara's leading Jewish banking family. The conversion of the building into the first permanent place of worship for the members of Ferrara's Jewish community had been authorized by Duke Ercole I of the House of Este, which had generously (and sometimes bravely) been extending protection and support to both resident and refugee Jews since the middle of the fifteenth century. In 1473 Ercole I had extended such protection to resident Jews in opposition to papal demands, and two decades later he allowed twenty-one families of Spanish exiles to settle in Ferrara under rather favorable conditions. This policy had been reaffirmed by his son, Alfonso, in 1506. Ferrara, in the early sixteenth century, was a modest sized, though fairly heterogeneous Jewish community, which despite periodic tensions with the local Christian populace, had benefited from unusually good relations with the ruling dynasty.[1]

---

[1] Parts of this article were first presented as a lecture on "Modes of Jewish Confraternal Piety in Pre-Expulsion Spain and their Impact upon Mediterranean Jewry," presented at the Sorbonne in the spring of 1992. David Ruderman was kind enough to read various versions. The final one was completed during my stay as a Skirball Fellow at the Oxford Centre for Hebrew and Jewish Studies.

For an overview of relations between the Jews and the House of Este see Balletti, *Gli Ebrei*, and on the history of the community of Ferrara, Pesaro, *Memorie storiche*. For a more up to date treatment of the history of Ferrarese Jewry during this period see Ruderman, *The World of a Renaissance Jew*,

The *Gemilut Hasadim* (hereafter *GH*) society founded there is the earliest Italian Jewish confraternity whose documentation has survived. It has survived, moreover, not only from the initial stages of the confraternity's organization but in a series of statutes continuing through the seventeenth century. Unlike some later Italian Jewish confraternities, however, the records of Ferrara's *GH* do not contain such serial information as the minutes and attendance lists of monthly meetings, but only the less frequent (though at times quite radical) revisions over time of the confraternity's statutes and membership roster. These sources, too, can be made to speak history, and through them can be reconstructed, if somewhat schematically, the shifting emphases and social contours of Jewish confraternal piety in sixteenth-century Italy as the phenomenon began gradually to take shape.

A concise and concrete description of its major aims are contained in the Ferrarese confraternity's inaugural statutes:

> for its members to care for the infirm poor when necessary, and to attend them day and night, nursing them, for the glory of God, until they regain their health. Also to attend the dying . . . and, after their deaths, to prepare a coffin . . . to wash their bodies, to carry them to the cemetery, to bury them, and, afterwards, to accompany the mourners home.[2]

Its primary orientation, then, was toward acts of benevolent piety connected with sickness and especially death. These concerns, common among contemporary Catholic confraternities in Italy, had also been dominant among the only Jewish pious (as opposed to mutual aid) associations known with certainty to have existed in late medieval times, those of Spain and southern France.[3] Ferrara's *GH*, founded not long after the expulsions of the Jews from Spain (1492) and from Provence (1500–1) and including among its ranks no small number of refugees from both, would seem to have drawn upon these traditions of confraternal benevolence. Duke Ercole I of Ferrara had invited twenty-one families of Spanish émigrés to settle in Ferrara in 1493, and Jews from southern France had been making their own way to the city.[4] The Jews arriving from some of these areas, moreover, had

---

21–6, Segre, "Sephardic Settlements," 122–6, and Bonfil, "Spanish and Portuguese Jews in Italy," 219–20. The primary manuscript source to be cited in this article is the Minute-book (Pinkas) of *Hevrat Gemilut Hasadim*, Ferrara, ms. Haifa University Ha 6 (microfilm Central Archive for the History of the Jewish People, HM 5231), hereafter, PHGH.

[2] Ruderman, "The Founding," 236. The Ferrara society has also been discussed by Rivlin, *Mutual Responsibility*.

[3] On Jewish burial societies in late medieval Spain see now Assis, "Welfare and Mutual Aid," 333–8. On Arles see most recently Ben-Shalom, "Communal Life," 25–31.

[4] On the arrival of Spanish exiles see Modena, "Les exiles," 117–21, and on the movement of Jewish exiles from Provence to Italy see Milano, *Il Ghetto*, 214–15.

witnessed a proliferation of Christian confraternities in their midst. Abraham Farissol, the first scribe of Ferrara's *GH*, had come to Italy from Avignon, where sixty-four Christian confraternities had emerged during the fifteenth century alone.[5] In Rome two confraternities for Torah study emerged among the Spanish exiles in the city before 1540, one associated with the Aragonese community and the other with that of the Castilian Jews.[6] Thus, Jews coming from these areas to Ferrara in the late fifteenth or early sixteenth centuries seem to have brought with them certain Mediterranean habits of sociability that had been translated, in their former communities, into forms of confraternal piety.[7] Their own inclinations in this direction could only have been fortified by the Italian environment, in which during that same period there was, as has widely been noted, "a proliferation of various societies within many areas."[8]

Whereas its Jewish predecessors in Spain and southern France devoted themselves to the care of the sick *or* the dead, the Ferrarese confraternity chose to widen its focus so as to provide both kinds of charity to the wider community, providing burial in all instances and sick-care in cases of financial need. Yet, not all of the services provided by Ferrara's *GH* were directed towards the larger community – some, as was also the case in Italian Catholic confraternal piety,[9] were reserved for its members alone. This symbolically important distinction had also been part of the late medieval traditions of confraternal piety among Spanish and southern French Jewry. Thus, the inaugural statutes of Ferrara's *GH* stipulated that upon a member's death the confraternity would care for and comfort the mourners, and see to it that ten members were present twice daily at the services held in their home during the week of mourning. Such provisions for after-death care were not included in the services offered by *GH* to the Jewish community of Ferrara. In 1517 an amendment was added to the statutes, requiring ten fellow members (chosen by lot) to fast for one

---

[5] Their number had grown from two in the thirteenth and thirty-one in the fourteenth. See Chiffoleau "Les confréries," 790–1. In the neighboring Comtat Venaissin, Chiffoleau points to the emergence of fifty-three new confraternities during the first half of the fifteenth century and fifty-five in the second half, whereas only two had existed before 1300 (*ibid.*, 791–3). On Farissol in Avignon and Ferrara see Ruderman, *The World of a Renaissance Jew*, chs. 1–3.

[6] It is possible that they were in existence even before 1520. See Schwarzfuchs, "Un episodio," 133–43.

[7] On the role of sociability in confraternal piety recently the important comments of Weissman, "Cults and Contexts," 203, 216.   [8] Black, *Italian Confraternities*, 31.

[9] See Terpstra, *Lay Confraternities*, 75.

whose end appeared to be near[10] – reflecting how the confraternity could become an artificial kin group.[11] Members of GH who declined to fast could pay a fee instead, which would go to the person who would fast in their place. No indication was given, however, that the confraternity was already divided in such a way that its poorer members would earn money by performing various duties in place of its wealthier ones. Aside from the matter of age, with those over thirty being given more power in the amendments of 1517,[12] the members of GH shared, in its initial stages, equal status and equal responsibilities.

No criteria were stated for admission, other than the willingness to abide by the confraternity's statutes (including payment of monthly dues), and no selection process for new members was mentioned. None of the seventy-one names listed in its inaugural statutes was preceded by an honorific of any sort. The manifestly evident egalitarian character of the confraternity – in a community where oligarchical rule by a small number of banking families had prevailed for decades – seems to have been perceived by some as a threat. Among the amendments to its statutes GH introduced in 1517 was a long one concerning "those unbridled ones from among our people who open their mouths to speak badly of this confraternity, and others who extend their hooves [like swine] declaring 'I am pure...'"[13] In response to these it was decided that any individual found guilty of verbally offending the confraternity would have his name, together with the offending words, publicized upon the walls of Ferrara's (only) synagogue. Furthermore, such a person, as well as his family, would be denied even the most minimal aid from the confraternity's coffers until he recanted. Although no indication is given as to the precise identity of those "unbridled ones" who spoke badly of the confraternity, it is likely that they were connected with the community's wealthy families, such as the Norzis, who had kept their distance from GH and had the most to lose from the emergence of a Jewish institution which might serve as a competing base of power.

The egalitarian character of the confraternity diminished considerably by 1552 (the year of the next statutes), and the distinction between the

[10] Ruderman, "The Founding," 260–1, 263. Compare, on fasting for a fellow member, Rivlin "The 1547 [sic] Statutes," 365, 379.

[11] On confraternities as artificial kin-groups see, for example, Chiffoleau, "Les confréries," 811; Bossy, "The Counter Reformation," 58–60.

[12] Ruderman, "The Founding," 263, pars. 21–2. On the association of the age of thirty (for better or worse) with maturity see Horowitz, "The Worlds of Jewish Youth," 87–8.

[13] Ruderman, "The Founding," 264 (par. 24).

services offered to members and those offered the general community widened further. Whereas originally funeral attendance was seen as a part of the confraternity's general service to the community, by 1552 attendance was required only upon the death of a fellow member or a member of his (or her) family. Another of the exclusive services offered then to members was that confraternal officials were required, when visiting a member who had been ill (with fever) for three days "to encourage him to confess his sins before God and to deliver his final testament before his family."[14] In the latter case the confraternity saw itself as standing somewhere between God and the family, dutifully reminding the moribund member to fulfill his responsibilities towards both. And in involving itself in a member's deathbed confession, as in fasting for his recovery, the confraternity used ritual as a means of both reflecting and intensifying the fraternal bonds between its members. The concern with confession went beyond the functional level, however, for the Jews of post-Tridentine Italy were much concerned with this aspect of the deathbed rite, mirroring a basic shift with regard to this "sacrament" which had occurred in the surrounding environment.[15]

This increasing concern with the soul and its salvation seems to have displaced some of *GH*'s concern with the body and its interment. Though most of the confraternal fines were raised substantially between 1515–52, the only one which remained constant (making it a relative bargain in the latter year) was the fine to be paid upon failure to arrive, after being duly summoned, to help prepare a body for burial.[16] Whereas the inaugural statutes had seen burial as a core, and perhaps the most central, activity of the confraternity, those of 1552 no longer regarded it as a task in which all members need, at some time or another, take part. It was assigned rather to "a Jew from among the non-paying members," who would perform the burial free of charge.[17]

[14] PHGH, 5b (par. 7), 7a (par. 20).

[15] On this shift in post-Tridentine Catholicism, whereby confession became "a regular occurrence in the devout life" rather than a once yearly affair see Evennett, *The Spirit of the Counter-Reformation*, 37–8; Bossy, "The Social History of Confession," 31–5. On the stress upon the sick confessing before death see the 1542 confraternal statutes from Salò quoted by Pullan, *Rich and Poor*, 275. On the impact of this development upon Jewish rituals see Horowitz, "The Jews of Europe," 271, and the sources cited there.

[16] This remained a modest two *bolognini*. By contrast, the failure to attend monthly meetings, which had been half that amount in 1515, shot up fivefold by 1552 (See Ruderman, "The Founding," 263–4, and compare PHGH, 6b [par. 14] 7b, [par. 26]). A *bolognino grosso*, which is here intended, was also known as a *soldo*. A master mason in nearby Modena (also under Este rule) earned approximately 14 *soldi* a day during the period 1530–60. See Felloni, "Italy," 26.

[17] PHGH, 6a (par. 13).

In the inaugural statutes, moreover, there had been no such thing as non-paying members, and consequently no set of activities reserved for a confraternal underclass. By mid-century membership had fallen nearly 40 percent to thirty-six men and only eight women, but within that smaller group there was now greater differentiation than among the original seventy-one members. According to the revised statutes of 1552 those who did not pay monthly dues were expected to perform a wider range of activities than those who did, some of them (such as burial) quite demanding. Whereas the original statutes granted only confraternal officers the option of declining to perform tasks assigned to them by lot, at mid-century this privilege was allocated on a strictly financial basis. Members paying monthly dues could decline so long as they found themselves a replacement, whose remuneration was their responsibility. If they were unsuccessful in their efforts the confraternity, according to the 1552 statutes, would send "one of the members absolved from payment." The latter would receive four *bolognini* (twice the monthly dues) for waking during the summer nights and twice that amount for waking during the (colder) nights of winter. Ferrara's *GH* was thus becoming a confraternity in which membership, while it had its rewards for all, meant different things to different people. Although it was not quite divided along the neat lines of "those who paid and those who prayed,"[18] the rich, if they wished, could maintain themselves as upstanding members without ever visiting the sick or caring for the dead. For those poor "who were absolved from payment" membership was a more demanding affair, but its rewards (financial if not spiritual) could also be concomitantly greater.

In establishing what were, in effect, separate orders for rich and poor, Ferrara's *GH* was following a pattern which had emerged elsewhere in Italian confraternal piety – most famously among the Catholic *Scuole* of Venice.[19] In Venice, the Catholic Scuole maintained what Pullan has called their "stranglehold" upon the poorer members through the medium of alms, thus providing them with an economic incentive. Membership in Ferrara's *GH* did provide opportunities for the poor to earn money on the side, but there also existed other incentives for them to join the confraternity.

At mid-century the confraternity placed even greater emphasis upon the maintenance of social ties between its members than it had in 1515. Physical violence between the members was also carefully controlled. Whereas the inaugural statutes had imposed a maximal

[18] See Weissman, "Cults and Contexts," 213–14.
[19] Pullan, *Rich and Poor*, ch.2. esp. 66–7, 76–7.

fine of only fifteen bolognini for striking a fellow member and drawing blood, by 1552 the fine had skyrocketed to six (gold) *scudi* whether or not bleeding was caused. Such violence between members was considered so severe an offense that the victim was permitted to bring the offender before a non-Jewish court.[20]

The confraternity's otherwise maximal fine of two gold scudi was imposed in 1552 for three offenses, all related to its internal affairs rather than to the services it offered the public. These were failing to reconcile within three days after a quarrel with a fellow member, leaving its ranks without special dispensation, and failure to attend the funeral of a fellow member or a member of his family.[21] The original statutes had seen funeral attendance as part of the confraternity's general service to the community, but by 1552 it became a special obligation to fellow members. *GH* was thus retreating from the complex commonweal of Ferrara's growing but increasingly stratified community, and turning inwards into itself more and more.

In parallel manner it shifted away from direct contact with the body of the deceased and became more interested in the rituals surrounding death. Dues-paying members were, in 1552, no longer even invited to participate in burials, and were offered an attractively low fine (considerably lower than that paid for missing a monthly meeting) for failing to report for the washing and preparation of a dead body for burial.[22] The members of the poorer class were largely entrusted with the performance of these messy activities, allowing the others to cultivate ritual and sociability, both of which had become higher priorities for the confraternity. This was, all things considered, a better arrangement for *GH* than retreating entirely from such activities as the washing and burial of the dead. Doing so would have invited the emergence of a competing confraternity devoted to those activities, thus ending the monopoly *GH* had enjoyed in Ferrara for almost four decades.

How can we see that *GH* had become an increasingly elite confraternity by mid-century? A cursory comparison of the 1552 membership list with that of 1515 reveals that whereas none of the fifty-seven males who were charter members bore honorifics before their names, three of thirty-six were so honored in 1552, as were two of the eight women who were there listed. This does not necessarily mean that none of the

---

[20] On the 1552 fine for striking a fellow member see PHGH 6b, (par. 16), and compare Ruderman, "The Founding," 262 (par. 18). On the matter of the recourse to non-Jewish courts see Bonfil, *Rabbis and Jewish Communities*, ch. 5.   [21] PHGH, 5b (pars. 4, 6, 7).

[22] *Ibid.*, 6a, 7b (pars. 10, 26).

original members were deserving of such honor, but it does indicate that no point was then seen in officially distinguishing between one member and another, just as no distinction was yet made in 1515 between paying and non-paying members.

The three male members bearing honorifics in 1552 were placed by the new scribe at the very top of the page. Gracing the top of the right hand column appear the names of Don Jacob and Don Judah Abravanel, each with the princely epithet *ha-Sar* preceding their Iberian-style honorific.[23] These two brothers, scions of "what was perhaps the outstanding [Jewish] family in all Europe in that age" were grandsons of the exegete, philosopher and statesman Don Isaac Abravanel.[24] Their parents, the illustrious couple Samuel and Benvenida Abravanel, had moved north upon the expulsion of the Jews from the kingdom of Naples in 1541, settling in Ferrara, where Samuel died before the end of May 1547.

Samuel Abravanel was referred to by the former Marrano author, Samuel Usque as "the foremost and distinguished man among the Spanish Jews," and his wife Benvenida has been compared with "the great noblewomen of the age." Among Samuel's three sons Isaac, Jacob, and Judah, the latter two (who joined Ferrara's *GH*) were, as sons of Benvenida, treated more favorably in his will than Isaac, who had been born to a woman to whom Samuel was not married.[25] Jacob, the elder of the two, seems, together with his mother, to have taken over the family's lucrative loan-banking business which extended as far as Tuscany. There, mother and son were on especially close terms with the ducal family, Jacob with Cosimo I and Benvenida with his wife Eleonora, whose tutor she is reported to have been during her sojourn in Naples.[26] It was more, then, than the letter "Aleph" at the beginning of their family name which prompted *GH*'s scribe to place Jacob and Judah Abravanel at the head of the confraternity's membership list in 1552. Their name was associated with wealth, pedigree, and learning, and their standing could only have been heightened by the publication, in Ferrara itself, of a short biography of their grandfather Don Isaac just the year before.[27]

---

[23] *Ibid.*, 8a.

[24] For this characterization of the family see Roth, *Renaissance*, 54. On the Abravanel family in Italy see the pioneering article of Margulies, "La famiglia," 97–107, 145–54, and recently Leoni, "Nuove notizie," 153–206.

[25] Samuel was Isaac's youngest son and brother of the philosopher Judah (Leone Ebreo) author of the celebrated *Dialoghi di Amore*. On Samuel and Benvenida see Roth, *Italy*, 189, 192, 208, 215, 279, 285, and 310.   [26] See Margulies, "La famiglia," 99; Roth, *Renaissance*, 54.

[27] This was written by R. Baruch Hizketto and appeared in the first edition of Isaac Abravanel's *Ma'ayanei ha-Yeshu'a* (Ferrara, 1551).

The third member whose name was singled out for prominence at the head of the 1552 list was Isaac Fano, whose father Joshua had been one of the confraternity's founders. Isaac, whose name headed the left-hand column of the membership list (directly across from the two Abravanels) was later to be called by the polymath Azariah dei Rossi "the greatest of his generation," and was to be singled out by the latter, together with Don Isaac Abravanel, for his munificent hospitality to the Jewish refugees of the 1571 earthquake in Ferrara.[28]

Like the two Abravanel brothers, he was accorded a double-honorific by the scribe who composed the membership list at the end of *GH*'s 1552 statutes. The latter placed his name prominently at the head of the left column, where, somewhat differently from the Iberian titles which accompanied the names of the Abravanels, it was preceded by the words *he-hashuv kevod morenu*, suggesting both social eminence and advanced rabbinical erudition. Although Isaac's father Joshua, who was still alive in 1552, was no longer then a member of *GH*, two Fano women – Rosa and Jochebed, (evidently Joshua's wife and daughter-in-law) were to be found among its eight female members in 1552 – the only two whose names were preceded with honorifics.

Their family was truly one of the most illustrious ones among Ferrara Jewry in the 1550s. Isaac's uncle, Raphael Elhanan Fano, was selected as one of the local delegates to the synod of Italian communities which took place there in 1554. Two years later, together with his brother and business partner Joshua (Isaac's father), he established a charitable foundation worth 1,500 gold scudi (of which Isaac was to be sole executor) in return for God's having granted them "wealth and property and honor."[29]

The leading members of the Norzi clan, the first family of Ferrara's Jewish community, were conspicuous in their continued absence from *GH* in 1552. Isaac Norzi, described by a contemporary as "a powerful figure in his town, deferred to on account of his wealth and fortune, and feared by all," never joined *GH*, nor had his father before him, the legendary and equally feared Emmanuel.[30] True to family tradition, Isaac's sons (the eldest of whom, Abraham Emmanuel, had

---

[28] Rossi, *Meor 'Enayim*, 20–2, 293.

[29] On Isaac Fano as Joshua's son see Bonfil, "New Information," 134–5, who provides a useful family tree. On Raphael Elhanan as a delegate to the 1554 synod see Finkelstein, *Jewish Self Government*, 302–3.

[30] On Emmanuel and Isaac see Norsa, *Una famiglia* II, chs. 1–2. On the fear of the former see Diena, *Responsa* II, 27, and on the fear of Isaac see the responsum published by Kupfer, "R. Abraham Rovigo," 151–5. On the latter as delegate in 1554 see Finkelstein, (previous note).

been ennobled by Duke Ercole II in 1543) also remained outside the ranks of the confraternity, as did their brother-in-law, Joshua Modena. The latter's father, Eliezer, was one of the most respected members of the community, having distinguished himself through both learning and philanthropy, yet he too seems to have kept his distance from Ferrara's only Jewish confraternity.[31]

Those Norzis (Ben Zion and Yom Tov) who appeared among the members of *GH* in 1552 were, like Eliezer Modena's younger son Jacob, the less (or not yet) distinguished sons of a distinguished family. Yet the more prestigious line of the family – Isaac's ennobled son Abraham Emmanuel Norzi and his sons – had not joined by 1552. Whereas some of Ferrara's leading Jewish families, such as the Fano's and Abravanels, were represented in *GH* by their best and perhaps brightest, others, like the Norzis and Modenas, refrained from putting their weight behind the confraternity, and were represented in its ranks at mid-century only by those situated at some remove from the family's seat of power.

We may also note the two boys who, for the first time, appeared among the members of *GH* in 1552. One was listed as "the blessed child 'Oh that *Ishmael* might live' (Gen. 17:18) b. Azariah Finzi, may God protect him," suggesting that, at the time, he suffered from rather delicate health. Ishmael's father, who was not himself a member, evidently enrolled his young son in the hope that the spiritual benefit conferred by membership would improve the latter's chances of survival. Ishmael did indeed survive, long enough, at least, to still be listed among the members of the Ferrarese confraternity in 1583. He proved, in fact, in line with the prophecy for his biblical namesake, to be something of a "wild man" (cf. Gen. 16:12), being provoked in 1577, after no less than fifteen years' membership in a pious confraternity, to slay his sister on account of her alleged sexual misconduct. Azariah Finzi, the girl's father, saw fit to defend this action by his only son, asserting that it was "inappropriate for one calling himself a Jew, especially a member of one of the best families, to suffer a veil of shame upon his face, being mocked by all who see him for the blemish attached to his family's reputation."[32]

---

[31] On Isaac Norzi's sons see Norsa, *Una famiglia*, 2, ch. 3. On Abraham Emmanuel's ennoblement, which applied also to his heirs, see Simonsohn, *Mantua*, 32 n. 115. On Joshua Modena see Boksenboim (ed.), *Jewish Teachers*, 22 and the sources cited there. On his father Eliezer see Diena *Responsa*, 1, 279 ff. and 2, 172, as well as Boksenboim (ed.), *Matnot ba-Adam*, 389.

[32] Abraham Yagel, *Bat Rabim* ms. Moscow-Guenzberg 129, no. 67 [Institute of Microfilmed Hebrew Mss, Jewish National and University Library, Jerusalem no. 6809], 57a–b. The incident has been mentioned by David Ruderman, who graciously made the manuscript available to me, in his, *Kabbalah, Magic and Science*, 21. See now also Adelman, "Servants and Sexuality."

Family honor was carefully cultivated and protected among Italy's Jews just as it was among the country's Catholic population.[33] Concern with a family's reputation thus influenced its members in deciding which institutions to embrace or to refrain from embracing no less than in deciding which measures to take against women who knew not when to refrain from embracing. Families who either put their full weight behind a new institution such as *GH*, or withheld their support from it, or allowed themselves minor representation in its ranks, played a crucial role thereby not only in determining its chances of survival but also in influencing the particular course it might be led to take.

In the case of the Ferrarese confraternity this course, between 1552 and 1583 (the date of the third statutes), involved both continuity and change. So far as membership is concerned, the absolute number remained unchanged, but there was a significant shift in the confraternity's social composition. Women, whose numbers had fallen sharply (to eight) by mid-century from their zenith (of fourteen) at the time of the confraternity's inception, had disappeared entirely by 1583.[34] The forty-four males, whose numbers had grown since the previous statutes by more than 20 percent, now enjoyed an absolute monopoly.

It is unlikely that the women had left *GH* out of sisterly solidarity with the murdered Ms. Finzi, whose brother Ishmael, her confessed assassin, had been permitted to remain a member in good standing. But those same circumstances which shaped the young Ishmael's entry into the confraternity in 1552 would seem, indirectly, to have played a role in the departure of its women from its ranks. For confraternal membership had become, at least in Ferrara, a more sacral affair, a form of affiliation which could be regarded as conferring spiritual benefit upon a babe in arms, but which could, at the same time, render highly problematic the continued presence of women alongside men in such a "holy society."

At a certain point there seems to have emerged a tacit recognition on the part of members of both sexes that women were as out of place in a pious confraternity such as *GH* as they would be in the mens' section of any of Ferrara's by then numerous synagogues.[35] It was never explicitly stated in the confraternity's statutes, however, that

---

[33] See, for example, Burke, "Insult and Blasphemy," 95–109.

[34] This was noted by Rivlin, *Mutual Responsibility*, 113, who calculated the dates of the statutes somewhat erroneously, however, as 1553 and 1584.

[35] On the process of masculinization compare Chiffoleau, "Les confréries," 804.

women would be officially barred from its ranks. This may have been because no compelling reason could be given for such exclusion, and because some women were still needed to perform, whether voluntarily or for payment, certain services for the female dead for which, for reasons of modesty, male members were ineligible.

The confraternity's third statutes (of 1583) are the first in which it implicitly treated confraternal organization as a self-justifying activity rather than as a means toward the performance of pious or benevolent deeds. The first and second statutes had granted its officers authority to assign responsibilities to its members by lot and to organize them into shifts *le-to'elet gemilut hasadim*, that is, "for the benefit of [performing] acts of lovingkindness." Those of 1583, however, radically altered the design of this authority through the interpolation of a single word. They empowered the officers to go about their duties "for the benefit of *hevrat gemilut hasadim*," that is, towards the purpose of the proper functioning of the *confraternity*.[36] Although this might have been a scribal slip,[37] it would appear, if this were indeed the case, to have been one of the Freudian variety, for other paragraphs of the 1583 statutes also point clearly to a shift of the sort sociologists have called "goal displacement."

When this occurs, "the actual activities of the organization become centered around the proper functioning of organization procedures, rather than upon the achievement of the initial goals."[38] Thus, it may be noted that in 1583 the penalty for disobeying the confraternity's officials was doubled, whereas some others which had previously been raised steeply, such as the fine to be paid for failing to reconcile with a fellow member, remained virtually unchanged after three decades. The emphasis now was less upon members interacting with each other, and more upon their interaction with the institution. From 1583 meetings were to be held only once every two months, half as frequently as before (with a concomitant decline in face-to-face contact among the members), but the fine to be paid for non-attendance at meetings, like that for disobedience to the confraternity's officials or leaving its ranks, was then doubled.

In 1552 *GH* had indeed regarded abandonment of its ranks as a major offense, imposing its then maximal fine of two scudi upon the offender – the same imposed for failure to reconcile with a fellow member. This suggested that the confraternity had then placed an equally high premium upon maintaining amicable relations between

---

[36] Ruderman, "The Founding," 259; PHGH, 5a, 10b (par. 5).
[37] This, however, appears unlikely since the 1603 statutes preserved the same formulation (*ibid.*, 16a [par. 6]).   [38] See Sills, *The Volunteers*, 62, and "Voluntary Associations," 369–70.

fellow members and insuring their institutional loyalty. In 1583, as we
have noted, the fine regulating relationships remained unchanged, but
the one to be extracted from a member departing the confraternity
without its express consent was doubled. The person departing was to
pay four gold scudi "on account of his insolence." Moreover, it was
decided then that one leaving even with the confraternity's permission, "shall not depart freely, but shall pay only two scudi, *in order
to atone for the thought which he had harbored in his heart.*" The striking
language together with the hefty fines indicates that the very act of
belonging had for *GH* become the central aspect of confraternal piety,
pushing all others to the margins. Affiliation with the confraternity
had increasingly taken on sacral significance so that leaving its ranks,
even with official consent, became a kind of ritual transgression
requiring its own sin-offering.

It is not surprising that women came to be excluded from this sort
of Jewish ritual brotherhood. It is also hardly surprising that, as it
became more concerned with its organizational features, the confraternity drifted even further from its original goals. Burial, which
had been perhaps the primary activity for which *GH* had been
founded, was no longer performed by *any* of its members, even its less
wealthy ones. Whereas the inaugural statutes had required every
member, by lot, to participate in burials and those of 1552 had
relegated the act of interment to the confraternal proletariat, in 1583 it
was decided that if a death should occur "the coffin shall be constructed by members of the confraternity and the grave shall be dug by *a Jew*
(emphasis added)."[39] The members of *GH* were willing, it appears, to
incur the risk of splintery hands but not that of muddy feet, which
might have lowered their social standing. Evidently there were none
among them willing to perform burials even for payment. The task
would have to be farmed out, from 1583, to a (Jewish) non-member,
whether the deceased was male or female.

"A man's feet/ will make him fleet/ a dead man's grave/ to dig..." So
wrote, nonetheless, Samuel Rieti, one of five recently arrived members of that clan to join Ferrara's *GH* by 1583,[40] in the celebratory
poem which preceded the confraternity's statutes of that year. Although Rieti obviously allowed himself a measure of poetic license in
composing it, his poem does reflect some of the basic changes which
had taken place in the confraternity's orientation in the three decades

---

[39] PHGH, 11a–b, pars. 8, 10, 15.
[40] On the Rietis see Simonsohn, "I banchieri," 406–23, 487–99, [= "On the History," 310–315 (n.v)].

since 1552. Its members are referred to in the second (prose) introduction to the 1583 statutes as "rich and poor together" (Ps. 49:3) and indeed, the distinction between rich and poor which had been central to the previous statutes was quietly eradicated in the third version. Members of both groups, as Rieti indicated in the introductory poem's third line, could be called upon at all times to attend the sick.[41] Similarly, the sixth line declared proudly that "to clothe the dead/none shall dread" and, in fact, the fine for failure to arrive when summoned to prepare a body for burial was quintupled from the bargain rate of two bolognini in 1552 to ten in 1583 – equaling the steep fine to be paid by members for such "serious" offenses as non-attendance at meetings and disobedience to the confraternity's officials.[42] Care of the sick and of the dead (if not the act of burial itself) had become a more respectable form of piety among Italian Jewry at the end of the sixteenth century, by which point confraternities devoted to these activities had emerged in every major community, and even members of an exclusive confraternity could be expected to do their share.

In contrast to 1552, when some members paid dues and some did not, the statutes of 1583 exempted no one from payment, and consequently, assigned no tasks to a non-paying proletariat. Dues were set on a sliding scale, however, "at least two bolognini per month and four from him whose heart so moves him" (Cf. Ex. 25:2). How many hearts were so moved we do not know, but a marked turn does appear towards more "capital-intensive" forms of piety, such as the provision of dotal aid for needy brides and support for Torah study, both of which were alluded to by Rieti towards the end of his introductory poem.[43] Their inclusion in the 1583 statutes testifies not only to the relatively well-heeled character of the confraternity at that point, which was expressed in other ways as well,[44] but to the increasing eclecticism of its concerns.

By the early 1580s Ferrara's *GH*, although probably the earliest of Italy's Jewish confraternities, was in a position to be influenced by developments in the sphere of confraternal piety which had occurred in other communities. Of perhaps greatest relevance in this matter was the presence in its midst of a sizable number of Bolognese Jews,

---

[41] PHGH, 9b. The prose introduction, evidently written also by Samuel Rieti, appears on 10a.

[42] *Ibid.*, 9b, 11b (par. 17).   [43] *Ibid.*, 9b, 12a (par. 25).

[44] Such as the purchase of a meeting place and hiring of a physician (*ibid.*, 11b, [par. 18]). The medical expenses of the poor, moreover, would be paid for "at least three days" (*ibid.*, 11a, [par. 11]) in contrast to a maximum of two days in 1552.

especially those belonging to the aristocratic Rieti family, who arrived in Ferrara in the wake of the 1569 expulsion from the Papal States.[45] Of the five Rieti's who were listed among its members in 1583, two (both grandsons of the illustrious Ishmael Rieti of Siena) served on the influential board which drafted the new set of statutes approved in that year. The Rieti affiliation with *GH* of Ferrara is reminiscent of the association of leading Catholic families with particular confraternities – such as that of the Bentivoglio's of Bologna with S. Maria della Pietà.[46] Samuel b. Moses Rieti, who composed the introductory poem in which he inscribed his name acrostically, signed the prose introduction with characteristic literary flair, describing himself as a "long-term" (literally "pierced-ear") slave to *Havurat Gemilut Hasadim*. Some of these Rieti's, as well as others among the 1569 exiles who joined Ferrara's *GH*, had probably previously been "enslaved" to one of the two Jewish confraternities which had existed in Bologna before the expulsion. Although we know little about the membership of Bologna's Jewish confraternities, it has been estimated recently that "by the middle of the sixteenth century Bologna's confraternities gathered possibly 20 percent of the adults," in that city of 55,000.[47]

Of these *Rahamim* and *Nizharim*, the two Bolognese Jewish confraternities of which we have knowledge, considerably more is known of the latter, whose 1546 statutes have recently been published. Even a brief perusal of their fifty-five paragraphs reveals the eclecticism of the confraternity's pious orientation. The first four, for example, are dedicated to distancing its members from such diverse vices as taking God's name in vain, blasphemy,[48] late arrival for morning prayers, and idle chatter in the synagogue. As in Ferrara's *GH*, sickness and death are addressed, but these hardly constitute the primary focus (if there was one) of the Bolognese confraternity.[49]

Nizharim was allowed the luxury of pursuing so diverse an agenda largely because it was founded alongside a Rahamim society (whose name may have been inspired by Catholic *Misericordia* confraternities),

---

[45] On the 1569 exile and the subsequent move of many Bolognese Jews to Ferrara, where they signed a special agreement with the local community in 1573 see Sonne, *Mi-Pavlo*, 222, 228–9; Carpi, "The Expulsion," 145–65; Ruderman, "A Jewish Apologetic Treatise," 253–75.

[46] Terpstra, *Lay Confraternities*, 126, who notes that "all the legitimate males of the Bentivoglio family had joined it soon after it began in 1503."   [47] *Ibid.*, 132.

[48] The prominence of these transgressions in *Nizharim's* statutes would appear to be linked to the emergence, among Bologna's Catholic population, of a Nome de Dio confraternity intended to counter the sin of blasphemy. See Prodi, "The Application of the Tridentine Decrees," 238; Black, *Italian Confraternities*, 64, 69.

[49] Ms. New York Public Library, Jewish Items 34/12, published by Rivlin, "The 1547 [sic] Statutes," 357–96. On the treatment of death and the dying in Bologna's Catholic confraternities see Terpstra, "Death and Dying," 68–82.

which was presumably devoted to caring for the victims of sickness and death.[50] *Gemilut Hasadim* of Ferrara, too, was sometimes referred to as Rahamim, since both names (meaning "loving kindness" and "mercy" respectively) suggested similar modes of piety.[51] The founders of Nizharim in Bologna could therefore take for granted that the needs of the sick and the dead in their community would be seen to, and could enjoy considerable latitude in setting the aims of confraternal piety. These included, for the women, special attention not only to the three classic feminine commandments (monthly ablutions, the taking of *hallah* when baking bread, and the lighting of Sabbath candles), but also to modest appearance and bearing in public.[52]

Significantly, the 1546 statutes devoted two consecutive paragraphs to provisions for aid to needy brides and support for Torah study – two concerns which would reappear (in the same order!) in the 1583 statutes of Ferrara's *GH*.[53] Since Nizharim was still in existence, albeit as a "small confraternity," as late as 1567,[54] it is likely that some of the Bolognese Jews who joined *GH* after arriving in Ferrara had been initiated into confraternal piety as members of Nizharim.

This would also help to explain the appearance of yet another novel feature among the statutes of Ferrara's *GH* in 1583 – the confraternal *beit va'ad*, or "meeting house," which also served as a warehouse. A separate confraternal space of this sort had not been mentioned in any of the previous statutes of Ferrara's *GH* (whose members seem to have met in the main synagogue) but had been maintained by both the *Nizharim* and Rahamim confraternities in Bologna,[55] in keeping with the conventions of Bologna's Catholic confraternities. As Nicholas Terpstra has recently noted: "Unlike contemporary Florence, where four out of five confraternities met in an existing church, two-thirds or more of Bolognese confraternities ... through the first half of the sixteenth century met in their own oratories or ospedali. Companies interested in safeguarding their independence set out immediately buying, adapting, and adorning properties for their communal needs."[56] The Bolognese exiles of 1569 were therefore probably

---

[50] On S. Maria della Misericordia in Bologna see Terpstra, *Lay Confraternities*, 16–18. For Venice, see Pullan, *Rich and Poor*, 38, 48.   [51] See Horowitz, "*Yeshiva and Hevra*," 124–5.

[52] This is the subject of the last of the nine paragraph appendix for female members. See Rivlin, "The 1547 [sic] Statutes," 393–396. On women in Bologna's Catholic confraternities see Terpstra, *Lay Confraternities*, 116–132.

[53] See Rivlin, "The 1547 [sic] Statutes," 381–2 (pars. 29–30) and compare PHGH, 12a (par. 25).

[54] See Boksenboim (ed.), *Jewish Teachers*, 50, 276, for letters mentioning Bologna's *Nizharim* as late as July of 1567.

[55] PHGH, 12b (par. 26); Rivlin, "The 1547 [sic] Statutes," 374, 376 (pars. 14, 18).

[56] Terpstra, *Lay Confraternities*, 164–5.

instrumental in Ferrara's *GH* acquiring such a confraternal property. This development dovetailed also with the greater financial strength and enhanced self-image of the confraternity in 1583, and may have reflected a growing need to stake out for itself a separate space, however modest, in a community which by the late sixteenth century boasted nearly a dozen synagogues.

Although less is known of the Rahamim confraternity in Bologna, it can be established that members of the Rieti family had been associated with it before 1569. In fact, even some of those Rietis who resided in Siena joined Rahamim as "corresponding members," including, apparently, the famed banker Ishmael himself. Confraternal affiliation seems, therefore, to have become an integral part of the Rieti family's style and social identity even before many of its members moved to Ferrara.

Like the five Rieti's, there were also five members of Ferrara's Levi family among the ranks of *GH* in 1583, one of whom, the banker Joseph Levi, was placed by the scribe at the head of the list. Joseph's father Isaac (who had also been a member) received a recommendation from Don Francesco d'Este, in 1555, enabling him to extend his banking activities southward to Naples. In a further expansion of the family business, Joseph and three of his brothers were able, in 1572, to take over the bank in San Felice sul Panaro which had previously belonged to the Norzis, for decades Ferrara's leading (and often most feared) Jewish family.[57] And in 1573 Joseph Levi served with Isaac Norzi and the eminent Isaac Fano as one of the three *parnasim* of the "Italian" community of Ferrara who presided over its union with the Ashkenazic.[58] It was no mere coincidence that his name headed the roster of *GH*'s members in 1583, nor that he was joined there by a brother and three nephews.

The youngest of these, however, Ishmael Levi, was among the three children at the very bottom of the list, representing the opposite end of the spectrum in terms of the confraternity's membership. Although appearing there as Ishmael, he had at birth, it may be learned, been given the name Isaac Jedidiah by his parents Samuel Levi and the former Stella Diana Norzi. Three years previously his mother had sent a moving letter to R. Abraham of Sant' Angelo, her former tutor, requesting that he prepare an amulet to safeguard the health of her only son, whose name had been changed with his first illness but who

---

[57] See Simonsohn, *Milan*, 1285, 2928; Norsa, *Una famiglia*, 2, 23. On Joseph and his brothers see also the documents in the appendix to Bonfil, *Ha-Rabanut be-Italya*, nos. 57–60.

[58] Sonne, *Mi-Pavlo*, 223.

was again facing danger.[59] Whether or not an amulet was dispatched and whether or not it proved effective we cannot tell, but it is quite telling that after attempting to improve the child's delicate health through such methods as changing his name and hanging an amulet around his neck his parents eventually took the step of enrolling him in a pious confraternity.[60] Since it is unlikely that they were interested in having him pay nocturnal visits to the sick or construct coffins for the dead, it would appear that they were drawn to *GH* in 1583 (and motivated to pay its monthly dues) by the belief that confraternal membership itself possessed potentially redeeming sacral significance.

They were not the first to take such a step. Some three decades earlier the parents of the equally fragile Ishmael Finzi had enrolled him as a boy in Ferrara's *GH*, and the latter had recovered sufficiently to kill his (allegedly) sluttish sister in order to protect the family's honor. Significantly, the father of neither of the two Ishmaels was himself enrolled in the confraternity, nor were the fathers of any of the other three boys who between 1552 and 1583 were present in its ranks. In all these cases the children seem to have been enrolled in *GH* *instead* of their parents. The latter, it may be presumed, footed the bill, but preferred to have their children receive the spiritual benefit that was believed to accrue as a consequence of membership in a pious confraternity. The belief in the spiritual advantages of confraternal membership would also seem to have motivated those parents who, some years later, entered their infant sons into Ferrara's *GH* on the very day of their circumcision.[61]

This was a belief to which, as noted above, the confraternity itself gave tacit expression as well, and this belief undoubtedly contributed also to its enhanced self-image, as did the clustering of increasing numbers of Ferrara's Jewish elite among its ranks. Relatedly, from 1583 *GH* was no longer willing to open its doors to all comers, but became rather a confraternity of the selective variety. Neither the original statutes nor those of 1552 had mentioned any acceptance procedure, implying that its doors were open to all – provided they were willing to pay the monthly dues or to perform certain services in their stead. In 1583, however, it was stipulated that "anyone whose heart shall move him" to enter the confraternity must first be approved by two thirds of its council, after which he would pay an

---

[59] For their marriage in 1571 see Boksenboim, *Jewish Teachers*, 388, and for Stella Diana's moving letter to R. Abraham (which may have been written on her behalf) see *ibid.*, 310–11.

[60] R. Abraham had been affiliated with Bologna's *Nizharim* as its "preacher" (*darshan*) in the 1560s. See Rivlin, "The 1547 [sic] Statutes," 359 and Horowitz, "Speaking of the Dead," 135–42.

[61] See PHGH, 14b; Bonfil, *Rabbis and Jewish Communities*, 320.

entrance fee. Not surprisingly, a similar arrangement had previously
existed in Bologna, where as early as 1546 prospective members of
Nizharim needed to be approved by a majority of two thirds before
being accepted into its "covenant," a practice which may have been
influenced by the local flagellant confraternities, which also required
approval by a two-thirds.[62] In Bologna's *Nizharim*, however, members
were to pay a considerable admission fee of half a *scudo*, whereas the
"offering" to be made upon joining the Ferrarese confraternity was
left open.[63] The latter's new selective posture would seem to have
come as a result both of the influence of Bolognese exiles who had
joined the confraternity and of its generally enhanced self-image
vis-a-vis the Ferrarese community.

    In the meantime, however, new members continued to stream into
GH. Six joined at once shortly before *Rosh ha-Shana* of 1584, perhaps
hoping to enhance their spiritual merit before the days of judgment.
These included Isaac Rieti of Bologna, who joined the five other
members of his family in *GH*, and Abtalion del Bene, another Bologna exile, who had been in Ferrara since at least 1573. In late 1592
nine new members joined at one fell swoop, one of whom (Menahem
del Bene) would seem to have been Abtalion's son.[64] Parents, even
those not resident in Ferrara, continued to enter their young sons into
the confraternity. Two sons of the eminent kabbalist R. Menahem
Azariah Fano then residing in nearby Reggio, Yohai and Elisha Itai,
joined Ferrara's *GH* (separately) in the early 1590s, although neither
youth was older than ten years when joining its ranks. Between 1598
and 1601 four new members joined the confraternity, all of them
children. Three of these entered its ranks on the very day they were
circumcised, entering its covenant simultaneously with their entry
into the covenant of Abraham.[65] Although *GH* was hardly becoming a
youth confraternity,[66] it was becoming increasingly popular as a repository for fragile young souls precisely at the point when it was
drawing away from the care of the sick and the dead.

    If by 1583 the confraternity's members were no longer involved in the
burial of the dead, two decades later they seem to have abandoned the
deathbed as well. In the 1603 statutes, the third revision and the last

[62] Terpstra, *Lay Confraternities*, 86–8.
[63] PHGH, 10b (par. 6); Rivlin, "The 1547 [sic] Statutes," 385 (par. 37).
[64] PHGH, 14a–b. For Abtalion (son of the deceased Menahem) del Bene as one of the Bolognese
      exiles in Ferrara in 1573 see Sonne, *Mi-Pavlo*, 229. On Menahem (the elder) having been jailed in
      Bologna in 1567 see Boksenboim, *Jewish Teachers*, 274.
[65] PHGH, 14b. See also Bonfil, *Rabbis and Jewish Communities*, 318–20.
[66] On this phenomenon see Horowitz, "A Jewish Youth Confraternity," 36–97.

that shall concern us here,[67] the paragraph dealing with deathbed confession which had been introduced a half-century earlier, and which had been retained in 1583, is omitted. Since it is highly unlikely that deathbed confession was becoming a lower priority among Ferrarese Jews precisely when in most Italian communities it was becoming a central concern, especially among death-related confraternities, it would appear that a separate confraternity devoted to such rites had, by 1603, already appeared on the scene. This was probably *Marpe la-Nefesh* ("Cure for the Soul"), which is otherwise known only from 1626 as having been one of the "principal confraternities" of Ferrara Jewry when they entered their Ghetto in that year.[68]

A similar shift in the 1603 statutes would seem to point to the existence of yet a third Jewish confraternity in Ferrara at that time. Those of 1583 had stated that in the case of a pauper's death the confraternity would provide only a coffin, letting the remainder of his burial expenses fall upon "the shoulders of the community of Ferrara."[69] Two decades later, however, *GH* remained adamant in its refusal to provide more than a coffin in such cases, but was silent about which shoulders would bear the additional expenses. Here, too, it would appear that one of the confraternities otherwise known only from 1626, when Ferrarese Jews entered their Ghetto, was already in existence in 1603. This would be *Kabbarim*,[70] which, like the Spanish and Provençal confraternities of the fourteenth and fifteenth centuries bearing that name, was devoted to burial, and was thus a natural candidate for sharing with *GH* the expenses for the burial of the poor. The fourth confraternity referred to by a later chronicler as having been in existence in 1626 was *Bikkur Holim*, which concerned itself with the care of the sick. It, too, may have appeared initially before 1603. All three of the newer confraternities, it should be noted, took on responsibilities which had previously belonged exclusively to *GH*. This shift to more narrowly specialized confraternities was identified by Weissman as a characteristic of Baroque piety. *GH* seems ultimately, as Pesaro noted long ago, to have become a kind of "archconfraternity," an institution which developed among Catholic confraternities in Italy during the course of the sixteenth century, and which contributed, according to some scholars, to greater standardization and control from above.[71]

---

[67] These were erroneously calculated by Rivlin as being from 1647(!). See *Mutual Responsibility*, 113.

[68] This according to the testimony of Manini Ferranti, *Storia sacra*, 4, 180–2, who reports that its purpose was "di assistere agl'infermi negli ultimi periodi di vita."   [69] PHGH, 11b (par. 15).

[70] See Manini Ferranti, *Storia sacra*, 4, 180–2, and contrast Pesaro, *Memorie*, 48.

[71] See Weissman, "Cults and Contexts," 215. On archconfraternities in Italian Catholic confraternal piety see Bossy, "The Counter-Reformation," 59–60; Pullan, *Rich and Poor*, 272; Black, *Italian Confraternities*, 72–4; Terpstra, *Lay Confraternities*, 219–20.

The existence of other Jewish confraternities in Ferrara may have pressured *GH* to become less selective. Whereas it had, in 1583, taken the step of requiring new members to be approved by two thirds of its council, two decades later it retreated to a position whereby approval by a majority alone was sufficient.[72] But probably more significant in this regard was the ongoing decline in Ferrara's Jewish population, resulting in a smaller pool of potential applicants for membership. From a peak of some 2,000 Jews in 1590, the number of Jews in Ferrara fell to 1,530 in 1601. The community's decline was precipitated by the death of Duke Alphonso II in 1597, after which point Ferrara was lost to the Este dynasty and incorporated into the Papal States. As a result of the stricter measures imposed upon the community by the new authorities, which included a drastic reduction in the number of synagogues, Jews began to leave Ferrara in considerable numbers.[73] From the early seventeenth century, as Cecil Roth has observed, it "ceased to be a great center of Jewish life."[74]

But paradoxically, decline in some aspects of Jewish life seems to have given rise to revitalization in others. Moses Alatino of Ferrara had the sense, after 1597, of "dwelling in another country and another world, with its constant flow and ebb of innovations,"[75] not all of which were entirely negative. As the number of synagogues declined radically (from ten down to three)[76] the need arose for an alternative means by which to provide the "small-group" affiliation which they had for decades afforded Ferrara's Jewish males. Confraternities, like synagogues, were institutions whose social composition would reflect both the idiosyncrasies of individual choice and, as we have seen, the subtle constellations arising from such larger factors as class, kinship, and ethnic origin. Moreover, like synagogues they could function as hubs of male sociability while providing simultaneously a sense of sacred purpose. Ferrara's *GH* had, in the late sixteenth century, become increasingly synagogue-like in character as it attached itself to a specific locus (its meeting house), gradually shed its women, and, in a variety of ways (such as the absorption of sick children and infants) allowed confraternal membership to acquite an aura of inherent sacrality. It is no wonder, therefore, that as Ferrara's synagogues declined

---

[72] PHGH, 16a (par. 7).

[73] For the figures see Pesaro, *Memorie*, 34, following Frizzi, *Memorie per la storia di Ferrara*, 5, 46 [1809 edn, 5, 44]. For the community's decline in the wake of Duke Alphonso's death see Baron, *Social and Religious History of the Jews*, 89–90.   [74] Roth, *Italy*, 320–1.

[75] Quoted by Baron, *Social and Religious History*, 14, 90.

[76] Azariah de Rossi referred to the ten synagogues of Ferrara at the time of the earthquake of 1571 (*Meor Enayim*, 21) and this number has been generally accepted by scholars. See Shulvass, *Renaissance*, 192.

in number its confraternities actually multiplied, and with the contraction of its Jewish population *GH*, the senior of these confraternities, expanded by 45 percent from forty-four members in 1583 to sixty-four three decades later.

Yet this quantitative leap indicated little about the qualitative nature of *GH* in 1603. The only fine to be increased significantly from its 1583 level was that to be paid for refusing to serve in confraternal office – which was raised five-fold,[77] suggesting a dearth of individuals who were willing to become seriously involved in its activities. As the confraternity became less selective it seems also to have attracted a generally younger membership. The paragraph stipulating the donation to be made by a member upon the marriage of a son or daughter, which had remained substantially unchanged between 1515 and 1583, was now expanded to include the occasion of a member's own marriage – suggesting that more such occasions were now anticipated.

The confraternity's significant expansion in size, proved, however, to be rather short-lived. Thirteen of the sixty-four officially listed members of *GH* in 1603 are also described as having left town, effectively cutting its actual membership down to only fifty-one.[78] Although this number was still quite impressive in light of the Jewish exodus which had begun in 1597, the confraternity's best days, like those of the Ferrara Jewish community as a whole, were behind it. Early in the sixteenth century it had introduced the confraternal mode of piety to Italian Jewry, late in the sixteenth century it had absorbed influences from confraternities elsewhere (notably Bologna), but by the seventeenth century it was the community of Venice which had become the trendsetter in confraternal matters,[79] as in many others, for Italian Jewry as a whole.

---

[77] PHGH, 16a.   [78] *Ibid.*, 16b, 17b.

[79] See Horowitz, "Jewish Confraternal Piety in the Veneto," 301–13, "The Dowering of Brides," 347–71, and "Coffee, Coffeehouses," 17–46.

THE SCUOLE PICCOLE OF VENICE: FORMATIONS
AND TRANSFORMATIONS

RICHARD MACKENNEY

In assembling his "further thoughts" on the *Scuole Grandi* of Venice, Brian Pullan recalled that when he had embarked on Venetian social history in 1959 he had been "much influenced by the doctrine of 'il faut compter'."[1] There can be no doubt that one of the features that makes *Rich and Poor in Renaissance Venice* such a landmark in the historiography of the city (and indeed the state) is the amount of hard data it contains.[2] By focusing on social institutions and the lives of the people whom they touched both directly and indirectly, Professor Pullan's work took the focus of Venetian history away from characterizations of the constitution and placed it on the inhabitants of the city who were not nobles. The Scuole Grandi were, of course, the half-dozen major brotherhoods in the city, and for anyone interested in the characteristics and functions of confraternities in Venice, *Rich and Poor* remains the essential starting point. Certainly this is a book which answers many questions and asks others.

Among the most important was the extent to which such institutions drew off, as it were, the political aspirations of the Venetian citizen class, the *cittadini*. According to Gasparo Contarini, the offices available in the Scuole Grandi played a critical role in maintaining the stability of the state:

they are all restrained under the power and authorities of the Councell of

---

[1] Pullan, "Further Thoughts," 273. All documentary references are to the Archivio di Stato di Venezia, and to its index Provveditori di Comun (PC). The sources used are PC serie Matricule Scuole, registri N, Sestiere di Cannaregio, vol. 1; reg. O, Cannaregio, vol. 2; reg. P, Sestiere di Castello, vol.1; reg. Q, Castello, vol. 2; reg. R, Sestiere di Santa Croce, vol. 1; reg. S, Santa Croce, vol. 2; reg. T, Sestiere di San Marco, vol. 1; reg. U, San Marco, vol. 2; reg. V., San Marco, vol. 3; reg. Z, Sestiere di San Nicolò, vol. 1; reg. AA, San Nicolò, vol. 2; reg. BB, Sestiere di San Polo. In order to keep references as simple as possible, the notes list the letter identifying the relevant register and then appropriate folios (f.). Other references are to the index Scuole Piccole (SP). I am very grateful to the British Academy for its support.   [2] Pullan, *Rich and Poor*.

ten, so that they may not in any thing make any alteration, nor assemble together, unless it be at appointed seasons, without their leave and permission, such honours doe the plebeians of eyther sort attaine unto in this commonwealth of ours, to the end that they should not altogether thinke themselves deprived of publike authority, and civile offices, but should also in some sort have their ambition satisfied, without having occasion either to hate or perturbe the estate of the nobilitie.[3]

Professor Pullan's work demonstrated that there was much more to the activities of the Scuole Grandi than to act as substitutes for political power, and emphasized the importance of organized charity in the maintenance of the social and political order. However, in an extended and searching review article, Reinhold Mueller pointed out that the Scuole Grandi may not have offered support to more than about 10 percent of the Venetian population, which prompted the question of what other agencies may have existed for their support and welfare.[4] Subsequent research and its publication have begun at least to address the question of what sorts of institutions figured in Venetian society more broadly defined.[5]

Within this complex of concerns, the specific role played by the confraternities known as *scuole piccole* to distinguish them from the Scuole Grandi remains shadowy. This is especially so when one seeks to offer a quantitative answer to basic questions such as how many people were members of the scuole and how many scuole were there for them to join. In a modest way, such questions open up broader methodological problems which in turn reflect shifts in the interests of historians in the course of the past three or four decades. This is particularly the case in questions of mentalities (ideas, attitudes, and assumptions) and identities (self-perception and self-awareness), which were constantly in flux. In some ways, what were once seen as continuities over the longue durée were themselves the creation of innumerable sources of mobility.[6] In the specific context of Renaissance Italy, such methodological problems have been confronted (and conquered) in Samuel K. Cohn's quantitative study of wills from six cities in the center of the peninsula, the evidence expansively analyzed in tabular form yet used to sample the "psychological subsoil" of the Renaissance.[7]

As one reviews the character of the scuole piccole and their relation to the social order in Venice, one must acknowledge the frustrations

---

[3] Contarini, *Commonwealth*, 146.   [4] Mueller, "Charitable Institutions."
[5] Romano, *Patricians and Popolani*; Rapp, *Industry*; Davis, *Shipbuilders;* Mackenney, *Tradesmen and Traders.*   [6] The changes are very acutely identified in Burke, "Overture," esp. 5 and 15.
[7] Cohn, *Cult of Remembrance*, quotation from 288.

involved in following the principle "il faut compter." However, the
evidence examined in this chapter is suggestive of a moving reality
which gave the scuole and their members their identities and the
capacity to change them. The autonomy of these institutions in
creating identity perhaps provides food for thought. Professor Greenblatt sets his concept of "self-fashioning" in a context of dawning
individual awareness in the Renaissance partly generated by "a new
assertion of power by both family and state."[8] However, the formation of a new definition of private and public spheres, identified with
the family and the state respectively, cannot be said to have occurred
suddenly. Venetians did not see the sudden invention of such a
separation. In Venice, there survived many agencies which mediated
between family and state. How can we locate and contextualize
confraternities, which we must number among such entities? We
should be cautious about classifying them as public in that they were
clearly not the creation of the state, yet they were public in the sense
that private individuals otherwise excluded from the political processes of public life created their own avenues into the religious space
of a church or the public space of a procession. In that sense, perhaps
they provide evidence of the social construction of public life, and that
in itself may tell us something about their contribution to the maintenance of the social order. While the construction of identity in the
Renaissance may have been generated by "the discovery of the
individual" and of his or her "psychic mobility," it may also be worth
asking whether the history of Venetian confraternities suggests that
the fashioning of identity could also be a collective phenomenon, as
Professor Cohn's analysis of very different evidence seems to indicate.[9]

If we are seeking to give substance to the scuole piccole, then some
form of quantification is essential – "il faut compter" – yet if we
underscore mobility then characterizing structures becomes infinitely
more difficult because they are not static. This means that in what
follows, counter-examples, exceptions, and even contradictions
abound. In order to make sense of them, it is perhaps appropriate to
reflect that while quantification remains fundamental, this is a world in
which perceptions, attitudes, and identities shift and change to such a
degree that the official documentation – which lays down what is
"statutory" and "normal" – is often subverted or led in a dance. With
that in mind, one may begin to see how the confraternities of Venice
were constructed from below rather than merely imposed from
above, and precisely because of this they do not stand still in order to

[8] Greenblatt, *Self-fashioning*, 2.   [9] Cohn, *Cult of Remembrance*, e.g. 243, 247, 286.

be turned into statistics. In this way, one hopes to evoke the social life of Venetians rather than treat "Venice" as an abstract entity with a life of its own, and to relate the history of the scuole to the life cycles of successive generations of humans rather than stressing the continuity of institutional "structures." In an attempt to make sense of evidence which seems quite lacking in pattern, particular attention is given to the degree of government control. For, given the powers which the Venetian state is often thought to have exercised – following the lead given by Contarini quoted above – it is particularly striking that its control of the scuole piccole seems to have been less marked than that in other states which seem to have been less "stable."

In order to underscore the way in which the confraternities were socially constructed rather than politically imposed, one might point to the rather surprising disparities which occur in the records of different government bodies. This is particularly pertinent given the emphasis which Contarini laid upon the role of the Council of Ten as a supervisory body with vigorous regulatory powers. Some years ago, Lia Sbriziolo cataloged the decisions of the Council of Ten relating to the formation and activities of the confraternities between 1310 and 1476.[10] These can be compared with the foundations and records of the comparable period as preserved within the records of the *Provveditori di Comun* on which this paper is based.[11] It seems a rather futile exercise to try to tabulate what the disparities were – the precision would be misleading – and some few comments should suffice. There were thirty-seven entries for various of the scuole piccole over this period in the records of the Ten. Only eight of these confraternities match the data in the statutes compiled by the Provveditori di Comun. Six more are entered in both sets of records, but with different foundation dates. Thus, the Provveditori give a foundation date for the *Scuola di San Lunardo* at San Salvador as 1453, yet it appears in the records of the Ten as 1368.[12] There were two references to scuole formed for different "nazioni" – and whether or not the Provveditori di Comun had any responsibility for these is unclear. Most important of all, no fewer than twenty-one of the Council of Ten's references to scuole – more than half the citations – are not entered at all by the other magistracy. In the case of the scuole piccole,

[10] Sbriziolo, "Confraternite veneziane."
[11] The starting point here is the collection of statutes compiled in the eighteenth century for the Provveditori di Comun. These were surveyed and sampled in Mackenney, "Continuity and Change," but have now been amplified and supplemented by other references to produce a chronological catalogue which is too long to be published here.
[12] U, f. 1r; Sbriziolo, "Confraternite veneziane," 420.

the lack of co-ordination between the Ten and the Provveditori di Comun strongly implies a considerable degree of autonomy in how members – whoever they were, and however few or however many they may have been – fashioned the scuole.

That said, one need not juxtapose a Contarini-style vision of strict order with a reality of chaos and mayhem. What emerges from the documents is that the state's involvement with the scuole piccole is hard to characterize in any simple way. This is perhaps because the scuole take their character from those who formed them rather than fitting a template imposed by the authorities. There is no evidence of growing – or lessening – state involvement. Yet this does not mean that anarchy ruled. Rather, it poses the question of whether the social order was socially created.

The social construction of the confraternities is manifested in a wide variety of ways which roughly correspond to the "formations" and "transformations" of the title. The former include the numbers of people who decided to join a particular scuola, the foundation date and its relationship to the date of the scuola's statute, and the types of scuola which were formed in this way. "Transformations" came about through renewal and refoundation, amalgamation, and agreements – or the reverse – with the church which housed each scuola.

There was certainly no expected "norm" for membership on the part of either government or members: variation is simply enormous. Thus, the *Sovegno della Beata Vergine e San Matteo* clearly refers to 250 members present at a general meeting in 1604, though in 1583 the corresponding figure was only forty-five.[13] The *Sovegno di San Polo* had five founders, recorded twenty-one members present at a general meeting in 1548 but noted in 1559 "siamo al no. di 200." No fewer than 114 votes were cast at what was probably the first meeting of the *Sovegno della Presentazione della Beata Vergine* in 1569 – but only twenty-three were recorded the previous year.[14] In such cases, which is the representative figure? 250 or 44? 5, 21 or 200? 114 or 23?[15] Very few of these organizations record a membership of less than twenty active members attending meetings, and many go much higher than that. There were 142 members at the general meeting of the *Scuola della Beata Vergine e San Cristoforo dei Mercanti* in 1555.[16] The *Scuola di San Cristoforo* at the Giesuiti recorded 304 votes in 1566 – though this is an exception in that membership was compulsory for all makers of velvet.[17]

There are variables of similar proportions when one tries to estab-

---

[13] U, fs. 402r, 376r. [14] B, f. 578r. [15] BB, fs. 2r, 5v, 11r. [16] N, f. 577r.
[17] N, fs. 686v, 687r.

lish precise dates of formation. The Provveditori di Comun for instance list a *sovegno* or mutual aid scheme under the title of *Santa Maria della Celestia* founded at that church in 1707.[18] However, the Scuola della Celestia dates back to 1337, as recorded in its statute in the Archivio di Stato.[19] The *Scuola della Beata Vergine del Rosario* at San Domenico in Castello has a statute in the compilation dated 1619, but Professor Pullan cites evidence of a foundation "soon after 1480."[20]

In some forty cases, there is a clear gap between the foundation of a confraternity and the drawing up of its statute. However, the kind of clarity which the Florentine documentation offers, and which has been so lucidly tabulated by John Henderson, simply cannot be paralleled from the Venetian records.[21] The relationship between foundation and statute is too complicated. Given Venice's reputation as the city of order, and the Florentine record of instability and upheaval, the contrast in the regulation of social institutions is para-doxical.

Among the scuole the gap between foundation and statute is sometimes unremarkable: a foundation of 1525 and a statute of 1530 in the case of the *Beata Vergine Assunta* at San Stin.[22] But it could be much wider. The *Scuola della Madonna* at San Marzilian has a statute of 1420 but dates its foundation to 1402, for instance.[23] In other cases the time lag could be truly extraordinary. The *Scuola di San Giuliano e Carlo* was established in 1277 yet the first recorded government intervention dates from 1559.[24] The oldest of all the foundations was at San Mattia on Murano in 1247, but this is recorded in a statute of 1415 by which time the confraternity had moved to San Bartolomeo at the Rialto.[25] Even in the seventeenth century, there could be a considerable lag.

---

[18] Q, fs. 478r–501r.   [19] SP, b. 726, Santa Maria della Celestia, mariegola, 1337–1764.

[20] Q, fs. 428r–52r; Pullan, "Further Thoughts," 275 and n. 11.

[21] Henderson, *Piety and Charity*, 39.

[22] BB, f. 331r; *mutatis mutandis* 1538 and 1541 for the Scuola di San Felice, PC, O, f. 195r; 1616 and 1619 for the Scuola dell'Inventione della Santissima Croce at San Moise, Q, f. 334v; 1648 and 1653 for the Santissimo Rosario at the Angelo Raffaele, AA, 304r; 1656 and 1663 for the Suffraggio dei Morti at Sant'Agnese; AA, f. 1r. The gap was slightly wider – a foundation of 1596 and a statute of 1607 – in the case of the Beata Vergine delle Grazie at San Marcuola, 1581 and 1590 for the Santissimo Nome di Dio at San Domenico, O, f. 19r; P, f. 263r.

[23] N, f. 413r. About the same applies to San Giuseppe at San Silvestro, founded in 1499 but with a statute from 1515, BB, f. 80r. "Fu dato principio" to the scuola di San Valentin at San Simeon Profeta in 1601, but the mariegola dates only from 1613, R, f. 350v

[24] U, f. 584r. The Scuola di Santi Raffaele e Nicheta has a statute from 1580 which refers back to a foundation exactly 300 years earlier, Q, f. 323r.

[25] V, f. 389r. Less vast a gap, but in its way just as vague, existed in the case of the Scuola di San Giuseppe (Santa Fosca), with a statute from 1642 which refers back to 1580, O, f. 517r. The Scuola di San Leonardo has no precise date before 1626, but we know that the foundation was approved by the Council of Ten in 1395, N, f. 700r; Sbriziolo, "Confraternite veneziane," 421–2.

Santa Maria Elisabetta, a sovegno at San Simeon Profeta, recorded sixteen votes at a meeting of 1616, yet the Council of Ten only gave permission in 1671.[26]

In some cases one finds several stages of foundation itself, epitomizing the theme of formation and transformation around which this essay is organized. For how does one classify the *Scuola della Nattività della Beata Vergine*, which met at Sant'Aponal, but which was begun in 1526 at San Silvestro "by some flour merchants" then moved in 1528 and acquired a statute in 1532?[27] Another shift of corporate identity occurs in the case of the Presentazione della Beata Vergine founded as a scuola in 1533 but as a "new fraternity joined with the Scuola di Madonna Santa Maria" at Sant'Ubaldo, changing to a sovegno or mutual aid society in 1568 and acquiring a new statute in 1591.[28]

For reasons such as these, as analysis proceeded, it rapidly became apparent that the chronology should be based on the first recorded mention of a confraternity rather than the date of its statute. Table 1 is therefore crudely numerical, but includes a loose typology of scuole divided between those devoted to the Virgin, those which celebrated the cult of the Eucharist, and those associated with saints and other holy cults.

The general developmental pattern across time is fairly plain. In the early period, the confraternities tended to take their name from the church in which they met. In the years after 1500 there is a positive avalanche of eucharistic foundations, the full scale of which is only really apparent when one realizes that comparatively few of any other type were founded in that period.

The eucharistic foundations are quite sharply defined, sixty-eight described as "Scuola del Venerabile," two as "Corpo di Cristo," one

---

[26] S, fs. 237r–v. In the case of the suffraggio of the Santissimo Crocefisso at San Gieremia, the date of foundation appears to be 1615, but the statute dates from 1659, N, f. 18v. The sovegno di Sant'Ermolao "set up in the year 1626" in the scuola di San Provolo has a statute dating from 1692, S, f. 421v.

[27] BB, f. 361r. There is a confraternity based round a common occupation in the case of the Sovegno di San Vettor, which seems to have met as a scuola in 1377, though the Ten only gave their permission thirty years after that, and the statute for the mutual aid society dates from 1548, AA, f. 17v. More confusing still is the example of the Scuola di San Rocco e Margarita which met not at a church in Dorsoduro but at San Samuele, and still more perversely had links with the Scuola Grande di San Marco. It appears to have been founded in 1455, yet the statute opens in 1555 with a reference to a mariegola of 1492, U, fs. 421r–2r. The Scuola di Sant'Alvise in the church of that name was founded in 1402 and renewed in 1608, but its statute dates from 1723, N, f. 325r, 326v.

[28] BB, f. 572r. The sovegno of the Beata Vergine and San Matteo at San Samuele apparently dates from 1408, though there was a further change in 1498 when the Scuola di San Matteo e San Samuele came into existence, with the sovegno taking part of its title from the Virgin "renewed and founded" in 1580, U, fs. 368r, 378r.

Table 1. *Confraternity foundations in Venice*

Dates	Marian	Eucharistic	Other	Total
1247–1300	3		7	10
1301–50	3		14	17
1351–1400	5		11	16
1401–50	6		14	20
1451–1500	4	1	15	20
1501–50	13	57	8	78
1551–1600	20	9	24	53
1601–50	23	2	20	45
1651–1700	16		38	54
1701–27	15	1	21	37
1727–63?	13	1	13	27
Totals	121	71	185	377

as "Santa Veneranda." However, the looseness of the other two categories is striking. While "Other" may seem vague, it is a classification which includes much more than merely confraternities named after saints. The titles name sixty-six different saints singly – the most numerous being San Giovanni Battista (six), San Nicolo (six), San Giuseppe (five) and Sant'Antonio (four). A further ten foundations were named after two saints. In this category, however, one also finds forty-two foundations not named after saints: twenty-two associated with the Cross or Crucifix, three with the Trinity, three with the Buona Morte, three with the Nome di Dio.

Of the 121 Marian confraternities, there were thirteen dedicated to the Beata Vergine or the Madonna, ten to the Virgin of the Rosary, eight to the Annunciata, eight to the Nattività, seven to the Assunta, six to the Concezione, five each to the Parto, the Grazie and the Pietà, four to the Carmine, three to the Sette Dolori. Of the eleven cases in which the Virgin was paired with another saint, five were with Sant'Elisabetta.

All three categories contain scuole founded for a specific purpose – "for the extirpation of heretics" was the stated aim of the *Scuola della Beata Vergine del* Rosario at San Giovanni e Paolo – or in commemoration of a special event, such as the Beata Vergine del Terremoto at San Bartolomeo which followed the "greatest and most dangerous earthquake" of 1511.[29] The *Scuola di Sant'Antonio* at Sant'Angelo was founded in 1645 to commemorate the survival of a child thought to have drowned in one of the canals.[30] The *Scuola di San Bernardino* at

[29] Q, f. 34v; V, f. 103r.   [30] T, f. 191r.

San Giobbe, founded in 1450, commemorated the saint's visit to Venice in 1443. (And, to show that the elite was not entirely cut off from such institutions, one might note incidentally that the confraternity benefited from property given by Doge Cristoforo Moro, who was also a member at San Cristoforo.[31])

Moving to transformations, there are twenty-two cases of refoundation or renewal of a statute, with wide variations in the length of time between the original establishment and the renewal. The ancient Scuola di San Stefano at the church of that name was founded in 1299, though the mariegola appears to date from 1493.[32] The corporation in the name of the Beata Vergine Assunta at Sant'Eustachio was first formed in 1400. It was renewed in 1726 but had become a sovegno in 1559.[33] At least those dates are precise, but the *Scuola di San Nicolo* at San Salvador, founded in 1425, recorded that "this blessed congregation was renewed" at an unspecified time, perhaps close to 1545, and there is a similar vagueness in other cases.[34]

The renewal itself could be due to force of circumstance rather than reflecting a more intense popular piety. *The Scuola della Madonna* at Santa Maria Formosa was in existence in 1489, but a new statute was drawn up in 1523, because of theft, as had been the case in "in many other sacred places of monasteries in Venice." The scuola had lost "silverware and altar decorations and silk cloth" as well, "so that our scuola is stripped naked."[35]

Further complications concerning formation and transformation

---

[31] Gramigna and Perissa, *Scuole*, 123–4; Mackenney, "Trade Guilds," 97.

[32] T, fs. 503r, 504r. The Scuola della Beata Vergine Annuntiata dei Zotti dates from 1392, but was renewed in 1527, T, f. 364r. Similarly, the Scuola di San Giobbe apparently began in 1395, but was renewed in 1556, N, f. 124r. The Scuola della Beata Vergine Annuntiata (at Santa Maria Mater Domini) was founded in 1423 and renewed in 1553, S. f. 207r.

[33] R, fs. 101r, 122r. This may be compared with the Sovegno della Beata Vergine e San Matteo, which was founded in 1580, though the foundation incorporates an amalgamation with the Scuola di San Matteo which goes back to 1408, U, fs. 368r, 378r. Similarly, the Scuola di Sant'Alvise has a statute dated 1723, but that had been renewed in 1608 from an original foundation of 1402, N, fs. 325r, 326v. Sometimes, renewal might be the replacement of a tattered statute. Just to illustrate that there was no precise "shelf life" for a mariegola, one might note that the Scuola di San Magno (at San Gieremia in Cannaregio) drew up its first statute in 1423 but did not renew it until 1598, O, f. 31r. San Maurizio e San Gallo degli Albanesi (at San Maurizio) was founded in 1442 but was "newly revised" in 1552, U, f. 33r. The Scuola di San Sebastiano at San Giacomo dell'Orio, which dates from 1463, acquired a new statute in 1553, R, f. 161r. The Scuola della Beata Vergine del Terremoto was founded in 1513 but renewed its statute in 1605, V, f. 104v. One of the very earliest of the Scuole del Venerabile, that at Santa Margarita, dates from 1503, but there are complaints in 1636 about "an old and battered statute book," Z, f. 85r.

[34] T, f. 238v. In the same church, the Scuola della Beata Vergine was founded in 1439 but renewed at some later date, T, f. 289v. The statute of the scuola di Santa Cecilia (at San Cassiano) of 1522 is to "renew and once more raise again [sic] the scuola," though the original foundation is not recorded, S, f. 458v   [35] P, f. 131r.

are generated by the fluid relations between the scuole piccole and other institutions. While it is natural to classify the confraternities of Venice as Scuole Grandi, scuole piccole, and scuole delle arti, it is important to acknowledge the looseness of those categories. It was only in 1467 that the "Scuole Grandi' began to be classified as such – more than 200 years since their earliest foundations.[36] There was a penumbra between the different categories of confraternity. The *Scuola della Beata Vergine e San Cristoforo dei Mercanti* met at Santa Maria dell'Orto, where San Cristoforo moved in 1570 after a dispute with the friars at the Frari – though its foundation date is 1261, and it clearly regarded itself as the equivalent in standing and prestige.[37] The *Scuola di Santi Apostoli* was founded in 1350, but it had been connected with *Santa Maria della Carità* as early as 1288.[38] The mobility of identity is further illustrated in the case of the *Scuola della Beata Vergine del Rosario*, which met at San Giovanni e Paolo. It was dominated by mercers and had links with the *Scuola Grande di San Teodoro* which had been elevated to this status in 1552. The Rosario in turn became a Scuola Grande in 1765 – and one should note that there was a similar late elevation in the status of the *Scuola di Santa Maria dei Carmini*.[39] So, even at the highest level there is evidence of institutions which were "on the move."

With regard to the relationship to the *arti* or trade corporations, in a number of instances, the confraternities had a clear occupational bias. From its foundation in 1337, the Scuola di San Nicolo was reserved for those from the parishes of San Nicolo and San Raffaele who sold fish at Rialto or San Marco.[40] The *Scuola di San Vettor*, which was based at Santa Margarita, was reserved for the boatmen of the traghetto there.[41] Flour merchants founded the Scuola della Nattività at San Silvestro, wine merchants moved it to Sant'Aponal.[42] The mercers dominated at the Santissimo Rosario in San Giovanni e Paolo, and had a strong presence at San Felice.[43] The *Scuola di San Rocco* which met at San Zulian did so in the meeting place of the mercers' guild.[44] The Venerabile, founded at the same church at the very early date of 1502, acknowledged in 1525 that it existed "in the [meeting] place of the mercers' scuola."[45]

Within the jurisdiction of the Provveditori di Comun, there were organizations described as something other than scuole, very occa-

---

[36] Pullan, "Further Thoughts," 274.
[37] Mackenney, "Continuity and Change," 400 and n. 34.   [38] Mackenney, "Trade Guilds".
[39] Q, fs. 32r, 38r, 39v; Gramigna and Perissa, *Scuole*, 100, and on the Carmini, 70.
[40] Z, f. 148v.   [41] AA, f. 21r.   [42] BB, f. 361r.   [43] Q, 32r, 38r; eg. O, fs. 200r, 203r.
[44] U, f. 213r.   [45] U, f. 284v.

sionally the sussidio or suffraggio, more often the mutual aid society or sovegno.[46] Again, a rigid classification is thwarted by change, flux, and interaction. The *Scuola di Santa Catterina*, for example, was founded at Sant'Eustachio in 1324, but the sovegno of the same name and place began only in 1677.[47] The *Scuola di San Michiel Arcangelo* at Santa Maria dell'Orto was first formed in 1452, the corresponding sovegno in 1706, though the latter had grown out of the *Scuola del Venerabile* at Santa Sofia dating from 1507.[48]

The transformation was reversed in the case of San Nicola which met at San Stefano from 1652, when it was a sovegno, though it became a scuola twenty years later.[49] But there is no need to assume that the typology had to be progressive over time: the two types of corporation were not mutually exclusive. Permission was given for a sovegno in the name of Sant'Ermolao at San Simeon Profeta in 1692, acknowledging that there had been a "sovegno nella scola di San Provolo" in 1626.[50] San Giovanni Battista, which met at San Giovanni on the Giudecca, was described as a "sovegno della scuola."[51] The scuola and sovegno of San Sebastiano at the church of that name referred to "the brethren and sisters both of the scuola and the sovegno."[52]

But sometimes the institutions were more strictly separated. The sovegno of San Nicolo was designed for members of the "ancient scuola," membership of which was obligatory for joining the sovegno – a provision repeated at San Vicenzo, San Pietro Martire e Santa Caterina da Siena – yet the Provveditori di Comun ruled that the gastaldo of the Scuola di San Nicolo was *not* in charge of the sovegno.[53]

---

[46] Mackenney, "Continuity and Change," 395.

[47] R, fs. 40r, 417r. The Scuola di Santa Marina in the church of that name was founded in 1324 and the sovegno in 1595, Q, fs. 210r, 225r. The Scuola della Madonna at Santa Maria Formosa was in existence by 1489, acquired a new statute in 1523 and was complemented by a sovegno of the same name in 1594, P, fs. 136v, 131r, 664r.

[48] O, fs. 582r, 227r. Although the Scuola della Beata Vergine degli Angeli at Santa Trinità dated its foundation to 1621, the sovegno was formed only in 1720, Q, fs. 69r, 411r. A scuola del Rosario was founded at San Paternian in 1669 but it became a sovegno in 1698, V, fs. 244r, 250v. The Scuola di Sant'Apollonia at San Barnaba was founded in around 1559, but became a sovegno in 1673, Z, fs. 505r, 519r. The Scuola di Santa Caterina da Siena at the Servi, formed in 1599, became a sovegno in 1686, N, fs. 168r, 186r.   [49] V, fs. 134r, 134v.   [50] S, f. 421v.

[51] AA, f. 490r.   [52] Z, f. 9r.

[53] AA, fs. 256v, 259r; P, f. 214v. On this mobility of identity, one notes also the Scuola della Beata Vergine Assunta at Sant'Eustachio, founded in 1400, with a "scola di sovegno" set up in 1559 and a "restoration" in 1726, and similarly, the Beata Vergine e San Matteo was "renewed and founded" in 1580 as a sovegno, yet dates back to 1408 as a scuola, R, fs. 122r, 101r; U, fs. 368r, 378r. For other examples, see the Scuola della Presentazione della Beata Vergine which was founded in 1533, became a sovegno in 1568 and dated its statute to 1591, BB, fs. 572v, 574r, 572r; and Santa Maria

The interaction of scuole and sovegni is symptomatic of a broader phenomenon of amalgamation, absorption and indeed some conflict, as is evidenced by a dozen or so cases. The *Scuola della Beata Vergine e San Matteo* with a statute of 1580, for example, represents an amalgamation with the *Scuola di San Matteo e San Samuele* founded in 1408.[54] The *Scuola della Madonna* which dated back to 1402 disputed its title with *Santa Maria dei Mercanti*.[55] As a mixture of types, the *Scuola di San Giuseppe* at San Silvestro is particularly involved. It was founded in 1499, though it only obtained approval in 1515. It emphasized the importance of the Eucharist as a protection against the devil. It stored its valuables with the *Scuola di Santi Alessandro e Vicente* at the same church, and acknowledged the desirability of joint meetings given that the majority of brethren were members of both associations.[56]

The compatibility of the cult of the Eucharist with the traditional devotions of the scuole is striking. The eucharistic foundations, which represent a decisively new type of confraternity – parish-based with strong Roman associations – show no sign of being monitored, still less policed, with any extra scrutiny. That new types of scuola were not regulated any more closely is suggested by the example of the Venerabile at San Vitale, which was in existence by 1520, has records from 1546 but no written rules or constitution.[57] The Venerabile at Sant'Angelo had been in existence "for many years" by 1522, that at Santa Trinità was among the large number founded in 1507, though the first date in the statute is 1623.[58] That was also the year in which the Venerabile at Santi Simeon e Tadeo received its statute, though the scuola was "begun many years ago," and the Provveditori di Comun had given permission for the formation in 1572.[59]

As table 1 shows, the Scuole del Venerabile made an overwhelming impact in the early part of the sixteenth century. All the same, these brotherhoods sometimes grew out of existing confraternities and there is clear evidence that the old and new institutions could accommodate each other. The Scuola del Venerabile formed in 1544 at Santa Maria Nova had previously been a *Scuola della Madonna*. It was no exception.[60] The eucharistic brotherhood at San Biasio was founded in

---

della Morte, founded as a suffraggio, which was a "confraternity called a suffraggio" and shared a chapel with the Scuola of the Sacrament at San Basso, V, fs. 1r, 2v.

[54] U, f. 378r.   [55] N, f. 441r.

[56] BB, fs. 8or, 72v, 82r. The Sovegno di San Vicenzo, San Pietro Martire and Santa Caterina da Siena was founded in 1594, but the scuola had existed since 1458 and membership of the scuola was a precondition of joining the sovegno itself, P, f. 214r; Q, f. 627r; P, f. 214v; see also Gramigna and Perissa, *Scuole*, 100.   [57] V, f. 466r.   [58] T, f. 110r; P., f. 51r.   [59] S, fs. 273r-v, 278v.

[60] O, f. 286v. The Scuola della Beata Vergine Assunta at Santa Sofia, its statute dated 1589, took an altar formerly tended by the Scuola del Venerabile which had moved to the chapel of

1544, yet permission was granted to "set up a scuola of the Virgin to be joined with this of the Most Holy Sacrament" in 1560. The latter was therefore formed and absorbed at one and the same time.[61] The Venerabile at Sant'Antonin was referred to as the "scuola del Venerabile e San Saba" in 1609, deriving part of its identity from the *Scuola di San Saba* which dated back to 1399.[62]

There was devotional assimilation as well. The *Scuola di Santa Catterina* at San Giminiano was founded as early as 1436 and combined traditional imagery of an uncertain voyage with a warning to beware of the devil and a reminder that man is made in the image of God, the latter two characteristics much more readily associated with the eucharistic confraternities of the early sixteenth century.[63]

The brotherhood which met in the church of Corpus Domini is even more of a mish-mash. It had its first meeting licensed by the Provveditori di Comun in 1644, though its statute may date from either 1696 or 1714. However, we know that this church was the home of the very first eucharistic brotherhood in Venice from 1395 – though that foundation is not recorded by the Provveditori di Comun. The foundation date is in fact given as 1504, but the statute emphasizes its links to the *Scuola di San Girolamo*.[64]

The cumulative effect of these examples prompts a question which may be obvious but which needs to be asked. What constitutes "formation"? A meeting? If so, of how many people, and how convened? In any case, what did people assemble for, and what made them come in the first place? In the case of the *Suffraggio della Santissima Croce* at Santa Maria Mater Domini, we know that an altar was dedicated in 1551, and the statute drawn up three years later.[65] "Fu eretta" the *Scuola del Santissimo Abito della Beata Vergine del Carmine* in 1594, with a statute following in 1597.[66] But what separates the fact that the *Scuola di San Valentin at San Simeon Profeta* "was given a start" in 1601, from the dating of its statute in 1613?[67] Santa Maria del Carmine, which met at Sant'Angelo di Concordia on the Giudecca,

---

Sant'Antonio, O, fs. 446v–7r. Similarly the Scuola di San Carlo at San Leonardo took over an altar when the eucharist was moved, presumably to the high altar, N, f. 139v. The Suffraggio di Santa Maria della Morte shared a chapel with the Scuola del Santissimo Sacramento at San Basso, V, f. 2v.

[61] Q, f. 463r. The Scuola del Venerabile at San Pantalon traced its origins back to the Scuola di San Pantalon, with which it was amalgamated in 1530, Z, f. 438v. The Venerabile at San Provolo was joined in 1517 with the Scuola di San Zaccaria e San Lizier, Q, f. 255r.

[62] P, fs. 120r, 102r. There was another ancient connection for the eucharistic confraternity at San Zuan in Bragora which linked itself to the Scuola di San Zan Battista dating back to 1322, P, f. 81r.

[63] T, f. 62r. There is a similar injunction in the case of the Scuola di San Giuseppe at San Silvestro BB, f. 72v.   [64] O f. 368r, 385r, 380v; Gramigna and Perissa, *Scuole*, 47.   [65] S, f. 105r.

[66] AA, f. 128r.   [67] R, f. 350v.

records that "the devotion was initiated" in 1607, though the statute is from 1635.[68]

What happened in the interim in each case? Were there regular meetings, elections of officers, collections of fees? Perhaps it is not always helpful to see the written document as driving the activity it records. From another point of view, that of how a confraternity was perceived, identity – seen as physical presence and material impact – may have developed in ways which a statute *acknowledged* rather than in ways which a statute *laid down*. There are some important traces of physical activity and material changes within the documentary record. There were processions, for instance.[69] The *Scuola della Beata Vergine delle Grazie* at San Marcuola had a procession in praise of the Virgin:

> with appropriate candlelight, saints, and music with the Most Reverend chapter of the aforesaid church, and other ceremonies, the picture from the altar raised on high by four subdeacons, and we exert ourselves with the aid of the Most Blessed Virgin making our way along the Fondamenta dei Servi and the Rioterra.[70]

The *Scuola di Sant'Antonio da Padova* (which met at the Frari) specified that to honor the saint's feast day, the following would need to be carried:

> the banner with six large candles adorned with greenery, then the [pictures of?] miracles of Sant'Antonio carried by children dressed as angels, and after them, the banner of the friars with the young friars dressed up and then those with the pluvials with the reliquaries in their hands. After them 12 torches of 2 or 3 pounds hoisted on supports with greenery and in the middle of them the float of Messer Sant'Antonio decorated as is required with silver, candlesticks and other ornaments ... and then the singers and the mass prepared by the reverend friars together and thus all the officers are to be accompanied ... and thus our brethren are to accompany one another after the officers according to their stations ... and are to go around Rialto as was the ancient custom and then return to our church.

And the event was to be publicized, for on the evening before,

> a decorated float must be sent and with a child dressed as an angel, and with trombones and pipes to San Marco and Rialto, and through the angel is to announce the feast to the people ... so that our feast is attended by the people and a reminder is given to our brethren to come.[71]

Such arrangements required the co-operation of the clergy in the

[68] AA, f. 467r.
[69] See the analysis of one route in Mackenney, "Public and Private."   [70] O, fs. 19r–v.
[71] BB, fs. 63r–v.

church in which a particular confraternity was housed. However, even in this matter there is evidence of movement, and some scuole shifted their location. San Mattia moved from the namesake church in Murano to San Bartolomeo and had done so by 1415.[72] Founded in 1346, the *Scuola di San Francesco* at the church of San Francesco della Vigna moved to the Frari ten years later.[73] The *Scuola di Sant'Antonio da Padova* first met in March 1439 at San Simeon Profeta, but moved to the Frari within a couple of months.[74] San Giacomo had originally met at San Salvador, but moved to San Giacomo dell'Orio at an unspecified date.[75] The *Scuola della Concettion della Beata Vergine de Ciechi* was founded in 1315 and met in the church of Santa Maria in Broglio, but it moved to San Moise, perhaps in 1595.[76] The *Scuola della Nattività della Beata Vergine* first met at San Silvestro in 1526 but transferred to Sant'Aponal in 1532.[77] The Beata Vergine della Salute moved from San Vio in 1638 because of lack of space, to the church of the Spirito Santo.[78]

The moves were not always practical and amicable. As we have seen, the Scuola di San Cristoforo moved from the Frari after a dispute with the friars there. And there was a real identity crisis in the case of the *Scuola della Presentazione*, which was founded at Sant'Ubaldo in 1533, revamped as a sovegno in 1568 and acquired a new statute in 1591. After quarreling with the priests in 1569, consideration was given to leaving the church, but this was rejected.[79]

There were considerations which may have militated against such moves. Among the most important were the embellishments which a scuola might make to the fabric of the church in which it met, and which might be difficult to transfer to another location either physically or contractually. Here again, one has a sense of extra laminations of objects and decorations being added over time, sometimes long periods of time, through the more or less modest patronage of the confraternities, but nonetheless contributing to a continuously evolving appearance.[80] There could be a physical transformation: the *Scuola della Santissima Trinità* at Santa Trinità was founded in 1418, but was knocked down to make way for the church of the Salute in 1631.[81]

There are other cases of change which can be measured in terms of material appearance. The *Suffraggio della Santissima Croce* met at San

[72] V, f. 389r.   [73] BB, f. 294r.   [74] BB, f. 52v.
[75] R, f. 323r.   [76] U, fs. 487v, 525r.   [77] BB, f. 361r.
[78] Z, f. 181v.   [79] BB, fs. 572r, 574r, 578v.
[80] On artistic patronage, see Brown, *Narrative Painting*, and, on the Scuole del Venerabile, see Cope, *Chapel of the Sacrament*.
[81] Gramigna and Perissa, *Scuole*, 62.

Salvador from 1500 (though it may have been a scuola at this early stage). It acquired a gilt cross in 1501, torch holders and candlesticks in 1505, supporting harness, a reliquary and a velvet cloth for the dead in 1512, a large carpet in 1516.[82] The *Scuola del Venerabile* at San Silvestro also recorded the way in which it had refashioned the interior of the church

> witness the expense on the said church, that is on the altar, on galleries, taking out the pulpit, removing it from the side of the Holy Sacrament to the side of [the chapel] of Sant'Alessandro, taking out the barriers in the small choir underneath, making the church spacious and light and also having taken out of it the sacristy which was down below the choir [?] for our own greater comfort, all at our cost, expense and interest, and this having been done by the Scuola del Santissimo Sacramento.[83]

Most revealingly, the eucharistic brotherhood at San Basso recorded the acquisitions and projects initiated by successive wardens between 1568 and 1626: a desk, a tapestry, gilding, a painting of the Last Supper with a protective cover, a brass lamp, an ivory pax. In 1602, Antonio Buffeli, bookseller at the Aquila Negra "seeing the pictures of this scuola completely ruined by being so old" offered to pay for

> the picture of Our Lord in the garden and that for no other purpose than zeal for things divine, and also to give heart to all the other Wardens who succeed him in their good works.

But his thirty ducats were not enough. In 1607, he offered "to make two windows in the said church," in 1614 another warden offered "two gilt candlesticks" and in 1626 was acquired "the gilt leather which serves as decoration for the altar of the Holy Sacrament."[84]

So often our views of Venetian "stability," or "continuity" are shaped by the finished or decaying face of the city in the nineteenth century, that it may be salutary to remind ourselves from time to time how the city's appearance was constructed over many years by many generations.[85]

In this attempt to write the history of the scuole piccole "from below," the very diversity of the materials can be confusing. In many

---

[82] U, fs. 111bisv–12v.   [83] BB, f. 492v

[84] The chronology runs as follows: 1568 – "the counter or desk of nutwood;" 1570 – "the large tapestry;" 1571 – "the picture of the [Last] Supper with the friezes," when also "the decoration on the picture of the Supper was gilded;" 1574 – "the cover of blue canvas which protects the picture of the Supper;" 1575 – "three racks;" 1577 – "the gilding of the four carved candlesticks and holders;" 1584 – "crystal windows with an image of the Holy Sacrament on them;" 1585 – "brass lamp;" 1588 – "the ivory pax gilded and framed in ebony." V, fs. 50r, 51r, 51v, 52r, 53r–v, 54r–v.

[85] Pemble, *Venice Rediscovered*.

ways, the scuole conform to general trends such as the "laicisation of religion" in the late middle ages.[86] Perhaps the diversity and vitality of their religion is a rather stronger expression of that process, and one wonders whether it owes something to the relatively slight influence of the Mendicant orders which proved to be so definitive elsewhere in determining the character of piety.[87] Moreover, there is little evidence of Tridentine discipline directly affecting the scuole in the later sixteenth century.[88]

Having pointed to the apparent autonomy of devotional initiatives among the Venetian laity from both the state and the church, one might return to the question of what, if anything, their collective self-fashioning contributed to the stability of the city's political life. At the start of this paper, one suggested that stability might be the product of movement. There is a sense in which that idea is sharpened by study of the scuole. In many ways they seem less organized, less policed even than confraternities elsewhere. But they pose a problem which takes us to the heart of Venetian historiography: the state and what it meant to the inhabitants of the city.

Here, the focus on mentalities and identities is of critical importance. People could identify with the name of the local church and any saint one might mention. In many cases, in the naming of confraternities, as in the decoration of the home, the Virgin Mary is ubiquitous. Nearly one third of all the confraternities (121 of 378) are associated with her cult. There may be nothing remarkable in that. However, other sources suggest that there may well have been a close but essentially non-political identification between the Virgin and Venice herself.

Yet – and what an extraordinary thought after 377 statutes which seem to offer no pattern at all – only one confraternity, and not one of the 377 scuole piccole, but the Scuola Grande which met near San Giovanni e Paolo, is named after St. Mark. Coupled with the absence of his image from the non-noble home, this serves to show what an uncompromisingly political figure he was.[89] "Marco" could be shouted in the streets in the support of the state, but the city's patron was really not the property of all of the city's inhabitants: he belonged firmly to those who fashioned the state.[90] Did it never occur to people who founded several hundred confraternities over more than three

86 Goldthwaite, *Wealth and the Demand for Art*, 104, 114–21.
87 Cohn, *Cult of Remembrance*, 201.
88 Cf. Black, *Italian Confraternities*; Torre, 'Politics Cloaked in Worship.'
89 Palumbo-Fossatti, "L'interno."
90 Mackenney, "Public and Private."

centuries that they might identify with the city's patron saint? He is mentioned in preambles, but no foundation among the scuole piccole takes his name. Did he perhaps represent the supreme collectivity with which all Venetians could identify, and did that lead to a sort of blanking out of his presence in the popular mind? That takes us much too close to anachronistic concepts of brainwashing, but it also brings home how hard it is to understand the thoughts and concerns of people in past time, especially in the case of how they related to each other and to the world around them. It may be the case that the scuole piccole helped to construct the Venetian social order, but there is also a sense in which their movement nourished the stability of a greater whole, and in that sense they may have been minnows within Leviathan.

RELAUNCHING CONFRATERNITIES IN THE TRIDENTINE ERA: SHAPING CONSCIENCES AND CHRISTIANIZING SOCIETY IN MILAN AND LOMBARDY

DANILO ZARDIN

"Christendom's true Paradise." According to the writers and travelers of the late sixteenth century, Lombardy, one of the wealthiest and most densely populated regions in Europe, retained its pre-eminence as "the richest and most civilised part of Italy." Within Lombardy, the western portion embraced by the State of Milan formed one of the key dominions in the network of the Habsburgs' "Monarquía universal," created after the conclusion of the wars in Italy and the decline of Charles V's dream of domination. With the disturbances of the long military conflict behind it and the end of alternating subjection to the French and Spanish crowns, Milan had rebuilt itself as a center for communications and as a focus for stability within a framework which encompassed the local political bodies of the surroundings and subordinated existing institutions and power structures by calling on them to cooperate with the new demands emanating from the "center," yet at the same time did not suppress entirely local independence, customs and privileges.[1]

Madrid was too distant for Spain to govern with absolutist despotism and bureaucratic thoroughness. It was obliged to submit to a continual process of negotiation and adjustment, from which each of the parties involved – those who wielded sovereign power on the one hand and the mass of civil society on the other – sought to gain advantage. All the protagonists of the region – the vigorous inheritors of the military and landowning aristocracy, those who controlled the complex feudal powers which held sway in the countryside, the patrician families of the leading

---

The following abbreviations are used in the notes: *Acta Ecclesiae Mediolanensis*, 1582 and 1599/2 (*AEM*); Archivio Storico Diocesano di Milano (ASDMi); Biblioteca Ambrosiana, Milano (BAMi).
[1] Sella, *Crisis and Continuity*, 1–23.

urban centers, the ministers and courtiers at the service of the Spanish representatives, and the Church hierarchy newly triumphant in its hold on religious power despite the attacks of Protestant reformers – all these groups had a role to play in the interlocking power games which took place in the space thus opened up between sovereign power and society. Here they could display their status, deploy their plans for action, and negotiate for recognition, delegation, favors, agreements, economic and moral support. In such a context and at a time when religious divisions were deepening and hardening, it was inevitable that the reforms of the Church and its post-Tridentine desire to oversee the whole of traditional Christian life took root in terrain which was promising but also difficult and delicately balanced. Within such a complex dialectical situation, priests, regular orders, and ministers of religion were expected to find the most effective ways of putting the Papacy's new religious strategies into practice, while at the same time making sure they did not go against the interests of the Spanish crown and of the social elites. In the interests of building a collective order based on the newly emergent logic of "raison d'état," the clergy had to establish a kind of osmosis with the other leading institutions of government and administration in Milan – the Spanish governor, the Senate, the civil magistrature, the municipal bodies – while at the same time seeking to rival and supplant their influence. As one of the proponents of such a theory, Giovanni Botero, declared with frank realism, reflecting the widespread anti-Machiavellian thinking of the time: "Religion is the root of all principalities, for all authority derives from God; since religion is the only way to obtain the grace and favor of God, any other foundation would be disastrous."[2]

A considerable part of the State of Milan under Spanish rule constituted the diocese of the archbishop of Milan, among the most extensive and heavily populated episcopal sees in the Mediterranean Catholic world. Set between the rivers Ticino and Adda, it spread from the fertile and intensely cultivated agricultural plains of the Milanese lowland to the hills and mountains of the pre-Alps between lakes Maggiore, Lugano, and Como, and extended outside the frontiers of the state itself, with the valleys of Blenio, Riviera, and Leventina, to take in the district of Airolo, at the foot of the Gotthard in Switzerland. Great distances and great diversity in social life and natural setting, all united by the ubiquity of human settlements and the closely interwoven threads of the ecclesiastical fabric, especially in the plains north of Milan and in the foothills of the Alps. The local communities of this latter area were known for their rootedness and strong sense of their own identity: tenacious in their

---

[2] See Borromeo, "La Corona spagnola," and "L'arcivescovo Carlo Borromeo." For the quotation from Botero, see Botero, *Della ragion di stato*, book 2, "Della religione," 74–5.

resistance to the intrusion of outside powers, proud of their own *campanile*, of the loyalty of the clergy whom they supported financially, and of the vitality of the various long-established lay associations active within the parishes. In total there were nearly 800 parishes, more than 2,000 churches (without counting those of the regular clergy), several thousand monks and nuns, in a total population estimated as not less than 600,000. At the centre of the diocese lay Milan with a population of approximately 120,000. Round Milan there were large towns whose inhabitants were engaged in the same manufacturing and commercial activities which had brought wealth to the capital, together with somewhat smaller towns, with no more than 3,000 inhabitants, which acted as centers for large parts of the surrounding countryside with their fairs and markets, the prestige of their noble families, and the religious and administrative facilities which they were able to provide.[3]

It was to take up in person his post as Archbishop of the diocese that Carlo Borromeo returned to Milan from Rome at the beginning of 1566, after the death of his uncle Pius IV, who had originally called him to serve in the Papal court. He had already decided to oppose the spirit of indulgence and compromise which had characterized his predecessors' approach to the secular authorities in a period when the episcopacy's jurisdictional authority had been obscured. With his energy and openness to the ideals of Catholic reform, Borromeo quickly showed that he was fully aware of the importance for the Church of establishing a firm hold over the laity and of strengthening its claim in opposition to others as an institutional authority fitted to rule over the lives of individual communities. Borromeo had already developed detailed ideas on these matters before he returned to Milan, in his frequent contacts with the representatives who acted for him while he was still in Rome. Such ideas are expressed in a letter dated April 1566 and addressed to Giovanni Francesco Bonomi, a prelate who had remained in Rome but was later to join Borromeo in his program of Church reform in northern Italy:

> My aim in governing the laity is to introduce as far as it is in my power to do so the habit of frequenting the sacraments as the most effective guard against all sins and evil behaviour; I have therefore already proposed establishing in every parish a company of the SS. Sacramento to which all the leading families of the place would belong and which would promote many rules to the benefit of their lives . . . I also propose setting up another company "della Carità" whose business it will be to discover all the parishioners' temporal and spiritual needs so that they can always be dealt

---

[3] *AEM*, 1599, statistical tables in appendix; Caprioli, Rimoldi and Vaccaro (eds.), *Diocesi di Milano*, 375–613.

with as far as possible by the local priest or by the Archbishop; this has the additional benefit that it involves the gentry in religious works.[4]

This declaration of intent already shows the fundamental principle which would guide Borromeo throughout his work: his wish to make more orderly the proliferation of lay associations which channeled local religious life by bringing them under the aegis of a few specially authorized organizations, set up for the benefit of the whole community and directly under the control of the parish. For this purpose, Borromeo was prepared to enter into conflict with the centuries-old tradition of autonomy and group privilege which these strong but always "centrifugal" lay associations had long enjoyed. He was firmly in favor of making membership of the confraternity dedicated to the celebration of the Eucharist obligatory, since this sacrament not only symbolized the renewed strength of Catholic identity but also brought the whole community of the faithful together in the parish churches. The confraternity's devotional practices would be simplified in their original spirit and it would be open to all the inhabitants of each parish. The eucharistic confraternities would, moreover, work together with the similarly publicly oriented and openly structured confraternities "della Carità," which, as their name implies, were established for the purpose of distributing alms and welfare. Both these organizations had already been singled out by the more pastorally oriented bishops of the early sixteenth century such as Gian Matteo Giberti in Verona, whose early attempts at reform would be taken up in the post-Tridentine period by successors who wished to apply them more generally and more widely.[5]

In the view of these churchmen, lay associations should not merely serve to protect and encourage the pious devotions of individuals, but seek to shape the whole of their behavior by opposing "religious works" and "rules beneficial to holy living" to the corrupting fascination of "sin" and "evil ways." In order to strengthen its power to transform, the program of redirecting individual and social behavior towards Christian values was to be aimed not at all believers without distinction but in the first instance to those placed at the head of the highly hierarchical society of the time: those whose prestige and worldly power reinforced their capacity to guide, command, and persuade (Borromeo's "gentlemen", or in more general terms "all the leading persons of the city").

[4] BAMi, cod. F 37 inf., f. 111–3. See Marcora, "Nicolò Ormaneto," 355–6. There are modern interpretations of Borromeo and his activities, together with up-to-date bibliographies, in Buzzi and Zardin (eds.), *Carlo Borromeo*. On Bonomi, see Headley, "Borromean reform."

[5] Sources and bibliography can be found in Zardin, "Solidarietà di vicini," 379–96, and "Il rilancio delle confraternite," 128–30.

The effects which Borromeo's proposals were intended to bring about can be clearly seen in Lombardy in the late sixteenth to seventeenth centuries. Obligatory and universal membership of what were to be firmly parish-based Corpus Christi confraternities became the lynch-pin of Borromeo's pastoral strategy; an importance which was already adumbrated in the decrees issued by the bishops of the ecclesiastical province of Milan in their first post-Tridentine council in October 1565, the year before Borromeo's return. Subsequent Church legislation in the years which followed confirmed these priorities; they were enforced in the instructions which the episcopal visitors left for each parish after they had carried out their inspection, and they came to bulk large in the treatises and practical manuals designed for the use of parish clergy, with all the subsequent work of revision and adaptation which fed into the broader Catholic tradition, beyond the diocese of Milan, of strategies for governing the faithful.[6] Alongside the new "scholae" where clergy could work to catechize the laity and instruct the young in the new and more austere model of Christian morality, the eucharistic confraternities spread rapidly to take in even the weakest and most marginal parishes, filling the gaps which had been left after they first emerged, before the Council of Trent, in the early sixteenth century. However old or new the confraternity was, Borromeo's ever-vigilant collaborators in the diocesan Curia were ready with a scheme of standardized rules printed on sheets which were to be widely distributed and applied without distinction in every locality. The text of the new "general rules" was made available as early as 1569 and was frequently reproduced as one of two columns of print, the other containing the rules for the twin-confraternity "della Carità." Both sets of rules were later inserted into the corpus of laws of the *Acta Ecclesiae Mediolanensis*, printed in 1582, the code which served as a framework of reference for much of the legislation on local church government throughout the post-Tridentine Catholic world.[7]

The success of this campaign in favor of the eucharistic confraternities, promoted by the episcopacy in support of the parishes, is well-documented. Diocesan statistics up to the end of the sixteenth century – which were probably gathered for inclusion in the reports presented periodically to the Papal authorities during the course of the "visitatio ad limina Sancti Petri" and which were later published as an appendix

---

[6] Zardin, *Confraternite e vita di pietà*, 24–5; "Solidarietà di vicini," 395; "Il rilancio delle confraternite," 130–1.

[7] Zardin, "Solidarietà di vicini," 375–6, 395; ASDMi, Sezione XIII, 49; *AEM*, f. 335rv.

to the second edition of the *Acta* in 1599 – show that in a total of at least 772 parish churches, there were 556 confraternities dedicated to the SS. Sacramento as opposed to 130 Marian and 133 flagellant confraternities (the latter usually had their own building and distinctive vestments, and their duties comprised weekly meetings to recite the Divine Office and participation in public processions). We find the same disproportion, as far as the city is concerned, reported in a religious guide to Milan written at the same time, the *Descrizione storica delle chiese, de' monasteri, delle confraternite e de' luoghi pii di Milano*, which also provides valuable information on the functions carried out by the eucharistic confraternities.[8] This predominance of eucharistic confraternities is confirmed in many other documents of the mid-seventeenth century, such as the census of diocesan confraternities set up by Archbishop Alfonso Litta in November 1656.[9]

As they spread from the leading cities and towns down to the poorest rural parish, far more successfully than the less popular confraternities "della Carità," the confraternities of the SS. Sacramento were also remarkable for their inclusiveness. They were open to men and women from all social classes in a move to include all the families resident within a particular neighborhood, parish, or quarter, initially at least by ensuring that the adult heads of families were members. In bringing families together in this way they were also a means of focusing local religious life on what was intended to be its active center, the parish church, although its authority was frequently either in need of reinforcement or had yet to be constructed. The power of the parish church was superimposed on the various meeting points and dividing lines of the more loosely organized and more flexibly structured religious life of the past. What figures are available, especially for the closing years of the sixteenth century when the initial wave of Borromeo's reforms throughout the diocese had begun to settle, show individual enrollments in the order of tens or frequently hundreds, with an average in certain areas of about 20 percent of the total population or, more precisely, 30–35 percent of the so-called "anime da comunione," the inhabitants aged ten years and over who could receive communion and from whom the regular membership of the lay confraternities was drawn.[10] The situation is much the same

---

[8] BAMi, cod. A 202 suss., f. 10v: "In each parish church, with the exception perhaps of two or three, there is a 'scuola' named after Corpus Domini to which the inhabitants of the parish belong..." The full citation can be found in Ratti, "Scuole," 53–4.

[9] ASDMi, XIII, vol. 34. See Zardin, *San Carlo Borromeo*, 59–61.

[10] ASDMi, Sezione X. See Zardin, *Confraternite e vita di pietà*, 70–2, and "Confraternite e comunità," 707–8, 723–4.

in Milan and in the larger outlying towns such as Monza, Busto, Gallarate, and Varese which shared many characteristics with the capital. In these places, the parish tended to break up into the various quarters of the city. Borromeo's new confraternities, like the brother-hoods which had preceded them and were on occasion absorbed into them, were able to merge into the structures of neighborhood author-ity and identity by bringing together the middle and higher-ranking families (ignoring the homeless and other marginalized groups but also excluding the aristocracy with their privileges) and thus transforming themselves into what were in effect territorially based organisations of co-ordination and representation rather than free and selective associ-ations presiding over a restricted number of the faithful. One such urban eucharistic confraternity, S. Giorgio al Palazzo, is described thus in the episcopal report of 1656: "It is governed by a prior and his deputy, a treasurer, a chancellor, and others from the parish; the number of members ('scolari') is not limited: all parishioners can vote at the chapter meetings, which are never held without the presence of the provost and the canon curate, or of one of them at least."[11]

In addition to their openness to the entire community and accom-panying disregard for its rigid distinctions of class, profession, or membership in privileged corporate bodies, the other striking feature of the great confraternities was their ability to build a form of religious practice which had mass appeal and which could influence public opinion and reshape local traditional customs and their calendar. They were able to play a leading part in the administrative and thus in a certain sense political control of collective life through the institutions which functioned within local society, the religious institutions ahead of all others. The confraternities provided a vehicle for the spread of certain ideas, values, rules and prohibitions: certain forms of behavior, obedience, and restraint in the interests of social harmony could be filtered through them; they could bring pressure to bear on the moral behavior of individuals and on the whole web of social relationships which operated round them; and they could work to co-ordinate the economic and material resources of the community. Both the secular and the regular clergy could use them to widen their field of influence and their audience. It was for these reasons that the bishops in the dioceses of central and northern Italy who were working alongside Borromeo to introduce the Tridentine reforms, sought like him to

---

[11] ASDMi, XIII, vol. 34, fasc. 2. See also Curatolo, "Notabili a Milano," 62, 66–8; for an example of this fusion of neighborhood and confraternal associations in a rural area, see Zardin, "Confraternite e comunità," 706. On recruitment of members for the confraternity, see Bottoni, "Per la storia," 66–117.

exploit the tradition of the local confraternities and focus it on the parish-based cult of the Eucharist, which lay at the heart of a Church whose institutions and organization – from the episcopal summit down to the poorest and most distant rural benefice – had been infused with new strength.[12]

But in order to teach these religious values and devotional disciplines it was not necessary to draw only on those confraternities which had been established by Church authorities for specific purposes, such as those of the SS. Sacramento, formed for the veneration of the Host, that compelling symbol of Christian unity, or those "della Carità," formed to carry out the charitable duties which were the direct ethical consequence of such veneration. Ecclesiastical authorities could not fail to take account of the whole lively tradition of confraternal activity inherited from the preceding two centuries, an inheritance which under new forms of management could be more effectively utilized for new educational and pastoral purposes. This is why the post-Tridentine church reformers did not simply impose a uniform and authoritarian discipline over lay confraternal activities but, faced with such robust and diversified traditions, tried a variety of approaches. They did not attempt to eliminate the living inheritance of the past but opened up a complex dialogue with it. The attempt to introduce hierarchical authority, to remove rooted traditions, to impose uniformity was bound up with a paternalist approach to governing men and institutions, one which was always ready to compromise and postpone for tactical purposes.

In Borromeo's gradual reforms of Milanese religious life, and in addition to his overt and energetic promotion of the parish-based eucharistic and charitable associations, there are clear signs of such a pluralist strategy. We find an assimilation and "recycling" of the traditions of the numerous confraternities which were linked to churches used for public worship (not only parish churches, but also minor oratories, sanctuaries, the churches and buildings which belonged to the regular clergy, schools and charitable foundations), whether they were protected under the independent rights enjoyed by the flagellant and penitential confraternities and "scuole segrete" or had merged into the corporative structures of the various professional or social groupings, often of compatriots from the same geographical area. Borromeo exploited and radically reshaped both the confraternities of Christian doctrine and those of the "Virgins of Saint Orsola," and encouraged their growth throughout the diocese. He took the lay

---

[12] For a general overview, see Zardin "Il rilancio delle confraternite."

associations for widows, noblewomen and bachelors under his protection. From the outset of his episcopacy, he promoted the laborious task of sifting and collating the statutes of the unruly flagellant confraternities. This led, after the second provincial council in 1569 and the publication in 1573 of a standard body of general rules, to clarifying and expanding their decisive role in the administration of public ceremonies. The outcome reflected a brokering of the supervisory concerns of episcopal authority and the vitality of autonomous groups which were made up of faithful laity. Borromeo recognized that the reordering of those parts of religious life overseen by brotherhoods had to proceed by recruiting the groups which most exemplified confraternal traditions, and so were more compelling and effective in the local scene. To this end, he proposed as early as 1567 to establish a new and prestigious "Compagnia dei Battuti" in the capital itself, comprising a select membership of fifty gentlemen chosen from among Milan's leading families.[13]

Borromeo and his followers pursued a strategy of extending their control over the traditional forms of popular devotion. They aimed more at gradually adapting these forms to the Church hierarchy's new purposes than at imposing total change. In order to absorb the devotional zeal of the married laity, for example, they proposed new organizational models which nevertheless echoed traditional voluntary associations centered on the most compelling symbols of Christian piety. After the outbreak of plague in 1576–7 and its miraculous disappearance, new "Compagnie della Croce" were established based around images of Christ's Passion and the cult of the Holy Cross. They took as their emblem the votive columns erected even before the onset of plague in the main squares and crossroads of the city and afterwards on similar sites in rural towns; religious services were held for the faithful assembled round these columns as a safer alternative to indoor gatherings. These interwoven strategies – the revival of traditional forms of lay association, the revision of statutes under episcopal authority, and the skilful didactic deployment of the printed word – are most apparent in the final years of Borromeo's rule. An example is the campaign of support in Milan, Monza, and other leading rural centers for the Rosary confraternities, which from their first flowering in the fifteenth century had remained the monopoly of the Domini-

---

[13] Archivio di Stato di Modena, *Cancelleria ducale, Carteggio degli ambasciatori*, Milano, b. 39, 8 ottobre 1567. See Rotelli, "La figura e l'opera," 142. On the flagellant confraternities, see Zardin, "La riforma delle confraternite di Disciplinati" and "Le confraternite bresciane," 130–42. The text of the revised general rules can be found in *AEM* (ed. 1582: fo. 329r–335r). On other aspects see Rimoldi, "I laici."

can friars, and as such quite marginal to the concerns of the secular clergy.[14]

Throughout Borromeo's diocese in the late sixteenth century, two different strategies came to overlap: the preservation of traditional forms of confraternal religious association and their absorption into new forms of organized religion which sought to influence individual behavior by working directly on private and domestic life as part of a wholesale Christian reform of social and political life. This conjunction underscored confraternities' willingness to act as instruments for the Church's goal of attracting believers to a revitalized faith. The confraternities' statutes, whether revised in the light of Borromeo's reforms or newly drawn-up, continued to underline the importance of certain customary duties, albeit with greater rigor and consistency than before, for all those "confratelli" who, although living in the world and subject to its demands, were anxious to lead a comparatively unblemished life: daily prayer, an orderly observance of the various duties appointed throughout the day, fraternal reproof of others' failings, prescribed mealtime prayers, the examination of conscience at the end of the day and frequent attendance at the sacraments. In the significant period of liberation when the threat of plague had lifted, these duties appeared unmodified in the form of a guideline for the daily life of the laity to be displayed on walls and later incorporated into the widespread tract entitled *Ricordi al popolo della città et diocese di Milano*, published no later than 1578.[15]

The *Ricordi* adapted the model of popular contemporary books of manners like Giovanni della Casa's *Galateo* towards a more explicitly religious life. They show quite clearly that the aim was to effect a deep-rooted and longlasting change in each individual's moral behavior by instructing the faithful to examine their consciences regularly and confess their sins thoroughly at least once a month, and not merely for appearance sake in compliance with the general Eastertide duty of confession. The teaching of preachers and other spiritual directors among the confraternities was directed to the same end. It should also be noted that such appeals to the faithful and the systematic effort to instruct them in religious and moral matters were no longer confined to sermons, the enactment of the sacraments and other mass rituals, which, although effective, were by their nature merely occasional. Through the medium of print, books and other printed aids could be made available to all with a minimum of education. The breadth of

---

[14] Olivieri Baldissarri, *I "poveri prigioni,"* 11–69; Gatti Perer, "Per la definizione."

[15] *AEM*, 1582, f. 312r–317v. For a commentary see Zardin, "La 'perfettione,'" 117–25.

distribution would have been inconceivable in the age of scribal copying or even during the early years of printing itself.

Intensifying concerns which had already begun to appear in the bureaucratic language of statutes, the rules drawn up for the confraternities in the post-Tridentine period aimed at promoting knowledge of the central tenets of the faith as a condition of membership of the various associations (the representative example are the episcopal rules for the flagellant confraternities). This was the case not only in Borromeo's Milan but wherever the wave of Church reform reached. The rules urged support for catechism schools on holy days as a meritorious work of spiritual mercy, and encouraged the merging of such catechetic instruction with the more general effort to disseminate good Christian habits of life, an effort which focused naturally on families. The rules drawn up for the "Compagnie della Penitenza" – which were promulgated in the diocese around 1570 before the new common rules for the flagellant confraternities had been made available – proposed spending the part of the day after lunch and the recitation of the vespers and compline of the Madonna in teaching Christian doctrine. Yet predating these rules and the advent of Borromeo as Archbishop, the 1565 *Ordini riformati della compagnia di Madonna Santa Maria di Passione al campanile dei reverendi canonici* – which had its headquarters in the prestigious basilica dedicated to the city's patron saint, Ambrose – specify in great detail the minimum doctrinal knowledge its members were expected to acquire: "In addition to the *Pater Noster* and the *Ave Maria*, all should know by heart the Creed, the seven deadly sins and the seven virtues opposed to them, the five senses, the seven corporal and seven spiritual works of mercy, the seven gifts of the Holy Spirit, the seven sacraments, the three theological and four cardinal virtues, the ten commandments, the precepts of the Church and the Confiteor." Reflecting an acute awareness of the communicative possibilities of print, the *Ordini* also contained practical advice on memorizing without difficulty the various formulas, lists and precepts which formed the framework of popular catechetical instruction: "In order that each person may learn, the above mentioned points are to be written or printed on a panel and kept always in sight in the confraternity's meeting place."[16]

---

[16] *Regola delle confraternità de i Disciplinati*, ch. 1, *AEM*, 1582, f. 329v; ASDMi, X, "Pieve di Legnano," vol. 20, fasc. 1; "S. Calimero," vol. 1, fasc. 22; "S. Ambrogio," vol. 49. In the source: "Oltra il Pater et l'Ave Maria, sappia ciascuno a mente il Credo, i sette peccati capitali, le sette virtù opposte a' sette peccati capitali, i cinque sentimenti del corpo, le sette opere della misericordia corporale, le sette della spirituale, i sette doni dello Spirito Santo, i sette sacramenti della Chiesa, le tre virtù teologiche e le quattro cardinali, i dieci commandamenti della legge, i precetti della Santa Chiesa et

Panels and "summaries" listing the fundamental elements of the catechism, *Regole di costumi christiani* which could be posted on walls, *Interrogatori* and *Dottrine* by various authors, couched in the characteristic form of a dialogue between master and pupil, could all be circulated or offered free to those who frequented the confraternities. These were distributed following pastoral visitations, during the preaching campaigns which took place at key periods of the liturgical calendar, or during rural missions. They started to appear as appendices to the rule-books which the wealthier confraternities were printing. Later, in order to reinforce their mnemonic power, they were enhanced by the addition of litanies and prayers, woodcut devotional images, vernacular hymns, and lauds to be sung in procession or at meetings.

Catechetical tracts, however, were not the only form of Christian training. In keeping with the spirit of the times, the surviving inventories of the city's booksellers and printers show a much wider and more diversified range of didactic and edifying literature for which the network of lay religious organizations provided channels to a lively market. The most significant of these publications were the collections of hagiographies (such as the *Vite de' santi padri* and the *Legendario de' santi* based on the celebrated Latin compilation of Jacobus de Voragine) and the devotional tracts and guides to prayer and meditation such as the *De imitatione Christi* or the works of sixteenth-century religious authors (such as the Jesuit Loarte, the *Guida dei peccatori* and other writings by the Dominican Luis de Granada, the *Prattica dell'oration mentale* of the Capuchin friar Mattia Bellintani da Salò), which were already well-known to the more committed confraternities as texts for collective reading during meetings or as alternatives to sermons.[17] The sixteenth- and seventeenth-century archives of the city's and region's "scholae" bear frequent references to books bought for devotional purposes and edificational reading in the wider sense, not simply for public prayer and worship. These were the same texts promoted by publishers for the general market as essential reading for individual faithful, encouraging a more direct and intimate approach to the sources of Christian piety in their free time and within their own family circle. There is also one example known to us – so far unique but certain to be rare in any case since only the wealthiest confraternities could have allowed themselves the facility – of a

---

il Confiteor"; "Et accioché ogn'uno le possa imparare, stiano del continuo le sudette tutte cose o scritte o stampate sopra una tavoletta ne i luoghi d'essa compagnia."

[17] Bottoni, "Libri e lettura," 251–76; di Filippo Bareggi, "Libri e letture," 47–70, 77–90; Stevens, "Vincenzo Girardone."

collection of texts held in common, the beginnings of a small library of devotional literature for the use of those astute enough to put up the funds. This belonged to a confraternity named after S. Maria della Passione, which had its headquarters in the basilica of S. Ambrogio and was distinguished from its namesake by its allegiance to the community of Cistercian monks. An inventory attached to the report of the pastoral visitation of November 1566 (just after Borromeo's return to Milan and the start of his reforms) listed the confraternity's assets, and included a dozen vernacular texts for reading, for meditation, and for learning the secrets of "living Christianly" (as the title of a work by Dennis the Carthusian, aimed at "people of differing conditions" puts it).[18]

The Borromean strategy for establishing control of the life of the laity thus adopted modes of religious instruction which were in use before the sixteenth century but enhanced their efficacy through the new and powerful medium of print. The effect was to endow the rituals and public functions of the confraternities with new devotional significance, in stark and polemical contrast to an inward-looking and exclusive conformism. The effect of such changes on the tenacious and centuries-old form of lay religious association must have been considerable. Together with the simultaneous application of new statutes and new forms of devotion introduced under the explicit aegis of Tridentine and Borromean reform, the impact not only affected the areas of local concern which were left untouched by the earlier developments in religious life, but realigned and absorbed the existing confraternities along with their places of worship, their rights of patronage and their organizational roles. Yet the image of a triumphal march of reform is false. The inertia and increasing marginalization of the more traditional forms of lay association do not mean that they disappeared altogether. By the same token, the successful expansion of new forms should not obscure the difficulties attending their reception, the constraints they encountered, and the compromises which had to be made so that local communities would absorb them and acknowledge their authority. The strategy as formally drawn up and propagated by those at the center of church power had in practice to be adapted to a network of social customs and relationships which were unforeseen and undesired by the architects of diocesan institutional reform. They had to engage in a dialogue with diverse inherited traditions with varying results, often involving compromise when they did not lead to disappointment or, on occasion, downright

---

[18] Bottoni, "Libri e lettura," 251–68; ASDMi, X, "S. Ambrogio", vol. 21, fasc. 7.

failure. In the longer term the effort to reform and renew confraternal traditions could reinforce the self-defining and self-protective identities of the familial and social groups which made up the confraternities, thus serving a tenacious past rather than advancing the cause of moral and institutional reform. Yet it is also unlikely that the reformers themselves intended that the spirit of Lent to triumph so thoroughly over the spirit of Carnival or that they allowed for no possibility of accommodation between the demands of religion and those of the human and natural world. If the Church were to fulfil its function in the world as an intelligible guide, then it had to adapt itself in a process of osmosis. Amidst the conflicts of the sixteenth century, the Church could not hope to speak convincingly to humanity if it placed itself beyond worldly expectations and set itself against all common ground of mutual compromise and adaptation. Such strategic adaptations did not entail any diminution of the Church's authority; they were the natural forms whereby new models and codes of association were introduced to the mass of the faithful. A careful reading of the merely descriptive accounts of pastoral visitations obliges us to revise the old historical myth of a Counter-Reformation Church which in its zeal for order and control demolished a centuries-old accumulation of abuses and muddle. Having reviewed the reformers' statutory revisions and the programs which expressed their aspirations for educational and disciplinary change, this essay concludes by looking at the tensions and conflicts which arose when they attempted to put these intentions into practice.

The introduction of the new Corpus Christi confraternities, the symbol of Borromeo's reforms, was far from uncontested by those in the parishes whose religious life they sought to reorganize. Alongside cases where the establishment of such associations, helped by special envoys from the Curia in Milan, was deeply rooted and durable, there are numerous other examples where the hierarchy's attempt to centralize proceeded slowly and uncertainly, thus demonstrating the difficulties of imposing a uniform programme on a diversity of local needs and (often modest) resources.

In the rural parishes, ten to fifteen years after their introduction in the wake of Borromeo's reforms, many of the SS. Sacramento confraternities are recorded as still being without rules; parish priests, visitors, and rural vicars complained continually of their negligence in celebrating monthly communion, keeping proper accounts, or putting themselves at the service of the parish or of the needs (including the economic needs) of the clergy. Some clergy were cool to the confraternities at the outset, while others withdrew their support temporarily. This in turn led public sympathy for the new brotherhoods to decline, and is frequently indicated as the reason why local parishioners, resistant to outside pressure and clerical interference, were slow to accept the new-style confraternities. Even in those cases where the confraternity had been successfully introduced, its day-to-day functioning fell far short of the expectations of the Milanese Curia and its local agents ("Adest scola Corporis Christi: frigida," Vergo, pieve di Agliate, 1578). Likewise in urban parishes, the growth of the SS. Sacramento confraternities was marked by resistance, conflict and misunderstanding, which opened up a division between neighborhood associations with their traditionally local and self-supporting loyalties and the parish clergy's rival and innovative claims for leadership.[19]

At the very end of the sixteenth century, for example, the "visini di Santo Georgio in Palazzo" turned without hesitation to the Vicar General to ask him to defend their rights in the "confusion which has arisen between the chapter of canons and the "'scolari del Corpus Domini'" (i.e., members of the Corpus Domini confraternity). Established in the first decade of the sixteenth century, this had been one of the earliest Corpus Domini confraternities founded in Milan. By the mid-seventeenth century, as their account incorporated into the episcopal report of 1656 makes clear, the parish canons considered themselves to be in control of the situation. A more direct account of 1623, which represents the views of both the parties to the conflict, reveals the long-established confraternity's conviction that it could claim immunity from ecclesiastical jurisdiction on the grounds that it had received official recognition from the Duchy's civil authorities long before the promoters of Tridentine reform appeared on the scene. When the Vicar suggested that the confraternity should nevertheless abide by the episcopal visitor's decrees, they courageously went on to appeal to the supreme tribunal of the city's Senate, declaring themselves to be an entirely lay association and claiming their officers could not carry out "actions totally contrary to the jurisdiction of His Majesty," the king of Spain, whose authority had superseded that of the Sforza duchy of Milan. Similar antagonisms, in the very midst of Borromeo's reforms, poisoned the relationship between the clergy of S. Babila and its equally venerable eucharistic confraternity which, determined to restrict membership to the aristocracy, drew its members from all over the city in opposition to the clergy who were trying to restrict it within the newly enforced boundaries of the parish communities. Conflict can also be found, under different circumstan-

---

[19] *Ibid.*, "Pieve di Agliate," vol. 26, fasc. 2; Zardin, "Confraternite e comunità," 708–9.

ces, in another parish in the center of Milan, S. Michele al Gallo, around 1581.[20]

The alliance which the Church sought to impose, or at least to strengthen, between the "popular" confraternities and the parishes (only one of the points, it must be remembered, especially in the cities, around which local religious life focused) was thus a cause of the confraternities' instability and internal weakness. Yet it could also become the driving force behind their growth. If in their weakness and reluctance to defend their original autonomy they allowed themselves to be taken over by the clergy assigned to advance the reforms, they proved ideal vehicles for the propagation of models of Christian living and of partnership with Church institutions in many areas of social life, including some which today we would think of as beyond the reach of their influence – relations between men and women, family and professional life, local politics and administration, holidays and popular traditions. To the ecclesiastical "militants" who sought to revitalize the Church's power over men's consciences and conduct, the reformed confraternities provided a way of bringing the magical and superstitious practices associated with popular religion under control. They appeared willing to enter into potentially fierce and polemical competition with the stagnant conformism of much traditional religious behavior at the service of vested interests and social prestige. The lay associations had a role to play in the contemporary debate over the different ways in which Christian ethics could be applied to social life, and particularly in the conflict between the popular faith of local traditions and the more austere and uniform Christianity promoted by the reformers. The confraternities which were more easily controlled could thus function as the "long arm" of the clergy who supported Borromeo's innovations. They were transformed into vehicles for "the complete and utter reform of the entire world,"[21] a task for which they provided consensus, human resources, and means of persuasion.

The decrees which issued from the Curia in Milan acknowledged the usefulness of calling upon "certos etiam aliquos laicos homines, Christianae sanctaeque disciplinae studiosos" as collaborators. The provincial council of 1579 commissioned them to keep a discreet watch on their neighbors and report promptly to the church authori-

---

[20] ASDMi, X, "S. Giorgio al Palazzo," vol. 2, fasc. 17; Ratti, "Scuole," 63; ASDMi, X, "S. Babila," vols. 9 (f. 36v–37v), 12 (fasc. 14–15), 16 (fasc. 2), and "S. Maria Segreta," vol. 6 (the last two examples are mentioned by Bottoni, "Per la storia," 73–6, 86–90). Other useful material can be found in "Metropolitana," vol. 37, fasc. 5.

[21] Written deposition of the Jesuit Achille Gagliardi, cited in Marcora, "Il processo diocesano," 642.

ties any circumstance which threatened to undermine the spiritual
well-being of the faithful by giving rise to scandal and bad example.
The legislation refers explicitly to concubinage or "living in sin,"
debauchery, obscene language, slander, and cheating, popular amusements involving lascivious dancing, excessive laughter, gluttony and
lust.[22] For some years before, enquiries into the abuses which needed
tackling and special surveys of local religious life carried out by the
Curia in Milan had emphasized the need to bring in "huomini di bona
vita" and "persone amorevoli" in every parish in order to combat the
most ingrained vices such as swearing, gambling, and the neglect of
marriage vows; such persons were either to intervene themselves to
correct such "wrongdoers" or, when they were powerless to deal
with them directly, report back to the local clergy, in effect acting as
spies in helping to extend the Church's control and power of sanction
over immoral behavior.[23]

It is not surprising that members of the new Tridentine confraternities and of the "scuole" formed to teach Christian doctrine on
Sundays and feast days proved ideal collaborators for such a campaign
of moral surveillance. The Milanese carpenter Giambattista Casale
came from these ranks; his surviving diary shows his religious mili-
tancy alongside his membership in his trade guild and his neighborhood association. In addition to carrying out his duties as a father and
head of his family, he also taught reading and writing through membership in a Company of Christian Doctrine. A perfect match for
Casale can be found in the anonymous figure of "messer Orlando," a
"teacher of Christian life" who in 1582 antagonized the officers of the
flagellant confraternity of S. Quirico, S. Rocco, and S. Maria Maddalena by trying to get them to punish severely their more dissolute
members (addicted gamblers, frequenters of taverns, those disrespect-
ful of authority or inclined to abuse their administrative powers).[24]
Another example of a layman co-opted into the fight against wrong-
doing and the profane traditions linked to the Church calendar was
Francesco Rinaldi, a leading member of the Milanese Company of
Christian Doctrine. On being sent to Melegnano on a mission from
Borromeo, he persuaded the local authorities to censure "the prohibited game of dicing" ("gioco prohibito delli ossi") and punish a
certain mountebank ("cirlatano") who "by exhibiting a monkey in
the middle of the piazza detained many from going to morning mass"

---

[22] *AEM*, 1582, f. 109r.

[23] ASDMi, Sezione XIV, vol. 67, fasc. 5 (edited in Lurati, "Pene ai bestemmiatori," 43–7).

[24] BAMi, cod. Trotti 413, and Marcora, "Il diario di Giambattista Casale," 209–11, 220–2, 348, 363;
ASDMi, X, "Miscellanea città," vol. 14, fasc. 23.

("il qual in mezzo la piazza facendo atteggiar una [scimmia] fu ragion che molti quella matina perdessero messa").[25] Those who failed to respect holy days, frequented taverns, attended dances and popular entertainments were reprimanded and sometimes fined, with part of the proceeds going to the coffers of the local S. Sacramento confraternity. The threat of financial sanction was often combined with a process of rehabilitation designed to soften the hardened hearts of sinners who found themselves caught.[26] They had to participate in a ceremony of reconciliation in front of the church doors and before the entire assembled community and agree either to enrol in the "scuola" or to attend regularly the lessons in Christian doctrine. It is obvious how disputes – on occasion, bitter ones – could arise between the institutions working for Borromeo's reform of community life and those who supported the traditional organizations and balance of power. At the head of the latter we find those who had most to lose from the innovations: riotous youths who remained outside the new confraternities, loose-living men and women, tavern-keepers, musicians, the local gentry and nobility who were determined to keep their rights and their old ways of life.

There is incontestable evidence that the closing decades of the sixteenth century were filled with discontent and, on occasion, open resistance to the great wave of innovations which swept in with the Tridentine reforms. It was the local clergy and rural vicars who paid the price of such latent conflict when they dared to question the monopoly of power held by oligarchies of local notables clustered around those described unflinchingly in contemporary sources as "oppressors of the churches" ("tiranni delle chiese"). New educational and devotional initiatives were also affected: colorful processions, edifying spectacles with musical accompaniment designed to fascinate, hymns and chants, religious drama organized by the doctrinal "scuole" became the targets of sabotage and mockery from local youths, who combined natural indiscipline with the desire to protect their traditional holiday amusements. The Church hierarchy's proposals for the formation of new religious companies, sometimes introduced "ex lege" into communities which found themselves ordered to reorganize their traditional associations, met with similar resistance. In such complex disputes, the new confraternities frequently came into conflict with their traditional equivalents, of which they were

---

[25] *Ibid.*, "Pieve di Melegnano," vol. 7, fasc. 2.

[26] ASDMi, XIV, vol. 67, fasc. 3–5 (edited in Lurati, "Superstizioni lombarde," 232–49, and "Pene ai bestemmiatori," 43–7). A further example can be found in de Boer, "Sinews of discipline," 176.

intended to be a reformed and more tractable version. It is obvious
that in cases where confraternities wished to break free of such
imposed constraints, the Church hierarchy always supported the new
institutions which underpinned the parish church and its authority.

Such antagonisms – which only very gradually settled back into a
renewed framework of tradition in which the Borromean confraternities were finally absorbed – can be seen very clearly in the rural center
of Caronno, in the plains to the north of Milan. The formal accusation
sent to the Curia in 1569 states:

> Just as holy and blessed commandments bring consolation to the good
> spirits so they cause disgust, annoyance and diabolical agitation to the evil
> and wicked. So in Caronno, district of Nerviano, a school of Christian
> Doctrine has been set up together with the confraternity of Corpus
> Domini. In order for them to make good progress, an attempt has been
> made to abolish the devil's schools of music-making and public dancing,
> since these are so contrary to the spirit of the former that the two cannot
> exist together. But the enemy of mankind together with the children of
> iniquity has opposed our efforts and continues to resist, so that the poor
> rector is obliged to turn to Your most reverend Grace for help.[27]

The conflict in Caronno was sharp. On one hand, a curate who was
antagonistic towards popular amusements, and the pious laymen lined
up in support of a local "schola" of Corpus Domini which was
depicted as growing vigorously. On the other hand, those inhabitants
described as the "enemies of reform": men who feared that they
would no longer "have the time they desired for their profane pleasur-
es." Among the latter were two virulent peasants "full of vices," and
behind them the Omati brothers from Caronno's leading noble family, who owned land and property, held rights of burial and church
patronage, and were the undisputed arbiters of the ancient and by then
dying confraternity of S. Maria della Purificazione.[28]

This example of anti-Borromean resistance shows how the reforms

---

[27] ASDMi, X, "Pieve di Nerviano," vol. 24, fasc. 15: "Sicome le ordinationi sante, et benedette
portano consolatione a i boni spiriti, così li malegni, et cattivi generano nausea, fastidio, et furor
diabolico; quinci aviene che nella terra di Carono pieve di Nerviano essendosi instituita la scuola
della dottrina cristiana, et quella del Corpus Domini; acciò che elleno havessero bon progresso si è
cercato di levar le scuole diaboliche del sonare, et ballare publicamente, sicome quelle che di diletto
sono contrarie all'altre, talmente che è imposibile che l'une et l'altre insiememente stiano. A questo
sforzo l'inimico del genere humano insieme con i figliuoli dell'iniquità si è opposto, et si oppone
tuttavia, di modo che il povero rettore di essa terra [. . .] è sforzato di ricorrere a Vostra Signoria
illustrissima et reverendissima."
[28] Ibid., fasc. 16 and vol. 30, fasc. 2. For more detailed discussion see Zardin, Riforma cattolica, 85–106.
Examples of conflict between 'old' and new-style confraternities can be found in Zardin,
"Confraternite e comunità," 707, 716; "Solidarietà di vicini," 402–3.

of the lay confraternities – designed to make them a support for the construction of a unified parish and a vehicle for the propagation of a Christian reform of individual consciences and social relationships – could not eliminate the diversity of traditions and pluralistic system of lay associations which actually they sought to reinterpret. The Borromean strategy was absorbed into a dialectical and turbulent confrontation with a continuing tradition which hindered its wholesale advance; the persistence of the past meant that it was the people's collective traditions which absorbed and reshaped the innovations until the crises and discontinuities of more recent times.

THE DEVELOPMENT OF JESUIT CONFRATERNITY ACTIVITY IN THE KINGDOM OF NAPLES IN THE SIXTEENTH AND SEVENTEENTH CENTURY

MARK A. LEWIS

INTRODUCTION

"Spies ... are for sovereigns, not for religious bodies... Therefore you ought to rid yourself of your spies [among the companies]."[1] The image of a vast network of tightly controlled and highly disciplined cadres infiltrating every level of society under the direction of Jesuits has been a popular myth since at least the eighteenth century. Political intrigues, blood oaths, and secret surveillance on the part of Jesuit-sponsored confraternities have been some of the elements which make up these grand conspiracy theories. While considerable ink has been spilt in proving and disproving these conspiracies, much of the early data on Jesuit–lay collaboration has only recently begun to receive critical examination. Perhaps some kernels of truth emerge to support the dark interpretations of universal Jesuit control; nevertheless, the efforts of the Society of Jesus appear to have remained much more modest.

Historians of early modern Catholicism have often interpreted the advent of the educational systems and their related institutions as a response to the crisis of the Protestant Reformation. For conspiracy theorists, Jesuit control of education was a means to control society, and Jesuit sponsored companies extended that control even further. Increasingly, however, emphasis is being placed on these schools as essentially part of the Catholic formula for reform. In the first years of the Jesuit

Archival sources cited in this article: *Archivum Neapolitanum Societatis Iesu (ANSI)*; *Archivum Romanum Societatis Iesu (ARSI)*; and *Monumentum Historicum Societatis Iesu (MHSI)*. Translations, unless otherwise noted, are my own.

[1] *Lettera d'un Cavaliere*, 43.

enterprise, their schools sought to strengthen and adapt many existing Catholic practices, among them lay confraternities. These organizations, in turn, provided support and helped to propagate new Jesuit schools. As these schools became a more important aspect of Jesuit activity, they integrated other aspects of Jesuit practice already present in Jesuit-spon-sored companies into their educational program. The clearest instance of this can be seen in the use of elements from the *Spiritual Exercises,* authored by Ignatius Loyola, first in the companies and later in student-based *Marian congregations.* While this article will not address the grand conspiracy theories, it will examine the developments of Jesuit activity with the laity in the context of their developing system of schools in the Kingdom of Naples in the sixteenth and seventeenth centuries.

Because of its importance as an imperial city, as well as its location vis à vis Rome, Naples became the logical proving ground for many of the developments of the new Order. Administrators at the Roman College often had their first experience in office at the Jesuit College in Naples. In Naples the Jesuits encountered existing lay confraternities already active in Church reform. Jesuits joined these groups and received assistance from them. As the Jesuit College in Naples developed, Jesuits began to form their own style of confraternity, the company. The hallmark of this new style of confraternity was its preference for Jesuit spiritual practices. While Jesuits remained active in the older confraternities, the companies con-stituted a new level of Jesuit activity with lay confraternities. In 1577 another subset of confraternity emerged in Naples, the Marian congrega-tion. The distinctive feature of this type of organization was its affiliation with the *Prima primaria* congregation of the Roman College. Many, though not all, of the Jesuit-sponsored companies became affiliated with the Prima primaria. Yet Jesuits continued to direct and assist those which did not. In general, the Marian congregations brought a centralizing authority and uniform statutes to the diverse and worldwide membership of the companies. The growth of Jesuit-organized companies, and the later Marian congregations in Naples, indicate the maturation of the Jesuit apostolic mission into a more integrated program. The lay confraternity influenced the Jesuits in their earliest period; the Jesuits in turn modified the formula for the confraternity to produce the new companies; and these companies promoted the emerging Jesuit educational system.

The religious and moral situation in Naples at the arrival of the Jesuits was ripe for change. Antonio Illibato paints a dire picture of Naples freshly emerged from the struggles that led to Spanish and imperial dominance.[2] In the aftermath of war, the civil government had lost much

---

[2] Illibato, «*Liber Visitationis*», Introduction.

control over the behavior of its subjects in Naples. Religion too, had suffered. Non-residency of the archbishops of Naples, and the dominance of teenagers in the cathedral chapter provide just two examples of the absence of leadership from the higher clergy.[3] The situation was worse among the lower clergy. Inflation had forced many into other part-time work in order to eat. Concubinage was a constant problem through the first half of the century, and not completely eradicated in the second half. The advantage of clerical immunity from civil persecution also produced a particular problem for Naples. Common criminals often obtained minor Orders in order to avoid civil authorities. These so-called "*diaconi selvaggi,*" recognized by their "*abati di mezza sottana,*" had become the scourge of the city.[4]

Yet in the midst of these crises, various movements toward reform had also emerged. The Capuchins arrived in Naples in 1530 and were followed by the Theatines three years later. Bonsignore Cacciaguerra, active in the promotion of religious education and frequent communion, arrived in 1541. Less orthodox reformers also influenced the situation in Naples. Juan de Valdes, Bernard Ochino, and Peter Martyr Vermigli all preached there at mid-century. Thus while abuses were endemic, the climate of reform was also present. Illibato's thesis maintains that the confraternities in Naples were instrumental in providing this atmosphere for reform. He also suggests that Naples had more active confraternities than most other cities in Italy at this time.[5]

From the time of their arrival in the city of Naples in 1552, the Jesuits involved themselves in the activities of the kingdom's confraternities. Their initial activities appear to be confined to giving support to the reform elements within the organizations, and in receiving some of the material and spiritual benefits usually derived from their activity. Evidence suggests that religious practices supported by the Jesuits, especially frequent use of the sacraments of Confession and Communion, became part of the reforms of some of these confraternities.[6] While not abandoning their older associations, Jesuits founded new companies among neighbors and benefactors. While retaining many characteristics of the older confraternities, these associations reflected more clearly Jesuit concerns for reform. Elements taken from Ignatius of Loyola's *Spiritual Exercises* can also be discerned among them.[7] Finally, the schools adapted

---

[3] *Ibid.*, xviii.   [4] *Ibid.*, xx.   [5] *Ibid.*, xxi.

[6] The presence of Bonsignore Cacciaguerra in Naples in 1541, and his promotion of the frequent reception of Confession and Communion (found especially in his *Trattato della Communione* of 1557) make it difficult to attribute Jesuit authorship to these reforms. See Black, *Italian Confraternities*, 14.

[7] Maher, "Reforming Rome," draws an interesting parallel between directories for the first week of the *Exercises* and the matter suggested for these groups' meditations.

the rules of these groups for the benefit of their students. With the creation of the Marian congregations, the pious association of the confraternity was transformed into a centralized instrument of apostolic labor. The student-based Marian congregations, as a refinement of the companies of laity and secular clergy, represent a variation on the older confraternity model that had proven so popular and effective in Naples.

The "layered" development of Jesuit activity with confraternities in Naples would indicate less a desire to create groups which could be used for greater control and influence in the city, and more the experimentation, acquisition, modification, and propagation of an existing model of reform. Work and membership in the older organizations were not abandoned nor discouraged by the Jesuits. Rather, the new forms of confraternities sought to implement means similar to the older ones in a context more explicitly Jesuit.

INITIAL ACTIVITIES WITH EXISTING CONFRATERNITIES

Francesco Schinosi, in *Istoria della Compagnia di Giesù appartenente al Regno di Napoli,* makes it clear that confraternities in Naples supported the work of the first Jesuits to arrive in the city.[8] This began when the first Jesuits in Naples joined and contributed to already existing confraternities. Hence, while the focus of this essay will be on the early companies formed by the Jesuits in Naples and on their student-led counterparts, a brief review of this initial activity is necessary. The early confraternity activity of the Jesuits provided models for their own later inventions, opened opportunities for new ministries, and provided sustenance for the first Jesuit school in Naples.

Jesuit interest in confraternities dates back to the first years of the Order. Ignatius Loyola enrolled himself and the first ten companions in the Confraternity of the Holy Spirit (an organization supporting the Hospital of the Holy Spirit) in Rome. Pierre Favre began the first Jesuit ministry to a confraternity in 1540 when he was sent to Parma to reform the statutes of a confraternity there.[9] Yet the first Jesuit actively involved in the confraternities of Naples was Alfonso Salmerón. In 1552 he was brought into the membership of the recently reformed Confraternity of the Bianchi of Justice by two of the major benefactors of the new Jesuit school in Naples, Girolomo Vignes and Ettore Pignatelli.[10] Because the primary activity of the Bianchi involved accompanying the condemned to their place of execution, the presence of Salmerón (and later, other

---

[8] Schinosi, *Istoria,* 1, 25.   [9] *MHSI, Fabri Monumenta (Mon. Fab.),* 37 ff.

[10] *MHSI, Epistolae Salmeronis (Epist. Salm.)* 1, 106–7. The *Bianchi* were made up of the elite of Neapolitan society.

Jesuits) among their members brought the Society of Jesus into this ministry in Naples. The Jesuits also became chaplains to the prisons and ultimately founded companies among the prisoners themselves.

There are indications that the Bianchi had reformed in the direction of more frequent reception of the sacraments before the arrival of the Jesuits. Their Rule, as revised in 1519, called for Communion and Confession four times per year.[11] Frequency had subsequently increased by mid-century, but there is no evidence to indicate that the Jesuits originated the new custom among the Bianchi more than that they simply supported and encouraged an existing practice. Nevertheless the promotion of the practice of frequent reception of the sacraments tightened the bonds between the Bianchi and the Jesuits. It was the Bianchi member Vignes who underwrote the publication of the treatise *De frequenti usu Sanctissimi Eucharistae sacramenti libellus*, authored by the Jesuit Cristóbal Sánchez de Madrid in 1556.[12]

The Bianchi also became one of the major benefactors of the College of the Jesuits in Naples. While their principal financial responsibility remained the Hospital of the Incurables, they never limited themselves to just one charity, as during this period both the Capuchins and Theatines received support as well.[13] When the viceroy of Naples, Pedro Cardinal Pacheco re-authorized the confraternity to beg publicly in 1553, the proceeds of their weekly mendicancy were divided equally between the Jesuit College and the Hospital of the Incurables.[14] Salmerón objected to this division of the Bianchi's largesse, complaining to his superiors, "[The Hospital] has 10,000 ducats of endowment . . . and six small houses . . . We have neither a house nor endowments, not even the smallest lodgings."[15] Whether or not the division was fair, the Jesuit school became the recipients of roughly 300 ducats a year from this source.[16]

Even after the foundations of Jesuit-sponsored organizations, Jesuits remained active in the Bianchi of Justice and other confraternities. The Bianchi, who underwent another reform in 1595 (becoming a confraternity exclusively for clerics), allotted posts for six Jesuits and six Theatines among their regular enrollment.[17] Thus, Jesuits who were active in ministry in Naples remained in contact with an elite and reformed confraternity with a strong tradition of activity. Giovanni Battista Buoncuore, a noted canonist at the University of Naples and a

---

[11] Mascia, *La confraternita dei Bianchi*, 68.   [12] *MHSI, Monumenta Ignatiana (Mon. Ig.)* 11, 13.

[13] Mascia, *La confraternita dei Bianchi*, 72.

[14] Pacheco's predecessor, Don Pedro de Toledo, had suspended their license to beg two years earlier during unrest in the city.   [15] *MHSI, Epist. Salm.*, I, 106–7.

[16] Errichetti, *"L'antico Collegio Massimo,"* 200.

[17] The number of members was also limited to one hundred, further making the confraternity into a "spiritual elite," (Black, *Italian Confraternities*, 52).

member of the Bianchi, entered the Society of Jesus in 1563. He was the first vocation from this confraternity for the Society of Jesus, and had frequented the sacraments of Confession and Communion at the Church of the Jesuit College before his entrance in the Order. Thus, the relationship between the Bianchi and the Jesuits produced at least some vocations to the Order.[18]

EARLY COMPANIES

Among the first Jesuits sent to open the College at Naples in 1552 was a young scholastic named Giovanni Francesco Araldo. He had charge of the first-year Latin students there, and had also introduced the teaching of catechism to the school. But Araldo did not confine his energies simply to his classroom duties. From the outset he organized groups of lay people concerned with religious practice of the city. The first such group, for men, known as the Company of Communicants, were encouraged in the practice of frequent confession and communion as well as hidden works of charity. The *Zitti*, as they came to be known (for their "silent" charity), were made up primarily of men from the neighborhood. Although Araldo drew up their statutes, they received official approval from Ignatius in Rome, who changed their name to the Company of the Veneration of the Blessed Sacrament.[19] At almost the same time, Araldo started a similar group for women. The *Congregazione delle divote al Gesù*, in addition to the charitable work of visiting hospitals and catechizing their servants, promised to avoid the use of jewelry, rouge, and other "vanities." The women, however, did not follow the move of the College out of the neighborhood and into its new site in 1554. Instead, they transferred to the nearby Theatine Church of St. Paul where they eventually died out.[20] These first two Jesuit-formed confraternities would be joined by dozens of others in the course of the first generation of the Jesuit presence in Naples, providing much of the basic organization for the dissemination of the practices and devotions fostered by the Society of Jesus. The *Spiritual Exercises* provided the primary foundation for the Jesuit promotion of frequent reception of communion, inasmuch as it encourages, "weekly confession of sins and, if possible, the reception of the Eucharist every two weeks."[21] The Zitti remained faithful to Ignatius' spiritual legacy for over a decade. In response to a recommendation that

---

[18] *ANSI*, Araldo, *Cronica della Compagnia di Giesù di Napoli (Cronica)*, III, ff. 89r–v. Buoncuore helped maintain good relations with both the archdiocese and the University.

[19] *ANSI*, *Cronica*, I, 13v. Their documents repeatedly refer to this approval by Ignatius.

[20] *Ibid.*, 15v. It appears, contrary to Chatellier, *Europe of the Devout*, 15, that the genders were segregated into two distinct companies.   [21] Ganss (trans.), *Spiritual Exercises*, [18], 126.

the group be moved from the College, Salmerón reported in 1560 to
Father General Laynez:

> It has been many years since Father Master Ignatius, our father, gave
> permission for a Company of men to meet in this house . . . It has appeared
> to Father Madrid that they should leave the house. I am certain that should
> they be forced to leave, there will be much discontent and murmuring,
> and that devotion to frequent Communion and Confession will be
> cooled.[22]

By the first decades of the seventeenth century, however, Araldo's
original Company had declined in both numbers and apostolic activity
to the point that the Jesuit Provincial of Naples transferred it to the
Gesù Nuovo (Professed House) in order that it might be reinvigorated.[23] The rules for the "gentlemen's congregation" of the
Blessed Virgin of the Nativity (founded at the Gesù Nuovo in 1605)
also echo the counsels of Ignatius in the *Exercises*: "The end of this
Congregation is to attend, . . . with all diligence to the direction of the
Fathers of the Society of Jesus, the salvation of the member himself, . . .
that of his family (household), and his neighbor."[24]

The Jesuit-founded companies sought to accomplish more than
simply the fostering of personal devotion among its members. Not
only did it promote more frequent reception of the sacraments, but it
tied that practice to the daily spiritual and charitable activities of its
members. In this too, the practices originated in the spiritual practices
of the Jesuits themselves. Araldo urged his company to do secret acts of
charity each day and offered them an examination of conscience to be
made each day along with other prayers. The means listed to accomplish the ends of the Nativity congregation included: 1. daily mental
prayer; 2. mortifications; 3. seeking the virtues; and, 4. works of
charity. Each member was required to make the examination of
conscience "according to the five points" offered by their Jesuit
directors.[25] The spiritual works of charity assigned to the *Zitti* were to
include giving instruction in Christian Doctrine to children and
unlettered adults, as well as monitoring the community for evidence

---

[22] *MHSI, Epist. Salm.*, I, 415.
[23] Lopez, "*Una congregazione laica,*" 6–8. There was considerable discussion between Naples and
Rome concerning the possibility of their consolidation with another company already in existence
at the Gesù Nuovo. That the decision interested the General in Rome indicates the extent to
which control, even of the companies, had been centralized.
[24] *ANSI, Congregatio*, IV, "Regole," 2. The ends also resonate with the ends for the Society of Jesus as
found in the *Formula of the Institute.*
[25] *Ibid.*, 3–7. Cf. *Spiritual Exercises*, [18], 126. Ignatius expressed in many letters his view of the
importance of the daily examination of conscience as a means for spiritual growth.

of Protestant or heretical activity.[26] This too, had its roots in the Jesuits' own activities. The concern for Christian Doctrine and the instruction of children and the unlettered finds explicit reference in the Jesuit *Constitutions* which includes, "special care for the instruction of children" in the formula for the final profession of the Jesuit.[27] Thus, in a very concrete way, the new companies participated in the primary ministries of the Society. Jesuit priests continued to provide spiritual direction and supervision of members of companies as they extended the apostolic potential of the Order and encouraged its growth.

The use of lay companies to extend the labor of the Jesuits can also be seen in the popular rural missions throughout the Kingdom of Naples.[28] In the city of Lecce in Apulia, for example, Jesuit missionaries established a company of artisans to encourage pious practices during their first visits there in the 1570s. In 1574 three Jesuits went to found a residence for rural missions. By 1575 plans for a college had been submitted to Rome.

> In the year 1590 Father Bernardo Ottaviano, S.J., finding himself in Lecce, began with the permission of his superiors to institute a very necessary work for the poor, namely they were taught the things necessary for salvation. For this purpose he chose a church across from our College under the title of St. John the Baptist ... in which were congregated the poor.[29]

Ottaviano called on members of the earlier company of artisans to help support and succor this new congregation. The artisans sought alms in the city on Saturdays which they would distribute to the poor on Sunday in the Church. But before the alms were distributed, the artisans' company taught catechism. On feast days the poor organized processions through the city "to the great consolation of all the city." When the demand for confessions increased beyond the ability of the available Jesuits, the artisans' company elected a chaplain who would be responsible for the Sunday Mass and confessions of the poor "who confessed at least once a month."[30] The report concludes:

> Not only was a stable place established for all this [activity], but many people heard Mass who might not have otherwise been so diligent in these exercises; and further, many go to Confession at least once a month, and they are taught the things necessary for salvation: Some of the poor, having now been instructed, in turn teach others the Christian Doctrine.[31]

---

[26] Schinosi, *Istoria*, I, 66. Perhaps this is the origin of the myth of Jesuit "spies".
[27] Ganss, (trans.), *Constitutions S.J.*, [527], 202.
[28] See Selwyn, "Jesuits' Civilizing Mission," 5–34.   [29] *ARSI, Neap.*, 72, f. 42.   [30] *Ibid.*
[31] *Ibid.*

In the city of Naples, Jesuit companies formed among most of the classes to whom the Order ministered. Jesuit activity among those condemned to death, which began with the Bianchi confraternity, led to expanded activity in the city's prisons. Jesuits reported back to Rome at the beginning of the seventeenth century concerning the difficult conditions to be found there. The central prison of the *Vicaria* of Naples held more than one thousand men who were required to pay for both their bedding and food.[32] Two Jesuits were involved with that prison. At Christmastide of 1609, when the two Jesuits found their accustomed prison closed (with most of the prisoners paroled for the holiday), they decided to stop instead at the prison of Santa Maria d'Agnone. Seeing the lack of pastoral care there, one of the two, Pietro Ferraguto, S.J., decided to organize a company to remedy the situation by providing full-time chaplains. The company provided seven ducats monthly for the services of "two secular priests of good life, literate, and confessors."[33] Ferraguto continued to work among prisoners, organizing a company for the "*carcerati del popolo*" under the patronage of the *Madonna del Carmine*. The seat of the company was the prison chapel.[34] The congregation began on Pentecost of 1611 and, according to reports, met with quick success. Drawing on the success of the Carmine company, Gerónimo Marchese, S.J., founded another company there, the *Annunziata*, in 1616. Two years later, the magistrates at the nearby courts organized the *Congregazione della Santissima Trinità dei Tribunalisti* to "help sick prisoners, protect the women condemned to the penitentiary, and to have particular care for the three wards reserved for youthful offenders."[35] A public defender (*avocato dei poveri*) was instituted through their largesse. These groups also worked to improve the physical conditions of the prisons combating extortion, and reducing the practice of prostitution which had become an endemic problem in the prisons of Naples.

It is not surprising, given the emphasis on the sacraments of confession and communion, that Jesuits would also sponsor companies of clergy in Naples. In addition to the spiritual and charitable dimensions of the companies, the clerical groups also sought to improve their pastoral skills. In Aquila, a company of priests was founded by Sertorio Caputa, S.J., in 1607. This company of the Blessed Virgin Mary *Assonta* met "each Tuesday to be instructed in the practical ways of administering the sacraments and of assisting the dying." The group also studied the Church canons and Sacred Scripture, practiced preaching, and celebrated the Divine Office together.[36]

---

[32] *ARSI, Neap.*, 77, 1–65.   [33] *Ibid.*, 6–7.   [34] *ARSI, Neap.*, 78, 1.   [35] *Ibid.*

[36] Santagata, *Istoria*, 3, 254. The Jesuit College in Naples taught cases of conscience to its own students

The companies also generated much of the popular support for the expansion of the Jesuit educational enterprise in the seventeenth century. In the first half of the seventeenth century several new Jesuit schools were founded in Naples. Two of these schools directly emerged from the activities of Jesuit-founded companies. The first school, the Collegio Sant' Ignatio al Mercato, began as a professed house (residence) in 1611 to care for the needs of the *Congregation of the Assonta*, a company of merchants. The transition began with the Jesuit directors of the company teaching elements of Moral Theology to the clergy of the neighborhood. Such a course helped provide better confessors to serve the members of the *Assonta*. In 1623 the residence became a college and began to develop an endowment. By 1660, the college offered the full course of grammar instruction, primarily for the children of the company. The members of the Assonta company continued to meet at the school throughout the rest of the century.

The second school sprang from the *Real Congregación de Cavalleros Españoles*. The origins of the congregation date back to 1614 when Iñigo de Mendoza, S.J., organized a group for the Spanish officials of the viceregal palace. Originally titled in honor of the Blessed Sacrament, the company took the patronage of Francis Xavier in 1622 immediately after his canonization. In that same year, a residence and chapel were built for the congregants. Within the year, the residence became a college for children of the Spanish officials of the city. Enrollment in the grammar course reached 100 students by the following year.[37]

On the first of May 1584, Father Pierantonio Spinelli baptized two slaves at the Gesù Vecchio. This was the culmination of another type of apostolic activity being engaged in by the congregations founded by the Society of Jesus.[38] The next two decades would see local Jesuit activity among the slaves increase. This both fed, and was fed by, an increasing awareness of foreign mission activity. In 1601 a specific congregation was founded at the College for slaves.[39] Made up primarily of converts, their number often was augmented by catechumens who were awaiting baptism and the possibility of membership in the company. Emerging from these activities in 1603 was an Academy

from the beginning. By 1567 instruction was also given to the secular clergy and members of other religious Orders.

[37] Errichetti, *"L'antico Collegio Massimo,"* 245–46. *ANSI* conserves the rules for "The Royal Congregation of Spanish Gentlemen of the Jesuit College of St. Francis Xavier" but places its foundation in 1624 rather than 1622.   [38] Nardi, *"Opere per la conversione,"* 48.

[39] *Ibid.*, 45–7. Nardi, following Santagata, argues that the company was formed in 1601, however archival documents report the date as 1609 (*ARSI, Neap.*, 172, 110–13).

of Languages to prepare future missionaries in the languages of the
Middle East, Africa and the Orient.

Neapolitans were keenly aware of the needs of the foreign missions,
perhaps because of the close proximity of the Ottoman Empire. The
conversion of Turkish slaves and their public baptisms served to
remind the various congregants of their mission to evangelize. The
Academy of Languages, supported by several of the congregations,
served priests and seminarians eager to go to the foreign missions.
Much of the initial impetus for the school came from the congregations concerned with catechism and the preparation of catechumens.[40]
The *Congregazione di Maria Ss. Regina degli Apostoli* at the cathedral of
Naples was founded in 1646 for secular clergy interested in serving the
missions. It was not a Jesuit-sponsored congregation, but its founder,
don Sansone Carnevale, had been active as a member, then prefect, of
the congregation of priests at the Collegio Massimo.[41]

Other congregations raised funds for the missions. A letter from the
Jesuit General Mutio Vitteleschi in 1627 to the Congregation of the
Immaculate Conception thanks them for a gift of 200 ducats for "il
Collegio di Madure" in India.[42]

Two companies were founded in Lecce with the purpose of aiding
in the conversion of the Turkish slaves.[43] The Congregation of the
Epiphany of the Lord founded in 1605 counted slaves converted from
Islam as their members. The *Monte* of *Sta. Fede* was founded in 1631
for the financial relief of these converted slaves and for others who
were poor and in need.[44]

Jesuit-sponsored companies spanned the range of classes in Neapolitan society. From the nobility of the Zitti and *Javieristas* to the
converted slaves of the congregations of the *Purification* and *Epiphany*,
the Jesuits offered access to their own spirituality of Church reform
and encouraged the reception of the sacraments. Educational institutions provided the foundation and support for the companies which in
turn financed the existing schools and encouraged new Jesuit foundations.

In an ambience such as early modern Naples, already rich in the
tradition of lay confraternities, the number of Jesuit-sponsored companies mushroomed. Saverio Santagata, in his continuation of

---

[40] Errichetti, *L'antico Collegio Massimo*, 243–5.   [41] Nardi, "*Una congregazione missionaria*," 4.
[42] *ARSI, Neap.*, "*Pii Sodales*," 77.   [43] Schinosi, *Istoria*, 1, 429–30.
[44] *Ibid.* A *monte di pietà* was a financial organization closely affiliated with confraternity activity.
Because Jesuits were forbidden by the General from participating in any of the financial dealings of
the companies, the administration of funds was often transferred to separate *monti* founded and
governed by officers elected from the sponsoring company. They took responsibility for raising
and administering charitable funds in the interest of the company.

Schinosi's *Istoria*, indicates that by 1607, sixty-seven Jesuits were involved in the direction of fifty-six congregations throughout the Kingdom of Naples, serving a total of 5,633 congregants.[45] The Collegio Massimo counted thirteen of these congregations serving some 1,800 members. From a partial report of congregational activity at the College in the same year, we can chart the following statistics:[46]

Name	Founded	Clientele	Number	Affiliated[A]
Ss. Sacrament	1554	nobility	c. 20	no
Immaculate Conception	1577	theology students	349	yes (1577)
Annunciation	1579/80	younger students	130	no
Assumption	1582	merchants	899[B]	yes (1595)
Nativity	1600	sons of artisans	140	no
Annunciata	1601	grammar students	122	yes
Purification	1601–9	slaves	22	no

[A] Affiliated with the Prima primaria congregation at Rome (after 1563).
[B] This sodality was divided into four smaller sections.

The professed house, too, sponsored congregations. Their five congregations can be charted thus:[47]

Name	Founded	Clientele	Number	Affiliated
Nativity	1587	nobility	200	yes (1587)
Purification	1595	clergy	50	yes (1595)
Annunciation	1595	magistrates	80	yes (1595)
Assumption	1593?	artisans	500	no
Angels	1595?	servants	?	no

A sixth congregation was added when "the Guardian Angels" were founded in 1611. Intended for children of the nobility it counted twenty-four "*putti*" in its first year.[48] This data also indicates the final transition of the confraternity/company under Jesuit guidance – the organization of the Marian congregation and its centralization through the Prima primaria congregation in Rome.

THE MARIAN CONGREGATIONS

Among the fruits found among the externs, I say the most important one is that of a congregation of young students from the College of Naples,

[45] Santagata, *Istoria*, 3, 251. Santagata reports the founding of three more congregations by the beginning of 1608.   [46] *ARSI*, Neap. 172, 110–13.
[47] Santagata, *Istoria*, 3, 251; Chatellier, *The Europe of the Devout*, 18. Cf. *ARSI, Neap.*, 72, 85–107, 108–12.   [48] Santagata, *Istoria*, 3, 441.

which both in quantity and quality are a singular thing. There are 130 ordinary members, and another sixty who wish to join ... all of them confess and receive communion every eight days together in an oratory, they hear spiritual conferences, recite the Office of Our Lady, and they give great examples of virtue, ... devotion, and purity.[49]

Carlo Reggio, the official Visitor from Rome who made the above report to Father General Mercurian in 1580, was referring to the first Marian Congregation founded at the school in Naples. In 1577, Pierantonio Spinelli founded the Congregation of the Immaculate Conception, drawing from among his theology students at the school.[50] Spinelli, who had gained his experience of the Marian Congregations from his time at the Roman College, followed the same pattern that his confrére Jan Leunis had used there. He began first with only a few of his best students meeting privately after lectures for private devotions. What began with nine members in 1577 reached nearly 200 by the end of the decade. Spinelli limited membership in this congregation exclusively to Philosophy and Theology students. As their work became more visible other, younger students clamored to be admitted. The growing popularity of the Immaculate Conception congregation led to the establishment, in 1580, of a second one for students too young to be eligible for the first. The Congregation of the Annunciation imitated its predecessors at the school and supported many pious extracurricular activities. In this way they provided an important part of the school's spiritual presence in the city even after the professed house had come into existence. In 1601 a third student group, for those in the grammar course, was established. While other classes and ages would become involved in the movement, the Marian congregation remained primarily a student institution.

The new Marian congregations had originated in the Congregation of the Blessed Virgin Mary (*Annunciata*) formed at the Roman College in 1563 by the Belgian Jesuit Jan Leunis. This congregation, founded in the prototype school for Jesuit education, became the Prima primaria congregation to which all other Marian Congregations would come to be affiliated. Affiliation to the central congregation in Rome implied a spiritual unity between head and members that paralleled the reform plans of the Church and endorsed by the Society of Jesus. The benefits of this union, as well as its symbolic value for the Church were not missed. The lay Marian congregations reflected the Jesuits' identification with papal authority in the Church. By 1576 some thirty-thousand youth throughout the world were involved in Marian

---

[49] ARSI, *Fondo Gesuitico*, 13, 2.   [50] ARSI, *Neap.*, 80, 33.

congregations.[51] There was little doubt, then, that the young Neapolitans would seek to be affiliated with Rome. Spinelli's Immaculate Conception congregation joined a growing international band of students destined to provide additional laborers for Jesuit activities – not only during their student years, but often as later vocations to the Order.

Gregory XIII gave further impetus to the Marian congregations by granting canonical recognition of the pious association in 1584. Claudio Acquaviva, the Jesuit General who sought this recognition from the pope, had seen first-hand the work of the congregations in both Rome and Naples (where he had been rector and provincial). In 1587 he helped author and established "common rules" for all of the affiliated Marian congregations, further strengthening their sense of unity and cohesion.[52] Theoretically at least, the General controlled the naming of all spiritual directors of the Marian congregations, though usually it was delegated to the provincials. By obtaining formal papal approval for the Congregations of the Blessed Virgin Mary, and by codifying their basic structure, Acquaviva helped to create a worldwide society that over the next two centuries would include c. 2,500 affiliates.[53]

Spinelli's theology students, joined by congregations of younger students, changed the way Jesuit confraternities were organized in Naples. The question of affiliation with the Prima primaria soon confronted even the non-student organizations. Even when companies did not affiliate with Rome, they still had a model rule to follow, a new sense of apostolic purpose, and perhaps most importantly a specific spiritual identity. Reports to Rome from Naples point to three distinct ways in which these Jesuit-sponsored organizations had an impact on the city and local Church: 1. in the specific charitable and spiritual activities of the congregants in the local neighborhoods; 2. in the religious vocations fostered among their members; 3. in the establishment of new schools within the city. Through their animation of a larger population of the laity, particularly young students, the Jesuits considerably augmented their own impact throughout the city. In doing so, they created structures that would expand and develop well beyond the lives and expectations of the individuals who began them.

In his report in 1580, the Visitor Reggio identified the following activity accomplished by the Immaculate Conception congregation founded by Spinelli:

[51] Bangert, *History SJ*, 57.   [52] Chatellier, *Europe of the Devout*, 25.
[53] Bangert, *History SJ*, 107.

Some of these congregants went into the piazzas to "fish" for some and
send them to Church, and this exercise succeeded so well in Naples, where
until now it had not been tried, that they sent at times six hundred and
eight hundred people, from hill and house, to Church. There they taught
them some spiritual things, led them in prayer, and many confessed, as
many as were able with the number of confessors. This exercise is followed
on Sundays... And the city remains very edified by this work, and it
appears to everyone that a great deal of fruit is derived from it. Some of
these student congregants also go to preach in some of the churches of
Naples and nearby hamlets. These are places that would be difficult to
refuse given the arguments they make for having us.[54]

The success of "fishing" activity in Rome in 1559 could be seen in the
400 confessions heard in about five days. If Reggio is accurate in his
figures, the Immaculate Conception congregation at Naples matched
or surpassed the feat in a single weekend in 1580.[55]

That students could be found preaching in churches in Naples and
nearby towns was not too surprising given the concern at the College
for the preparation of good preachers. Jesuit scholastics were expected
to preach in the refectory and in public in order to hone their skills, so
it is likely that no exception would have been made for the theology
students of the congregation, most of whom were also preparing for
ecclesiastical careers. Once again, their presence extended Jesuit influence much farther afield than could have been possible had preaching
been confined only to the Jesuits themselves.

In the Annual Letters of the 1590s, regular mention was made of the
activities of the Marian congregations at the College. Often the report
would record the number of members and also the religious vocations
which emerged from them. In 1592, for example, 300 students belonged to the two sodalities, "from which 63 entered into various
religious communities this year."[56] The year 1593 saw eight members
of the Immaculate Conception congregation enter the Society of
Jesus, while another twenty-two entered other Orders.[57] By the last
years of the decade (1597–9 were summarized in one report), the
Collegio Massimo could count seven congregations. Religious vocations in those years included nine to the Jesuits and seventeen to other
Orders.[58] Studies indicate that many Jesuits joining in the first gener-

[54] ARSI, Fondo Gesuitico, CI, 169r.
[55] O'Malley, First Jesuits, 112–13. Grendler, Schooling in Renaissance Italy, 335, traces this method of
    "fishing" back to the works of the schools of Christian doctrine in the north of Italy in the late
    1530s.
[56] ARSI, Neap., 172, 56v. This was more than double the number reported as entering the religious
    life ten years earlier. See Villaret, Les congrégations Mariales, 189.   [57] Ibid., 73r.
[58] Ibid., 91v.

ation of the Order did so seeking the solaces of a life in a well-ordered and pious community.[59] The Marian congregations offered an introduction to this kind of ordered and pious life, so it follows that religious vocations would emerge from them.

The image of the world as a dangerous place served the purposes of the congregations. The choice of commitment to the congregation meant mutual support for a reformed life in the midst of a troubled world. "For the 'at-risk' adolescent, the Marian congregation was an asylum of security."[60] Those who found such a style of life appealing provided an important pool for vocations to the religious life.

The foundation of new Jesuit schools often followed Jesuit confraternity activity. Both the Colleges of Sant' Ignatio al Mercato and San Francisco Javier de Toledo arose out of existing congregations founded and directed by Jesuits. A third Jesuit college in Naples, however, emerged from the activities of one of the student congregations. The College of San Giuseppe a Chiaia, located on the northern shores of Naples in a neighborhood populated by fisherfolk, began in 1609 when theologians from the Collegio Massimo were transferred to the novitiate at the Nunziatella, a hill overlooking the shore of Chiaia. As part of their usual congregation activity, the students went down the hill to teach catechism to the children of Chiaia. Even after the theologians' return to the Collegio Massimo, the catechism courses continued to flourish and a congregation was established there for those students. In January of 1623 the college was founded there. While the school never thrived, it continued to teach the rudiments of Latin grammar and catechism to the children of Chiaia until the end of the century.[61]

The teaching of Christian doctrine, as a primary work of the Marian congregations, brought the need for more permanent financial and physical arrangements for its support. A letter from Father General Acquaviva in June of 1585 solicited the provincial's opinion on the sale of property to provide for the building of "an oratory for the instruction of Christian doctrine."[62] Jesuits established congregations and encouraged the foundation of 'monti' to support the activities of their members. The Congregation of Christian Doctrine (founded in 1573) merged with the Company of Catechumens (founded in 1576) in 1592. This brought the non-Christian Turkish slaves of Naples to the Collegio Massimo for catechetical instruction and marked a new function for the school. Student congregations, by teaching cat-

[59] Cohen, "Why Jesuits Joined," 237.   [60] Santagata, Istoria, 3, 392.
[61] Errichetti, "L'antico Collegio Massimo," 246–50.
[62] ARSI, Neap., 3, 91r. This might have been to serve the Congregation of Christian Doctrine.

echism, formed the basis for new congregations; these in turn, founded new schools, or created new curricula in existing ones.

CONCLUSIONS

Jesuit confraternity activity developed along three different lines. The earliest activity concerned Jesuit memberships in existing confraternities. Jesuits in Naples joined and contributed to the Bianchi confraternity from the 1550s. As other forms of Jesuit activity developed, Jesuits remained active with them. Yet the Jesuit members appeared not to have taken an active leadership role in this confraternity.

From 1552 onward, Jesuits organized their own confraternities in Naples according to their own perceived reform needs. The Zitti, with their devotion to frequent communion, commitment to secret acts of charity, and concern for orthodoxy among their neighbors, represent the new thrust of the Order. No doubt the company was loyal to its Jesuit sponsors, and zealously monitored communal behavior, but it would be difficult to read into these activities the sinister plots of later propagandists. Jesuits organized these companies and directed them along their own spiritual lines. But the membership retained control of offices and finances in the company. The multiplication of these companies indicated the popular support enjoyed by the Society of Jesus in Naples. The success of the companies in Naples can be most clearly seen in the new Jesuit schools which emerged from their activities.

From 1577 (in Naples) the Jesuit-sponsored company began to be transformed. Beginning with the theology students at the Collegio Massimo, a new form of Jesuit confraternity emerged, the Marian congregation. From the start these organizations were overtly tied to the Society of Jesus and its apostolic priorities. Tied to Rome through the Prima primaria, the Marian congregations received their Rules and Spiritual Directors directly from the hierarchy of the Order. As the Marian congregation movement spread through the classes of Neapolitan society, Jesuit attitudes were diffused more widely. Growing interest in the foreign missions and evangelization mark the success of the Marian congregation. Vocations to the Society of Jesus and other religious Orders helped justify their designation as a "seminary for the religious life."[63]

The confraternities administered by the Jesuits, then, exerted a significant impact on the Kingdom of Naples. After learning from the various reformed confraternities already in existence in the city, the Jesuit-

---

[63] Santagata, *Istoria*, III, 392.

sponsored company and the later Marian congregations were formed to help change religious behavior in Naples. Jesuits adapted the existing model of the lay confraternity with its devotions and organization to include the reform concerns of an increasingly centralized Church. They introduced their own particular devotions, created a centralized structure of authority tied to the Jesuit General at Rome, and used the congregations to promote their growing educational apostolate. The primary and immediate purpose of the Marian congregation was spiritual and for the benefit of the members. They made the *Spiritual Exercises* of Ignatius Loyola and participated in other devotions encouraged by the Jesuits.[64] Yet the outward, apostolic thrust of the confraternities increasingly gained prominence. Work with the sick, imprisoned, poor, even girls whose virtue was endangered, all provided corporal works to benefit both the congregant and society.[65] Teaching Christian doctrine, preaching, and spiritual conversations ("fishing"), made up the spiritual repertoire of the congregations. Towards the end of the sixteenth century, work for the conversion of non-Christian slaves became another sphere of activity. Fed by missionary zeal, this activity expanded into an academy for language study in 1603, and into congregations with specific concern for missions and conversions later in the century. Finally, the initial organization of a congregation planted seeds for future generations. Vocations to the religious life were fostered among their members, and the seventeenth century would see new Jesuit schools established within the city and throughout the Kingdom, the fruit of the activities of Jesuit confraternities. None of these activities originated in or were unique to Naples. Nevertheless, Neapolitans responded to them favorably. By organizing their students effectively into bands with clear ties to the central Jesuit authorities in Rome, the Jesuits were able to extend their influence throughout the city and into the hinterlands of the Kingdom.[66] While they never attained the tight control and discipline of legend, Jesuit activity with confraternities proved to be an effective tool for the Jesuits' desires for reform.

[64] Chatellier, *Europe of the Devout*, 37, asserts that the Forty Hours' Devotion originated from sodalities in Naples in 1580. *ARSI, Neap.*, 17, 21, notes that the *Exercises* were given to congregants as early as 1582.

[65] According to Chatellier, *Europe of the Devout*, 45, in 1593 the Confraternity of the Refuge was founded in Naples to protect young girls from the evils of prostitution.

[66] Villaret, *Les congregations Mariales*, 100, notes that the congregants from the Collegio Massimo, on their return to their native towns, founded similar congregations in Potenza, Thieta, Catanzaro, and Abruzzi.

CORPUS DOMINI: RITUAL METAMORPHOSES AND SOCIAL CHANGES IN SIXTEENTH- AND SEVENTEENTH-CENTURY GENOA

CLAUDIO BERNARDI

The Genoese staged civic-religious processions in celebration of two eucharistic feasts: the first took place on Holy Thursday and the second on the feast day of Corpus Domini. On Holy Thursday, a number of confraternal processions made their way towards the cathedral of San Lorenzo where the sepulchre which housed the Holy Sacrament was to be found, but on Corpus Domini only a single procession carried the Eucharist in triumph through the city, one in which confraternities had a secondary role. The liturgical reforms which were introduced in the wake of Vatican II modified the feast of Corpus Domini since it was regarded as a mere replica of Holy Thursday. During the middle ages, however, so many rituals and services marked Holy Thursday (the Reconciliation of Penitents, the Blessing of the Holy Oils, the Pedilavium), that a new liturgical feast day was created in order to celebrate the Eucharist with greater and more appropriate ceremony: this was the argument of Urban IV's 1264 bull *Transiturus de mundo* which promulgated the celebration of Corpus Domini throughout Christendom after its beginnings in the diocese of Liège.[1] This article will trace the development of the two feasts, and seek to demonstrate how the evolution of religious norms, political institutions, and the brotherhoods themselves made confraternities central to the public celebration of one feast, while they had no influence on the other.

Despite the fact that it was not originally part of the liturgical office for the day, the procession became, in the course of the fourteenth century,

---

Archival abbreviations employed in the notes which follow: Archivio di Stato di Genova (ASG), particularly three collections: Archivio Segreto (A Se); Giunta di Giurisdizione (G Gi); Sala Senarega (S Se); and Archivio Storico Civico di Genova (ASCG) and its Fondo dei Padri del Comune (F PaC).
[1] Rubin, *Corpus Christi*, 164–81.

the distinguishing event of Corpus Domini, and for many cities in western Europe the most important religious and civic occasion of the year. Such success can probably be ascribed to the way the event encapsulated the tension between the Christian ideal of brotherhood and its actual manifestation; for one day in the year at least, the earthly city sought to transform itself into its heavenly version. The celebration of Christian unity in the body of Christ did not seek to conceal the divisions of everyday life. Corpus Domini was an opportunity to express faith in what Bossy has called the "social miracle,"[2] the slow creation of a spiritual brotherhood in which feuds, rivalries, civil wars and hostility would cease, to be replaced by material and spiritual assistance shared freely among members of the same family in the first instance and then among members of the same social groups. The health of the social body, of the city, and of the state was dependent upon the health of its individual members. The mystery of the Eucharist showed that God was not a concept but a body, three persons in one, and the suffering, death, and resurrection in the Christian story applied both to individual and social bodies. Heaven and earth, the ideal and the actual, influenced each other.

The first accounts of the Corpus Domini liturgy in Genoa date from the early decades of the fourteenth century. The custom of holding a procession was probably introduced during the same period, since it is known that the doge Simon Boccanegra (1339–44) used to accompany the Eucharist in person carrying a flaming torch. As in other cities, the procession, despite its religious significance, was dominated by laymen rather than the clergy: the principal evidence for this is a ruling of the Genoese synod of 1375 which made clerical participation in all the principal feast-day processions obligatory, but omits all mention of Corpus Domini. The civic significance of the event is further borne out by the existing records (for example, those relating to 1412) of the contributions made by the *Comune* and by private citizens towards the costs of decorating the streets with tapestries, branches of oak and myrtle, and sprays of broom. The 1459 statutes drawn up by the *Padri del Comune*, or city elders, provide for the annual gift of twelve torches and the election of twelve citizens dressed in ceremonial robes to carry them. The political importance of the event is also revealed by the decision of several of the city's doges to take part in the procession in person (Barnaba Guano, for example, in 1415 agreed to carry one of the poles which held the *palio* or baldacchin aloft, a task which his predecessors had never performed).[3]

Edoardo Grendi has shown how the public ceremonies in the cathedral of San Lorenzo carried a special symbolic significance on account of

---

[2] Bossy, *Christianity in the West*, ch. 4.   [3] Cambiaso, *L'anno ecclesiastico*, 63–6.

the very close connection between the religious and political life of the
city. The structure of the Genoese Republic was reflected in the intri-
cately balanced formation of the so-called *mobbe*, composed of *bianchi* and
neri, *nobiles*, *populares*, and *artifices*, who did the carrying in the most
important processions of the time: the Invention of the Cross, Corpus
Domini, and the feast days of St. Sebastian, St. John the Baptist and the
Virgin Mary. In the specific case of the Corpus Domini procession there
is a regulation dating from the end of the fourteenth century which states
that the privilege of bearing the palio should be given to twenty-four
citizens, twelve each from the city's Guelf and Ghibelline factions.[4] The
factions were reconciled for this celebration of Christ the bringer of
peace. In 1416 the doge and the elders approved the "long-established
and beneficial custom" of electing twenty-four "antiquos and probos
cives" to carry the palio. With the increasing importance of the eucharistic cult in the fourteenth century, however, there was a danger that the
fierce hostility between the factions would be transformed into zealous
competition for ceremonial prestige. In 1439, forty-seven of the city's
nobles came together to donate a preciously carved wooden coffer for the
Corpus Domini procession; the archbishop of the time, Imperiale,
granted two of their number in return the honor of joining those who
carried the palio. The same privilege was extended by the doge Campo-
fregoso in 1448 to a *societas* of youths who had contributed a sum of more
than 600 florins towards the tabernacle in the cathedral.[5]

Grendi has also linked the increase in the number of confraternities
dedicated to Corpus Domini in the fifteenth century to the waves of
intense political activity in the city during the same period, especially
when led by the younger generation in unsuccessful attempts to oust the
ruling elders. In 1528, after many years of conflict and discord, Andrea
Doria's reforms of the Republic established an aristocratic oligarchy
under which the government of the city was entrusted to twenty-eight
families, of which twenty-three were to be *antiche* and the remaining five
populari. The houses which could prove their descent from a single
founder were called *famiglie*; those in which various branches shared the
same surname were called *alberghi*. The constitution introduced in 1576
abolished the distinction between the ancient and new nobility and made
all the posts in the government elective. The settlement of 1528 had
proved possible in part because the city's self-governing associations,
among which the *societates Sanctissimi Corporis Christi* were prominent,
had been successfully marginalized. Such associations differed from the
post-Tridentine SS. Sacramento confraternities. They were freely for-

⁴ Grendi, *La repubblica aristocratica*, 114.   ⁵ Grendi, "Le compagnie del SS. Sacramento," 456–7.

med organizations of laymen who sought to gain the support of the various churches in the city for the promotion of the Eucharistic cult, in the process giving rise to intense competition over both the places where the rituals were held and all their trappings (choir-stalls, chapels, furnishings, altars, works of art, etc.) and the celebration of the rituals themselves (especially the visits to the sepulchre on Holy Thursday and Good Friday). Since these associations of private citizens were formally established societies, with their own statutes, legal autonomy, and assets used to support their charitable work (and buy influence), the Republic regarded them as groups outside its control which encouraged factionalism and threatened to destabilize the new and hardwon balance of power. The early sixteenth century saw a proliferation of these *Compagnie del Corpo di Cristo*, of both noble and plebeian origin.[6] Alongside them there were numerous noble and "popular" companies or associations which took such names as *della Pace*, *della Carità*, *della Concordia*, *dell'Unione*, and *della Fraternità*, and which were frequently linked to the cult of the Eucharist.[7] In these associations, the struggle between the city's old and new nobility again took the form of competitiveness over the cult and possessiveness of consecrated spaces: they were the particular targets of Doria's reforms in 1528. The central authority succeeded in reclaiming for public use the most prestigious church in the city, the cathedral of S. Lorenzo, and in transforming the associations into Eucharistic companies or expropriating their assets for the public purse.[8] The noble companies before the reforms of 1528 can be seen as vestiges of an outworn political system, essentially factions ruled by clans, and their religious activity motivated principally by the need to acquire social prestige and political influence. It must be noted, however, that the intense competition for the control of religious ritual which these groups inspired was nonetheless a considerable advance in civilized behavior over the cruel massacres and vendettas of former times.

The Compagnie del Corpo di Cristo as transformed into confraternities of the *SS. Sacramento*, the model of lay association in the Counter Reformation, introduced considerable changes to confraternal activity throughout Liguria.[9] They differed from the older flagellant confraternities known in Genoa as *casacce* in having no place of their own for meeting and for worship; they were usually based instead in the parish church and took care of all aspects of the cult of the Eucharist, taking it to the sick, setting up the altar of repose on Holy Thursday, conducting processions

---

[6] Grendi, "Le società dei giovani," 509–28.   [7] Grendi, *La repubblica aristocratica*, 105–6.
[8] *Ibid.*,128.
[9] On the model and the fundamental role played by the SS. Sacramento confraternities in the modern period see Zardin, "Il rilancio delle confraternite," 129–31.

annually on Corpus Domini (and later monthly), and practicing the Forty Hours' Devotion, or *Quarantore*.[10] Unlike the nobility's devotional associations, these parish confraternities aimed to reach many more people than the members of family groups, oratories, and trade guilds, and their purposes were primarily religious and spiritual. Their local roots were strong because of their connection with the parish church which acted as a unifying focus for the community's social and religious differences (of class, between nobility and plebeians, of ritual, between laymen and clergy, and of religious devotion, between its public and private forms).[11] The close co-operation in matters of worship between the confraternities and the parish clergy often extended into administrative responsibilities and thus enhanced the former's social role, unlike the autonomous associations which worked as a rule to protect their own interests, activities, and prestige.[12] From the sixteenth century onwards and not only in Genoa, the Christian ideals of charity and social harmony were expressed in a variety of activities, institutions and forms – public ceremonies, charitable work,[13] a more inclusive sense of spiritual brotherhood, schools for religious instruction, an interaction between the Church's universalism and local autonomy – all of which tended to overcome traditional conflict and divisions among families, neighborhoods, confraternities, trade and craft guilds, and civil and religious authorities.[14]

If the cult of the Eucharist was to be a source of unity, it had to be the object of universal rather than private devotion. In order to achieve public responsibility for the cult, the Genoese pursued a policy of gradually excluding the private associations. The administration of the cathedral of San Lorenzo was entrusted to the *Padri del Comune* in the 1500s. The two most important cults – St. John the Baptist and the Holy Sacrament – thus came under the direct control of the Genoese Republic and the various associations and their claims on spaces within the cathedral were either transformed or abolished, such as the *Vera Pace e Concordia* company which was the last such association in charge of the cult of the Eucharist.[15] The abolition of the companies' private cult in the

---

[10] An exception to this rule may be found in the Compagnia del SS. Sacramento e delle Cinque Piaghe in Marassi, a suburb of Genoa, whose statutes as approved by the civil authorities have survived (in ASG, G Gi, 130). The company had its own oratory and its activities were completely different from the liturgical duties carried out by the "SS. Sacramento" confraternities (see Ginella, "Le confraternite della Valbisagno," 255–62).

[11] Raggio points out that the parish church was not necessarily a focus for local integration but, as a public place where social prestige and political power could be displayed, it provoked contention, especially in the small rural centers of the Ligurian hinterland: see *Faide e parentele*, 138.

[12] See Grendi's discussion of the parishes in Cervo, *Il Cervo e la repubblica*, 44–6.

[13] Savelli, "Dalle confraternite allo Stato," 171–216.   [14] See Raggio, *Faide e parentele*.

[15] Grendi, *La repubblica aristocratica*, 129.

Cathedral of S. Lorenzo also brought an end to factional rivalry for ceremonial prestige. In 1553 the city elders commissioned a silver chest bearing a tabernacle in which the Host would be carried; unlike previous tabernacles, the chest was a public and not a private gift. Public funds also went towards the baldacchin in 1564.[16] The Genoese Republic was now responsible for all the organizational aspects of the procession from proclamations about cleaning and decorating the streets to arranging, through the official master of ceremonies, the order of procession.

After the Council of Trent, the presence of the Church authorities began to be felt. In the provincial synod of 1567 the guiding principles decided at Trent were given local form: profane images and spectacles which served to delay or distract were to be banned from all religious processions, including Corpus Domini.[17] Their elimination testified to the need to rid Catholic devotion of all those aspects which had been the object of Protestant attack: the pagan accretions, the love of visual display, the rituals and spectacles designed to enhance personal prestige. At the same time the Church did not wish to commit the iconoclastic excesses of the evangelicals and their puritanical approach to ritual; in the effort to abandon the corporative and private aspects of medieval piety, carefully defined divisions between the sacred and the profane needed to be established. Examples of the abolition of practices considered to be unChristian, or at least impure, can be found in the reform of the rules of the flagellant confraternities which Archbishop Sauli took over from Borromeo with the addition of a few local regulations.[18] While recognizing spheres of lay autonomy, the Church claimed full control and authority over religious content. Such a claim was uncontentious within churches and monasteries, but matters were more complex when it was a question of public ceremonial where the jurisdictions of the civil and ecclesiastical authorities overlapped. In the case of Corpus Domini, the most urgent measure needed was to ensure the participation of the clergy as guarantors of the cult's universal and not merely local appeal. Archbishop Agostino Salvago in 1564 applied the very recent Tridentine ruling that the regular and secular clergy were obliged to participate in public processions; he urged the Genoese clergy, on pain of excommunication and other penalties, to present themselves in solemn array at the tenth hour on the feast day of Corpus Domini in the cathedral. His only concession was that one or two priests could be left behind in the monasteries to hold mass for the sick and frail.[19]

---

[16] Locatelli, *La processione del Corpus Domini*, 9–15.
[17] *Synodi Diocesanae et Provinciales editae atque ineditae S. Genuensis Ecclesiae* (Genova, 1833), 102.
[18] Cambiaso, "Casacce e confraternite," 92–4.
[19] Locatelli, *La processione del Corpus Domini*, 19–20.

The order of the procession as described by the official master of ceremonies in 1588 (and found more or less unvaryingly in all the subsequent official ceremonials) reflected a traditional tripartite social division: the procession was led by the regular and secular clergy positioned in hierarchical order and headed by the bishop walking immediately in front of the coffer containing the Holy Sacrament. The middle section of the procession was divided jointly between the religious and civil authorities. The coffer was escorted by the "Padri del Comune," half of them preceding with music and the rest following behind. The clergy was nominally responsible for carrying the coffer but, because of its weight proper porters were needed. These wore white hoods and worked in teams of four which took turns to bear the load; a white cloth fixed round the coffer hid them from view. The official representatives of the Republic followed behind: first the senators, accompanied by the civil militia and soldiers carrying halberds; the mace-bearers, the page, registrars, the sword-bearer and the master of ceremonies preceded the doge, the ambassador of Spain and other officials, all walking two by two. The third part of the procession was made up of the guild members. They were instructed not to bring with them boys to pick up the wax which dripped from their torches, since their presence was not only regarded as unseemly but might also hold up the procession.[20]

At first sight the tripartite division into orders or estates seems to perpetuate the old hierarchical categories of priests, warriors, and workers, but the numerous conflicts which arose over precedence and the general organization of the procession present a different picture. The three orders were not seen as hierarchically linked but as distinct and autonomous entities acting in co-operation. The parity between civil and religious authorities is clear; the disputes and rivalries which inevitably arose were dealt with by a special magistrature, the *Giunta di Giurisdizione*, set up by the Republic to oversee relations between the city and the Church. A less obvious feature is the contractual power wielded by private associations and individuals. Private citizens' relations with the religious and secular authorities were founded on the principle of their voluntary commitment to saving their souls or working for the *res publica*. The traditional image of a pyramid-like social organization is misleading; relations between the component orders or estates were polyphonic, as in a choir or orchestra. It is significant that the Italian word used whenever

[20] In the *Diurnale nel quale si contiene tutto quello che si fa dalla Serenissima Repubblica quando esce di Palazzo et come se ricevono le visite e se visitano altri Serenissimi in nome di lor Signorie Serenissime fatto dal R. Hieronimo Bordonio Sermonetano primo mastro di cerimonie. L'anno 1588* can be found the *Ordinanza del modo che se doverà far per la città il giorno del Santissimo Corpo de Christo, ordinata dal mastro de cerimonie et approvata da tutti due gli Serenissimi Colleggi il di 14 di giugno del 1588*, ASG, A Se, 474.

the procession was disrupted by conflict or dispute is "sconcertata," literally "dis-concerted." In 1589 a dispute among the clergy over precedence aroused the indignation and disgust of the Senate. The *maestro di cappella* was at odds with the cathedral chaplains and walked off with the choir, leaving the procession without music and thus "much disrupted because it failed to move" (*molto sconcertata perché non se caminava*).[21] In 1592 the master of ceremonies complained that the procession had been *alquanto sconcertata* because of the length of time needed for the change-over between the different groups of bearers and because the streets lacked decoration.[22] Serious disorders were recorded in 1590 when conflict broke out among the guilds;[23] in 1591 the procession divided into two at the gates of the jetty, with the clergy marching on to the jetty-point and the Senate and other civic officials refusing to go, despite a former agreement.[24] In 1593 the captains of the civic guard, heedless of the doge's commands, re-occupied their prestigious position immediately behind the coffer, although three years before they had made way for the senators.[25] The princes of Church and State soon came into open conflict over their relative status. Archbishop Alessandro Centurione had taken it upon himself to place the episcopal throne in the cathedral in a more prominent position than the doge's seat. No compromise seemed possible and in 1597 the Senate decided to boycott the procession and refused to allow the doge's standards to be displayed within the cathedral. At the time appointed for the church service to begin, the civil authorities did not take up their usual position in the choirstalls but waited outside seated in the piazza for the procession to begin. When the baldacchin had reached a point midway down the nave, the senators took the supporting poles as custom required and accompanied the Host into the piazza. The guilds were placed between the Archbishop and the Host, and on the return to the cathedral, Centurione had to wait a considerable time for the coffer surmounted by the tabernacle with the Host to arrive. When the civil authorities arrived, they escorted the Host as far as the first bay of the nave and then left by the central door and returned to the doge's palace.[26] The question of which power took priority was only one among many contentious issues which divided the civil and religious authorities which characterized the Ancien Régime; for the purpose of the present essay it is enough to understand that Church and State represented

---

[21] *Ordinanza del modo che si doverà far per la città il giorno del Santissimo Corpo de Christo . . . 1589*, ASG, A Se, 474.

[22] *Procession del S.mo Corpo de Christo dell'anno 92 con l'intervento del Reverendissimo Arcivescovo*, ASG, A Se, 474.   [23] *Procession del S.mo Corpo di Christo* (1590), ASG, A Se, 474.

[24] *Procession del S.mo Corpo di Christo dell'anno 1591*, ASG, A Se, 474.

[25] *Procession del S.mo Corpo de Christo l'anno 1593*, ASG, A Se, 474.

[26] *Procession del S.mo Corpo de Christo dell'anno 1597*, ASG, A Se, 474.

different constituencies, the universal and the local, and worked towards the shared goal of social unity in different ways. Their agreement was considered to be essential for the smooth running not only of daily life but also of exceptional events like the Corpus Domini celebrations.[27]

Unlike the Church or the ruling patrician class, the third estate and the city's population in general had no tribunals, no powers of enforcement, no magistrature and officers, no means or men at their disposal, but they were nevertheless aware that the success of the procession – as of the broader social consensus which underlay it – depended on their agreement and active participation. The official ceremonials make the reason clear. In 1589, many places in the city were praised for the cloths and hangings which were fittingly displayed while at the same time other sites were criticized for their failure to comply.[28] In 1590 the poverty of the street decoration led the authorities to devise a scheme whereby artisans asked nobles to lend them hangings and pictures to display on the facades of their houses "regardless of owner, as is the custom in Rome" ("senza guardare a case di nessuno, come se costuma a Roma."[29]) In 1591 there was again a proposal that special provision should be made to see that the streets were decorated adequately, as was the custom "throughout Christendom" and also in Genoa "where everyone agrees but few do

[27] A notable conflict between State and Church in Genoa affected the Corpus Domini procession: this was occasioned by the refusal of the Cardinal Archbishop of the time, Stefano Durazzo, to recognize the doge's claims to royal status after the Virgin Mary had been proclaimed Queen of Genoa in 1637 and the Republic's dominion in Corsica had been transformed into a kingdom. The Republic had adopted this stratagem in order to give the doge equal if not superior status to the Cardinal, whose title (as a prince of the Church) was higher than the doge's but still less than royal. The dispute focused on where to seat the Cardinal and the doge in the cathedral. The laity stood in the nave, the clergy sat in the presbytery, the civil authorities sat in between; the doge, as the highest civil authority sat with the clergy, but this opened up a separate question of precedence. The authority with the higher rank sat in the more prominent Gospel side to the right of the altar, with the other relegated to the Epistle side on the left. Cardinal Durazzo refused to recognize the doge's claim to royal status, since this would entitle the doge to sit on the Gospel side. The parties reached a compromise eight years later by moving the doge's throne to the Gospel side but leaving it in a position slightly below the cardinal's throne. Durazzo's successor, Giovanni Battista Spinola, rejected this compromise after he became Archbishop in 1664. The Republic renewed its claim that the doge should occupy the most prominent position on the Gospel side, and a new and lengthy legal battle was joined. For an account of this episode and its effects on the procession, see Locatelli, *La processione del Corpus Domini*, 62–86, and Franchini Guelfi, *Le Casacce*, 62. For documentary evidence on the processions in the seventeenth century, see the annual accounts recorded by the masters of ceremonies in ASG, A Se, 474 to 1614; filza 475 to 1638; filza 476 to 1658; filza 477 to 1671; filza 478 to the end of the century, when on 20 June 1698 the master of ceremonies declares that describing the Republic's ceremonies each year no longer serves any useful purpose since they "are always the same" and having been already fully described in the past, are no longer "worth recording."   [28] ASG, A Se, 474 (1589).

[29] "Procession del S.mo Corpo di Christo" (1590), ASG, A Se, 474.

anything about it."[30] The Genoese Republic can be seen as made up of different bodies whose co-operation for the most important civic-religious ceremony of the year required careful stage-management.

The city elders each year issued a proclamation which, as we can read in the text for 1661, ordered the streets to be cleaned and rubbish or other obstructions to be removed and urged citizens to decorate their houses with hangings and religious paintings; those who were responsible for constructing the arches under which the procession passed were re-minded to leave enough space for the baldacchin to get through; the *consoli delle arti* were asked to come to the cathedral piazza in time to organize the guilds' parade and distribute candles and torches (which were to cost no more than 15 lire in accordance with the decree passed in December 1659). Any attempt at self-display on the part of the guilds was firmly discouraged. The musicians too were to assemble with their instruments early in the cathedral; if they failed to comply, they incurred strict penalties. Finally all the inhabitants and shopkeepers in the streets through which the procession was due to pass were ordered to hang awnings above the street both to protect the procession from the sun's rays and to lend the event an air of greater decorum.[31] The commune also fixed the stopping-places along the route where the bearers of the baldacchin changed hands. The 1661 text also lays down the order of precedence for the ninety-six guilds for the benefit of the consoli delle arti in charge of them.[32]

Despite the recurrent legal wrangles, the disputes over precedence, the complaints about the lack of enthusiasm and the disorders of various kinds, the impression of a stable equilibrium underlying the Corpus Domini ceremony persists. If we are to judge from the rare instances of internal conflict in the 300-year history of the Genoese Republic, it was the festive symbol of a socio-political system successfully founded on the substantive agreement of diverse powers.

The flagellant confraternities proved more resistant to the model of peaceful co-existence among different social categories which the Corpus

---

[30] "Procession del S.mo Corpo di Christo dell'anno 1591," ASG, A Se, 474.

[31] ASCG, F PaC, 297, no. 98. The "filza" contains the various regulations laid down by the "Padri del Comune" for the Corpus Domini procession from 1657 to 1696. There is a list of the names of all those residents in the relevant neighborhoods who had been chosen by lot to take charge of the street decoration. The names of the musicians involved are also specified. In 1696 there were seventeen singers in the choir (sopranos, contraltos, tenors and basses) and eighteen players in the orchestra on violas, violins and harps (no. 454).

[32] ASCG, F PaC, 297, doc. no. 98. The number of guilds represented, listed on occasion in the order of the position in the procession and at other times alphabetically, changes from year to year: there are 85 in 1666 (no. 151) and 1668 (no. 201), 86 in 1662 (no. 133) and 1669 (no. 215), 89 in 1670 (no. 242), 90 in 1675 (no. 310), 91 in 1676 (no. 314).

Domini procession came to symbolize. The Genoese flagellants directed their energies to quelling civil discord and promoting good works, but after the reforms of 1528 they began to foster among the city's working population a sense of the other great theme of the Corpus Domini festivities: food for the spirit. For the educated classes, such symbolic nourishment was constituted by literature, politics, philosophy, theatrical and courtly entertainments; for the illiterate populace, public festivity was the highest expression of heavenly food.

The Genoese casacce came into being for the most part with the flagellant movement of 1260 and were fully established and reformed under the movement of the "Bianchi" in 1399 and the apostolic work of S. Vincenzo Ferreri at the beginning of the fifteenth century: nineteen are recorded in a list drawn up in 1410.[33] According to the chronicler Giustianiani, their principal collaborative ritual was the Good Friday procession. Five thousand confratelli clothed in sackcloth traversed the streets in total silence calling at churches and beating themselves until the blood ran in a spectacle which moved the sinful and the pious alike.[34] The casacce initially met in the churches from which they took their names, but in the course of the fifteenth and sixteenth centuries they acquired their own permanent oratories and thus became independent of the parish churches and the religious orders. Together with the nobility's confraternities, the casacce, whose members were drawn mainly from the city's lower classes, were the target of the 1528 reforms. The Republic set up a *collegio* consisting of five annually elected syndics whose responsibility it was to tackle all the problems associated with the casacce and to organize their part in the ceremonies held on Holy Thursday, regarded as potentially the most disruptive occasion in the year. The success of the Eucharistic cult in the fifteenth century had led the flagellant confraternities to move their main public ritual from Good Friday to Holy Thursday. The visit to the sepulchre in San Lorenzo led to bouts of fierce competition among the casacce, which centered not only on the rival displays of coffers, vestments, singing and crucifixes, but often ended in fighting which led to violent assault and even on occasion murder.[35] The event was judged to be in need of serious reform and in 1602 the Senate

---

[33] Cambiaso, "Casacce e confraternite," 83.   [34] *Ibid.*, 95–6.

[35] A vivid description of the carnival-like and on occasion violent mayhem caused by the procession of the casacce can be found in an unusual text: a documentary novel by the Genoese nobleman Giovanni Ambrosio Marini, *La Settimana Santa ben avventurosamente sfuggita* (Genoa: 1657), 316–21. Marini inveighs against the disorder which occurred regularly each year causing injuries and deaths and blames the "confratelli" who are only intent on dressing for display, make changes to the established route and compete to carry the cross so that they can be "admired by the ladies." He supports the abolition of the casacce, originally formed for devotional purposes but now increasingly dissolute.

issued a series of decrees to bring it under control.[36] It was forbidden to carry weapons during the procession; a route to and from the cathedral was fixed for each casaccia and care was taken to avoid the possibility of any encounter between the casacce who most detested each other, such as the three dedicated to St. James – S. Giacomo delle Fucine, S. Giacomo della Marina, and SS. Giacomo e Leonardo.[37] The arrivals of the casacce at the sepulchre in San Lorenzo were timed precisely with an interval of fifteen minutes left between them.[38]

In the 1528 reforms, the twenty casacce were the only confraternities to be officially recognized by the Genoese Republic; despite their later acceptance of the rules laid down for them by Archbishop Sauli in 1587, this meant that they came under the jurisdiction of the civil rather than the ecclesiastical authorities and were thus a striking exception in Counter-Reformation Italy. In 1748 the then Archbishop Saporiti was astonished that such an obvious breach of the provisions of canon law had not raised any objections on the part of his predecessors.[39] The State's control and defense of the casacce had a twofold motive: the first was to limit the power of the Church and the second was to control the populace. Anonymous accusations at times of public catastrophe or profound social unrest urged the suspension or outright abolition of the confraternal processions, but only on very rare occasions did the authorities move to suppress the casacce; their role as a comparatively safe outlet for the discontents of the most oppressed social stratum in the city's aristocratic oligarchy was too valuable to discard.[40]

---

[36] Alfonso, "Casacce e confraternite," 43–4.

[37] In 1772 government officials banned the three casacce from going under the name of S. Giacomo Maggiore or S. Giacomo Galiziano and from using it in speech, in songs, on coats of arms and mottoes. All three wished to use the name and it was a source of fierce rivalry and jealousy. Their protests at the ban forced the doge to intervene personally with little result; the widespread and ostentatious disregard of the ban meant that it had to be lifted; the battle between the supporters of the white and the black S. Giacomo casacce continued (the first was S. Giacomo della Marina and the second S. Giacomo delle Fucine): see Levati, *I dogi di Genova*, 4, 416–20. See also the "biglietti di calice" for 6 May and 19 August 1772, ASG, A Se, 95.

[38] Numerous regulations concerning times and routes for the "casacce" from each of the five neighborhoods can be found in ASG, G Gi, 124.

[39] Levati, *I dogi di Genova*, 3, 341–2 relates how Saporiti re-invigorated the traditional Corpus Domini procession, but also introduced some innovations in the order of precedence, in particular promoting the cathedral canons over the nobility. He had a fresco painted in his palace depicting the procession and all the positions of the ecclesiastical and civil ranks who participated in it to serve as a kind of permanent record. On his death in 1767 the Republic ordered the fresco to be painted over and the order of procession which existed before Saporiti to be restored.

[40] Grendi, "Morfologia e dinamismo," 295. Levati, *I dogi di Genova*, 3, 358–62 mentions the "popular unrest" of 1768. In a short space of time three people had been killed for no good reason by the city's police; the authorities had taken no action against them. General indignation was running high and it was feared the casacce would take revenge on the "casaccia di S. Antonio," whose members were drawn from the police force, during the Holy Thursday procession. Despite

The casacce were thus allowed to grow and flourish: in the eighteenth
century at the height of their splendor, a wide variety of rich objects was
to be found among the trappings accumulated for their processions: the
coffers for the confraternity's patron saint, wooden sculptures created by
famous artists such as Anton Maria Maragliano, huge crucifixes in tor-
toiseshell and the arms embossed in gold and silver, richly ornamented
lanterns, cloaks for the priors with great trains for attendant pages to carry,
maces surmounted by silver figures of the patron saint, robes and capes,
embroidered silk handkerchieves, splendid banners.[41] The rich costumes,
the beautiful coffers and the splendor of the processional trappings were
accompanied by the public displays of the confratelli themselves. On-
lookers could admire the strength and dexterity of the young men
carrying the massive crosses,[42] the concerts with songs sung by the most
beautiful local girls known as *pellegrine*, the theatrical performances such
as that of the youth in the role of St. James who went round the city on
horseback preaching in Spanish.[43] This late eighteenth-century opulence
and the fierce competition to outdo each other in splendor and display
tended to obscure, like the hoods worn by the confratelli, the social role
of the casacce: their roots in the city's poorest quarters, their ability to
draw their local neighborhood together, their systems of mutual aid and
support for the most despised classes of laborers such as porters and dyers.
This underlying social function can most clearly be seen in their collaboration with the civil authorities at times of famine or great hardship,[44] the
use of the oratories as hospitals and the help given by the confratelli
during the terrible outbreak of plague in 1657–8.[45] In the eighteenth
century the casacce also provided schooling on workdays for children
from the poorest families.[46] Performances and other recreational activities

warnings, however, the gathering was allowed to proceed and passed off without incident, except
for a dispute which broke out when a group of soldiers tried to block the way of a hooded
confratello. A large number of confratelli from the SS. Pietro e Paolo casaccia rushed to his aid and
in the tension unguarded words were spoken. Two people were arrested but almost immediately
released.   [41] Grosso, *Le casacce genovesi*, 5–7.

[42] For an account of the antics of the nobleman Domenico Spinola with the crucifix belonging to the
casacce of S. Giacomo delle Fucine and S. Giacomo della Marina and the mishaps which occurred
in 1780, see Levati, *I dogi di Genova*, 4, 407–8. On the competition between crucifixes and the
restrictions of the authorities, *ibid.*, 422–6.

[43] On 29 February 1752, the official representatives of the casacce prohibited the former custom of
bringing horses into the cathedral of S. Lorenzo and forbade the singing of songs and lauds which
had not been specially approved; these vetoes were directed especially against the confraternities
"sotto titolo de SS. Giacomo ed Antonio," ASG, G Gi, 124.

[44] Alfonso, "Casacce e confraternite," 47.

[45] Cambiaso, "Casacce e confraternite," 100. For the outbreak of plague in 1743, see also ASG, A Se,
1639B, the "biglietti di calice" for 5, 23, and 28 March 1743.

[46] Father Lorenzo Garaventa's success in 1757 in setting up free schooling for the children of poor
families led to suggestions that the large oratory belonging to the "casaccia" of S. Andrea could be

were also held for the entire local community in the oratories.[47] The oratories also housed other confraternities and pious associations: at least four can be found in each casaccia.[48]

Confraternal associations were very numerous in Genoa: in addition to the casacce, there were eighty-three secret oratories recorded by the "Giunta di Giurisdizione" in 1751 and the church confraternities.[49] The influence of the Counter Reformation together with the growth of new religious orders and new spiritual attitudes encouraged a more inward form of devotion and the spread of confraternities which, as Weissman has pointed out, preferred a less external expression of spiritual discipline.[50] Yet the pious exercises, the veneration for the Eucharist, the assiduous frequenting of the sacraments and the daily examination of conscience, did not serve to develop the spiritual growth of the individual confratelli and their associations alone; they also led to the creation of rituals which were more centered on the church than the confraternity itself. The history of Genoese confraternities reveals a growing hostility towards the casacce, especially in the eighteenth century, and not only on the part of the nobility; the city's artisans and middle classes began to see them as superseded forms of religious association.[51] The festive opulence of the casacce at the end of the eighteenth century can thus be seen as the dazzling sunset of an essentially unorthodox model of religious association: juridically secular, doctrinally Catholic, ritually "popular."

The year 1797 marked a watershed. For some time life in Genoa had been affected by events in revolutionary France. On 26 April the aristocratic government prohibited the processions of the casacce for fear of popular uprisings.[52] 14 June was the eve of Corpus Domini: in the Piazza dell'Acquaverde the *Libro d'oro*, the register of the city's noble families kept in the Palazzo Reale, was burnt. Over the ashes of its pages, which had depicted coats of arms and aristocratic emblems, there was raised a Tree of Liberty, marking the end of the Genoese Republic.[53] The casacce

---

used for the purpose. In 1770 the school moved to the oratory of S. Stefano and then to S. Ambrogio. In the meantime two other schools had been established: in 1761 in the casaccia of SS. Giacomo e Leonardo and in 1762 in the oratory of S. Giacomo della Marina. See Cambiaso, "Casacce e confraternite," 100–1. See Levati, *I dogi di Genova*, 3, 375–7, for an account of the way the casaccia boycotted the initiative at S. Andrea delle Fucine. The doge had to intervene in order to obtain the use of the oratory of S. Stefano.

[47] *Ibid.*, 185. In 1750 the Senate ruled that the "casacce" of S. Giovanni Battista and S. Bartolomeo were to remove the theatres from their oratories in order to allow confratelli to perform their devotions undisturbed.

[48] ASG, S Se, 3132: this contains the statutes of various casacce and associated companies. The latter's rules occasionally include a clause on their obligations towards the principal confraternity in the Holy Thursday procession to S. Lorenzo.   [49] Grendi, "Confraternite e mestieri," 239.

[50] Weissman, "Cults and contexts," 214.   [51] Grendi, "Confraternite e mestieri," 263.

[52] Levati, *I dogi di Genova*, 4, 672.   [53] Levati, *I dogi di Genova*, 4, 685–8.

entered their final phase: suppressed in 1811, restored after 1814, only to be abolished again in 1835[54], they failed to flourish under the new middle-class state with its doctrines of equality, fraternity, and liberty and with no time for the obscurantism of the flagellant confraternities. A new chapter opened with the Savoy dynasty and the Church working together to eliminate their independence by bringing them under the control of the parishes, preventing their public processions and displays, and demolishing their oratories. With the disappearance of the old regime which had protected them, the casacce had no means of survival except for the accumulated material treasury of their devotion in the past. This artistic patrimony was rapidly dispersed in the nineteenth century only to be recovered on occasion in the present one for exhibitions and museums, organized events and anniversaries, in short, the cultural sites and rituals of our postmodern religion.[55] Yet the charitable ideals of the old casacce and confraternities still live on in the voluntary associations found in Genoa and throughout Italy today which can be seen as a new expression of the ideals underlying Corpus Domini.

[54] Grendi, "Morfologia e dinamismo," 302.
[55] See the catalogues of the exhibitions held in 1939, *Le casacce e la scultura*, and in 1982, *La Liguria delle casacce*, and Franchini Guelfi, *Le casacce*.

FAITH'S BOUNDARIES: RITUAL AND TERRITORY IN RURAL PIEDMONT IN THE EARLY MODERN PERIOD

ANGELO TORRE

1. Local religion has often been analysed largely as expressions of *mentalités* or as a set of spiritual attitudes.[1] This seriously distorts the sources on this subject which have come down to us; it abstracts beliefs from the context in which they were recorded and separates them from the institutions which have inventoried and classified them. Such a selective approach reflects a conviction that the religious behavior of rural and urban populations under the Ancien Régime can be analysed without reference to other forms of activity. The actual practices of particular individuals or of groups are subsumed under their religious aspirations,

This essay is based on the reports of pastoral visitations kept in the diocesan archives of Alba, Asti, and Mondovì, and employs the following archival abbreviations: *Archivio della Curia Vescovile di Alba (ACV Alba)*, m. 26, Visita di Mons Marino, 1573–80; visita apostolica di mons. Montiglio, 1585; Visita di mons. Capriano, 1590; m. 27, mons. Pendasio, 1607–12 and mons. Brizio, 1643–47; m. 28, mons. Della Chiesa, 1667, 1680 and 1689; m. 29, mons. Provana, 1692 and mons. Roero, 1713; m. 30, mons. Natta, 1753 and mons. Vagnone, 1773. *Archivio Capitolare di Alba (AC Alba)*, m. 110, Decreti della visita apostolica di mons. Ragazzoni, 1577. *Archivio della Curia Vescovile di Asti (ACV Asti)*, Armadio I, I, visita di mons. Della Rovere, 1570; II, visita apostolica di mons. Peruzzi, 1583; III, visita di mons. Panigarola, 1588; IV–V, mons. Aiazza, 1597–1606; VI, mons. Pentorio, 1621; VII–IX, mons. Broglia, 1626, 1633 and 1645; XI and XIII, mons. Roero, 1656 and 1661; XIV–XV, mons. Tomatis, 1667 and 1676; XVII, mons. Migliavacca, 1696; XVIII–XIX, vicario Icardi, 1708 and 1728–37; XXI, mons. Felissano, 1743; XXII, mons. Sammartino, 1760; XXIII, mons. Caissotti, 1768. *Archivio della Curia Vescovile di Mondovì (ACV M)*, Visita apostolica di mons. Scarampi, 1583; visite di mons. Castruccio, 1593 and 1599; mons. Argentero, 1607 and 1620–8; mons. Ripa, 1633, 1635–7 and 1640; mons. Beggiamo, 1658; mons. Solaro, 1665; mons. Trucchi, 1669 and 1677; mons. Isnardi, 1698, 1707, 1710, and 1720; vicario Vasco, 1728; mons. Sammartino, 1743, 1750, and 1753; mons. Casati, 1755. Material relating to Valsesia is kept in the *Archivio di Stato di Vercelli, Sezione di Varallo Sesia (ASVS)*; within this archive, *Congregazioni di Carità (CDC)*, and material relating to the *Archivio dell'Ordine Mauriziano di Torino (AOM)* are unpublished. The essay develops certain suggestions which were made in my previous work *Il consumo di devozioni*.

[1] See the arguments and criticisms put forward in Lloyd, *Demystifying Mentalities*, "Introduction" and ch. 1.

without considering the fact that these practices are only known to us through the mediation of the ecclesiastics and professionals who have recorded them.[2] The approach presupposes that daily life was able to find full expression in religious idealism: it assumes a seamless continuum between practices and beliefs.[3]

This essay proposes to analyse local religion as a group of practices which interact systematically with local cultural, political and social life. On such a reading, ritual kinship groups should not be analysed through some abstract institutional identity, but must be approached through the rituals by which their members stake out power and territory in the community. This article considers four groups through which social kinship was expressed in early modern rural Piedmont: *confrarie, disciplinati, societates,* and *consortie.* Far from offering a static institutional analysis, it aims to retrace the dynamics inherent in the practice of rituals and ceremonies, and so consider local religious life not just in the light of generalized sociological categories such as "the family" or "the community" but in connection with two other aspects of society under the Ancien Régime: its jurisdictional culture and its territorial politics. Both these aspects require some explication. The new legal historiography has emphasized that medieval and early modern Europeans perceived and identified power through jurisdiction.[4] A variety of powers manifested itself in a variety of jurisdictions which intersected and overlapped within one territory. This complex of jurisdictions was accompanied by a multiplicity of legal procedures ranging from ordinary justice to summary proceedings.[5] The majority of these procedures were based on what we can call "possessory rulings,"[6] that is to say, on a plaintiff's request for official recognition from the magistrature of what was a "de facto" or existing state of affairs. Demonstrating possessory rights was critical to the use of resources,[7] given the fact that customary law recognized many forms of access (collective, corporate, individual)[8] to such resources.

Where jurisdictional culture had such a strong grip, ritual had legitimizing function in at least two senses. Rituals established both the

---

[2] The most mature results of this approach can be found in Prosperi, *Tribunali*, 366.

[3] Needham, *Belief, Language and Experience*, 41 n. 5, 102–3, and 106–7.

[4] Costa, *Iurisdictio*; Hespanha, "Magistrales populaires," 806–7. On the new legal history, see Clavero, *Antidora*. Grossi, *Il dominio*; Grossi, *L'ordine giuridico*; Schaub, review of Clavero, 367–70. The implications for the historical interpretation of the modern age are spelled out by Hespanha, *Visperas del Leviatan*; Raggio, "Costruzioni delle fonti e prova," 135–56; Torre, "Percorsi della pratica," 799–829. On symbolic interpretations of certain aspects of customary law: Grinberg, "Don, prélèvements, échanges," 1413–32, and "Le nouage rituel/droit," 247–62.

[5] Cerutti, "Giustizia e località," 447, 453 ff.   [6] Silvestrini, *Politica, religione e giustizia*, ch. 3.

[7] Raggio, "Forme e pratiche," 158.

[8] Moreno, *Dal documento*, 181–205. Moreno and Raggio (eds.), "Risorse collettive," 614.

significance of actions, and the justification for them. In other words, they gave legitimacy and status to those who performed them. More than that, they also served to legitimate the institutions which recorded them. The transcription of social rituals, which is so prevalent in historical documentation, certainly served to validate the "practical purposes" of those who are described – or who describe themselves – in the act of saying or doing something. But this transcription also expressed the "practical purposes" of the one who, in recording these acts, validated them and confirmed his own prerogative over them.[9]

2. The capacity of social ritual to legitimize becomes clearer on a closer examination of the internal structure of local politics and their territorial organisation. A new historical anthropology of European rural communities has led us to discard one of the most potent historiographical myths of the twentieth century: the idea of the peasant community as the organic nucleus of rural society. A topographical analysis of Italian villages, whether in Piedmont, Liguria, Tuscany, or Campania,[10] has revealed an internal fragmentation, the implications of which have yet to be fully understood. Patterns of settlement, for example, reveal the persistence in certain areas of peripheral neighborhoods under the domination of particular families; more generally, they also show how many villages were broken up into outlying areas and districts. Alongside such patterns as these we can also find areas where the villages are more unified, but whose precise territorial and chronological development remain to be analysed.

Villages with patterns of fragmented settlement were particularly common in Liguria and Piedmont, and can also be found in Lombardy.[11] This allows us to draw some initial generalizations. First, there is a close connection between this pattern of settlement and what amounts to a political system based on the family-dominated neighborhoods. A series of different factors distinguishes the various kinship groups. Such groups distribute themselves variously among the different settlements,[12] and these patterns of distribution have a profound influence on the way marriages and alliances are formed.[13] Within each kinship group the number of affines and their position in the hierarchy of wealth varied considerably, giving them in turn varied abilities to access material and

---

[9] Torre, "Percorsi della pratica," 799–829; Cottereau, "Justice et injustice," 25–59.

[10] Grendi, "Il sistema politico," 98–103; Grendi, *Il Cervo,* 41–72; Levi, *Inheriting power,* 44–79; Torre, "Le visite pastorali" 162, 164, 180; Raggio, *Faide e parentele,* 88–96; Angelini, "L'invenzione epigrafica," 658–64; Pazzagli, *Famiglie e paesi,* 28–43; Delille, *Famiglia e comunità,* 93–111; Ciuffreda, "I benefici di giuspatronato," 37–72; Lombardini, "Family, kin," 227–57; Palmero, "La costruzione del territorio." [11] Toubert, "Les statuts communaux."

[12] Raggio, *Faide e parentele.* [13] Lombardini, "Family, kin."

symbolic resources. Out of this there developed a "social awareness of territory," which functioned as a powerful matrix in local politics.[14] The asymmetry of local powers resulted in social fragmentation, and we can then see the villages themselves as aggregates of such fragments – each potentially based on kinship – co-existing in constant tension. Secondly, it is noteworthy that the feuding which is recorded in such fragmented settlements persists under different political-institutional frameworks:[15] the Genoese aristocratic republic in the case of the Ligurian villages, the Holy Roman Empire for the imperial fiefs of Langhe, or the duchy of Savoy for the outlying villages round Ceva and Mondovì.

The reasons for such fragmentation are numerous and sometimes difficult to identify. Recent research has abandoned the attempt to define the origins of such patterns of settlement and concentrated instead on their more or less natural character.[16] However, it is still possible to identify certain factors which may have made this type of settlement so common in the region under consideration. Even though individual circumstances vary considerably, it can be said that in general the emergence of centers from which the single villages of Liguria and Piedmont took their bearings was a tortuous process. The process was difficult for many reasons. The development, especially in Piedmont, of the late medieval *villenove* accompanied by the only partial disintegration of previous territorial organization[17] increased the complexity of intersecting jurisdictions to the extent that such complexity became one of the defining characteristics of the region. It was rendered even more acute by two further processes, working independently but concomitantly: the creation of fiefdoms and the dissolution of the *pieve*, the geographical and jurisdictional unit of the Italian church before the parish.

The first process, "feudalization," seems particularly to have intensified fragmentation. It was driven forward by the diversity of territorial powers and the multiplicity of seigneurial families in each locality, and drew these together as *consortili* or unions of local lords characterized by fierce internal tensions.[18] An extreme fragmentation of separate jurisdictions and an ensuing competition to claim jurisdictional authority were the results of such a process. The second process, dissolution of the pieve and the growth of the rural parish, had a similar impact on territorial development in Piedmont.[19] This process was still under way in early

---

[14] Grendi, "Cartografia e disegno locale." On the internal development within Italian microhistory of the view of peasant communities, see Torre, "Società locale e società regionale," 113–24.

[15] Raggio, *Faide e parentele*; Torre, "Feuding, factions and parties."

[16] Moreno, *Dal documento*, 127–59.   [17] Guglielmotti, "Territori senza città," 769–77.

[18] On the feudalization of Piedmont: Bordone, *Città e territorio*; Bordone, "Lo sviluppo;" Sergi, "La feudalizzazione;" Sergi, "Anscarici, Arduinici, Aleramici;" Guglielmotti, *I signori di Morozzo*; Provero, *Dai marchesi Del Vasto*; Provero, "I marchesi Del Carretto."

modern Piedmont and underlies the continual conflict among different territories and jurisdictions over control of sacramental practices for each local population. The "territorialization of the rights of burial" is said to lie at the root of the development of rural communes in eleventh- and twelfth-century Tuscany.[20] Such claims took effect in Piedmont only feebly or partially; even in the late sixteenth century, papal and pastoral visitations make clear that acknowledgment of a recognized parish church, both as a building and as an administrative center, was still highly contentious. Most Piedmontese villages still had several churches which could lay claim to such a prerogative, either because they held tithe rights, or were in charge of a local congregation, or because certain local community rituals were held there.[21]

Persistent overlapping and interlinking of jurisdictions, together with social and political fragmentation affect the very meaning of religious expression. It appears peculiarly adapted to the symbolic enactment of the tensions between various social groups and centers of power. To give only one example: even the development in Piedmont of what Jacques Chiffoleau has called "la comptabilité de l'au-delà"[22] is subject to fragmentation. The church and religious life provided an important means of expression for the various local kinship groups and their territorial claims,[23] ranging from straightforward legacies to the endowment of chaplaincies and simple benefices in the gift of lay patronage. Yet neighborhoods are also protagonists in the politics of parish formation in Piedmont; the concentration of legacies in peripheral sites of worship accentuated the plurality of such sites which is so characteristic of Piedmontese villages.

When taken together, these features – the lack of acknowledged centers, the fragmentation of settlements, the overlapping of jurisdictions – lend a distinctive character to the religious life of Piedmontese villages, which can be seen as an untiring process of negotiation among different settlements regarding their legal and jurisdictional rights. The villages in Piedmont take on the appearance of federations which express their internal tensions and solidarities by means of religious rituals articulated through multiple centers of worship.

3. A jurisdictional culture, the transcription of practices in historical sources, the importance of possessory acts, the territorial fragmentation of local politics: these are the elements which we can use to construct a

[19] Settia, "Crisi e adeguamento;" Andenna, "Unità e divisione territoriale."

[20] Wickham, Comunità e clientele, 78–92, and especially 89–91.

[21] Torre, Il consumo di devozioni, ch. 1.   [22] Chiffoleau, La comptabilité de l'au-delà.

[23] Torre, "Le visite pastorali," 164–72; Torre, "Politics cloaked in worship," 70–9.

topographical analysis of the surviving documentation which reflects the
priority that locals placed on space or territory. This is the key that
cultural and social historians and historical anthropologists alike have
disregarded, yet it is indispensable for unlocking the importance of rituals
and the significance put on them by participants and observers alike,
above all when it came to the construction on the ceremonial level of that
community which the tensions and asymmetries of power so frequently
obscured. The purpose of what follows is to analyse some of the most
widely diffused forms of the ritual construction of community in early
modern rural Piedmont.

The approach sketched above can help us understand the brotherhood
or *confraria* (from the Latin "confratria") of the Spirito Santo, which is the
most difficult to understand of all the ceremonial associations in late
medieval and early modern villages.[24] Occasional legacies dating from the
thirteenth and fourteenth centuries and brief descriptions from post-
Tridentine episcopal visitations reveal the existence of a medieval institution formed for the purpose of symbolically redistributing resources left
by the dead in their legacies. The primary form of redistribution was a
Pentecostal feast consisting of meatless dishes eaten in a secular building
dedicated to ceremonial purposes. It might be thought that the sheer
extent of such a ritual throughout the northern Mediterranean region,
from Portugal, parts of France and the Alps, to northern Italy, would have
led historians to examine it in the context of local institutions. On the
contrary, they have preferred to attempt to trace the mythical origins of
the ceremony and ignored its vast geographical diffusion from the thirteenth to the fifteenth century, with the result that the confraria has been
described as a proto-confraternity, as a municipal institution, or, from the
sixteenth century onwards, as a mere archeological relic.[25]

A topographical reading of ceremonial practices of the confraria as
transcribed by post-Tridentine episcopal visitors in the dioceses of southern Piedmont reveal a number of characteristic features. The brotherhoods are territorially organized but their territory does not necessarily
coincide with the community's juridical boundaries; they express the
social and political fragmentation of the villages. They demonstrate an
ability to survive through the course of the Ancien Régime, and occasionally preserve their repertory of ceremonial rituals and symbols –

---

[24] On the Spirito Santo "confrarie": Calvini and Cuggé, *La confraria di Santo Spirito*, 15–54; Duparc,
  "Confréries du saint-Esprit;" Bernard, "Les confréries communales;" Comino, "Sfruttamento;"
  Comino, "Per una storia;" Hoffman, *Church and community*, 59–68 and 104–8. For examples in
  Veneto and Trento: Nubola, *Conoscere per governare*, 145–48, and Knapton, "Istituzioni ecclesiasti-
  che," 403–5.

[25] Valduggia provides evidence to the contrary: the registers from 1575 to 1600 have been preserved
  and contain a striking number of small legacies: "Inventario dei legati 1557–1770," *ASVS*,
  Congregazioni di Carità, Valduggia, Confraria di Santo Spirito, b. 1.

including a Trinitarian iconography peculiar to them – well into the nineteenth century.[26]

Despite the accumulation over the years of property deeds and rents bequeathed in legacies, the confrarie identified themselves through the fact that they *made* (lit. *fare*) the Pentecostal feast. Post-Tridentine episcopal visitors expressed this with the terms: "confratria fietur...," and even lay authorities identified the confrarie with an *activity*. In the course of an enquiry of the Ordine dei Santi Maurizio e Lazzaro, the delegates sent by the duke of Savoy tried to discover the existence of a 'confraria' which locals were attempting to conceal, by asking to see "the place where Pentecost was enacted."[27]

If we look to the actual staging of the Pentecostal feasts (in spite of the somewhat laconic sources), we can see that it was precisely the local variations that gave a voice to segments of the population who were otherwise mute: groups of neighbors or of kin, depending on the kind of settlement.[28] Seen in this light, the confraria served to express the identity of a local group by means of the symbolic redistribution of food among its own members. In reality, the organization of the Pentecostal supper took a variety of forms along a continuum ranging from one ceremony for the whole community to a more generous distribution which usually involved from seven to nine confrarie per locality. In between these two extremes there was a proliferation of localized practices corresponding to geographical designations such as "soprano/sottano" (or "upper/lower"). To give only one example: when the men of the community of Agnona in Valsesia met to elect the confrari who would organize the supper (or *Carità*) di Santo Spirito, they did so according to the locally recognized boundaries: in 1694, for example, we read that they "agreed that for Croso di Garlotto and the country above, the afore-mentioned Procurators and confrari should elect one person in Agnona and another in Casosso to administer one Carità; and that for Croso and the country below they were to elect the other two Procurators to administer the other Carità, electing one person in Agnona and the other in Cascine."[29]

These choices were not independent of the formal authority structures

---

[26] In a curious process which remains to be studied (and on which I am currently working), it was paradoxically the nineteenth- and twentieth-century scholars of regional folklore who contributed to the disappearance from view of the "confrarie" and the traditions related to them, since they based their research on literary rather than administrative sources; while the former are scarce on the confrarie, the latter are numerous.

[27] AOM, *Confrarie*, m. 1, n. 24, *Sommario delli beni instrumenti et altre scritture delli beni di Santo Spirito*, s.v. Cardé.

[28] Comino, "Sfruttamento," 687–9, 697–700. On Valsesia, where the phenomenon is even more marked, see Torre, "Confraria e comunità."

[29] "Libro della Carità di Santo Spirito," *ASVS, Congregazioni di Carità*, Agnona, b. 1.

which held locally. Communities controlled by a powerful lord tended to have a single feast, regardless of how fragmented their settlements were.[30] Yet through the confrarie we can see a diffuse village structure which could almost be called federative, similar to the above-mentioned but more restricted type of the *comunità di valle*.[31] Close analysis of these federative structures would allow us in any event to see in the confraria one of the matrixes of the rural parish. Even in the middle of the seventeenth century, it is the presence of more than one confraria that gave rise to more than one parish rather than the other way round.[32]

Are the Piedmontese S. Spirito confrarie simply one of the variables in the patterns of settlement found in Mediterranean villages? In reality, the choice of terms used to celebrate Pentecost, the interpretative categories used to describe the activities of the confrarie, and the symbols used by contemporaries to identify them would all seem to indicate a cultural self-awareness and definite institutional structure which it is still almost wholly impossible for us to reconstruct.

While rural Piedmontese communities celebrated Pentecost with a range of activities from games and dances to the celebration of Mass, the language used to express them is always the same: charity. The association of these activities with charity is a longstanding one familiar to scholars,[33] but it has always been understood in terms of Christian doctrine rather than the symbolism of local politics. Observations regarding the confrarie of Varallo Sesia (on the borders with Lombardy) made by one of the more sensitive episcopal visitors of the time, Mons. Carlo Bascapé,[34] bishop of Novara and a member of Cardinal Borromeo's circle, allow us to understand the institution more in terms of local sociability than of theology. According to Bascapé, the confrarie were charitable organisations located "not merely in single parishes, but in villages ... Many from the same village or area form an association which meets to eat together or to distribute bread as if it were one brotherhood or fellowship, a true confraternity gathered for the sake of Christian charity; this explains why these acts of piety are known, here and elsewhere, as 'carità' and why many ecclesiastics call the custom of eating together "fare la carità.""[35]

---

[30] Torre, *Il consumo di devozioni*, 102–3.

[31] These are the initial results of a collective research project on the origin of commune boundaries, carried out for the Piedmontese regional authorities and coordinated by R. Bordone, *Schedario storico-territoriale*. On the "comunità di valle": Vaccari, *La territorialità*, 42 ff.; Santini, *"I comuni di pieve;"* Valetti Bonini, *Comunità di valle*.

[32] 'Transazione nella causa vertente tra gli uomini di Valduggia e S. Maria per la carità di S. Spirito," 1660, *ASVS, CDC*, Valduggia, b. 1.   [33] Coulet, "Les confréries du Saint-Esprit."

[34] On Bascapé and the territorial rule of the diocese: Andenna, "Eredità medioevale."

[35] Bascapé, *Novaria* (Novara: 1612), I, "Terminatio Varalli," 133–6. Ravizza (ed.), *La Novaria sacra*,

Bascapé's observation is crucial: the Pentecostal feast during which the confraria is *enacted* is charity insofar as it binds participants (or at least those who believe themselves entitled to attend) together as brothers. It thus becomes essential to know who participates in the feast. In the midst of the endless variations which characterize the confrarie, Bascapé singles out one in particular as a kind of explicit *leit-motif*: "The administrators call many to undertake this task each year; they go from door to door asking for grain which the various local institutions make into bread; they add beans which are cooked and distributed to be eaten in public, not only for the poor, but all who happen to be passing including people from outside the locality."[36]

Thus a group of entitled persons gathers food provisions – due to them either as rent or under the terms of a legacy or simply given as alms – and redistributes them within their own circle (however defined) while *inviting* outsiders – the inhabitants of neighboring villages, foreigners, strangers, the poor – to partake of the public provision of prepared food. This ritual legitimizes those who are entitled to provide, and distinguishes them from those who are provided for, recipients may include the poor, but not the destitute. Bascapé's observation tends to confirm the theory advanced by social historians over the past thirty years that charitable activity serves to define the community or social group,[37] but it also reveals the dynamics which underlie this process of legitimization, in particular the public aspect of the ceremony.

In the fragmented context of Piedmont, Bascapé's observations serve to render the interpretative framework even more complex. The assemblies which came together to exercise Pentecostal charity were not based on administrative communities. On the contrary, they created communities by giving a name to places, instituting them as spaces in which a public ritual is enacted – the public distribution of food performed according to rules which are exclusively local.[38] It could almost be said that the place was transformed into a body of people, in the sense that the place itself holds a *quasi ius*.[39] This group or body of people took on juridical status which enabled it to gather and to distribute, to receive

---

149. Bascapé continues with the description of two other types of Carità, the *Carità dei poveri*, and the *Carità di San Marco*; on these see: Torre, "Confraria e comunità."

36. Bascapé, *Novaria*. Ravizza, *La Novaria sacra*, 149.

37. Trexler, "Charity and the defense;" Henderson, "Charity in late medieval Florence," 68; Henderson, *Piety and charity*, 9.

38. The documents in the diocese of Mondovì and Novara (Valsesia) show us that the confraria tended to *create* its own area of influence, a space which did not correspond to the existing administrative areas: see Torre, *Consumo di devozioni*, 130–2, and Torre, "Confraria e comunità."

39. The expression was used by Mons. Della Chiesa in 1667 with reference to the village of Cairo ("Visita mons. Della Chiesa," *ACV Alba*, m. 28, s.v.).

legacies and to hold possession (in Valsesia, from which most of our evidence comes, there is explicit mention of the "jurisdiction" of a confraria).[40] Taken in this sense, the confraria is an institution of sociability or neighborhood, expressing territorial loyalties which may fragment official administrative boundaries. Fragmentation can occur even in apparently unitary localities, such as a single fiefdom or a single administrative unit.[41]

But there is another way of expressing these characteristics of Pentecostal charity, one suggested by a lesser-known aspect of the confrarie: their iconography. The "charity" of Santo Spirito refers to a particular iconographic representation of the Trinity as three distinct persons in human form. Such a depiction of the Trinity is found in other parts of Europe,[42] but in Piedmont it became the explicit symbol of the confrarie. It went under various names, such as the *Tre Santi Spiriti* and *Tre Salvatori col mondo in mano*, showing how flexibly or broadly the underlying myth could be used.[43] Certainly there needs to be further research into this concept of the Trinity as a model of social relations.[44] Given its suggestions of equal status and political representation, the theological sources (both Biblical and patristic),[45] the chronological development, the geographical diffusion, and the eventual decline of this image need to be established more clearly.[46]

4. The fragmented nature of the *confrarie dello Spirito Santo* throughout north-western Italy can help to illuminate some of the obscurities which stand in the way of understanding how lay people of the Ancien Régime constructed their religion. The recognition of such fragmentariness enables us to interpret anew much documentary material which relates to local religious life. The following pages present a highly abbreviated account of this new interpretation.

[40] "Elenco delle famiglie domiciliate nella 'giurisdizione' della carità di Santo Spirito di Valduggia per la scelta dei confrari, 1699–1806," *ASVS, CDC*, Valduggia, b. 1.
[41] Torre, *Consumo di devozioni*, 119–20; Comino, "Per una storia."
[42] Boefsplug, *Dieu dans l'art*, 162–5.
[43] "Sommario delli beni instrumenti et altre scritture delli beni di Santo Spirito," *AOM, Confrarie*, under the headings Murello (where the description "three saviors holding the World and representing the Holy Trinity" is added), Polonghera, Casalgrasso, Roddino ("Santi Spiriti"). Analogous images can be found at Valgrana, Melle, Bellino, Scarnafigi, Martiniana Po and Vallepietra (old province of Saluzzo).
[44] Vernon, "Introduction," *Christianity in the Renaissance*, 26–7; Boefsplug, *Dieu dans l'art*, 270–98.
[45] Following Black, *Council and Commune*, 69, 160: the Trinitarian inspiration of conciliar theory saw corporate associations as a synthesis of egalitarianism, love, and works.
[46] There is a striking contrast between the situation in Piedmont and the picture drawn by Froeschlé-Chopard, *Espace et sacré en Provence*, 47, 108, based on the geographical extent of the *cult* rather than the ceremony.

The characteristics of the confraria help us to understand the development of the rural parish in new terms. This was not the natural consequence of the dissolution of the pieve, but a deliberate historical construction of a jurisdictional nature. The institution of the parish involves
the definition of prerogatives, the demarcation of territory, and a designated body of the faithful.[47] In rural Piedmont this construction took
place gradually and contentiously; the parish always had to be imposed on
a set of rival institutions.

The first of the local religious institutions which a topographical
reading reveals as rival to the parish were the flagellant confraternities or
disciplinati. Episcopal and papal visitors of the post-Tridentine Church
thought that certain rituals, especially the feast, the foot washing in Holy
Week,[48] and other characteristics of the flagellants could be traced back to
the confrarie. The flagellants' oratories were called *domus* exactly like the
buildings of the confrarie[49] and in some the meetings of the local council
took place.[50] In addition, the flagellants' ceremonies also centerd round
the distribution of food; this was not carried out only during Holy Week,
as has usually and wrongly been assumed.[51] It was common to find
flagellants' oratories in the late sixteenth century which were not dedicated to a saint; in other words, they were not as fully or exclusively part
of the world of devotional practice as the bishops thought they ought to

---

[47] Torre, *Il consumo di devozioni*, ch. 1.

[48] Out of the 250 parishes examined at the end of the sixteenth century, only four (Bagnasco,
Garessio, Castino and Saliceto, all in the diocese of Alba) won the visitor's approval by not
performing the Holy Week foot washing.

[49] "Visita Apostolica di mons. Scarampi," *ACV* Mondovì, Frabosa Soprana and Roburent. Reports
of visits in the diocese of Albi only rarely mention the names of the confraternities, while those
from the diocese of Asti invariably do. "Visita di mons. Della Rovere," *ACV* Asti, *passim*.

[50] The meetings of municipal councils in the confraternity's "domus" took place in Monforte,
Neive, Millesimo (diocese of Alba); Govone, Canale d'Alba (Asti); Boves (Mondovì).

[51] In Cuneo (diocese of Mondovì), on the feast of the Circumcision, the confraternity of San
Francesco di Cuneo prepared "a meal for the brothers." Bagnasco (diocese of Alba) claimed to
have abolished the Easter feast, but feasts were held on several other occasions throughout the year.
In Saliceto (diocese of Alba) two distributions took place (Christmas and Corpus Domini); at Boves
(diocese of Mondovì) at Pentecost; at Roccavione (diocese of Mondovì) bread and chickpeas were
distributed on several occasions and to all comers, not only the poor; this was also the practice at
Serralunga (diocese of Alba) on Holy Thursday; bread and beans were distributed at Castelletto and
Montanera (diocese of Mondovì). At Monforte (diocese of Alba) it was remarked in 1573 that the
distribution of food was not to the poor but to everyone ("Visita di mons. Marino," *ACV Alba*, m.
26, s.v.), while in 1583 at Bastia ("Visita Apostolica di mons. Scarampi," *ACV* Mondovì, s.v.) the
poor received only the unwanted left-overs. What Santa Vittoria was told in 1621 was true: in
reality the "alia opera Charitatis" practiced by the "confratelli," apart from reciting Divine Office,
amounted to nothing but feasts ("Visita mons. Pentorio," *ACV Asti*, cc. 71v–75). For another area
of Piedmont, see Lebole, *Storia della Chiesa Biellese* vol. 1, 96, 104–12, 161, 187, 405, 441, 535, 559;
vol. 2, 436; *La pieve di Cossato*, vol.1, 6, 104; vol. 2, 48, 208, 306 (at Torrazzo salt was distributed,
1652); *La pieve di Puliaco-Giflenga*, 330.

be.[52] This explains the visitors' persistent complaints about the unorthodox furnishings found in the oratories.[53]

Other aspects of the confraternities suggest that they were a different
kind of association than the confrarie. The fact that in rural Piedmont
there was never more than one flagellant confraternity in each parish
indicates a unitary or centralizing tendency in contrast to the fragmentation of the villages.[54] Moreover, in the few cases where a confraternity
split into two groups, the new organization was invariably dedicated to
the Turin brotherhood named after San Giovanni Decollato or "della
Misericordia."[55] Such duplication was part of the fierce factional struggle
taking place in rural Piedmont as the Savoy dynasty was taking control of
the peripheral areas, and it is a process which needs to be studied further.[56]

If the documents left us by visitors in the post-Tridentine period are
read with this in mind, they reveal how forcefully the flagellant confraternities attempted to support, sustain or even control the unity of the
village: in the words of the confraternity in Garessio in the diocese of
Alba, their purpose was to "*govern* the poor by charity."[57] Unlike the
confrarie, the confraternities could express this purpose in a variety of
ways. We can sense the underlying intention in such rituals as the
processions organized by the confraternities: these tended to cover the
whole of the village as an administrative unit[58] and had a clearly propiti-

---

[52] More revealing than a host of examples is the fact that whenever the episcopal visitors found that a
village had no oratory (or an inadequate one) they sought out a "domus" where they could stay.
"Visita mons. Peruzzi," *ACV Asti*, Cortandone.

[53] At San Michele in the diocese of Asti, the prior of the confraternity tried in vain to convince the
apostolic visitor that the bishop of Asti had given them explicit permission to use a wooden altar
("Visita Apostolica mons. Peruzzi," *ACV Asti*, c. 420r). In general, the altars of the flagellant
confraternities were found to be "wrongly formed": hollow (Peveragno, 1583, Cravanzana, 1643,
Frabosa Serro, 1583, Frabosa sottana, 1583); narrow (Monastero Vasco and Montaldo, 1583 – use
of the altar at Montaldo was forbidden in 1659); "pierced" (Montaldo Roero, 1626).

[54] The growth of flagellant confraternities is striking. At the end of the sixteenth century they were
present in a large number of parishes (in the diocese of Alba, in 1593 there was a total of sixteen
flagellant confraternities out of thirty-one villages visited; in 1643 this total had become forty-three
out of ninety-one. In the other two dioceses, the density was greater: sixty-nine out of ninety-nine
villages in the Asti diocese, and thirty-three out of fifty-one including the six confraternities in
Mondovì and Cuneo). When the number of members is given, they are substantial: about a
hundred in each parish comprising 600–700 inhabitants.

[55] On the Misericordia confraternities, see Prosperi, "Il sangue e l'anima"; Black, *Italian confraternities*;
Terpstra, *Lay confraternities*.   [56] Fresia, "Comunità e signori," 133.

[57] "Visita apostolica mons. Montiglio," *ACV Alba*, s.v. Garessio.

[58] "Visita mons. Della Rovere," *ACV Asti*, s.v. Sommariva Perno: the flagellants went in procession
"per terram." "Visita Apostolica mons. Scarampi." *ACV*, s.v. Montaldo: the flagellants'
processions visited all twenty-three rural chapels in the parish. Such efforts occasionally mask an
attempt to dominate festive rituals: the rural chapels were all controlled by the flagellants (Govone
in the diocese of Asti, Cairo in the diocese of Alba) or they were old parish churches used as
cemetery chapels (Bastia and Beinette in the diocese of Mondovì, Serralunga in the diocese of

atory function (e.g., to protect the harvest) which is quite absent from the feasts of the confrarie.[59] Other practices tend to reinforce a sense of internal social cohesion: singing, for example, but above all flagellation. It is rare, on the other hand, to find a confraternity managing an *ospedale*; religious associations in Piedmont were little inclined to practice this form of charity.[60]

The unifying thrust and universalizing language of the confraternities met with competition from the parishes, despite the latter's weakness in late sixteenth-century Piedmont. The rituals which marked the death of villagers were particularly contentious, since the approaches of con-fraternity and parish contrasted sharply. Death, whether of confratelli or of villagers, provided the occasion for a requiem Mass which even episcopal visitors condoned. But it also sparked additional rituals that the parish clergy strongly opposed. While parish rectors claimed their alms as a right or fee, the confraternities never assumed this was anything more than a free donation to help cover funerary costs. But practice created the precedent for a prerogative: on occasion the confraternities took advan-tage of their popular support in order to claim the right to carry the parish cross at funerals[61] or to allow villagers to kiss it in return for alms-giving. In other words, the confraternities claimed to represent the parish. The remarks made by episcopal visitors need to be read with this rivalry between the confraternities and the parish in mind. The confraternities were less in conflict with the religious attitudes of the established church hierarchy than involved with them in a battle of jurisdictional authority.

The flagellant confraternities were not the only organizations bent on welding together the fragmented territories of Piedmontese villages into a unity. In the second half of the sixteenth century, we can already find two prominent lay associations pursuing the same purpose. These were the societates of the Eucharist and the *consortiae* of the Virgin Mary which sought to base themselves in the parish church (though, as we have seen, many churches might compete for this title). These associations, or at least the groups who promoted and directed them, were more restrictive than the confraternities. They tended to occupy themselves with the organization of their specific cults and devotions in contrast to the

---

Alba). At Margarita, the flagellants are recorded in 1669 as having gone in procession to the chapel of the Visitation of the Virgin Mary where they distributed corn to "the poor." "Visita mons. Trucchi," *ACV* Mondovì, 1669, s.v.

[59] In 1667 we can still find the flagellants of Castiglione Tinella stressing to the visitor that their processions were held "pro conservatione fructuum" ("Visita mons. Della Chiesa," *ACV Alba*, s.v.).   [60] Cavallo, *Charity and Power*, 251.

[61] At Rocchetta Tanaro in 1621 ("Visita mons. Pentorio," *ACV Asti*, cc. 128r–9v).

penitential motives of the flagellants, at least during the second half of the
sixteenth century.

The societates of the Eucharist usually took the title of "Corpus
Christi," and were decidedly elitist. Since the associations themselves
have left no documents, we have to rely on the brief descriptions
provided by episcopal visitors. These reveal that the Corpus Christi
societates were usually allotted a peripheral space within the parish
church, and that they indulged in a precocious taste for rich furnishings
and devotional elaboration.[62] This specialization contrasts with the diversity of ritual practices centered on the Eucharist elsewhere in late sixteenth-century Europe.[63] Elsewhere it had an irenic significance,[64] which
sometimes led to some confusion between the Eucharist and Pentecost.[65]
In Piedmont it became a potent element within the fragmented and
jurisdictional culture that we have described. It could become the center
of an authentic "ritual pact," an intense negotiation of status and relations
between clergy and laity, especially on the occasion of Easter communion.[66] This ritual pact also explains why the Eucharist was associated
with the distribution of food, at least until the mid-eighteenth century.[67]

Yet the real force behind eucharistic symbolism appears to be connected to a specific situation relating directly to the fragmented nature of
Piedmontese villages. Episcopal visitors were insistent that the consecrated host be kept continually in the tabernacle.[68] The practice was new
to rural Piedmont, and its implications were such that it only gradually
became established. Keeping the consecrated host within the tabernacle
meant that it could be carried to the houses of the sick and the dying.
Such a ritual was certainly not unknown, but post-Tridentine bishops
laid an unprecedented degree of ceremony on it. To this end they

---

[62] Torre, *Il consumo di devozioni*, 258–60.   [63] Rubin, *Corpus Christi*, 210–347.

[64] Sabean, *Power in the Blood*, ch. 1. "Visita Apostolica mons. Scarampi," *ACV* Mondovì, Cuneo, c.
140 v, e Vico, c. 208r; "Visita Apostolica mons. Peruzzi," *ACV*, Monticello, cc. 385v–98r, e Santa
Vittoria, cc. 399r–401v.

[65] In 1588 at Montechiaro the parishioners of Santa Caterina carried out their Eastertide duties during
Pentecost ("Visita mons. Panigarola," *ACV* Asti, cc. 248–52).

[66] Torre, *Il consumo di devozioni*, 57–64.

[67] All examples associating the Eucharist with the distribution of food can be interpreted in this way,
as at Rocca de Baldi until 1669 ("Visita mons. Trucchi," *ACV* Mondovì, cc. 379ff.) and at Govone
until 1761 ("Visita mons. Sanmartino," ACV Asti, s.v.).

[68] At the end of the sixteenth century, the practice is totally unknown in the parishes of Cortandone,
Frinco, and Rocchetta Tanaro in the diocese of Asti and Trezzo, and Benevello in the diocese of
Alba. The reason given at Moline (diocese of Mondovì) in the middle of the seventeenth century
was the poverty of the place; at Montechiaro and Peveragno, on the other hand, the uncertain
demarcations of parish jurisdiction made it impossible to organize the conservation of the host
("Visita mons. Panigarola," ACV Asti, c.249 and "Visita Apostolica mons. Scarampi," *ACV*
Mondovì, c. 89v.). It should also be noted that in 50 out of 250 parishes, the conservation of the
host was only temporary, during certain periods of the year, rather than permanent.

provided for a *societas* attached to the high altar of the parish church which would accompany the consecrated host on its journey round the dispersed areas of the villages.[69] The eucharistic *societas* seemed to project parochial symbolism beyond the main or central settlement. The ritual of accompanying the host had distinct forms depending on whether it took place in the center of the village or in the outlying quarters, but in either case rendered the celebration of masses for the dead in the chapels and other sacred buildings of the outlying wards and farms redundant. The eucharistic *societas* thus assumed and promoted a hierarchical and centralizing view of the parish.[70] Yet the *societas* took root more or less gradually as local circumstances permitted, and closer examination of their activities always shows them to be limited to the central part of the village. If we look beyond the official confirmation that a eucharistic *societas* existed in a district and focus instead on its liturgical rituals and furnishings, we find that for much of the Ancien Régime the sick continued to receive communion from various places of worship in the village, and not just in the parish church or from the parish clergy.[71]

The association linked to the worship of the Virgin Mary was by contrast fairly widespread in the Piedmontese countryside (it can be found in just under a third of the rural parishes in the second half of the sixteenth century)[72] but the form it took was less easily defined. It was commonly designated a *consortia*. Dedicated to the Blessed Virgin Mary, these were not highly organized, but had a long tradition of encouraging a general worship of the Virgin (no particular Marian feast-day was celebrated more than the others) with an occasional miracle-working element.[73] Their defining feature was the promotion of a *public cult* which could not be identified with any of the different clans or areas of the village; in the words of Mons. Panigarola, its altar "ad nullum pertinet."[74] With their systematic diffusion through the parish and their frequently strong female component,[75] they seemed intended more to promote

---

[69] Torre, *Il consumo di devozioni*, 254–69.

[70] Barbero, "Apparati e strumenti liturgici," 164–5, 169.

[71] The practice was described at La Morra in 1698: communion for the sick in the outlying wards "was carried from the country chapels where mass is said to this purpose" (*ACV Alba, Risposte*, vol. 3, cc. 137r–8r).   [72] Torre, *Il Consumo di devozioni.* 270.

[73] In twelfth-century Andenna ("Unità e divisione territoriale," 291, 306 n. 121) the *consortia* brought priests, clergy and laymen together round the pieve for common prayer, the celebration of anniversaries and the exercise of fraternal charity with annual feasts and the distribution of bread and wine to the poor. Andenna follows Meersseman, *Ordo Fraternitatis*, v. 1, 37, in stating that "consortia" is a synonym for "confratria" and that its members are called "confratres." The antiquity of the *consortia* dedicated to the Virgin is emphasized in "Visita Apostolica mons. Peruzzi," *ACV Asti*, Govone, and in "Visita Apostolica mons. Scarampi," *ACV Mondovì*, Sant'Albano.   [74] "Visita mons. Panigarola," *ACV Asti*, Castellinaldo.

[75] "Visita mons. Pentorio," *ACV Asti*, Cortandone.

communal control of female religiosity than to reflect established kinship
groups or civic factions.[76] In a process that was at least in part sponta-
neous, these confraternities of the Virgin adopted the devotional exercises promoted by the Dominican order and transformed themselves into
Companies of the Virgin of the Rosary.[77] The new organization became
more formalized and was generally controlled by the rector. They became exclusively parish-based associations and until the middle of the
seventeenth century were responsible for the most elaborately adorned
altars in the parish church.

5. After these brief observations, we can look at the initiatives proposed
by the post-Tridentine episcopacy in light of the structure and the way of
life of Piedmontese villages. The bishops, especially those influenced by
Borromeo's ideas, tended to discourage fragmentation. There are occasional explicit assertions of this intent: Mons. Bascapé, for example,
declared his support for the confrarie as long as all possible confusion
between the eucharistic supper and profane gatherings could be elimin-
ated.[78] The decisions taken by the episcopal visitors on individual practices of the confrarie are more often revealing. These seem to be guided by
two distinct strategies: the transformation of charity into welfare and the
ritual construction of the parish. The first meant establishing the pawn-
shops known as "Monti di pietà" or their rural equivalent, the grain
stores known as "Monti frumentari." Both were chronically short of
funds and were destined to remain so throughout the deepening economic crisis which overtook Piedmont in the seventeenth century.[79] Yet
there are innumerable indications in the accounts left by the episcopal
visitors that charity and welfare were incompatible. "Monti Frumentari"
tended to be under the direct control of the municipal council. When
confrarie opposed this, the municipal administrative body became negli-
gent;[80] their management frequently aroused suspicions of usury and thus
sharpened internal divisions within the community, opening the way for
the local lord's jurisdictional intervention.[81]

    The second strategy – the ritual construction of the parish – met with

---

[76] Grendi, "Le confraternite liguri," 24.
[77] On the transformation see Torre, *Il consumo di devozioni*, 274–6 and table 3.
[78] Bascapé, *Novaria*, 136.   [79] Cerutti, *Mestieri e privilegi*, ch. 3.
[80] Mallare is an example of open opposition to the transformation of the *confraria* into a "Monte di
    Pietà" (*ACV Alba, Relazione*, 1657, cc. 34r–37v). See *Risposte*, 1698, v. 2, n.p. "Visita mons. Della
    Chiesa," *ACV Alba*, Serralunga, 1667, for an example of municipal negligence.
[81] An evident case of usury can be found in the "Visita Apostolica mons. Montiglio,"*ACV Alba*,
    Bagnasco (1585). "Visita mons. Brizio," *ACV Alba*, Cairo (1644), cc. 107r–9v: the local lords were
    called upon to judge the internal disputes in the "Monte." Other examples can be found in Torre,
    Il consumo di devozioni, 108–10.

greater success in Piedmont. In the 1580s the apostolic visitors continually urged the confrarie to abandon the rituals of preparing and eating the Pentecostal supper in favor of acquiring the tabernacle with the Host.[82] The crucial passage from a Pentecostal to a eucharistic ritual can be seen in the local establishment of a *societas Corporis Domini* or a *schola Sanctissimi Sacramenti* intent on reconciling and reintegrating the diverse loyalties of village groups in a solidarity based, at least in principle, on the centrality of the parish.

Secular political authorities also waged a campaign against the fragmentation of Piedmontese villages by attempting to establish communal administrative control. The fact that both ecclesiastical and secular authorities, the sources of most of our surviving documentation, were suspicious of the confrarie has led researchers to ignore the continuing history of these institutions. The framework of local and regional authority undoubtedly had a bearing on their survival. To take only one example, the Dukes of Savoy were responsible for the greatest interference in the internal affairs of charitable institutions: their more or less effective threats of suppression encouraged the confrarie to turn to the church authorities.[83] The direct contrary can be seen in the neighboring region of western Liguria, where the fierce ecclesiastical attacks on the confrarie led them to seek the protection of the Genoese magistrature.[84]

Yet external pressures appear to have had only a limited impact on the confrarie, particularly on their activities. In some areas of Piedmont, especially in the so-called *comunità di valle*, their presence can be traced even into the present century.[85] Nor was this presence merely dormant: at the beginning of the nineteenth century, for example, we find a debate being carried on between Piedmont and Lombardy on the criteria by which various settlements within a commune take part in the management of a confraria. The most controversial issues have to do with the possible consequences of an unequal population growth of the various settlements, the criteria for adjusting the membership rates for "brothers who are separated and living in their own houses," and the rights to be bestowed on "new households."[86]

However, the sources yield abundant evidence that the activities of the confrarie in the eighteenth century continued even in areas where they were no longer supposed to exist, such as those under the control of the

---

82 The "Decreti della Visita Apostolica Mons. Ragazzoni," *AC Alba, make this suggestion on innumerable occasions.*

83 Erba, *La chiesa sabauda,* 237–47; Torre, *Il consumo di devozioni,* 103–23.

84 Calvino and Cuggé, *La confraria di Santo Spirito,* 28–48.

85 Comino, "Per una storia" is based on this kind of documentary evidence.

86 "Elenco delle famiglie," *ASVS, Congregazioni di Carità,* Valduggia, Carità di Santo Spirito, controfrontespizio, 1822.

Savoy dynasty. In 1721 the Santo Spirito confrarie were officially suppressed and their assets incorporated into *Congregazioni di Carità* established – on paper at least – in every village in the kingdom of Sardinia.[87] A close analysis reveals that throughout the eighteenth century, these congregations were an exact reconstitution of the old local confraria.[88] The unclearly defined assets of the confrarie, on the other hand, had been sold off from the 1620s onwards[89] and were certainly inadequate for the provision of welfare to the destitute in rural areas. In reality such assets as there were supported the ceremonial redistribution of bread on occasions which more often than not coincided with the feast of Pentecost.[90]

6. The survey sketched out above has shown how the fragmentation characteristic of Piedmont exercised a strong influence on the political and cultural developments in the region's rural areas. The religious renewal which followed in the wake of the Council of Trent, for example, was seen in Piedmont as sanctioning the co-existence of different forms of worship, or moving towards a parish life characterized by the co-existence of the rector, the confrarie, the societates and consortie dedicated to the Eucharist and the Virgin Mary, and the flagellant confraternities. This co-existence is not to be understood simply as multiple initiatives in a restricted territory.[91] Its full significance can only be understood in the light of the prevailing jurisdictional culture which we started by describing. Devotional zeal inspires each local group, but each is also aware that its individual status and prerogatives are defined by its particular ritual practices: if others can perform these rituals, the identity of the group is damaged or diminished. As a result, in some villages the *Compagnia del SS. Sacramento* opposes alms collection by the *Compagnia del Rosario* on the grounds that it impedes their own collection for the Eucharist lamp. In other places the rector believes that his own rights as the celebrant of Mass at the high altar are threatened by the masses held at the other altars maintained by the companies.[92] This in turn

---

[87] For the edicts which established the "Congregazioni di Carità" and suppressed the confrarie see: Duboin and Muzio, *Raccolta per ordine*, tom.XII, v.14, 34–92 and tom.XIII, v.15, 528–30. Cavallo dates the real beginning of the *congregazioni* to the 1760s: *Charity and power*, 184.

[88] Torre, *Il consumo di devozioni*.123–49.

[89] Erba, *La chiesa sabauda*, 225–47; Torre, *Il consumo di devozioni*, 124–8, in particular table 1.

[90] Torre, *Il consumo di devozioni*, 143–50, and in particular tables 6 and 7: these show how long the *congregazioni* retained possession of the furnishings which belonged to the confrarie and went on practicing the latter's rituals.

[91] Quaccia, "Lo spazio sacro" Dardanello, "Spazio religioso."

[92] "Visita mons. della Chiesa, 1667," *ACV Alba*, Castiglione Tinella; "Visita mons. Trucchi, 1669," ACV Mondovì, Piozzo, c. 223r.

explains the opposition of the episcopal hierarchy to all ceremonies seen as "novas et insolitas."[93]

Such attitudes reveal the working of a highly significant historical and cultural process: liturgical and devotional practices and the objects employed in them are seen as instruments for asserting prerogatives.[94] As the ecclesiastical hierarchy generates new devotional practices, particularly after Trent,[95] these are seized on by local groups as offering new opportunities for changing the existing framework of their rights and prerogatives. The new devotional forms were neither merged syncretically nor manipulated politically. They were absorbed into a system of fragmented parochial jurisdiction where they became vehicles for the further assertion of autonomous and competing prerogatives. This explains how, for example, S. Giovanni Nepomuceno, promoted by post-Tridentine ecclesiastical authorities as the focus of an anti-heretical cult, could be transformed locally into the patron saint who protected the harvest from frost.[96] Contemporaries justified such evolutions and appropriations of ritual by saying that they served to "increase the people's devotional zeal." It is difficult today to gauge the effect of these devotional politics. What we do know for certain, however, is that these rituals had the ability to increase the powers of the patrons who appropriated and exercised them.

---

[93] "Visita mons. Della Chiesa, 1667," *ACV Alba, Castiglione Tinella: dispute over processions between the flagellant confraternities and the rector.*

[94] See Torre, *Il consumo di devozioni,* 308–12, for an analysis of the distribution of furnishings and liturgical apparatus among the villages in the dioceses of Alba and Asti in the first half of the eighteenth century.

[95] Rosa, "La Chiesa meridionale," 295–345.

[96] "Libro de' Conti della Veneranda Confraternita di San Giovanni decollato," Archivio Parrocchiale di Canale d'Alba, c. 78 (1774).

THE SUPPRESSION OF CONFRATERNITIES IN ENLIGHTENMENT FLORENCE

KONRAD EISENBICHLER

No sooner were confraternities established than governments sought to suppress them. This may have been, in part, simply a knee-jerk reaction on the part of the authorities who had earlier sought to disperse the flagellant and penitential movements, those popular waves of public pietism that had spread like wildfire across Italy in the thirteenth and fourteenth centuries. As was the case then, so later the attempt to suppress confraternities was often motivated by political reasons.

In fifteenth-century Florence, the major precedent for direct government intervention had been set by the Senate on 19 October 1419 when, suspecting that confraternities had become dens of dissent and political subversion, it decreed their general closure.[1] Lorenzo Mehus, the late eighteenth-century apologist for Grand Duke Peter Leopold's own unilateral action against lay religious organizations, considered this decree to be so important and so exemplary that he actually devoted two chapters to it in his volume *Dell'origine, progresso, abusi, e riforma delle confraternite laicali*, one discussing the circumstances and aims of the decree (ch. 20), and another transcribing it in full in its original Latin (ch. 21).[2] The 1419 decree was both severe and extensive: every type of confraternity, whether flagellant, laudese, or otherwise, meeting in Florence or within a

---

The following archival abbreviations will be employed in the text: Archivio Arcivescovile di Firenze (AAF); Archivio della Compagnia di San Girolamo di Firenze (ACSG); Archivo di Stato di Firenze (ASF).

On the flagellant movement of 1260 see the two fundamental volumes *Il movimento dei disciplinati nel settimo centenario dal suo inizio (Perugia – 1260)* and *Risultati e prospettive di ricerca sul movimento dei disciplinati*. For the penitential movement of the Bianchi of 1399 see Daniel E. Bornstein, *The Bianchi of 1399*.

[1] ASF, Provvisioni, Registri 109, ff. 160v–2v. See Mehus, *Dell'origine*, 136–63; Weissman *Ritual Brotherhood*, 165–6; Polizzotto, "Confraternities, Conventicles and Political Dissent," 238–40. There had been, already, previous suppressions in 1377, 1381, and 1381; see Weissman, *Ritual Brotherhood*, 165.   [2] Mehus, *Dell'origine*, 146–63.

mile of the city limits was suppressed; all confraternity account and record books were to be brought to the Chancellor of the Commune or to two of his deputized ministers who, by the end of October, were to burn them; by the end of November all sacred objects, books, and whatever other possessions confraternities owned, were to be confiscated and distributed among religious houses and persons in the city; all their furniture was to be destroyed and their oratories converted to secular use; no confraternity was allowed to meet again in any location either inside or outside the city; any citizen who took part in such a meeting would be excluded from public office; any citizen who lent his house, or clergyman who permitted a convent or monastery to be used for such a meeting would have his house or his parsonage (*canonica*) confiscated; no new confraternities were to be established within three miles of Florence without the explicit permission of the Republic; and the Republic retained the right to allow and approve, within the month of October, the continuation of old or the creation of new confraternities, as long as such groups did not meddle in the affairs of the Commune.[3] Though the decrees were very severe, the application was desultory at best, so much so that Ronald F. E. Weissman notes that "no company is known to have been dissolved for good, and all major companies founded in the thirteenth and fourteenth centuries survived beyond 1419."[4] Mehus is not certain about the reasons why the decree failed to have its desired effect and suggests either that the Commune was too generous in allowing and approving current confraternities to continue, or that a change in government brought to power many of the seventy-two elected officials who had previously voted against that decree.[5]

Though ineffective in the long run, the suppression of 1419 set the precedent for several subsequent bans. In 1426 and 1458 the government again closed confraternities in response to perceived threats and political crises of the moment. At other times (1443, 1455, 1471) it sought to prevent possible confraternity interference in politics by prohibiting all franchised males over the age of 24 who had been either *seduti* (that is, who had held one of the three highest offices in the Republic: the Signoria, the Twelve Good Men, and the Sixteen Captains of the Standard-Bearing Companies), or who had been *veduti* (that is, who had been determined to be eligible for these offices) from participating in any way in confraternity life on pain of exclusion from office. However, as Weissman again points out, "despite a history of prohibition against confraternal activity by the Florentine political class, the veduti and their

---

[3] For a selective English translation from these decrees, see Weissman, *Ritual Brotherhood*, 165–6.
[4] Weissman, *Ritual Brotherhood*, 166. [5] Mehus, *Dell'origine*, 163–4.

kinsmen continued to participate and did so in great numbers.''[6]

It may well have been because of this inability on the part of the Republican government to deal effectively with confraternities that Lorenzo de' Medici approached the problem of perceived clandestine confraternity involvement in the political life of the city in a completely different manner. Instead of distrusting confraternities and closing them down, as the Republic had sought to do in the first half of the century, he joined them with a vengeance. Over the course of his brief life (1449–92), Lorenzo became a member of at least six different and differing confraternities, including those of San Domenico, San Paolo, the Magi, Gesù Pellegrino, the Neri, and Sant'Agnese.[7] In his youth he may even have been a member of the youth confraternity of San Giovanni Evangelista, in which he later enrolled his own children, Giovanni and Giuliano, and possibly also his eldest son and heir, Piero.[8] Not only did he enroll his children in confraternities, but he also strategically placed his clients and supporters in them.

Lorenzo's handling of internal problems in the Congregazione dei Neri, a subgroup of fifty men from the confraternity of Santa Maria della Croce al Tempio, illustrates this approach very well. On 23 June 1476 the Neri invited Lorenzo to join their group in the hope that his presence and participation would help resolve irreconcilable differences that had arisen within the membership. In the following twelve years, however, Lorenzo never did anything to resolve the group's problems nor did he take part in its devotions or its charitable activity of comforting condemned criminals. In early 1488, when the situation clearly would not resolve itself, he finally took action by appointing a committee of two trusted external agents who unilaterally ejected all current members (except for Lorenzo and his son Piero), enrolled a new crop of men drawn, for the most part, from Medici sympathizers, and placed Pandolfo di Giovanni di Pagolo Rucellai, a relative of Lorenzo by marriage, in charge of the reformed Congrega dei Neri. These changes were notarized at the Signoria, the confraternity's new statutes were approved by the archbishop and his vicar, and the newly reconstituted Neri duly thanked Lorenzo for his splendid work on their behalf. Clearly, Lorenzo had infiltrated and gained control of the group, so much so that, when the Medici were driven out of Florence in 1494, the Neri, concerned about their close affiliation with the ousted regime, promptly rescinded all of

---

[6] See Weissman, "Lorenzo de' Medici."

[7] The list is drawn from Hatfield, "The Compagnia de' Magi," 124; it has been cited or repeated by subsequent scholars.

[8] On the confraternity of San Giovanni Evangelista and Lorenzo's children see Eisenbichler, "Confraternities and Carnival."

Lorenzo's reforms and returned to their pre-1488 structures, thereby betraying their previous political stripes.[9]

The variety inherent in the confraternities Lorenzo joined suggests an attempt to cover all bases, from the neighborhood *laudese* confraternity of Sant'Agnese, well known for its production of the elaborate Ascension play in the church of the Carmine, to the city-wide festive confraternity of the Magi, who organized the Epiphany cavalcade; from the charitable Congrega dei Neri, who comforted condemned criminals and buried their bodies, to the *buca* of San Paolo, where strict discipline, overnight devotions, and self-flagellation were the order of the day on Saturday nights.[10]

Lorenzo's successful "participatory" approach to the problem of perceived confraternity interference in politics was not followed by the Republican governments that came after him. In late 1494, the growing instability of the political situation in Florence, brought about by the imminent collapse of the Medicean regime, the meteoric rise of the Savonarolan party, and the threatening advance into Italy of King Charles VIII of France, led the government to close for a time all confraternities in the city (22 September).[11] In 1513, the same context in reverse – that is, the collapse of the Soderini republic and the rise of the Medici faction, led the Council of Eight to issue another edict, again closing all confraternities (4 September).[12] For the most part, these closures lasted only a few months – in 1494 the buca of San Girolamo, for example, reopened six months later on 4 April 1495, while in 1513 it reopened one year later on 25 November 1514.[13] Nonetheless, the turmoil of the Savonarolan period, the ensuing political uncertainties of the following years, and the

---

[9] For a detailed analysis of this event see Eisenbichler, "Lorenzo de' Medici e la Congregazione dei Neri nella Compagnia della Croce al Tempio," and "Lorenzo de' Medici and the Confraternity of the Blacks in Florence." Lorenzo also "reformed" the *buca* of San Paolo; see Weissman, *Ritual Brotherhood*, 117.

[10] For the confraternity of Sant'Agnese and its Ascension play, see Newbigin, *Feste d'Oltrarno*; for the Magi and its festive processions see Hatfield, "The Compagnia de' Magi," 107–61; for the Neri see Eisenbichler, "Confraternity of the Blacks in Florence," 85–98; for the *buca* of San Paolo (and other confraternities) see Weissman, *Ritual Brotherhood*, 107–61, and *passim*. For a definition of the term *buca*, indicating an adult confraternity that met overnight and practiced flagellation, and on the *buca* of San Girolamo in particular, see Sebregondi, *Tre confraternite fiorentine*, 3–23.

[11] ASF, Provvisioni, Registri 185, f. 6v and ASF, Provvisioni, Registri 186, f. 91v. See Polizzotto, "Confraternities, Conventicles," 247–8.

[12] ASF, Otto di Guardia e Balìa, Epoca Repubblicana, Registro 223, Minute di Bandi, ff. 26r. See Weissman, *Ritual Brotherhood*, 177–80 and Polizzotto, "Confraternities, Conventicles," 251.

[13] For 1494 see ACSG, "Memorie," f. 13; cited by Sebregondi, *Tre confraternite fiorentine*, 5, 69. For 1513 see ACSG, Deliberationi e Partiti 1500–1562, ff. 60v, 63r; cited by Sebregondi, *Tre confraternite*, 5, 69. Drawing on the records of the adult confraternity of the Archangel Raphael Weissman gives a very detailed list of eleven occasions in which this confraternity was closed for longer or shorter periods between 1513 and 1544; Weissman, *Ritual Brotherhood*, 179–80.

random closures did disrupt the smooth functioning of all confraternities in Florence.[14]

From 1494 to about 1540 confraternities were suppressed or closed not only for political, but also for sanitary reasons. On 3 June 1527, an edict from the Officers of Sanitation closed them for fear of the plague that had struck the city (3 June).[15] Though the plague may have been the official reason, the recent sack of Rome (6 May) and subsequent expulsion of the Medici from Florence (19 May) may also have been determining factors in the decision against confraternities. The length of this closure varied from confraternity to confraternity – in the case of Santa Maria della Croce al Tempio it lasted for about sixteen months, while for the buca of San Girolamo it continued for fifteen years.[16]

Although in the fifteenth century Archbishop Antoninus and the Florentine clergy had come to the defense of confraternities against the closures and prohibitions imposed by the government, in the early sixteenth century the current archbishops – Rinaldo Orsini, Cosimo Pazzi, and Giulio de' Medici – took no apparent interest in defending the lay religious organizations of their diocese. During the Savonarolan regime and then, later, during the Medici protectorate, the reason for such disinterest may be obvious – Church and State were far too closely tied to differ. During the intervening Soderini Republic, however, ecclesiastical authorities could have defended the interests of lay religious organizations with a certain degree of detachment from the current government, but did not do so. Although I do not have firm evidence that would shed light on the reasons for this failure on the part of the clergy, the generally troubled nature of the times may perhaps be held at fault. These were, after all, uncertain years, rendered all the more chaotic first by the intense emotions of the Savonarolan period, then by the ineffectual Soderini Republic and concurrent machinations of the Medici faction, and finally by the malaise of the Medicean rule of Pope Leo X and his cousin Pope Clement VII, who governed Florence through appointed vicars and through their two young, incompetent nephews, Ippolito and Alessandro.[17]

---

[14] For a discussion of this turbulent half-century in the life of Florentine confraternities, see Weissman, *Ritual Brotherhood*, 137–79, and Polizzotto "Confraternities, Conventicles," 237–58.

[15] ASF, Otto di Guardia e Balìa, Epoca Repubblicana, Registro 205, f. 2r. See Polizzotto, "Confraternities, Conventicles," 251–52.

[16] Santa Maria della Croce al Tempio reopened on 18 October 1528; see ASF, Compagnie Religiose Soppresse da Pietro Leopoldo 1646, fasc. 8, f. 279v. The *buca* of San Girolamo reopened in 1542; see ACSG, "Deliberationi e Partiti 1500–1562," f. 112v, cited and discussed by Sebregondi, *Tre confraternite*, 5.

[17] Cardinal Giulio de' Medici was made archbishop of Florence in 1513 by his cousin Pope Leo X and continued to be its archbishop even when he ascended to the See of Rome (1521–32).

With the establishment of a stable hereditary Medici government (1532) and the changing religious atmosphere of Tridentine Italy, Florentine confraternities once again enjoyed the support of the government and the clergy. Like Lorenzo the Magnificent, Duke Cosimo I de' Medici (r. 1537–74) also found it more profitable to infiltrate confraternities and use them to his advantage.[18] The Medici children were once again enroled in the youth confraternity of San Giovanni Evangelista, which once again busied itself more with spectacles than with devotions. Starting in the mid-century, the Vangelista, as it was popularly known, once again became noted for the plays it staged for the entertainment not only of its members, but also of the court and the city. A *Memoria* at the Archepiscopal Archive in Florence recalls that

> In the year 1569 the theatre of the Confraternity, having developed a taste for comedy and having started to present comedies without any desire or hope for reward, was honored on several occasions by the Most Serene Cosimo I and the Most Serene Eleonora of Toledo his wife, and their children, all of whom came to see the comedies staged in the said theatre, and especially the one mentioned in Vignola's book on perspective, commented by Fr. Ignazio Danti of the Order of Preachers, which [performance] so pleased the Sovereign that he not only deigned to bestow his high patronage on both the confraternity and the theatre, but he also was pleased to enrol himself among its brothers, and his example was followed by all the succeeding Grand Dukes of the glorious house of Medici up to the Most Serene Grand Duke [Gian] Gastone.[19]

Given such high patronage, it comes as no surprise that the confraternity was asked to put on plays for important state occasions such as the 1569 visit to Florence of Archduke Karl von Hapsburg, brother-in-law of Francesco de' Medici, or the 1589 wedding of Duke Ferdinando I with Christine of Lorraine.[20]

[18] Cosimo I did, however, suppress one confraternity, and an important one at that – the Compagnia di Santa Maria del Bigallo, which had been founded in 1244 and had quickly come to administer several hostels in Florence for pilgrims and the poor. The manner of Cosimo's 1542 suppression is quite revealing: he amalgamated the Bigallo into his newly founded magistracy to oversee about 200 hospices throughout the duchy and then he transferred not only the assets, but also the name of the Bigallo to his new magistracy. For a detailed discussion of this suppression see Terpstra, "Confraternities and Public Charity." For the Bigallo in general see Saalman, *The Bigallo.*

[19] AAF, Compagnie, VII.II fasc. 1, ff. n.n. 1v–2r. The reference is to Jacopo Barrozzi detto Il Vignola, *Le dve regole della prospettiva pratica di M. Iacomo Barozzi da Vignola. Con i comentarij del RPM Egnatio Danti* (In Roma, 1583), 92.

[20] On both occasions the youths performed plays by the Florentine notary and dramatist Giovan Maria Cecchi (1518–87). For the 1569 visit they staged *La coronazione del re Saul*, and in 1589 *L'Esaltazione della croce*. Both plays were five-act religious dramas enlivened by elaborate *intermezzi* accompanied by music and dancing. A detailed description of the 1589 stage set and *intermezzi* is extant; see Baccio Cecchi, "Descrizione dell'apparato."

Confraternities clearly had nothing to fear from the government and the clergy. Temporary closures were no longer predicated by political fears, but by purely sanitary concerns during time of plague. In January 1631, for example, confraternities were closed because of the current epidemic, and then again in June 1633. Apart from these temporary crises, they continued to prosper and grow throughout the sixteenth and seventeenth century with the blessing of Church and State.

With the advent of the eighteenth century, however, the new spirit of "enlightenment" that spread across Europe from France and Germany brought about a drastic change in attitudes towards lay religious organizations. Danilo Zardin rightly points out that, although critical attitudes towards confraternities had always existed, in the eighteenth century they reached a level probably never seen before, indicative of a much more profoundly complicated relationship between learned and popular culture, between ecclesiastical and lay society, and between the ruling classes and the masses.[21] This was especially true in Tuscany and Lombardy, regions that had now come under the rule of the Hapsburg family and its reforming rulers. The Empress Maria Theresa closed confraternities in the smaller and less important dioceses of Lombardy and then carried out a surgical suppression of selected confraternities in Milan itself, not without some initial opposition from the local archbishop and clergy.[22] Her sons, Grand Duke Peter Leopold and Emperor Joseph II soon followed her example with sweeping closures of their own in Tuscany and Lombardy respectively.

The cultural climate supporting such drastic action had already been prepared by some of the most eminent intellectuals of the period. In Italy, the prolific thinker/writer/historian Ludovico Antonio Muratori (1672–1750) strongly criticized certain types of external, popular religiosity, including confraternities and their practices. In his *Antiquitates Italicae Medii Aevi, sive Dissertationes de moribus, ritibus, religione, regimine* . . . (1742), Muratori devoted an entire discourse, the Seventy-Fifth Dissertation, to "The pious Confraternities of the laity, and about their origins, about the Flagellants, and about sacred Missions."[23]

---

[21] Zardin, "Le confraternite in Italia settentrionale," 119. See also, Rosa, *Riformatori e ribelli.*
[22] For the Milanese suppressions see Bottoni, "Le confraternite milanesi."
[23] Muratori, *Antiquitates italicae medii aevi,* 6, coll. 447–82. An Italian translation was published shortly thereafter under the title *Dissertazioni sopra le antichità italiane.* My translations of Muratori will be from this Italian translation where the Seventy-Fifth Dissertation "Delle pie Confraternità de' Laici" appeared in vol. 3, 592–607.

As the title indicates, Muratori's essay on confraternities was really an attempt to determine when and where the contemporary confraternal movement had its origins. He began by mentioning the ancient Greek and Roman brotherhoods, but then dismissed them saying that "in fact, I do not believe Christian confraternities were instituted on the example of pagan ones, but rather by the effort of pious people who, eager to increase the cult of God, undertook themselves to carry out certain religious rituals and duties. Thus, one must seek the origin of sacred confraternities within the bosom of Christianity."[24] He then considered pre-Carolingian brotherhoods from the fifth to the ninth century, but dismissed them as well, saying that there were far too many differences between the "pious societies" of that time and the "secular" ones of his day.[25] The confraternities and guilds of the ninth to the thirteenth century fared better, so much so that, as Muratori pointed out, "whoever does not see the establishment of pious confraternities of the laity already at the time of [archbishop] Hincmar [of Rheims], that is, in the ninth century, must be blind, for [these groups] sought to carry out those things that were of God and appropriate to Christian religion."[26] This is a strongly ironic statement, coming as it does fast on the heels of Muratori's observation that:

> Companies were thus instituted at that time [ninth century] so as to carry out certain pious and charitable works; that is, to make offerings at the temple, maintain its lights, accompany the deceased to burial, give alms, and carry out other pious duties in order to gain merit with God. What else, by your grace, do modern confraternities propose to do? And for this reason in these gatherings it is sometimes believed that feasts are celebrated more solemnly with a banquet and good wine; and, furthermore, fights and hostilities often arise here: it is useful to listen to Hincmar again, who confirms that in his time the same things occurred, and he seems to describe the customs of our own times. '[There are] even banquets, – he says – and meals, which divine authority forbids, where both fees and inappropriate taxes [are charged], and [there are] shameful and inane amusements and quarrels; and often, as we very well know, even murders, and hatreds, and dissensions are wont to occur there.[27]

In other words, Muratori acknowledged the pious and charitable origins of the confraternal movement, but then undermined its validity by pointing out the abuses that stained it from the very start. In the pages that followed, Muratori sought to identify the first of the "modern" confraternities in several Italian cities, often linking them

---

[24] *Ibid.*, 593.   [25] *Ibid.*, 594.   [26] *Ibid.*, 597.   [27] *Ibid.*, 596.

directly with the flagellant/penitential movements of the twelfth and thirteenth century or with the missionary efforts of the new penitential orders. Although in these pages he did maintain a certain historical distance, such was not the case in his abrupt conclusion to the dissertation:

> Sometime also, the end of a pestilence gave birth to some of these confraternities, about which we have only left to say that, just as their institution is highly praiseworthy, so we must wish that their rules be observed more religiously, and that there do not appear in them that turmoil and those stains that are with reason condemned by Nicolaus de Clemangiis in his treatise *De novis celebritatibus non instituendis* and by Fr. Théophile Raynaud, of the Company of Jesus, in his *Heteroclita spiritualia* part I and II.[28] The ancient Romans had the college of the *Epulones* who oversaw the games and certain sacrifices. And [Guillaume] Budé, dealing with the confraternities of his time in France, wrote: "They could perhaps be called *coëpulones* [gluttons], as they generally gather more for feasting than for divine office."[29]

Muratori's revival of Budé's stinging word-play against confraternity members of his day (*epulones/coëpulones*) points to the long tradition of derision heaped by learned and enlightened thinkers upon superstitious and superficial piety. Martin Luther, for example, had touched the same chord as Budé when he claimed that in confraternities "you have nothing but gluttony, drunkenness, useless squandering of money, howling, yelling, chattering, dancing, and wasting of time."[30]

Muratori's criticism weighed heavily on Italian confraternities. It came from the most eminent Italian intellectual of the time, a scholar whose knowledge and erudition were unparalleled in the peninsula, someone who was thoroughly versed in the Latin and vernacular literature of Italy from the middle ages to the present, the editor of the

[28] The theologian Nicolaus de Clemangiis, also known as Matthieu-Nicolas de Clamenges [or Clémangis] (b. *c.* 1367), studied at the Collège de Navarre in Paris, where he returned in his old age after an illustrious career as rector of the Academy in Paris, secretary of the anti-pope Clement VII, treasurer of Langres, and archdeacon of Bayeux. A friend of Jean Gerson and Pierre d'Ailly, he was a stong critic of contemporary vices and an avid proponent of moderate church reform. Théophile Raynaud (1583–1663), who became a Jesuit in 1602, taught philosophy and theology at the university in Lyons. He subsequently became confessor to Maurice of Savoy (1631), refused the bishopric of Chambéry, spent some time in Rome, and often became embroiled in controversies. His *Heteroclita spiritualia*, first published in Grenoble in 1646, is a description of religious practices that found their origin in ignorance, superstition, or a slackening of discipline.

[29] Muratori, *Antiquitates italicae medii aeri*, 6, 606–7.

[30] Luther, "The Brotherhoods," in *Luther's Works*, 35, 68; see 67–73 for his fuller thoughts on German confraternities. For another reference to Luther and a sixteenth-century German initiative to reform confraternities see Thiessen, "Hartmut von Cronberg's *Statutes of the Heavenly Confraternity*."

(still) fundamental collection *Rerum italicarum scriptores* (published in twenty-five volumes between 1723 and 1751) and its companion series, the *Antiquitates italicae Medii Aevi* (1738–42) and the *Annali d'Italia* (1744–9). Not to mention that Muratori was also a priest. He thus influenced the opinion of most, if not all, Italian thinkers in the second half of the eighteenth century, be they lay or clerical.

It is not surprising, therefore, to see that one of the most thorough attacks on Italian confraternities in the late eighteenth century was carried out by a learned priest with clear Muratorian roots, the Florentine abbot and *savant* Lorenzo Mehus (1716–1802). Mehus summarized the current lay intellectual view of confraternities in his *Dell'origine, progresso, abusi, e riforma delle confraternite laicali* (1785), a historical examination of the establishment and rise of confraternities, their periodic deterioration, and the recurring calls for their reform, both in Italy and abroad.[31] Mehus neither minced words nor hid his bias. His opening sentence was absolutely clear:

> My intention is to consider those Lay Gatherings commonly called Con-
> fraternities . . . and to show that they are contrary to Sacred Laws, harmful
> to Parish Jurisdiction, and offensive to that status which, by right of Divine
> Decree, is held among their flock by Rectors of churches, who in our day
> reside in them enjoying no respect and nearly insulted.[32]

Then, over the course of nearly 200 pages, Mehus pointed out that, although pious confraternities had existed since the fourth century and had contributed to the spiritual and physical well-being of Christians, secular or immoral imitations of these original groups had subsequent-ly been established and had given rise to inappropriate practices which, in turn, had badly misled innocent Christians. Mehus placed the fault for these abhorrent institutions and practices squarely on the shoulders of the mendicant orders and on "the scandalous and reckless Confraternity of the Flagellants of the thirteenth century." He then took to task Scholasticism itself, which he held accountable for "that superstitious licence in which barbarous education has led the World."[33] Mehus objected not only to the external, visible signs of the flagellant origins of contemporary confraternities – the ritual of self-flagellation, the wearing of hooded gowns, etc. – , but also to con-

[31] The presentation copy of this book from the author to the Grand Duke is now at ASF, Gabinetto di Segreteria, 51, together with an autograph presentation letter that mentions how the Grand Duke had intended to give a copy of the volume to "all the Archbishops, Bishops, General Vicars, Ministers and Pastors (*parroci*) of the Grand Duchy," but this unfortunately could not be done because the Grand-ducal Secretary, Riguccio Galluzzi, had had only 200 copies printed. On Mehus, see Rosa, "Per la storia dell'erudizione toscana del 700."

[32] Mehus, *Dell'origine*, 5–6.   [33] *Ibid.*, 105.

fraternal practices which he deemed to be heretical – in particular, the hearing of confessions and the granting of absolution by the laity. Mehus was clearly exaggerating with this last point: confraternity members did not hear each other's confessions and grant absolution in a sacramental manner, though they did acknowledge in front of the membership their personal failure to observe the confraternity's regulations and in turn received forgiveness for it from the appropriate confraternity officer. The public confession ritual, which existed more on paper than in practice, was enough for Mehus to accuse confraternities of heresy and disregard for the rights of the parishes and their priests.[34]

Mehus was a relatively minor intellectual of the late eighteenth century and his work had a limited impact. His volume against confraternities enjoyed a very small print run and a very restricted distribution – only 200 copies were printed and were distributed only within Tuscany (see n. 27). However, his views did reflect the general intellectual climate of the period, and especially the "enlightened" attitudes held not only by the laity, but also by some of the clergy itself. Mehus was a learned abbot whose clerical status did not stop him from criticizing cultic practices which he considered grounded in error and superstition.

Even some of the higher clergy espoused enlightened views and attacked, in both words and deeds, what they perceived to be false pietism. Mehus' contemporary and compatriot, Bishop Scipione de' Ricci (1741–1810), was spearheading at that very moment a thorough (and Jansenist) reform of religious practices in his twin diocese of Pistoia and Prato.[35] The diocesan synod he convened in Pistoia in September 1786 "proposed a variety of reforms designed to rationalize Catholic practice" and encouraged bishops "to reclaim their rights over a variety of matters that had been given to them by Christ but that had been usurped by the Roman Court."[36] Ricci's hope was that his initiative would be followed by the episcopate throughout Tuscany, Italy, and, eventually, by the Church Universal. In the words of a recent scholar, "Scipione de' Ricci and the diocesan Synod of Pistoia constitute perhaps the nearest to victory that Enlightened Catholicism came."[37] Ricci's motives were lofty, and his aspirations high, and both were fueled and sustained by their apparent affinity

---

[34] *Ibid.*

[35] On Ricci, see the recent collection *Lettere di Scipione de' Ricci a Pietro Leopoldo* and Miller, "The Limits of Political Jansenism in Tuscany."

[36] Carroll, *Veiled Threats*, 19, but see also 18–24 regarding Ricci's reforms.

[37] Miller, "Political Jansenism," 762.

with the intentions of the very active and efficient ruler of Tuscany, Grand Duke Peter Leopold.

The affinity was, however, not complete for, as Miller clearly points out, "Ricci's political theory was in many ways a throwback to the traditional concept of all sovereignty being of God with the prince being the worldly representative of divine authority, the Church being subject in all matters of this world to the sovereign's jurisdiction, in a word, an Erastian concept. On the contrary, the grand duke's political theory, if it can be said to have been derived from any one source, was indebted to contractual theories current in the eighteenth century, chiefly the ideas of Montesquieu."[38] Eventually, a well-concerted reform, carried out by the bishop and the grand duke acting in unison, failed to materialize for several reasons. One of these was the fact that the pace of Ricci's reform initiatives was too frantic for the grand duke's own keen sense of political realism which would not ignore the objections of the majority of Tuscan bishops. "The Assembly of the Tuscan episcopate in 1787 marks the point at which the fundamental lack of a similar ideology, perhaps more accurately the reluctance of the grand duke to ignore political reality ... becomes glaringly apparent. From that point on, Ricci's conviction that the prince would support him through thick and thin becomes more and more an exercise in self-deception."[39]

Even though a concerted reforming initiative on the part of the enlightened grand duke and the Jansenist bishop would not be possible, a reform of church and state was carried out after all. Grand Duke Peter Leopold (r. 1765–90), like his brother the Emperor Joseph II and his mother the Empress Maria Theresa, had a keen interest in reforming Church and State. During his reign in Tuscany, he abolished the right of sanctuary, suppressed a number of orders and convents, closed the courts of the Inquisition, subjected ecclesiastical decrees to his approval, and regularized the education of the clergy.

For our own interests, Peter Leopold is remembered mostly for his unilateral decree (*motu proprio*) of 21 March 1785 whereby he closed down all confraternities in the realm. His decree was swift and efficient to a degree no fifteenth-century Republican interdictions could have hoped for, or even imagined. Part of the reason for Peter Leopold's boldness was, without a doubt, his awareness of the "ambiguous alliance," as Diana Toccafondi characterizes it, that had been struck between high churchmen with strong Jansenist tendencies seeking to reform the Church from within and the grand duke, whose concept of

[38] *Ibid.*, 764.   [39] *Ibid.*, 765.

kingly rights easily encompassed both ecclesiastical and civil jurisdictions.[40]

Peter Leopold's interest in confraternities had already led him, in July 1783, to issue a grand-ducal decree ordering a thorough census of all confraternities, inquiring about their status, membership, and activities. This information was then compiled into a document for the use of the Grand Duke and his ministers.[41] The final report, signed by Carlo Giunti, ended with a few "General Observations" that pointed clearly to the perceived problems with confraternities. Among other things, it noted that the majority of the works of mercy carried out by confraternities were *"for their own institution"* (emphasis in the original), that is, for their own benefit, and that in many of these organizations officers and members received special gifts (rations of pepper, candles, bread, etc.) and other hidden profits, again for their own benefit.[42] Francesco Alfonso Tallinacci, Grand-Ducal Chancellor for Fiesole, echoed Giunti's words when he wrote in his report that, although confraternities had once had "praiseworthy and holy" intentions, nonetheless his inspections revealed that now, "as far as piety and devotion are concerned, there is not even a hint of them, but everything revolves around mundane pomp ... and display."[43] And, to aggravate matters, there had been a proliferation of lay religious associations that had gone beyond the bounds of reason. Tallinacci pointed to Campi, a small village six miles outside Florence, where he had located "very near each other, just a few steps away, four parishes with nine companies and four *centurie*." This same proliferation of lay-religious organizations was true for Florence where, within the walls, there were "152 *compagnie*, 64 *congregazioni*, 17 *centurie*, 6 congreghe, 5 *buche*, 4 *società*, 1 *aggregazione*, and 1 *confederazione*, for a total of 251 associations."[44]

All the different reports also revealed what everyone knew: that there was great wealth scattered among all the different confraternities of the realm. Not surprisingly, the Grand Duke followed this initial inquiry with an order that a detailed inventory of all confraternity

---

[40] Toccafondi, "L'Archivio delle Compagnie Religiose Soppresse," 108.

[41] ASF, Segreteria di Gabinetto 51, fasc. 7, containing the "Nota di tutte le Compagnie della città e regola loro" and the "Relazione sopra tutte le Compagnie, Congregazioni, Centurie, Buche esistenti in Firenze attualmente. Li 22 Ottobre 1783."

[42] ASF, Segreteria di Gabinetto 51, fasc. 7, f. 87r.

[43] ASF, Segreteria di Gabinetto 51, 6B, "Relazione sullo stato delle Compagnie che sono intorno a Firenze e di quelle del Vicariato di Firenzuola" [18 September 1784], unnumbered folios; cited in Sebregondi, "La soppressione delle confraternite fiorentine", vol. 3, 1042.

[44] Tallinacci in ASF, Segreteria di Gabinetto 51, 6B, f. n.n.; cited in Sebregondi, "La soppressione delle confraternite fiorentine," 1042. The tally of associations in Florence is also in *ibid*.

holdings be drawn under the supervision of a government official (17 July 1784). His interest in the extensive material wealth of confraternities was obvious, as was his intention to centralize it, rationalize it, and place it under the management of officials directly responsible to Church and State. Already in 1784 Peter Leopold had established the "Ecclesiastical Patrimonies," a series of diocesan treasuries charged with the central administration of parish revenues. One year later, these "Patrimonies" would became the central repository for all the funds, benefits, and material wealth of confraternities.

Once all the inventories had been compiled, Peter Leopold politely asked Archbishop Antonio Martini to draw up a list of Florentine confraternities to be exempt from the general suppression he was about to decree. In September 1784 the archbishop forwarded a list with nineteen names on it, and then the following November a second, revised list of twenty confraternities.[45] When the decree of suppression was finally issued, on 21 March 1785, the follow-up decree exempting certain organizations listed only nine, not twenty, confraternities: the buca of San Girolamo in via della Sapienza, the buca of San Iacopo nel Popolo di Santa Felicita, the confraternities of the Misericordia, the Bacchetoni (or Vanchetoni), the Stimmate, San Benedetto Bianco, San Salvadore, San Filippo Neri, and the youth confraternity of San Niccolò del Ceppo.[46] A tenth confraternity, the Buonuomini di San Martino, established at the time of Cosimo the Elder and Archbishop Antonino Pierozzi, was allowed to continue its work of assisting the "shamefaced poor," but was forced to remove the altar from its oratory, an indication that it was considered an organization of social assistance rather than a devotional confraternity. All other were permanently suppressed. The nine that survived were no longer to use hoods and banners (*stendardi*), not to take part in public processions, meet at night or on holy days, or bestow dowries on women. And they were to conform themselves with Peter Leopold's third *motu proprio* on confraternities establishing the new

---

[45] ASF, Segreteria di Gabinetto 51, fasc. 8bis "Nota data dall'Arcivescovo di Firenze delle Compagnie che crederebbe utili da conservarsi in Città," and ASF, Segreteria di Gabinetto 51, fasc. 9 "Seconda nota data posteriormente dall'Arcivescovo di Firenze di altre Compagnie che crederebbe utili di Conservarsi."

[46] *Bandi e ordini del Granducato di Toscana*, vol. 12, n. 99. There is a manuscript copy of the three separate decrees from the Granducal Cabinet dealing with (1) the suppression of all confraternities, (2) the exemption of nine confraternities, and (3) the establishment of new parish-based Confraternities of Charity in ASF, Segreteria di Gabinetto 51, fasc. 12 "Editto approvato e pubblicato per la Soppressione di tutte le Compagnie"; fasc. 13 "Motuproprio per le Compagnie che dovranno restare in Firenze, e loro Regolamento"; and fasc. 14 "Capitoli e Sistema dato alle nuove Compagnie in tutte le Cure." See also the *Gazzetta toscana*, no. 14 (2 Aprile 1785): 53–6. See also Mehus, *Dell'origine*, 185–94 for a ten-point resumé of the decree of suppression.

structure and practices of confraternities. In this third and final document, the Grand Duke decreed that new confraternities be established, one per parish, to assist in the needs of that parish, that they be known as "Confraternities of Charity" and that they take their name from the titular saint of their parish church.[47]

Peter Leopold's actions reveal a thorough sense of order and rationality. In closing down all confraternities and replacing them with only one confraternity per parish, the Grand Duke was introducing a sense of order into the confused confraternal map of the realm. No longer were confraternities to engage in a variety of charitable or devotional activities independently of religious or secular authority, or to exhibit themselves in a rainbow of colorful names, ceremonies or cloaks, but they were all to serve the immediate needs of their own parish community in partnership with their local priest and bishop.

The Grand Duke then ordered that all churches, houses, books, sacred objects, possessions, and funds belonging to confraternities be seized by the local ecclesiastical administrators, who were to dispose of them immediately. Real estate, funds, and goods were to be appraised and sold. Confraternity churches and oratories not suitable for parish religious service were to be deconsecrated and sold. In consultation with the local bishop, sacred objects and art works were to be distributed among needy churches throughout the diocese. Charitable subsidies were to remain within the parish where the confraternity had been located. All revenues from sales and any other wealth, including rental revenue, were to be deposited into the "Ecclesiastical Patrimony." This, and other subsidies, were to be distributed to needy churches by the ecclesiastical administrators in consultation with the local parish priest. This distribution of wealth was to be done simply and profitably, without partiality or scheming.[48] On many points Peter Leopold's orders seemed to echo those of 1419, but, unlike the Republican rulers of earlier times, he had both the will, the power, and the co-operation necessary to implement his reforms fully.

Unlike the initial situation in Milan, Peter Leopold's extensive

---

[47] Although it might be tempting to compare these Confraternities of Charity with the sixteenth-century Confraternities of the Most Holy Sacrament, the exercise may not yield results. The principal duties of the Leopoldine Confraternities of Charity revolved around assisting the parish priest in the proper care of altars and churches, whereas the principal motivation of the earlier Confraternities of the Most Holy Sacrament centered on the affirmation of, and devotion to, the Divine Presence in the Eucharist (especially in light of Protestant denials of such a presence).

[48] *Bandi e ordini del Granducato di Toscana*, vol. 12, n. 99. For the dispersion of confraternity art works, see Ludovica Sebregondi, "Tracce per la ricostruzione del patrimonio artistico delle confraternite fiorentine soppresse." For a detailed history of the newly created archive of documents from the suppressed confraternities see Toccafondi, "L'Archivio delle Compagnie Religiose Soppresse."

reform of confraternities was carried out without any significant opposition from the local ecclesiastical hierarchy. Such compliance may have been motivated by the fact that the archbishop of Florence, Antonio Martini, was himself a reformer, or that the higher clergy was also keen to gain control of confraternities and their wealth. Whatever the case, the suppression went smoothly enough for Peter Leopold to take pride of this deed in a *pro memoria* he composed for the benefit of his son and successor, Ferdinand III (r. 1790–1824). This private document offers an insight into the reforming Grand Duke's personal view of what confraternities had been like:

> They gathered on feast days and recited the Office, and for the most part they served to waylay the people from the parishes and from [Christian] instruction, and they constantly fomented dissension with the parish priests on account of the authority the brothers thought they had over churches, functions, processions, etc. In the countryside they served as a pretext for festive meals. In Florence, then, there were also many night companies, where they gathered to eat all night long, and even slept there, and they heard Mass on feast days very early, before daylight, and they spent the rest of the day hunting, or at the inn, or loafing around, and they did a thousand knavish things in the distribution of the many dowries that were given out by these confraternities, and were of a respectable amount.[49]

Peter Leopold then noted that, because of his extensive reform of confraternities, "fanaticism" had been reduced in Tuscany, a sizable ecclesiastical patrimony had been established to provide for poorer churches, and new parish-based confraternities of charity had been established to look after the local churches. His advice to Ferdinand III, briefly put, was that "whoever will head the government of Tuscany will do well ... not to permit the introduction of new companies or confraternities, to which the country is much inclined, and abolish even those that have been left in Florence,"[50] and his final comment was that, although he had allowed a few to survive because of the valid charitable work they carried out, "these, too, should be abolished in order to dispel the thought of establishing new ones."[51]

Peter Leopold's suppression in 1785 was both immediate and, in the case of the majority of confraternities, final. The reforming Grand Duke had assessed correctly the religious climate of his realm, and carried out the deed neatly and swiftly. He had also succeeded in tying new confraternities more closely to the parishes, and in giving a boost to poorer parishes through a more equitable distribution of religious

[49] Leopold II, *Relazioni sul governo della Toscana*, 3, 176–7.   [50] *Ibid.*, 1, 7.   [51] *Ibid.*, 1, 177.

objects and wealth. And, through it all, he had managed to avoid the suspicion of self-interest or personal profit.

His victory, however, was only temporary. Within a few years the religious and political climate of Tuscany changed dramatically. The reforms spearheaded, on the ecclesiastical side, by Bishop Scipione de' Ricci and the Diocesan Synod of Pistoia (1786) had met their match in the people, the Grand Duke, and the Pope. The general population and the local clergy were not Jansenist, and therefore did not take kindly to the destruction of their cherished pietistic beliefs (or the loss of income from pietistic practices). When, in the spring of 1787, rumours spread in Prato that the bishop was about to remove from the duomo the town's prized relic, the Girdle of Our Lady which she had let fall as she ascended into heaven, a popular revolt broke out against him. Similar revolts occurred in other locations where religious images were under threat. In the wake of one such uprising in 1790 the Jansenist bishop was forced to flee and, one year later, resign his bishopric. In 1794 Ricci saw his dreams for reform come to an end when Pope Pius VI issued a bull condemning eighty-five of the Pistoian propositions and declaring seven of them heretical. By then, the French Revolution had broken out and hardened attitudes against reform. The death of Emperor Joseph II (20 February 1790) had elevated his brother, Grand Duke Peter Leopold, to the archducal throne and imperial dignity in Vienna. Tuscany had been left in the hands of a much more moderate Council of Regency. Shortly after it came to power in 1790, and just five years after the Leopoldine suppressions, the Council had succumbed to the veritable wave of protest from the "Viva Maria" movement and allowed some confraternities to re-open. Then, in January 1792, the new Grand Duke, Ferdinand III, apparently keen to undo his father's ecclesiastical reforms, decreed the re-establishment of suppressed confraternities — without, however, returning to them all the wealth and benefices that had been confiscated in 1785.[52]

In the long narrative of Tuscan lay religious associations, it seemed history was poised to repeat itself.

---

[52] Turi, "*Viva Maria*", 4–9; Toccafondi, "L'Archivio delle Compagnie Religiose Soppresse," 113; Miller, "Political Jansenism," 766–7; Carroll, *Veiled Threats*, 22–3.

BIBLIOGRAPHY

Acta Ecclesiae Mediolanensis tribus partibus distincta. Quibus concilia provincialia, conciones synodales, synodi dioecesanae, instructiones, litterae pastorales, edicta, regulae confratriarum, formulae, et alia denique continentur, quae Carolus S. R. E. cardinalis tituli S. Praxedis, archiepiscopus egit (Milan, 1582 and 1592).

Adelman, H., "Servants and Sexuality: Seduction, Surrogacy, and Rape: Some Observations Concerning Class, Gender, and Race in Early Modern Italian Jewish Families," in T. M. Rudavsky (ed.), *Gender and Judaism: Transformation of Tradition* (New York, 1995), 81–97.

Agnoletti, A. M. E. (ed.), *Statuto dell'arte della Lana di Firenze (1317–1319). Fonti e studi sulle corporazioni artigiane del medio evo* 1 (Florence, 1940).

Ahl, D. C., *Benozzo Gozzoli* (New Haven, 1996).

Ait, I., *Tra scienza e mercato. Gli speziali a Roma nel Tardo Medioevo* (Rome, 1996).

Alberigo, G., "Contributi alla storia delle confraternite dei Disciplinati e della spiritualità laicale nei secc. XV e XVI." in *Il Movimento dei Disciplinati* (Perugia, 1962 and 1986), 156–252.

Alexander, J. J. and A. C. De La Mare, *The Italian Manuscripts in the Library of Major J. R. Abbey* (London, 1969).

Alfonso, L., "Casacce e confraternite fra Senato e Chiesa," in *La Liguria delle Casacce*, 43–52.

Altieri, M. A., *Li nuptiali*, ed. E. Narducci (Rome, 1873).

Alves, A. A., "The Christian Social Organism and Social Welfare: The Case of Vives, Calvin, and Loyola," *Sixteenth Century Journal*, 20 (1989): 3–21.

Andenna, G., "Eredità medioevale e prospettive moderne di riflessione carismatica nella 'Novaria' di Carlo Bascapé. Da Carlo Borromeo a Carlo Bascapé," in *La Pastorale di Carlo Borromeo e il Sacro Monte di Arona. Atti della Giornata Culturale*, Arona 12 settembre 1984 (Novara, 1985): 247–79.

   "Unità e divisione territoriale in una pieve di valle: Intra, Pallanza e la Vallintrasca dall'XI al XIV secolo," in M. L. Gavazzoli Tomea (ed.), *Novara e la sua terra nei secoli XI e XV. Storia, documenti, architettura* (Milan, 1980).

Angelini, M., "L'invenzione epigrafica delle origini familiari (Levante Ligure, secolo XVIII)," *Quaderni storici*, 93 (1996): 653–82.

Angelozzi, G., *Le confraternite laicali. Un'esperienza cristiana tra medioeva e età moderna* (Brescia, 1978).

Aranci, G., *Formazione religiosa e santità laicale a Firenze tra Cinque e Seicento: Ippolito Galantini fondatore della Congregazione di San Francesco della Dottrina Cristiana di Firenze (1565–1620)* (Florence, 1997).

Armellini, M. (ed.), "Origine d'alcune istituzioni di beneficenza in Roma nel secolo XVI," *Cronachetta mensuale di scienze naturali e di archeologia XIX* (1885): 155–60, 171–4.

Arnold, D., *Giovanni Gabrieli and the Music of the High Renaissance* (London, 1979).

"Music at the Scuola di San Rocco," *Music and Letters*, 40 (1959): 229–41.

"Music at a Venetian Confraternity in the Renaissance," *Acta Musicologica*, 37 (1965): 62–72.

Arrizabalaga, J., J. Henderson, and R. French, *The Great Pox: The French Disease in Renaissance Europe* (New Haven, 1997).

Assis, Y. T., "Welfare and Mutual Aid in the Spanish Jewish Communities," in H. Beinart (ed.), *Moreshet Sepharad: The Sephardic Legacy* (Jerusalem, 1992).

Balletti, A., *Gli Ebrei e gli Estensi* (Reggio Emilia, 1930).

Bandi e ordini del Granducato di Toscana (Florence, 1786).

Bangert, W., *Claude Jay and Alfonso Salmerón* (Chicago, 1985).

A History of the Society of Jesus (St. Louis, 1985).

Banker, J., "Death and Christian Charity in the Confraternities of the Upper Tiber Valley," in Verdon and Henderson (eds.), *Christianity and the Renaissance*, 302–35.

Death in the Community. Memorialization and Confraternities in an Italian Commune of the late middle ages (Athens, GA, 1988).

Barbalarga, D., "Gli atteggiamenti devozionali nei testamenti," in "Il rione Parione durante il pontificato sistino: analisi di un'area campione," in Massimo Miglio *et al.* (eds.), *Un pontificato e una città. Sisto IV (1471–1484). Atti del Convegno, Roma 3–7 dicembre 1984* (Rome, 1986), 694–705.

Barbée, P., "Von deutscher Nationalgeschichte zu römischer lokalgeschichte," *Römische Quartalschrift*, 86 (1991): 23–52.

Barbero, A., "Apparati e strumenti liturgici," in A. Barbero, F. Ramella, and A. Torre, *Materiali sulla religiosità dei laici. Alba 1698–Asti 1742* (Cuneo, 1981), xli–ci, 139–172.

Baron, H., *The Crisis of the Early Italian Renaissance* (Princeton, 1966).

Baron, S. W., *A Social and Religious History of the Jews*, 18 vols. (New York and Philadelphia, 1952–83).

Barone, G., "Il movimento francescano e la nascita delle confraternite romane," *Ricerche per la storia religiosa di Roma 5*, (1984): 71–80.

"Società e religiosità femminile (750–1450)," in L. Scaraffia and G. Zarri, (eds.) *Donne e fede. Santità e vita religiosa in Italia* (Bari, 1994), 61–113.

Barone, G. and A. M. Piazzoni. "Le più antiche carte dell'archivio del Gonfalone (1267–1486)," in *Le chiavi della memoria. Miscellanea in occasione del I Centenario della Scuola Vaticana di Paleografia, Diplomatica e Archivistica* (Vatican City, 1984), 17–105.

Barr, C., "Music and Spectacle in Confraternity Drama of Fifteenth-Century Florence: The Reconstruction of a Theatrical Event," in Verdon and Henderson (eds.), *Christianity and the Renaissance*, 376–404.

Bartolomei Romagnoli, A., "Santa Francesca Romana: un episodio di religiosità femminile nella Roma del Quattrocento," *L'ulivo*, NS 12/4 (1982): 21–9; 13/1 (1983): 31–7; 13/2 (1983): 27–32.

Bascapé, C., *Novaria seu de Ecclesia Novariensi libri duo. Primus de locis, alter de episcopis, Carolo episcopo auctore* (Novara, 1612).

Becker, M., *Florence in Transition*, vol. 1, *The Decline of the Commune* (Baltimore, 1967).

Ben-Shalom, R., "Communal Life in Arles...," *Michael*, 12 (1991).

Benvenuti Papi, A., «In castro poenitentiae». Santità e società femminile nell'Italia medievale (Rome, 1990).

"*Regularis familia*: il laicato alla ricerca della vita perfetta," In AA.VV., *Les mouvances laïcques des ordres religieux* (Saint-Etienne, 1996), 221–33.

Bernard, F., "Les Confréries communales du Saint-Esprit, leurs lieux de réunions et leurs activités du xe au xxe siècle," *Mémoires de l'Académie des sciences, belles-lettres et arts de Savoie*, 6th ser., 7 (1963): 16–79.

Bernardi, C., *Carnevale, Quaresima, Pasqua e dramma nell'età moderna (1500– 1900)* (Milan, 1994).

Bertelli, S., N. Rubinstein, and C. Smyth (eds.), *Florence and Milan: Comparisons and Relations*, vol. 2 (Florence, 1989).

Bertoldi Lenoci, L., "La sociabilità religiosa pugliese. Le confraternite (1500–1900)," *Ricerche di Storia Sociale e Religiosa*, 37–8 (1990): 213–37.

(ed.) *Confraternite, Chiese e Società. Aspetti e problemi dell'associazionismo laicale europeo in età moderna e contemporanea* (Fasano, 1994).

(ed.) *Le Confraternite pugliese in età moderna*, 2 vols (Fasano, 1988–9).

Black, A., *Council and Commune: The Conciliar Movement and the Fifteenth-Century Heritage* (London, 1979).

Black, C., "The Baglioni as Tyrants of Perugia, 1488–1540," *English Historical Review*, 85 (1970): 245–81.

"Confraternities," in Hans J.Hillerbrand (ed.), *The Oxford Encyclopedia of the Reformation*, vol.1 (New York, 1996): 406–8.

"Confraternities and the Parish in the context of Italian Catholic Reform," in J. Donnelly and M. Maher (eds.), *Confraternities and Catholic Reform in Italy, France and Spain* (Kirksville, MO., 1999) 1–26.

"Epilogue – European Confraternities," in K. Farnhill (ed.), *English Medieval Gilds* (forthcoming).

"'Exceeding Every Expression of Words': Bernini's Rome and the Religious Background," in A. Weston-Lewis (ed.), Exhibition catalogue for *Effigies and Ecstasies: Roman Baroque Sculpture and Design in the Age of Bernini* (Edinburgh, 1998), 11–21.

Italian Confraternities in the Sixteenth Century (Cambridge, 1989).

"Perugia and Post-Tridentine Church Reform," *Journal of Ecclesiastical History*, 35 (1984): 429–51.

Boefsplug, F., *Dieu dans l'art. Sollicitudini Nostrae de Benoit XIV (1745) et l'affaire Crescence de Kaufbeuren* (Paris, 1984).

Bogini, E. (ed.), *L'archivio della confraternita di Maria Santissima dei Miracoli di Castel Rigone* (Perugia, 1996).

Boksenboim, J. (ed.), *Letters of Jewish Teachers in Renaissance Italy* (Tel Aviv, 1985).

(ed.), *Responsa Matnot ba-Adam* (Tel Aviv, 1983).

Bonaini, F. (ed.), *Statuti inediti dell citta di Pisa dal XII al XIV secolo* (Florence, 1854).

Bonfil, R, *Ha-Rabanut be-Italya. be-Tekufat ha-Renessans* (Jerusalem, 1979).

"The History of the Spanish and Portuguese Jews in Italy," in H. Beinart (ed.), *Moreshet Sepharad: The Sephardic Legacy* (Jerusalem, 1992).

"New Information Concerning Rabbi Menahem Azariah da Fano and his Age," *Studies in the History of Jewish Society. Presented to . . . Jacob Katz* (Jerusalem, 1980).

Rabbis and Jewish Communities in Renaissance Italy, trans. J. Chipman (Oxford, 1990).

Bonini, F. V., *Comunità di valle in epoca signorile. L'evoluzione delle comunità di Valcamonica durante la dominazione viscontea (secoli XIV–XV)* (Milan, 1976).

Bono, S., *Corsari nel Mediterraneo: cristiani e musulmani fra guerra, schiavitu e commercio* (Milan, 1993).

Bordone, R., *Città e territorio nell'alto medioevo. La società astigiana dal dominio dei Franchi all'affermazione comunale* (Turin, 1980).

"Lo sviluppo delle relazioni personali dell'aristocrazia rurale del regno italico," in *Structures féodales et féodalisme*, 241–49.

Bornstein, D., *The Bianchi of 1399: Popular Devotion in Late Medieval Italy* (Ithaca, 1993).

"Corporazioni spirituali: proprietà delle confraternite e pietà dei laici," *Ricerche di storia sociale e religiosa*, 48 (1995): 77–90.

(trans.), *Dino Compagni's Chronicle of Florence* (Philadelphia, 1986).

Borromeo, A., "L'arcivescovo Carlo Borromeo, la Corona spagnola e le contro-versie giurisdizionali a Milano," in F. Buzzi and D. Zardin (eds.), *Carlo Borromeo e l'opera della "grande riforma"* (Milan, 1997).

"La Corona spagnola e le nomine agli uffici ecclesiastici nello Stato di Milano da Filippo II a Filippo IV," in P. Pissavino and G. Signorotto (eds.), *Lombardia borromaica, Lombardia spagnola. 1554–1659*, vol. 2 (Rome, 1995), 553–78.

Bortolami, S., "Comuni e beni comunali nelle campagne medioevali: un epi-sodio della Scodosia di Montagnana (Padova) nel XII secolo," *Mélanges de l'Ecole Française de Rome. Moyen Age-Temps Modernes*, 99 (1987): 555–84.

Bossa, M. I. (ed.), *Chiese e conventi degli ordini Mendicanti in Umbria nei secoli XIII e XIV. La serie Protocolli dell'Archivio notarile di Perugia* (Perugia, 1987).

Bossy, J., *Christianity in the West 1400–1700* (Oxford, 1985).

"The Counter Reformation and the People of Catholic Europe," *Past and Present*, 47 (1970): 51–70.

"The Social History of Confession in the Age of the Reformation," *Transactions of the Royal Historical Society*, 5th ser., 5 (1975).

Botero, G., *Della ragion di stato*, ed. Chiara Continisio (Rome, 1997).

Bottoni, R., "Le confraternite milanesi nell'età di Maria Teresa: aspetti e problemi," in AA.VV., *Economia, istituzioni, cultura in Lombardia nell'età di Maria Teresa*, 3 vols (Bologna, 1982), 595–607.

"Libri e lettura nelle confraternite milanesi del secondo Cinquecento," in N. Raponi and A. Turchini (eds.), *Stampa, libri e letture a Milano* (Milan, 1992), 247–77.

"Per la storia delle confraternite milanesi nell'età di san Carlo Borromeo" (Tesi di laurea: Università degli Studi di Milano, 1977–8).

Bowsky, W. M., *A Medieval Italian Commune: Siena Under the Nine, 1287–1355* (Berkeley, 1981).

Brandileone, F., *Saggi sulla storia della celebrazione del matrimonio in Italia* (Milan, 1906).

Brieskorn, N., 'Ignatius in Azpeitia 1535: Eine Rechthistorische Untersuchung," *Archivum Historicum Societatis Iesu*, 49 (1980): 95–112.

Brolis, M. T., "Confraternite bergamasche bassomedievali. Nuove fonti e prospettive di ricerca," *Rivista di storia della Chiesa in Italia*, 49 (1995): 337–54.

Brufani, S., "La fraternita dei disciplinati di S. Stefano," in U. Nicolini, E. Menestò, and F. Santucci (eds.), *Le fraternite medievali di Assisi: Linee storiche e testi statutari* (Perugia, 1989), 45–86.

Burke, P., "Insult and Blasphemy in Early Modern Italy," in P. Burke, *The Historical Anthropology of Early Modern Italy* (Cambridge, 1987).

"Overture: The New History, its Past and its Future," in P. Burke (ed.), *New Perspectives on Historical Writing* (Cambridge, 1991): 1–23.

Buzzi, F. and D. Zardin (eds.), *Carlo Borromeo e l'opera della "grande riforma". Cultura, religione e arti del governo nella Milano del pieno Cinquecento* (Milan, 1997).

Calori, G., *Una iniziativa sociale nella Bologna del '500: L'Opera dei Mendicanti* (Bologna, 1972).

Calvini, N. and A. Cuggé, *La confraria di Santo Spirito, gli Ospedali e i Monti di Pietà nell'area intemelia e sanremasca* (San Remo, 1996).

Cambiaso, D., *L'anno ecclesiastico e le feste dei santi in Genova nel loro svolgimento storico. Atti della Società Ligure di Storia Patria* 48 (Genoa, 1917).

"Casacce e confraternite medievali in Genova e Liguria," *Atti della Società Ligure di Storia Patria*, 71 (1948): 79–111.

Camerano, A., "Assistenza richiesta ed assistenza imposta: il conservatorio di S. Caterina della Rosa di Roma," *Quaderni storici* 82 (April 1993): 226–60.

Caprioli, A., A. Rimoldi, and L. Vaccaro (eds.), *Diocesi di Milano*, 2 vols (Brescia, 1990).

Carpi, D., "The Expulsion of the Jews from the Papal States during the Reign of Pope Pius V and the Inquisition Against the Jews of Bologna, 1566–1569," *Scritti in memoria di Enzo Sereni* (Jerusalem, 1971).

Carroll, M. P. *Veiled Threats: The Logic of Popular Catholicism in Italy* (Baltimore,

284   BIBLIOGRAPHY

    1996).

Le Casacce e la scultura lignea sacra genovese del Seicento e del Settecento (Genoa, 1939).

Casagrande, G., "Devozione e municipalità. La compagnia del S. Anello/S. Giuseppe di Perugia (1487–1542)," in AA.VV., *Le mouvement confraternel au Moyen Age* (Rome, 1987), 155–83.

    "La fraternita dei raccomandati di Maria," in Nicolini *et al.* (eds.), *Le fraternite medievali di Assisi*, 13–44.

    "Lettere d'indulgenza e di concessione di benefici spirituali. Forma vitae dei raccomandati della Vergine," in Nicolini *et al.* (eds.), *Le fraternite medievali di Assisi*, 187–98.

    "Monasteri, nuovi ordini, movimenti religiosi e spazi laicali (secc. xii–xv): uno sguardo di sintesi," in G.Casagrande (ed.), *Una Chiesa attraverso i secoli. Conversazioni sulla storia della Diocesi di Perugia. I. Le origini e l'età medievale* (Perugia, 1995), 81–104.

Religiosità penitenziale e città al tempo dei comuni (Rome, 1995).

    "Ricerche sulle confraternite delle diocesi di Spoleto e Perugia da visitationes cinquecentesche," *Bollettino della Deputazione di Storia Patria per l'Umbria*, 75 (1978): 31–61.

    "Statuto e matricola della fraternita dei raccomandati della Vergine," in Nicolini, *et al.* (eds.), *Le fraternite medievali di Assisi*, 199–232.

    "Women in Confraternities between the Middle Ages and the Modern Age: Research in Umbria," *Confraternitas*, 5/2 (1994): 3–13.

    and M. G. N. Ottaviani, "Donne negli statuti comunali: sondaggi in Umbria," *Annali della Facoltà di Lettere e Filosofia dell'Università di Perugia. 2. Studi Storico-Antropologici*, 17–18 (1993/4–1994/5): 15–36.

Castellini, G., *La congregazione dei nobili presso la chiesa del Gesù in Roma* (Rome, 1954).

Castracane, M. M., "Ricerche sulla natura giuridica delle confraternite laicali nell'età della Controriforma." *Rivista di storia del diritto italiano*, 55 (1982): 43–116.

Cavaciocchi, S. (ed.), *La donna nell'economia secc. XIII–XVIII* (Prato, 1990).

Cavallo, S., *Charity and Power in Early Modern Italy: Benefactors and Their Motives in Turin, 1541–1789* (Cambridge, 1994).

    "Conceptions of Poverty and Poor Relief in Turin in the second half of the Eighteenth Century," in Stuart Woolf (ed.), *Domestic Strategies: Work and Family in France and Italy, 1600–1800* (Cambridge, 1991), 148–99.

    "The Motivations of Benefactors: An Overview of Approaches to the Study of Charity," in J. Barry and Colin Jones (eds.), *Medicine and Charity Before the Welfare State* (London, 1991): 46–62.

    "Patterns of Poverty and Patterns of Relief in Eighteenth Century Italy," *Continuity and Change*, 5 (1990): 65–98.

Cecchi, B., "Descrizione dell'apparato e de gl'intermedj fatti per la storia dell'Esaltazione della Croce rappresentata in Firenze da' giovani della Compagnia di S. Giovanni Evangelista con l'occasione delle nozze delle Altezze Serenissime di Toscana nell'anno 1589," in A. D'Ancona (ed.), *Sacre rappresentazioni dei secoli XVI, XV e XVI*, vol. 3 (Florence, 1872), 121–38.

Cerutti, S., "Giustizia e località a Torino in età moderna: una ricerca in corso," *Quaderni storici*, 89 (1995): 445–86.

Mestieri e privilegi. Nascita delle corporazioni a Torino, secoli XVII–XVIII (Turin, 1992).

Chambers, D., *Patrons and Artists in the Italian Renaissance* (London, 1970).

Chatellier, L., *The Europe of the Devout: The Catholic Reformation and the Formation of a New Society* (Cambridge, 1989).

Chauvin, C., "Ignace et les courtisanes: La Maison Sainte Marthe (1542–1548)," in *Ignacio de Loyola y su tiempo*, ed. Juan Plazaola (Bilbao, 1992).

Chenu, M. D., "'Fraternitas': Evangile et condition socio-culturelle," *Revue d'histoire de la spiritualité*, 49 (1973): 385–400.

Chiacchella, R. (ed.), *Una Chiesa attraverso i secoli. Conversazioni sulla storia della Diocesi di Perugia. II. L'età moderna* (Perugia, 1996).

"La città della Controriforma: vescovi e ordini religiosi dopo il Concilio di Trento," in Chiacchella (ed.), *Una Chiesa attraverso i secoli*, 7–24.

Chiffoleau, J., *La comptabilité de l'au-delà. Les hommes, la mort et la religion dans la région d'Avignon à la fin du Moyen Age (vers 1320–vers 1480)* (Rome, 1980).

"Les confréries, la mort e la religion en Comtat Venaissin à la fin du moyen age," *Mélanges de l'Ecole française de Rome: Moyen Age-Temps Modernes*, 91 (1979): 785–825.

"Entre le religieux et le politique: les confréries du Saint-Esprit en Provence et en Comtat Venaissin à la fin du Moyen Age," in AA.VV., *Le mouvement confraternel*, 9–40.

L. Martines and A. Paravicini-Bagliani (eds.), *Riti e rituali nelle società medievali* (Spoleto, 1994).

Chittolini, G. and G. Miccoli (eds.), *La Chiesa e il potere politico dal Medioevo all'età contemporanea. Storia d'Italia*, 9 (Turin, 1986).

Ciamitti, L., "La dote come rendita. Note sull'assistenza a Bologna nei secoli XVI–XVIII," in AA.VV., *Forme e soggetti dell'intervento assistenziale in una città di antico regime*, vol. 2 (Bologna, 1986), 111–132.

"Fanciulle, monache, madri. Povertà femminile e previdenza in Bologna nei secoli xvi– xviii," in *Arte e Pietà. I patrimoni culturali delle opere pie* (Bologna, 1980), 461–99.

"Quanto costa essere normali. La dote nel conservatorio femminile di S. Maria del Baraccano (1630–1680)," *Quaderni storici* 53 (1983): 469–97.

Cipolla, C., *Fighting the Plague in Seventeenth Century Italy* (Madison, 1981).

Ciuffreda, A., "I benefici di giuspatronato nella diocesi di Oria tra XVI e XVIII secolo," *Quaderni storici*, 67 (1988): 37–72.

Clavero, B., *Antidora. Antropología católica de la economía moderna* (Milan, 1991 and Paris, 1996).

Clawson, M. A., "Early Modern Fraternalism and the Patriarchal Family," *Feminist Studies*, 6 (1980): 368–91.

Cohen, S., *The Evolution of Women's Asylums since 1500: From Refuges for Ex-Prostitutes to Shelters for Battered Women* (New York, 1992).

Cohen, T. V., "Why the Jesuits Joined 1540–1600," *Canadian Historical Association Historical Papers* (1974): 237–55.

Cohn, S., *The Cult of Remembrance and the Black Death: Six Renaissance Cities in Central Italy* (Baltimore, 1992).

Death and Property in Siena, 1205–1800: Strategies for the Afterlife (Baltimore, 1988).

Comino, G., "Sfruttamento e ridistribuzione di risorse collettive nel Monregalese: il caso delle confrarie dello Spirito Santo nel Monregalese dei secoli XIII–XVIII," *Quaderni storici* 81 (1992): 687–702.

"Per una storia delle confrerie dello Spirito Santo in diocesi di Mondovì," *Bollettino della Società per gli Studi Storici, Archeologici e Artistici della provincia di Cuneo*, 100 (1989): 45–69.

Constitutioni et capitoli della Venerabile Confraternita dell'Annunziata di Perugia (Perugia, 1587).

Contarini, G., *The Commonwealth and Government of Venice*, trans. L. Lewkenor, *The English Experience*, no. 101 (1599; repr. Amsterdam, 1969).

Cope, M., *The Venetian Chapel of the Sacrament in the Sixteenth Century* (New York, 1979).

Cosmacini, G., *Storia della medicina e della sanità in Italia. Dalla peste europea alla guerra mondiale. 1348–1918* (Bari, 1987).

Costa, P., *Iurisdictio* (Milan, 1969).

Costituzioni e capitoli della confraternita della Madonna de' Miracoli e Gonfalone di Castel Rigone (Perugia, 1634).

Cotterau, A., "Justice et injustice ordinaire sur les lieux de travail d'après les audiences prud'homales (1806–1866)," *Mouvement social* 141 (1987): 25–59.

Coulet, N., "Les confréries du Saint-Esprit en Provence: pour une enquete," *Mélanges R. Mandrou* (Paris, 1985), 205–17.

Crum, R. J. and D. G. Wilkins, "In the Defense of Florentine Republicanism: Saint Anne and Florentine Art, 1343–1575," in K. Ashley and P. Sheingorn (eds.), *Interpreting Cultural Symbols: Saint Anne in Late Medieval Society* (Athens, GA., 1990), 131–68.

Curatolo, P., "Notabili a Milano tra Cinque e Seicento: le confraternite nella parrocchia di S. Maria Segreta," *Archivio storico lombardo*, 117 (1991): 59–103.

D'Accone, F. A., "Alcune note sulle compagnie fiorentine dei laudesi durante il quattrocento," *Rivista italiana di musicologia*, 10 (1975): 86–114.

"Le compagnie dei laudesi in Firenze durante l'Ars nova," *L'Ars nova italiana del Trecento*, 3 (Certaldo, 1970): 253–80.

D'Addario, A., *Aspetti della Controriforma a Firenze* (Rome, 1972).

"Noti di storia della religiosità e della carità dei Fiorentini nel secolo XVI," *Archivio storico italiano*, 126 (1968): 61–147.

Dalarun, Jacques, «Lapsus linguae». La légende de Claire de Rimini (Spoleto, 1994).

D'Amelia, M., "Economia familiare e sussidi dotali. La politica della Confraternita dell'Annuziata a Roma (secoli XVII–XVIII)," in Simonetta Cavaciocchi (ed.), *La Donna nell'Economia. Secc. xiii–xviii* (Florence, 1990), 195–215.

Dardanello, P., "Spazio religioso e paesaggio devozionale: i casi di Villanova e Torre," in Garrone *et al.* (eds.), *Valli monregalesi*, 107–47.

Davidsohn, R., *Storia di Firenze*, vols. 1–4 (Florence, 1956–73).

Davis, C. T., "An Early Florentine Political Theorist: Fra Remigio de' Girolami," in C. Davis (ed.), *Dante's Italy and Other Essays* (Philadelphia, 1984): 198–223.

Davis, R. C., *Shipbuilders of the Venetian Arsenal: Workers and Workplace in the Preindustrial City* (Baltimore, 1991).

De Boer, W., "Sinews of Discipline: The Uses of Confession in Counter-Reformation Milan," (Ph.D. diss.: Erasmus Universiteit Rotterdam, 1995).

Dei Rossi, A., *Meor 'Enayim*, ed. D. Cassel (1866; repr. Jerusalem, 1970).

De La Roncière, C., "Les confréries à Florence et dans son contado aux xive–xve siècles," in *Le mouvement confraternel*, 297–342.

"Les confréries en Toscane aux xiv et xv siècles d'après les travaux récents," *Ricerche per la Storia Religiosa di Roma*, 5 (1984): 50–64.

"La place des confréries dans l'encadrement religieux du contado florentin: l'example de la Val d'Elsa," *Mélanges de l'Ecole Française de Rome. Moyen-Age – Temps Modernes*, 85 (1973): 31–77, 633–71.

Delcorno, C., *Giordano da Pisa e l'antica predicazione volgare* (Florence, 1974).

La predicazione nell'eta comunale. Scuola aperta, lettere italiane, 57 (Florence, 1974).

D'Elia, R., *Vita Popolare nella Napoli Spagnuola* (Naples, 1971).

Delille, G., *Famiglia e comunità nel Regno di Napoli* (Turin, 1989).

Delplace, L., *Histoire des Congrégations de la Sainte Vierge*. (Bruges, 1884).

De Luca, G., *Introduzione alla storia della pietà* (Rome, 1962).

Delumeau, J., *Vie économique et sociale de Rome dans la seconde moitié du XVIe siècle*, 2 vols (Paris, 1957).

De Molen, R. (ed.), *Religious Orders of the Catholic Reformation* (New York, 1994).

Demoustier, Adrien, SJ, "The first companions and the poor," *Studies in the Spirituality of Jesuits*, 21 (1989): 4–20.

de' Rossi, F., *Ritratto di Roma Moderna* (Rome, 1645).

De Sandre Gasparini, G., *Contadini, chiesa, confraternita in un paese veneto di bonifica. Villa del Bosco nel Quattrocento* (Padova, 1979).

"Il movimento delle confraternite nell'area veneta," in *Le mouvement confraternel*, 361–94.

Statuti di confraternite religiose di Padova nel Medio Evo (Padova, 1974).

Diena, A., *Responsa*, 2 vols., ed. J. Boksenboim (Tel-Aviv, 1977–79).

Di Filippo Bareggi, C., "Libri e letture nella Milano di san Carlo Borromeo," in N.Raponi and A.Turchini (eds.), *Stampa, libri e letture a Milano* (Milan, 1992), 39–96.

Di Leone Leoni, A., "Nouve notizie sugli Abravanel," *Zakhor: Rivista di Storia degli Ebrei d'Italia*, 1 (1997).

Dixon, G., "Lenten Devotions: Some Memoriae of Baroque Rome," *The*

Musical Times 124 (1983): 157–61.

Documenti inediti o poco noti per la storia della Misericordia di Firenze, 1240–1525 (Florence, 1940).

Donnelly, J. and M. Maher (eds.), *Confraternities and Catholic Reform in Italy, France and Spain* (Kirksville, MO, 1999).

Duboin, C. and R. Muzio, *Raccolta per ordine di materia delle leggi, cioè Editti, Patenti, Manifesti ecc. emanati negli Stati di Terraferma sino all'8 dicembre 1798 dai Sovrani della Real Casa di Savoia* (Turin, 1818–79).

Dudon, P., *St. Ignatius of Loyola*, trans. W. J. Young (Milwaukee, 1949).

Dunn, M. R., "Nuns as Patrons: The Decoration of S. Marta al Collegio Romano," *Art Bulletin*, 70.3 (September 1988): 451–476.

Duparc, P., "Confréries du saint-Esprit et communautés d'habitants au Moyen Age," *Revue Historique de Droit Français et Etranger*, 4th ser., 36 (1958): 348–67.

Eckstein, N., *The District of the Green Dragon: Neighbourhood Life and Social Change in Renaissance Florence* (Florence, 1995).

Edgerton, S., *Pictures and Punishment: Art and Criminal Prosecution During the Florentine Renaissance* (Ithaca, 1985).

Egidi, P., *Necrologi e libri affini della Provincia Romana*, vol. 1–2 (Rome, 1908–14).

Eisenbichler, K., "Angelo Poliziano e le confraternite di giovani a Firenze," in Luisa Secchi Tarugi (ed.), *Poliziano ne suo tempo*. Atti del VI Convegno Internazionale (Chianciano-Montepulciano 18–21 luglio 1994), (Franco Cesati Editore, 1997), 297–308.

The Boys of the Archangel Raphael: A Youth Confraternity in Florence, 1411–1785 (Toronto, 1998).

"Confraternities and Carnival: The Context of Lorenzo de' Medici's Rappresentazione di SS. Giovanni e Paolo," in C. Davidson and J. H. Stroupe (eds.), *Medieval Drama on the Continent of Europe* (Kalamazoo, 1993): 128–39; published contemporaneously in *Comparative Drama*, 27/1 (1993): 128–39.

"Italian Scholarship on Pre-Modern Confraternities in Italy," *Renaissance Quarterly*, 50 (1997): 567–80.

"Lorenzo de' Medici and the Confraternity of the Blacks in Florence," *Fides et Historia*, 26/1 (1994): 85–98.

"Lorenzo de' Medici e la Congregazione dei Neri nella Compagnia della Croce al Tempio," *Archivio Storico Italiano*, 150/2 (1992): 343–70.

"Nativity and Magi Plays in Renaissance Florence," *Comparative Drama*, 29 (1995–6): 319–33.

"Plays at the Archangel Raphael's," *Fifteenth Century Studies*, 13 (1988): 519–34

"A Playwright in the Pulpit: 'the Spiritual Discourses' of Giovan Maria Cecchi (1558)," in *Italian Culture*, vol. 6 (1987), 77–88.

"Ricerche nord-americane sulle confraternite italiane," in Bertoldi Lenoci (ed.), *Confraternite, Chiese e Società*, (Fasano, 1994), 289–301.

"Il ruolo delle confraternite nell'educazione dei fanciulle: il caso di Firenze," in L. Rotondi Secchi Tarugi (ed.), *L'educazione e la formazione intelletuale nell'età dell' umanesimo* (Milan, 1992): 109–19.

"Strutture amministrative di una confraternita di giovani a Florence prima e dopo Trento," in L. Borgia *et al.* (eds.), *Studi in onore di Arnaldo d'Addario,* vol. 3 (Lecce, 1992), 951–64.

(ed.) *Crossing the Boundaries: Christian Piety and the Arts in Italian Medieval and Renaissance Confraternities* (Kalamazoo, 1991).

Elam, C., "Lorenzo de' Medici and the Urban Development of Renaissance Florence," *Art History,* 1 (1978): 43–66.

"Il palazzo nel contesto della città: Strategie urbanistiche dei Medici nel Gonfalone del Leon D'Oro, 1415–1530," in G. Cherubini and G. Fanelli (eds.), *Il palazzo Medici Riccardi di Florence* (Florence,1990): 44–57.

Ellero, G. (ed.), *L'archivio IRE: inventario dei fondi antichi degli ospedali e luoghi pii di Venezia* (Venice, 1987).

Erba, A., *La Chiesa sabauda tra Cinque e Seicento. Ortodossia tridentina, gallicanesimo savoiardo e assolutismo ducale (1580–1630)* (Rome, 1979).

"Pauperismo e assistenza in Piemonte nel secolo xvii," in Politi *et al.* (eds.), *Timore e Carità,* 211–24.

Errichetti, M., "L'antico Collegio Massimo dei Gesuiti a Napoli (1552–1806)," *Campania Sacra,* 7 (1976): 170–264.

"La Nunziatella," *Societas,* 28 (1979): 35–41.

Esposito, A., "Apparati e suggestioni nelle 'feste et devotioni' delle confraternite romane," *Archivio della Società Romana di Storia Patria,* 106 (1983): 311–22.

"Le 'confraternite' del Gonfalone (secoli xiv–xv)," *Ricerche per la storia religiosa di Roma,* 5 (1984): 91–136.

"Le confraternite del matrimonio. Carità, devozione e bisogni sociali a Roma nel tardo Quattrocento (con l'edizione degli Statuti vecchi della Compagnia della SS.Annunziata)," in L. Fortini (ed.), *Un'idea di Roma. Società, arte e cultura tra Umanesimo e Rinascimento* (Rome, 1993), 7–51.

"Le confraternite e gli ospedali di S. Maria in Portico, S. Maria delle Grazie e S. Maria della Consolazione a Roma (secc. xv–xvi)," *Ricerche di storia sociale e religiosa,* nos. 17–18 (1980): 145–72.

"*Ad dotandum puellas virgines, pauperes et honestas*: Social Needs and Confraternal Charities in Rome in the Fifteenth and Sixteenth Centuries," *Renaissance and Reformation,* 18 (1994): 5–18.

"Gli ospedali romani tra iniziative laicali e politica pontificia (secc. xiii–xv)," in A. J. Grieco and L. Sandri (eds.), *Ospedali e città. L'Italia del Centro-Nord, XIII–XVI secolo* (Florence, 1997), 233–51.

"S. Francesca e le comunità religiose femminili a Roma nel sec. xv," in S. Boesch Gajano and L. Sebastiani (eds.), *Culto dei santi, istituzioni e classi sociali in età preindustriale* (L'Aquila, 1984), 539–62.

Un'altra Roma. Minoranze nazionali e comunità ebraiche tra Medioevo e Rinascimento (Rome, 1995).

Evennett, H. O., *The Spirit of the Counter-Reformation,* ed. J. Bossy (Cambridge, 1968).

Falvey, K., "The Italian Saint Play: The Example of Perugia," in C. Davidson (ed.), *The Saint Play in Medieval Europe* (Kalamazoo, 1986), 181–204.

Fanti, M., *La Chiesa e la Compagnia dei Poveri in Bologna* (Bologna, 1977).

"La confraternita di Santa Maria della Morte e la conforteria dei condannati in Bologna nei secoli xiv e xv," *Quaderni di centro di ricerca di studio sul movimento dei disciplinati*, 20 (1978): 3–101.

"Gli inizi del movimento dei disciplinati a Bologna e la confraternita di Santa Maria della Vita," *Bollettino della deputazione di storia patria per l'Umbria*, 66/1 (1969): 181–232.

"Istituzioni di carità e assistenza a Bologna alla fine del Medioevo," *Forme e soggetti* (Bologna, 1986): 31–64.

(ed.), *Gli archivi delle Istituzioni di carità e assistenza attive in Bologna nel Medioevo e nell'Età moderna* (Bologna, 1985).

Fanucci, C., *Trattato di tutte le opere pie dell'alma città di Roma* . . . (Rome, 1601).

Farrell, A., "Colleges for Extern Students Opened in the Lifetime of St. Ignatius," *Archivum Historicum Societatis Iesu*, 6 (1937): 287–91.

Fatica, M., "La reclusione dei poveri a Roma durante il Pontificato di Innocenzo XII (1692–1700)," *Ricerche per la Storia Religiosa di Roma*, 3 (1979): 133–79.

Felloni, G., "Italy," in G. Parker and C. Wilson (eds.), *Introduction to the Sources of European Economic History 1500–1800* (London, 1977).

Fenlon, I., "Music and Spirituality in Florence and Milan," in Bertelli (ed.), *Florence and Milan*, 297–302.

Ferrante, L., M. Paluzzi, and G. Pomata (eds.), *Ragnatelle di rapporti. Patronage e reti di relazione nella storia delle donne* (Turin, 1988).

Filannino, A. and L. Mattioli (eds.), *Biografie antiche della beata Angelina da Montegiove* (Spoleto, 1996).

Finkelstein, L., *Jewish Self Government in the Middle Ages* (New York, 1924).

Fiorani, L., "L'esperienza religiosa nelle confraternite romane tra Cinque e Seicento," *Ricerche per la storia religiosa di Roma*, 5 (1984): 155–96.

"Le Visite Apostoliche del Cinque-Seicento e la società religiosa romana," *Ricerche per la Storia Religiosa di Roma* 4 (1980): 9–79.

Fiori, D., "I necrologi del Salvatore: una fonte per la storia sociale della Roma basso-medievale" (Tesi di laurea: Università di Roma la Sapienza, 1991–2).

Fiorucci, F., "La fraternita di S. Maria del Mercato di Gubbio. Testi statutari e profilo storico (secoli xiii–xv)" (Tesi di laurea: Università di Perugia, 1996–7).

Firpo, M., *Riforme protestanti ed eresie nell'Italia del Cinquecento* (Bari, 1993).

Forme e soggetti dell'intervento assistenziale in una città di antico regime (Bologna, 1986).

Fortini Brown, P., "Honor and necessity: The Dynamics of Patronage in the Confraternities of Renaissance Venice," *Studi Veneziani*, 14 (1987): 179–212.

Venetian Narrative Painting in the Age of Carpaccio (New Haven, 1987).

Franceschi, F., *Oltre il "Tumulto": I lavoratori fiorentini dell'arte della Lana fra tre e quattrocento* (Florence, 1993).

Franchini Guelfi, F., *Le Casacce. Arte e tradizione* (Genoa, 1973).

Frati, L (ed.), *Statuti di Bologna dall'anno 1245 all'anno 1267*, 3 vols. (Bologna, 1877).

Fresia, R., "Comunità e signori nel Cinquecento. Un secolo di lotte degli uomini di Guarene," *Bollettino della Società per gli Studi Storici, Archeologici e Artistici della provincia di Cuneo*, 115 (1996): 81–173.

Frizzi, A., *Memorie per la storia di Ferrara* (Ferrara, 1791).

Froeschlé-Chopard, M.-H., *Espace et sacré en Provence (XVIe–XXe siècle). Cultes, Images, Confréries* (Paris, 1994).

Frugoni, A., "La devozione dei Bianchi del 1399," in A. Frugoni (ed.), *Incontri nel Medio Evo* (Bologna, 1979), 203–14.

Fubini Leuzzi, M., "'Dell'allogare le fanciulle degli Innocenti': un problema culturale ed economico 1577–1652," in Prodi (ed.), *Disciplina dell'anima*, 863–99.

Gabrijelcic, A., "Vescovi e cattedrale," in M. Pierotti (ed.), *Una città e la sua cattedrale* (Perugia, 1992), 521–38.

Ganss, G., "Jesuit Colleges for Externs and the Controversies about Their Poverty," *Woodstock Letters*, 91 (1962): 139–40.

—— (trans.), *Ignatius Loyola: The Spiritual Exercises and Selected Works* (New York, 1991).

—— and J. Padberg (trans.), *The Constitutions of the Society of Jesus and Their Complementary Norms* (St. Louis, 1996).

Garrone, G. G., S. Lombardini, and A. Torre (eds.), *Valli monregalesi. Società, cultura, devozioni* (Vicoforte, 1985).

Gatti Perer, M. L., "Per la definizione dell'iconografia della Vergine del Rosario. L'istituzione della compagnia del S. Rosario eretta da san Carlo e l'edizione figurata del 1583 delle Rosariae preces di Bartolomeo Scalvo," in F. Buzzi and D. Zardin (eds.), *Carlo Borromeo e l'opera della "grande riforma". Cultura, religione e arti del governo nella Milano del pieno Cinquecento* (Milan, 1997).

Gaudenzi, A (ed.), *Statuti delle societa del popolo di Bologna*, 2 vols. (Rome, 1889–96).

Gavitt, P., "Charity and State Building in Cinquecento Florence: Vincenzio Borghini as Administrator of the Ospedale degli Innocenti," *Journal of Modern History*, 69 (1997): 230–70.

—— *Charity and Children in Renaissance Florence: The Ospedale degli Innocenti, 1410–1536* (Ann Arbor, 1990).

Gazzini, M., "Solidarietà vicinale e parentale a Milano: le scole di S.Giovanni sul Muro a Porta Vercellina," in AA.VV., *L'età dei Visconti. Il dominio di Milano fra xiii e xv secolo* (Milan, 1993), 303–30.

Gemini, F., "Interventi di politica sociale nel campo dell'assistenza femminile: tre conservatori romani tra sei e settecento," in *La demografia storica delle città italiane* (Bologna, 1982), 615–28.

Gensini, S., *Roma capitale (1447–1527)* (Pisa, 1994).

Gentilcore, D., "Adapt Yourselves to the People's Capabilities: Missionary Strategies, Methods and Impact in the Kingdom of Naples, 1600–1800,"

Journal of Ecclesiastical History, 45 (1994): 269–96.

Geremek, B., *Poverty: a History*, trans. A. Kolakowska (Oxford, 1994).

Ghirardacci, G., *Historia di Bologna* (Bologna, 1657).

Giacomelli, A., "Conservazione e innovazione nell'assistenza bolognese del Settecento," in *Forme e soggetti*, 163–266.

Ginella, A., "Le confraternite della Valbisagno tra rivoluzione e impero (1797–1811)," *Atti della Società Ligure di Storia Patria*, NS 23/2 (1983): 193–320.

Glixon, J., "*Far una bella procession*: Music and Public Ceremony at the Venetian *scuole grandi*," in R. Charteris (ed.), *Altro Polo: Essays on Italian Music in the Cinquecento* (Sydney, 1990), 190–220.

"Music at the Scuole in the age of Andrea Gabrieli," in F.Degrada (ed.), *Andrea Gabrieli e il suo tempo* (Venice, 1985): 59–74.

Goldthwaite, R. A., *Wealth and the Demand for Art in Italy, 1300–1600* (Baltimore, 1993).

Gramigna, S. and A. Perissa, *Scuole di arti mestieri e devozione a Venezia* (Venice, 1981).

Greci, R., "Donne e corporazioni: la fluidità di un rapporto," in A.Groppi (ed.), *Il lavoro delle donne* (Rome, 1996), 71–91.

Greenblatt, S., *Renaissance Self-Fashioning from More to Shakespeare* (Chicago, 1980).

Grendi, E., "Cartografia e disegno locale. La coscienza sociale dello spazio," in *Lettere orbe. Anonimato e poteri nel seicento genovese* (Palermo, 1989).

Il Cervo e la repubblica. Il modello ligure di antico regime (Turin, 1993).

"Le Compagnie del SS. Sacramento a Genova," *Annali della Facoltà di Giuris-prudenza dell'Università degli studi di Genova*, 4 (1965): 454–80.

"Confraternite e mestieri nella Genova settecentesca," *Miscellanea di Storia Ligure*, 4 (Genoa, 1966): 237–65.

"Il disegno e la coscienza sociale dello spazio: dalle carte archivistiche genovesi," *Studi in memoria di Teofilo Ossian De Negri*, vol. 3 (Genoa, 1986), 14–33.

"Un esempio di arcaismo politico: le conventicole nobiliari e la riforma del 1528," *Rivista storica italiana*, 78 (1966): 948–68.

"Morfologia e dinamismo della vita associativa urbana: le confraternite a Genova fra i secoli XVI e XVII," *Atti della Società Ligure di Storia Patria*, NS 5 (1965): 239–311.

"Pauperismo e Albergo dei Poveri nella Genova del Seicento," *Rivista Storica Italiana*, 87 (1975): 621–75.

La repubblica aristocratica dei genovesi. Politica, carità e commercio fra Cinque e Seicento (Bologna, 1987).

"Il sistema politico di una comunità ligure: Cervo fra cinquecento e seicento," *Quaderni storici*, 46 (1982): 92–129.

"Le società dei giovani a Genova fra il 1460 e la riforma del 1528," *Quaderni storici* 27 (1992): 509–28.

Grendler, P. F., *Books and Schools in the Italian Renaissance* (Aldershot, 1995).

Schooling in Renaissance Italy: Literacy and Learning, 1300–1600 (Baltimore, 1989).

Grinberg, M., "Don, prélèvements, échanges. A propos de quelques redevances seigneuriales," *Annales ESC*, 43 (1988): 1413–32.

"Le nouage rituel/droit. Les redevances seigneuriales xive–xviiie siècles," in Chiffoleau *et al.* (eds.), *Riti e rituali*, 247–62.

Groppi, A., *I conservatori della virtù: donne recluse nella Roma dei Papi* (Rome, 1994).

"Il lavoro delle donne: un questionario da arricchire," in S. Cavaciocchi (ed.), *La donna nell'economia secc. XIII–XVIII* (Prato, 1990), 143–54.

Grossi, P., *Il dominio e le cose* (Milano, 1992).

L'ordine giuridico medievale (Bari, 1995).

Grosso, O., *Le Casacce genovesi del '600 e '700* (Genoa, 1968).

Guglielmotti, P., *I signori di Morozzo nei secoli X–XIV: un percorso politico del Piemonte medievale* (Turin, 1990).

"Territori senza città. Riorganizzazioni duecentesche del paesaggio politico nel Piemonte medievale," *Quaderni storici*, 90 (1995): 765–98.

Guidetti, A., *Le missioni popolari: i grandi gesuiti italiani: disegno storico-biografico delle missioni popolari dei gesuiti d'Italia dalle origini al Concilio Vaticano II* (Milan, 1988).

Guidicini, G., *Cose notabili della storia di Bologna*, 5 vols (Bologna, 1868–73).

Hall, E., *The Arnolfini Betrothal: Medieval Marriage and the Enigma of Van Eyck's Double Portrait* (Berkeley, 1994).

Hammond, F., *Music and Spectacle in Baroque Rome: Barberini Patronage under Urban VIII* (New Haven, 1994).

Haskins, S., *Mary Magdalen. Myth and Metaphor* (London, 1993).

Hatfield, R., "The Compagnia de' Magi," *Journal of the Warburg and Courtauld Institutes*, 33 (1970): 107–61.

Headley, J. M., "Borromean Reform in the Empire? La Strada Rigorosa of Giovanni Francesco Bonomi," in J. M. Headley and J. B. Tomaro (eds.), *San Carlo Borromeo: Catholic Reform and Ecclesiastical Politics in the Second Half of the Sixteenth Century* (Washington, 1988): 228–49.

Henderson, J., "Charity in Late Medieval Florence: The Role of Religious Confraternities," in Bertelli *et al.* (eds.), *Florence and Milan*, 67–84.

"Le confraternite religiose nella Firenze del tardo Medioevo: patroni spirituali e anche politici?" *Ricerche storiche*, 15 (1985): 77–94.

"Confraternities and the Church in Late-Medieval Florence," in W. Sheils and D. Wood (eds.), *Voluntary Religion* (Oxford, 1986), 69–83.

Piety and Charity in Late Medieval Florence (Oxford, 1994).

(ed.) "Charity and the Poor in Renaissance Europe," *Continuity and Change*, 3/(1988).

Herlihy, D., *Pisa in the Early Renaissance: A Study of Urban Growth* (New Haven, 1958).

"Women and the Sources of Medieval History: The Towns of Northern Italy," in J. T. Rosenthal (ed.), *Medieval Women and the Sources of Medieval History* (Athens GA, 1990), 133–54.

Hespanha, A. M., "Les magistratures populaires d'Ancien Régime," *Diritto e potere nella storia europea. Atti in onore di B. Paradisi (IV Congresso Internazionale della Società Italiana di Storia del Diritto)* (Florence, 1982), 807–22.

Visperas del Leviatan. Instituciones y Poder politico (Portugal, siglo XVII) (Madrid, 1989).

Hill, J. W., "Oratory Music in Florence," "I: Recitar Cantando, 1583– 1655" and "II: At San Firenze in the Seventeenth and Eighteenth Centuries," *Acta Musicologica*, 51 (1979): 108–36 and 246–67.

"III: The Confraternities from 1659 to 1785," *Acta Musicologica*, 58 (1986): 129–79.

Hills, P., "Piety and Patronage in Cinquecento Venice: Tintoretto and the Scuole del Sacramento," *Art History*, 6/1 (March 1983): 30–43.

Hoffman, P., *Church and Community in the Diocese of Lyon, 1500–1789* (New Haven, 1984).

Hoffmann, K., *Ursprung und Anfangstätigkeit des Ersten Päpstlichen Missionsinstituts: ein Beitrag zur Geschichte der Katholischen Juden und Mohammedanermission im sechzehnten Jahrhundert* (Munster, 1923).

Horowitz, E., "Coffee, Coffeehouses, and the Nocturnal Rituals of Early Modern Jewry," *AJS [Association for Jewish Studies] Review*, 14 (1989).

"The Dowering of Brides in the Ghetto of Venice: Between Tradition and Change, Ideals and Reality," *Tarbiz*, 56 (1987).

"Jewish Confraternal Piety in the Veneto in the Sixteenth and Seventeenth Centuries," in G. Cozzi (ed.), *Gli Ebrei e Venezia* (Milan, 1987).

"A Jewish Youth Confraternity in Seventeenth-Century Italy," *Italia*, 5 (1985): 36–96.

"The Jews of Europe and the Moment of Death in Medieval and Modern Times," *Judaism*, 44 (1995).

"Speaking of the Dead: The Emergence of the Eulogy among Italian Jewry of the Sixteenth Century," in D. B. Ruderman (ed.), *Preachers of the Italian Ghetto* (Berkeley, 1992).

"*Yeshiva* and *Hevra*: Confraternal Association and Educational Control in Sixteenth-Century Italy," in D. Carpi *et al.* (eds.), *Shlomo Simonsohn Jubilee Volume: Studies on the History of the Jews in the Middle Ages and Renaissance* (Tel-Aviv, 1993).

"The Worlds of Jewish Youth in Europe, 1300–1800," in J.-C. Schmitt and G. Levi (eds.), *A History of Young People* (Cambridge, MA, 1997).

Hughes, D. O. "Invisible Madonnas? The Italian Historiographical Tradition and the Women of Medieval Italy," in S. Mosher Stuard (ed.), *Women in Medieval History and Historiography* (Philadelphia, 1987), 25–57.

"Representing the Family: Portraits and Purposes in Early Modern Italy," *Journal of Interdisciplinary History*, 17/1 (Summer 1986): 7–38.

Humfrey, P., *The Altarpiece in Renaissance Venice* (New Haven, 1993).

"Competitive Devotions: The Venetian Scuole Piccole as Donors of Altarpieces in the Years Around 1500," *The Art Bulletin*, 70 (1988): 401–23.

Humfrey, P. and R. Mackenney, "The Venetian Trade Guilds as Patrons of Art in the Renaissance," *The Burlington Magazine*, 128 (1986): 317–30.

Hurtubise, P. "La présence des étrangers à la cour de Rome dans la première moitié, du XVIe siècle," *Forestieri e stranieri nelle città bassomedievali. Atti del Convegno internazionale, Bagno a Ripoli 4–8 giugno 1984* (Florence, 1988), 57–80.

Ignatius of Loyola, *Spiritual Exercises*, ed. Louis J. Puhl (Chicago, 1951).

Illibato, A., *Il «Liber Visitationis» di Francesco Carafa nella diocesi di Napoli* (1542–43) (Rome, 1983).

Jones, P., "Communes and Despots: The City State in Late-Medieval Italy," *Transactions of the Royal Historical Society*, 5th ser., 15 (1965): 71–96.

"Economia e società nell'Italia medievale: la leggenda della borghesia," *Storia d'Italia. Annali 1: Dal feudalesimo al capitalismo* (Turin, 1978), 185–372.

Jütte, R., *Poverty and Deviance in Early Modern Europe* (Cambridge: 1994).

Kent, D., "The Buonomini di San Martino: Charity for 'the Glory of God, the Honour of the City, and the Commemoration of Myself'," in F. Ames-Lewis (ed.), *Cosimo "il Vecchio" de' Medici, 1389–1464* (Oxford, 1992), 49–67.

The Rise of the Medici: Faction in Florence, 1426–1434 (Oxford, 1978).

Kent, D. and F. W. Kent, "Two Vignettes of Florentine Society in the Fifteenth-Century," *Rinascimento*, 23 (1983): 237–60.

Kertzer, D. I. and R. P. Saller (eds.), *The Family in Italy from Antiquity to the Present* (New Haven, 1991).

Klapisch-Zuber, C., *La maison et le nom: Stratégies et rituels dans l'Italie de la Renaissance. Civilisations et Sociétés*, 81 (Paris, 1990).

Women, Family, and Ritual in Renaissance Italy (Chicago, 1985).

and D. Herlihy, *Tuscans and their Families: A Study of the Florentine Catasto of 1427* (New Haven, 1985); translation of *Les Toscans et leurs familles* (Paris, 1978).

Knapton, M., "Istituzioni ecclesiastiche, culto, religiosità nella Valpolicella di età pretridentina e tridentina," in Varanini (ed.), *La Valpolicella*, 319–453.

Kosofsky Sedgwick, E., *Between Men: English Literature and Male Homosocial Desire* (New York, 1985).

Kuehn, T., *Emancipation in Late Medieval Florence* (New Brunswick, NJ, 1992).

Law, Family, and Women: Toward a Legal Anthropology of Renaissance Italy (Chicago, 1991).

Kupfer, E., "R. Abraham b. Menahem Rovigo and his Removal from the Rabbinate," *Sinai*, 61 (1967).

Lansing, C., *The Florentine Magnates: Lineage and Faction in a Medieval Commune* (Princeton, 1991).

La Sorsa, S., *La Compagnia d'Or San Michele ovvero una pagina della beneficenza in Toscana* (Trani, 1902).

Latini, pseudo-Brunetto, anonymous chronicle, in F. Schevill (trans.), *Medieval and Renaissance Florence*, vol. 1, *Medieval Florence* (New York, 1963): 106–7

Laude fiorentine: Il laudario della compagnia di San Gilio, ed. Concetto Del Popolo (Florence, 1990).

Lazar, L., "*E faucibus daemonis*: Daughters of Prostitutes, the First Jesuits, and the Compagnia delle Vergini Miserabili di S. Caterina," in B. Wisch and D. Ahl, (eds.), *Ritual, Spectacle, Image: Confraternities and the Visual Arts in Renaissance Italy* (Cambridge 2000).

Lazzarini, A., "Il codice Vitt. Em. 528 e il teatro musicale del Trecento," *Archivio storico italiano*, 113 (1955): 481–521.

Lebole, D., *Storia della Chiesa Biellese. Le confraternite. La pieve di Cossato. La pieve di Puliaco-Giflenga*, 6 vols. (Biella, 1972–81).

Le Bras, G., "Les confréries chrétiennes," in G. Le Bras, *Etudes de sociologie religieuse*, vol. 2 (Paris, 1956): 423–62.

Levati, L., *I dogi di Genova dal 1699 al 1797 e vita genovese negli stessi anni. Feste e costumi genovesi nel secolo XVIII* vol. 4 (Genoa, 1912–17).

Levi, G., *Inheriting Power* (Chicago, 1989).

Leopold II, Holy Roman Emperor, *Relazioni sul governo della Toscana*, ed. Arnaldo Salvestrini (Florence, 1969).

Lesnick, D. R., *Preaching in Medieval Florence: The Social World of Franciscan and Dominican Spirituality* (Athens, GA., 1989).

Lettera d'un Cavaliere Amico Fiorentino Al Reverendissimo Padre Lorenzo Ricci Generale de' Gesuiti Esortandolo ad una Riforma Universale del suo Ordine (Lugano, 1761).

La Liguria delle Casacce. Devozione, arte, storia delle confraternite liguri (Genoa, 1982).

Little, L. K., *Libertà, carità, fraternità. Confraternite laiche a Bergamo nell'età del comune* (Bergamo, 1988).

Religious Poverty and the Profit Economy in Medieval Europe (Ithaca, 1978).

Little, L. K. and B. H. Rosenwein, "Social Meaning in the Monastic and Medicant Spiritualities," *Past and Present*, 63 (1974): 4–32.

Liturgia, pietà e ministeri al Santo (Vicenza, 1978).

Lloyd, G. E. R., *Demystifying Mentalities* (Cambridge, 1990).

Locatelli, A., "La processione del Corpus Domini e la scena urbana a Genova nei secoli XVI e XVII," (Tesi di laurea: Università Cattolica di Milano, 1986–7).

Lombardi, D., "Poveri a Firenze. Programmi e realizzazioni della politica assistenziale dei Medici tra Cinque e Seicento," in Politi *et al.* (eds.), *Timore e Carità*, 165–84.

Lombardini, S., "Family, Kin and the Quest for Community," *History of the Family*, 1 (1996): 227–57.

"Appunti per un'ecologia politica dell'area monregalese nell'età moderna," in Garrone *et al.* (eds.), *Valli monregalesi*, 189–212.

Lombardo, M. L. and M. Morelli, "Donne e testamenti a Roma nel Quattrocento," *Archivi e cultura*, 25–6 (1992–3): 23–130.

Lopez, P., *Clero, eresia e magia nella Napoli del viceregno* (Naples, 1984).

"Le confraternite laicali in Italia e la Riforma Cattolica," *Rivista di studi salernitani*, 2 (1969): 153–238.

"Una famosa congregatione laica napoletana nel '600 e l'opera missionaria di Padre Corcione," *Rivista di Studi Salernitani*, 6 (1970): 1–43.

Riforma cattolica evita religiosa e culturale a Napoli (Naples, 1964).

Lori Sanfilippo, I., "Morire a Roma," in Maria Chiab *et al.* (eds.), *Alle origini della nuova Roma, Martino V (1417–1431)*. Atti del Convegno, Roma 2–5 marzo 1992 (Rome, 1992), 603–23.

Lurati, O., "Pene ai bestemmiatori, indulgenze, reliquie e 'immagini profane' nella diocesi milanese (e nelle Tre Valli) ai tempi di san Carlo," *Folklore suisse*, 60/4 (1970): 41–50.

"Superstizioni lombarde (e leventinesi) del tempo di san Carlo Borromeo," *Vox romanica*, 27 (1968): 229–49.

Luther, M., *Luther's Works*, ed. E. Theodore Bachmann (Philadelphia, 1960).

Maas, C., *The German Community in Renaissance Rome, 1378– 1523* (Freiburg, 1981).

Mackenney, R., "Continuity and Change in the *Scuole Piccole* of Venice, *c.*1250–*c.*1600," *Renaissance Studies*, 8 (1994): 388–403.

"The Guilds of Venice: State and Society in the Longue Duree," *Studi Veneziani*, 34 (1997): 15–43.

"Public and Private in Renaissance Venice," *Renaissance Studies*, 12 (1998): 109–30.

"Trade Guilds and Devotional Confraternities in the State and Society of Venice to 1620" (Ph.D. diss.: University of Cambridge, 1982).

Tradesmen and Traders: The World of the Guilds in Venice and Europe, c.1250–c.1650 (London, 1987).

Maher, M., "Reforming Rome: The Society of Jesus and its Congregations" (Ph.D. diss.: University of Minnesota, 1997).

Maiarelli, A. (ed.), *La Cronaca di S. Domenico di Perugia* (Spoleto, 1995).

Mancini, F., "I Disciplinati di Porta Fratta in Todi e il loro primo statuto," in AA.VV., *Il Movimento dei Disciplinati*, 269–292.

Mancini, G., *Cortona nel Medio Evo* (1897; repr. Florence, 1992).

Manini F. G., *Compendio della storia sacra e politica di Ferrara*, 6 vols (Ferrara, 1808–10).

Manno Tolu, R., "Ricordanze delle abbandonate fiorentine di Santa Maria e San Niccolò del Ceppo nei secoli XVII–XVIII," in L.Borgia *et al.*, *Studi in onore di Arnaldo D'Addario* (Lecce, 1995), 107–124.

Maragi, M., "Gli antichi statuti dello Spedale di Santa Maria della Vita," in Amministrazione degli Ospedali di Bologna (ed.), *Sette Secoli di vita ospitaliera in Bologna* (Bologna, 1960), 111–47.

Marcello, L., "Andare a bottega. Adoloscenza e apprendistato nelle arti (sec. XVI–XVII)," in O. Niccoli (ed.), *Infanzie* (Florence, 1993): 231–51.

Marcora, C., "Nicolò Ormaneto, vicario di san Carlo (giugno 1564–giugno 1566)," *Memorie storiche della diocesi di Milano*, 8 (1961): 209–590.

"Il processo diocesano informativo sulla vita di san Carlo per la sua canonizzazione," *Memorie storiche della diocesi di Milano*, 9 (1962): 76–735.

"Il diario di Giambattista Casale (1554–1598)," *Memorie storiche della diocesi di Milano*, 12 (1965): 209–437.

Margulies, S. H., "La famiglia Abravanel in Italia," *Rivista Israelita*, 3 (1906).

Marinelli, O., *Le confraternite di Perugia dalle origini al sec. XIX* (Perugia, 1965).

Maroni Lumbroso, M. and Antonio Martini, *Le confraternite romane nelle loro chiese* (Rome, 1963).

Martano, R., "La missione inutile: la predicazione obbligatoria agli ebrei di Roma nella seconda metà del Cinquecento," in *Itinerari Ebraico-Cristiani. Società, cultura, mito* (Fasano, 1987), 93–110.

Martin, A. L., *The Jesuit Mind* (Ithaca, 1988).

Martin, G., *Roma Sancta*, ed. G. B. Parks (Rome, 1969).

Martines, L. (ed.), *Violence and Civil Disorder in Italian Cities, 1200–1500* (Berkeley, 1972).

Marzola, M., *Per la storia della chiesa Ferrarese nel secolo XVI (1497–1590)*, 2 vols (Turin, 1976).

Mascia, G., *La confraternita dei Bianchi della Giustizia a Napoli "S. Maria Succure Miseris'* (Naples, 1972).

Matteucci, D., "'Se è mossa intrar in religione, o vero in questa casa, per passione o disperationi, o vero da qual spirito è guidata.' Gli ospizi di S. Maria Maddalena e S. Marta," in *L'ospedale dei pazzi di Roma dai papi al '900. Lineamenti di assistenza e cura a poveri e dementi*, vol. 2 (Bari, 1994): 331–7.

McCants, A., "Meeting Needs and Suppressing Desires: Consumer Choice Models and Historical Data," *Journal of Interdisciplinary History*, 26 (1995): 191–207.

McCrie, T., *History of the Reformation in Italy* (London, 1856).

Medici, M. T. G., *L'aria di città. Donne e diritti nel comune medievale* (Napoli, 1996).

Meersseman, G. G., "Nota sull'origine delle compagnie dei laudesi (Siena 1267)," *Rivista di storia della chiesa in Italia*, 17 (1963): 365–405.

"La riforma delle confraternite laicali in Italia prima del Concilio di Trento," in *Problemi di vita religiosa in Italia nel Cinquecento. Atti del Convegno di storia della chiesa in Italia* (Padua, 1960): 17–30.

Meersseman, G. G. and G. Pacini, *Ordo fraternitatis. Confraternite e pietà dei laici nel Medioevo*, 3 vols (Rome, 1977).

Mehus, L., *Dell'origine, progresso, abusi, e riforma delle confraternite laicali* (Florence, 1785).

Meloni, P. L., "Topografia, diffusione e aspetti delle Confraternite dei Disciplinati," in *Risultati e prospettive*, 15–98.

Meneghin, V., "Due compagnie sul modello di quelle del "Divino Amore' fondate da Francescani a Feltre e a Verona (1499, 1503)," *Archivum Franciscanum Historicum*, 62 (1969): 518–64.

Menestò, E. (ed.), *Le terziarie francescane della beata Angelina: origine e spiritualità* (Spoleto, 1996).

Menichetti, P. L., *I 50 ospedali di Gubbio* (Città di Castello, 1975).

Mezzanotte, F., "Le vicende del capitolo di S. Lorenzo nei secoli XI–XIII," in M. Pierotti (ed.), *Una città e la sua cattedrale* (Perugia, 1992), 109–35.

Miccoli, G., "La storia religiosa," *Storia d'Italia*, 2/1 (Turin, 1974), 431–1079.

Miglio, L., "Leggere e scrivere il volgare. Sull'alfabetismo delle donne nella Toscana tardo medievale," *Civiltà comunale: libro, scrittura, documento*. Atti del Convegno Genova 8–11 novembre 1988 (Genoa, 1989), 357–77.

"Scrivere al femminile," in A. Petrucci and F. M. Gimeno Blay (eds.), *Escribir y leer en Occidente* (València, 1995), 63–87.

Milano, A., "Battesimi di Ebrei a Roma dal Cinquecento all'Ottocento," in AA.VV., *Scritti in memoria di Enzo Sereni.* (Jerusalem, 1970), 133–167.

Il Ghetto di Roma (Rome, 1964).

Miller, S. J., "The Limits of Political Jansenism in Tuscany: Scipione de' Ricci to Peter Leopold, 1780–1791," *Catholic Historical Review*, 80 (1994): 762–7.

Mira, G., "Primi sondaggi su taluni aspetti economico-finanziari delle Confraternite dei Disciplinati," in *Risultati e prospettive della ricerca sul movimento dei Disciplinati* (Perugia, 1972), 229–60.

Mirri, G., *I vescovi di Cortona dalla istituzione della diocesi (1325–1971)*, ed. Guido Mirri (Cortona, 1972).

Mitterauer, M., *A History of Youth* (Oxford, 1992).

Modena, L., "Les exiles à Ferrara en 1493," *Revue des Etudes Juives*, 15 (1887).

Modigliani, A., "Li nobili huomini di Roma: comportamenti economici e scelte professionali," in S. Gensini (ed.), *Roma capitale (1447–1527)* (Pisa, 1994), 345–72.

I Porcari. Storie di una famiglia romana tra Medioevo e Rinascimento (Rome, 1994).

Molho, A., *Florentine Public Finances in the Early Renaissance, 1400–1433* (Cambridge, MA, 1971).

Marriage Alliance in Late Medieval Florence (Cambridge MA, 1994).

Mollat, M., "En guise de préface: les problèmes de la pauvret," in M. Mollat (ed.), *Etudes sur l'histoire de la pauvreté (Moyen Age–XVI siècle)*, vol. 1 (Paris, 1974).

The Poor in the Middle Ages: A Study in Social History, trans. Arthur Goldhammer (New Haven, 1986).

Monachino, V., M. da Alatri and I. da Villapadierna, *La Carità cristiana in Roma. Roma Cristiana*, vol. 10 (Bologna, 1968).

Monti, G. M., *Le confraternite medievali dell'alta e media Italia*, 2 vols (Florence-Venice, 1927).

Moranti, L., *La Confraternita del Corpus Domini di Urbino* (Ancona, 1990).

Moreno, D., *Dal documento al terreno* (Bologna, 1992).

Moreno, D. and O. Raggio (eds.), "Risorse collettive," *Quaderni storici*, 81 (1992).

Morghen, R., "Le confraternite dei Disciplinati e gli aspetti della religiosità laica nell'età moderna," *Risultati e prospettive*, 317–27.

Moroni, G., *Dizionario di erudizione storico-ecclesiastica. Da S. Pietro sino ai nostri giorni*, 103 vols (Venice, 1840–61).

Le Mouvement Confraternel au Moyen Age. France, Italie, Suisse (Rome, 1987).

Il Movimento dei Disciplinati nel Settimo Centenario dal suo inizio (Perugia–1260), Convegno internazionale, Perugia 25–28 settembre 1960 (Perugia, 1962 and 1986).

Mueller, R. C., "Charitable Institutions, the Jewish Community and Venetian Society: A Discussion of the Recent Volume by Brian Pullan," *Studi*

Veneziani, 14 (1972): 38–78.

Mullan, E., *History of the Prima Primaria Sodality of the Annunciation and Sts. Peter and Paul* (St. Louis, 1917).

The Nobles' Sodality of our Lady of the Assumption of the Gesù in Rome (St. Louis, 1918).

(trans.), *The Sodality of Our Lady: Studied in the Documents* (New York, 1912).

Muratori, L. A., *Antiquitates italicae medii aevi, sive dissertationes de moribus, ritibus, religione, regimine, magistratibus, legibus, studiis literarum, artibus, lingua, militia, nummis, principibus, libertate, servitute, foederibus, aliisque faciem & mores italici populi referentibus post declinationem Rom. Imp. ad annum usque MD* (Mediolani, 1742; repr. Bologna, 1965).

Dissertazioni sopra le antichità italiane (Milan, 1751).

Najemy, J. M., *Corporatism and Consensus in Florentine Electoral Politics, 1280–1400* (Chapel Hill, 1982).

Nardi, F., "Matteo Guerra. e la Congregazione dei Sacri Chiodi (secc. xvi–xvii). Aspetti della religiosità sense nell'età della Controriforma," *Bollettino Senese di Storia Patria*, 91 (1984): 14–135.

Nardi, G., "Una Congregazione missionaria a Napoli nel secolo xviii," *Asprenas*, 4 (1961): 4–35.

"Nuove richerche sulle istituzioni napoletane a favore degli schiavi: La Congregazione degli schiavi dei pp. Gesuiti," *Asprenas*, 14 (1967): 294–313.

Opere per la conversione degli schiavi a Napoli (Naples, 1967).

Navarrini, R. and C. M. Belfanti, "Il problema della povertà nel Ducato di Mantova," in Politi *et al.* (eds.) *Timore e carità. I poveri nell' Italia Moderna* (Cremona, 1982), 121–36.

Needham, R., *Belief, Language and Experience* (Oxford, 1972).

Nessi, S., "Storia e arte delle chiese francescane di Montefalco," *Miscellanea Francescana*, 62 (1962): 232–332.

Newbigin, N., *Feste d'Oltrarno: Plays in Churches in Fifteenth-Century Florence*, 2 vols., *Istituto Nazionale di Studi sul Rinascimento, Studi e Testi* 37 (Florence, 1996).

"Piety and Politics in the Feste of Lorenzo's Florence," in G. Garfagnini (ed.), *Lorenzo Il Magnifico e il suo mondo* (Florence, 1994), 17–41.

"The Word made Flesh. The Rappresentazioni of Mysteries and Miracles in Fifteenth-Century Florence," in T. Verdon and J. Henderson (eds.), *Christianity and the Renaissance. Image and Religious Imagination in the Quattrocento* (Syracuse, 1990), 361–75.

(ed.), *Nuovo Corpus di sacre rappresentazioni fiorentine del Quattrocento* (Bologna, 1983).

Nicolas, J., *La Savoie au XVIIIe siècle*, 2 vols (Paris, 1979).

Niccoli, O., "Compagnie di bambini nell'Italia del Rinascimento," *Rivista Storica Italiana*, 101 (1989): 346–74.

Il seme della violenza. Putti, fanciulli e mammoli nell'Italia tra Cinque e Seicento (Rome-Bari, 1995).

Nicolini, U., "Statuto della fraternita dei disciplinati di S. Rufino," in Nicolini *et al.* (eds.), *Le fraternite medievali di Assisi,* 305–329.

E. Menestò, and F. Santucci (eds.), *Le fraternite medievali di Assisi: linee storiche e testi statutari* (Perugia, 1989).

Norsa, P., *Una famiglia di banchieri: I Norsa,* 2 vols (Naples, 1959).

Novi Chavarria, E., "L'attività missionaria dei gesuiti nel Mezzogiorno d'Italia tra XVIe XVII secolo," in AA.VV., *Per la storia sociale e religiosa del Mezzogiorno d'Italia,* vol. 2 (Naples, 1982).

Nubola, C., *Conoscere per governare. La diocesi di Trento nella visita pastorale di Ludovico Madruzzo (1579–1581)* (Bologna, 1993).

Olin, J. (ed.), *The Autobiography of St. Ignatius Loyola, with Related Documents,* trans. J. O'Callaghan (New York, 1992).

'Erasmus and St. Ignatius Loyola," in J. Olin *et al.,* (eds.), *Luther, Erasmus, and the Reformation; a Catholic-Protestant reappraisal* (New York, 1969), 114–33.

Olivieri Baldissarri, M., *I "poveri prigioni". La confraternita della Santa Croce e della Pietà dei carcerati a Milano nei secoli XVI–XVIII* (Milan, 1985).

O'Malley, J., *The First Jesuits* (Cambridge, MA, 1993).

"How the Jesuits Changed: 1540–1556," *America,* 165 (July 1991): 28–32.

"Mission and the Early Jesuits," *The Way Supplement,* 79 (1994): 3–10.

"The Society of Jesus," in De Molen (ed.), *Religious Orders,* 139–63.

O'Regan, N., "Palestrina: A Musician and Composer in the Market-Place," *Early Music,* 22 (1994): 551–72.

Institutional Patronage in Post-Tridentine Rome: Music at the Santissima Trinità dei Pellegrini 1550–1650 (London, 1995).

Orioli, L., *Le confraternite medievali e il problema della poverta: lo statuto della compagnia di Santa Maria Vergine e di San Zenobio di Firenze nel secolo XIV* (Rome, 1984).

Paglia, V., "Le confraternite e I problemi della morte a Roma nel sei-settecento," *Ricerche per la storia religiosa di Roma,* 5 (1984): 197–220.

La morte confortata. Riti della paura e mentalità religiosa a Roma in età moderna (Rome, 1982).

"La Pietà dei Carcerati": Confraternita e Società dei Carcerati a Roma nei secoli xvi–xvii (Rome, 1980).

(ed.), *Confraternite e Meridione nell' età moderna* (Rome, 1990).

Palmero, B., "La costruzione del territorio in Alta Valle Tanaro (secoli XVI–XIX)," in AA.VV., *Orientamenti sulla ricerca per la storia locale.* Atti del Convegno di Mombasiglio, 1997 (forthcoming.)

Palumbo-Fossatti, I., "L'interno della casa dell'artigiano e dell'artista nella Venezia del '500," *Studi Veneziani,* 8 (1984): 109–53.

Papi, M., "Le confraternite fiorentine tra Medioevo e Rinascimento. Stato della questione e prospettive d'indagine," *Ricerche di storia sociale e religiosa,* 17–18 (1980): 121–33.

Parente, F., "Il confronto ideologico tra l'ebraismo e la Chiesa in Italia," *Italia Judaica* (Rome, 1983): 303–81.

Paschini, P., *Tre Ricerche sulla storia della Chiesa nel Cinquecento* (Rome, 1945).

Pastore, A., "Strutture assistenziali tra Chiesa e Stati nell'Italia della Controriforma," *Storia d'Italia. Annali 9: La Chiesa e il potere politico* (Turin, 1986), 431–65.

Patria, P. L., "Consortie, confrarie, società di devozione: la religiosità dei laici nella Valle di Susa tardomedievale," in A. Salvatori (ed)., *Spiritualità, culture, e ambienti nelle Alpi occidentali* (Stresa: Rosminiane, 1998): 71–136.

Pavan, P., "La confraternita del Salvatore nella società romana del Tre-Quattrocento," *Ricerche per la storia religiosa di Roma*, 5 (1984): 81–90.

"Gli statuti della società dei Raccomandati del Salvatore ad Sancta Sanctorum," *Archivio della Società Romana di Storia Patria*, 101 (1978): 35–96.

Pavone, F., *Statuti e Regole della Congragazione de' Chierici eretta in Napoli sotto il titolo della Beata Vergine nel Collegio della Compagnia di Gesù* (Naples, 1614).

Pazzagli, R., *Famiglie e paesi. Mutamento e identità locale in una comunità toscana: Buggiano dal XVII al XIX secolo* (Venice: 1996).

Pazzelli, R., *La vita claustrale nel Terzo Ordine regolare di San Francesco* (Rome, 1996).

Pecchiai, P., *I Barberini* (Rome, 1959).

Pelaez, M., "La fraternita di S. Maria delle Grazie e il suo statuto in volgare romanesco," *Archivio della Società Romana di Storia Patria*, 69 (1946): 73–89.

Pellicia, G., "Scuole di Catechismo e scuole rionali per fanciulle nella Roma del Seicento," *Ricerche per la Storia Religiosa di Roma*, 4 (1980): 237–68.

Pemble, J., *Venice Rediscovered* (Oxford, 1996).

Pesaro, A., *Memorie storiche sulla comunità israelitica ferrarese* (Ferrara, 1878).

Picasso, G. (ed.), *Una santa tutta romana* (Monte Oliveto Maggiore, 1984).

Piccialuti, M., *La carità come metodo di governo. Istituzioni caritative a Roma dal pontificato di Innocenzo XII a quello di Benedetto XIV* (Turin, 1994).

Pierotti, M. L. C. (ed.), *Una città e la sua cattedrale: il Duomo di Perugia* (Perugia, 1992).

Pizzoni, C., "La confraternita dell'Annunziata in Perugia," in AA.VV., *Il Movimento dei Disciplinati*, 146–55.

Polizzotto, L., "Confraternities, Conventicles and Political Dissent: The case of the Savonarolan "*Capi Rossi*," *Memorie Domenicane*, NS, 16 (1985): 235–83; 17 (1986): 285–300.

The Elect Nation: The Savonarolan Movement in Florence, 1494–1545 (Oxford, 1995).

"Lorenzo il Magnifico, Savonarola and Medicean Dynasticism," in B. Toscani (ed.), *Lorenzo de' Medici: New Perspectives* (New York, 1993), 331–55.

"Prophecy, Politics and History in Early Sixteenth-Century Florence: The Admonitory Letters of Francesco d'Antonio de' Ricci," in P. Denley and C.Elam (eds.), *Florence and Italy: Renaissance Studies in Honour of Nicolai Rubinstein* (London, 1988), 107–31.

Problemi di vita religiosa in Italia nel Cinquecento. Atti del Convegno di storia della chiesa in Italia (Padua, 1960).

Prodi, P., "The Application of the Tridentine Decrees," in E. Cochrane (ed.), *The Late Italian Renaissance* (New York, 1970), 226–43.

Il sovrano pontefice. Un corpo e due anime: la monarchia papale nella prima età moderna (Bologna, 1982).

(ed.), *Disciplina dell'anima, disciplina del corpo e disciplina della società tra medioevo ed età moderna* (Bologna, 1994).

Proietti Pedetta, L., *Le confraternite di Assisi tra Riforma e declino (secc. xvi–xviii)* (Assisi, 1990).

"Culto, devozione e carità nelle confraternite laicali," in R. Chiacchella (ed.), *Una Chiesa attraverso i secoli* (Perugia, 1996), 39–46.

Prosperi, A., "The Missionary," in R. Villari (ed.), *Baroque Personae*, trans. Lydia Cochrane (Chicago, 1995), 160–94.

"Parrocchie e confraternite tra cinquecento e seicento," in *Per una storia dell'Emilia-Romagna* (Bologna, 1985), 161–252.

"Il sangue e l'anima. Ricerche sulle compagnie di giustizia in Italia," *Quaderni storici*, 51 (1982), 960–99.

Provero, L., *Dai marchesi Del Vasto ai primi marchesi di Saluzzo. Sviluppi signorili entro quadri pubblici (secoli XI e XII)* (Turin, 1992).

"I marchesi Del Carretto: tradizione pubblica, radicamento patrimoniale e ambiti di affermazione politica," *Atti e memorie della Società savonese di Storia Patria*, NS, 30 (1994), 21–50.

Pugh Rupp, T., "Ordo Caritatis: The Political Thought of Remigio dei Girolami," (Ph.D. diss.: Cornell University, 1988).

Pugliese, O., "The Good Works of the Florentine "Buonomini di San Martino': An Example of Renaissance Pragmatism," in Eisenbichler (ed.), *Crossing the Boundaries*, 108–20.

Pullan, B., *The Jews of Europe and the Inquisition of Venice 1550–1670* (Totowa, NJ, 1983).

"Nature e carattere dell Scuole," in T. Pignatti (ed.), *Le Scuole di Venezia* (Milan, 1981), 9–26.

"The Old Catholicism, the New Catholicism, and the Poor," in M. Rosa (ed.), *Timore e carità: i poveri nell'Italia moderna. Atti del Convegno* (Cremona, 1982).

"Orphans and foundlings in early modern Europe," in *Poverty and Charity*, III: 5–28 (Aldershot, 1994).

"Povertà, Carità e nuove forme di assistenza nell'Europa moderna (secoli xv–xvii)," in Zardin (ed.), *La Citta e I Poveri*, 21–44.

Poverty and Charity: Europe, Italy, Venice 1400–1700 (Aldershot, 1994).

Rich and Poor in Renaissance Venice: The Social Institutions of a Renaissance State to 1620 (Oxford, 1971).

"The *Scuole Grandi* of Venice: Some Further Thoughts," in Verdon and Henderson (eds.), *Christianity and the Renaissance*, 272–301.

"A Ship with Two Rudders: Righetto Marrano and the Inquisition in Venice," *Historical Journal*, 20 (1977): 25–58.

"'Support and Redeem': Charity and Poor Relief in Italian Cities from the Fourteenth to the Seventeenth Century," *Continuity and Change*, 3 (1988): 177–208.

Puppi, L. (ed.), *Le Zitelle: architettura, arte e storia di un'istituzione veneziana*

(Venice, 1992).

Quaccia, F., "Lo spazio sacro a Ivrea in età moderna," *Bollettino Storico-Bibliografico Subalpino*, 88 (1990): 109–52.

Quattrone, S. *et al.* (eds), *Santa Caterina dei Funari. La chiesa, l'isolato, il restauro* (Rome, 1994).

Raccolta di orazioni le quali ordinatamente recitansi secondo le diverse funzioni solite a farsi tra l'anno in questa chiesa parrocchiale di S. Angelo (Perugia, 1793).

Raggio, O., *Faide e parentele. Lo stato genovese visto dalla Fontanabuona* (Turin, 1990).

"Forme e pratiche di appropriazione delle risorse," *Quaderni storici*, 79 (1992): 135–70.

"Costruzione delle fonti e prova: testimoniali, possesso e giurisdizione," *Quaderni storici*, 91 (1996): 135–56.

Rahner, H., *Saint Ignatius Loyola: Letters to Women*, trans. K. Pond and S. A. H. Weetman (Edinburgh and London, 1960).

Raponi, N. and A. Turchini (eds.), *Stampa, libri e letture a Milano nell'età di Carlo Borromeo* (Milan, 1992).

Rapp, R. T., *Industry and Economic Decline in Seventeenth-Century Venice* (Cambridge, MA, 1976).

Ratti, A., "Scuole o confraternite del SS. Sacramento," in A. Ratti, *Contribuzione alla storia eucaristica di Milano* (Milan, 1895), 53–75.

Ravizza, G. (ed.), *La Novaria sacra del Venerabile Vescovo Carlo Bescapé. Tradotto in italiano con annotazioni e Vita dell'Autore dall'Avvocato Cav. G. R* (Novara, 1878).

Ricci, G., "Poverta, vergogna e povertà vergognosa," *Società e Storia*, 5 (1979): 305–37.

Ricci, S., *Lettere di Scipione de' Ricci a Pietro Leopoldo*, 3 vols., eds. B. Bocchini Camaiani and M. Verga (Florence, 1992).

Rigon, A., *Clero e città*. «Fratalea cappellanorum», parroci, cura d'anime in Padova dal XII al XV secolo (Padova, 1988).

Riis, T. (ed.), *Aspects of Poverty in Early Modern Europe* (Stuttgart, 1978).

Rimoldi, A., "I laici nelle regole delle confraternite di san Carlo Borromeo (appunti)," *Miscellanea Carlo Figini* (Venegono inf. [Varese], 1964), 281–303.

Risultati e prospettive di ricerca sul movimento dei disciplinati. Atti del Convegno Internazionale di Studio, Perugia 5–7 dicembre 1969 (Perugia, 1972).

Rivlin, B., "The 1547 [sic] Statutes of 'Hevrat Nizharim' in Bologna," *Asufot*, 3 (1989).

Mutual Responsibility in the Italian Ghetto: Holy Societies 1516–1789 (Jerusalem, 1991).

Rocke, M., *Forbidden Friendships: Homosexuality and Male Culture in Renaissance Florence* (New York, 1996).

Rodocanachi, E., *Le Saint-Siège et les Juifs. Le Ghetto à Rome* (Paris, 1891).

Romani, V., "Vicende archivistiche romane del Settecento: Francesco Maria Magni e l'Archivio della Pia Casa degli Orfani," in *Studi in onore di Leopoldo*

Sandri (Rome, 1983), 783–92.

Romano, D., *Patricians and Popolani: The Social Foundations of the Venetian Renaissance State* (Baltimore, 1987).

Romeo, G., *Aspettando il boia. Condannati a morte, conforteria e inquisitori nella Napoli della Controriforma* (Florence, 1993).

Rondeau, J., "Prayer and Gender in the Laude of Early Italian Confraternities," in R. Trexler (ed.), *Gender Rhetorics: Postures of Dominance and Submission in History* (Binghampton, 1994), 219–33.

Rosa, M., "La Chiesa meridionale nell'età della Controriforma," in Chittolini and Miccoli (eds.), *La Chiesa e il potere politico*, 295–345.

"Geografia e storia religiosa per l'"Atlante Storico Italiano'," *Nuova Rivista Storica*, 53 (1969): 1–43.

"Pietà mariana e devozione del Rosario nell'Italia dell Cinque e Seicento," in M.Rosa, *Religione e Società nel Mezzogiorno tra Cinque e Seicento* (Bari, 1976).

"Per la storia dell'erudizione toscana del '700: profilo di Lorenzo Mehus," *Annali della Scuola speciale per archivisti e bibliotecari dell'Università di Roma*, 2/2 (1962): 41–96.

Riformatori e ribelli nel '700 religioso italiano (Bari, 1969).

(ed.), *Problemi e ricerche per la Carte Ecclesiastiche dell'Atlante Storico Italiano dell' età moderna* (Florence, 1972).

Rotelli, E., "La figura e l'opera di san Carlo Borromeo nel carteggio degli ambasciatori estensi," *Studia Borromaica*, 4 (1990): 133–45.

Roth, C., *The History of the Jews in Italy* (Philadelphia, 1946).

The Jews in the Renaissance (Philadelphia, 1959).

Rubin, M., *Charity and Community in Medieval Cambridge* (Cambridge, 1987).

Corpus Christi: The Eucharist in Late Medieval Culture (Cambridge, 1991).

"Small Groups: Identity and Solidarity in the Late Middle Ages," in J.Kermode (ed.), *Enterprise and Individuals in Fifteenth-Century England* (Phoenix Mill, 1991), 132–50.

Rubinstein, N., *The Government of Florence under the Medici, 1434 to 1494* (Oxford, 1966).

"Lay Patronage and Observant Reform in Fifteenth-Century Florence," in T. Verdon and J. Henderson (eds.), *Christianity and the Renaissance. Image and Religious Imagination in the Quattrocento* (Syracuse, 1990), 63–82.

Ruderman, D. R., "The Founding of a *Gemilut Hasadim* Society in Ferrara in 1515," *AJS Review*, 1 (1976).

"A Jewish Apologetic Treatise from Sixteenth-Century Bologna," *Hebrew Union College Annual*, 50 (1979).

Kabbalah, Magic and Science: The Cultural World of a Sixteenth-Century Jewish Physician (Cambridge, MA, 1988).

The World of a Renaissance Jew: The Life and Thought of Abraham . . . Farissol (Cincinnati, 1981).

Rudt de Collenberg, W. H., "Le baptème des Juifs à Rome de 1614 à 1798 selon les reistres de la 'Casa dei Catecumeni'," *Archivum Historiae Pontificiae*, 24 (1986): 91–231; 25 (1987):105–261; 26 (1988): 119–294.

Rurale, F., "L'attività caritativa degli istituti religiosi e il ruolo della Compagnia di Gesù," in Zardin (ed.), *La Città e I Poveri*, 253–72.

I Gesuiti a Milano. Religione e politica nel secondo Cinquecento (Rome, 1992).

Rusconi, R., "Confraternite, compagnie e devozioni," in Chittolini and Miccoli (eds.), *La Chiesa e il potere politico*, 469–506.

"Pratica cultuale ed istruzione religiosa nelle confraternite italiane del tardo medio evo: "libri da compagnia' e libri di pietà," in *Le Mouvement Confraternel*, 133–53.

Russo, C., "Parrocchie, fabbricerie e comunità nell'area suburban della diocesi di Napoli (xvi–xviii secolo)," in C.Russo, *Chiesa e comunità nella diocesi di Napoli tra Cinque e Settecento*, vol. 2 (Naples, 1984), 221–80.

Saalman, H., *The Bigallo: The Oratory and Residence of the Compagnia del Bigallo e della Misericordia in Florence* (New York, 1969).

Sabatine, B., "The Church of Santa Caterina dei Funari and the Vergini Miserabili of Rome" (Ph.D. diss.: University of California at Los Angeles, 1992).

Sabean, D. W., *Power in the Blood* (Cambridge, 1984).

Sannino, A. L., "Le confraternite potentine dal xv al xix secolo," in Paglia (ed.), *Confraternite e Meridione*, 119–40.

Santagata, S., *Istoria della Compagnia di Gesù appartenente al Regno di Napoli*, 2 vols. (Naples, 1756).

Santini, G., *'I comuni di pieve' nel Medio Evo italiano. Contributo alla storia dei comuni rurali* (Milan, 1964).

Savelli, R., "Dalle confraternite allo Stato: il sistema assistenziale genovese nel Cinquecento," *Atti della Società Ligure di Storia Patria*, NS, 24/1 (1965): 171–216.

Sbriziolo, L., *Le Confraternite Veneziane di divozione. Saggio bibligrafico e premesse storiografiche* (Rome, 1968).

"Per la storia delle confraternite veneziane: dalle deliberazioni miste (1310–1476) del Consiglio dei Dieci. Le Scuole dei Battuti," *Miscellanea Gilles Gérard Meersseman*, vol. 2 (Padua, 1970).

"Per la storia delle confraternite veneziane: dalle deliberazioni miste (1310–1476) del Consiglio dei Dieci. *Scolae comunes*, artigiane e nazionali," *Atti dell'Istituto Veneto di Scienze, Lettere ed Arti*, 126 (1967–8): 405–42.

Scaduto, M., "I carceri della Vicaria di Napoli agli inizi del seicento," *Redenzione umana* 6 (1968): 393–412.

Catalogo dei Gesuiti d'Italia, 1540–1565 (Rome, 1968).

L'epoca di Giacomo Lainez (1556–1565). Il governo (Rome, 1964).

L'epoca di Giacomo Lainez (1556–1565). L'azione (Rome, 1974).

L'Opera di Francesco Borgia (Rome, 1994).

Storia della Compagnia di Gesù in Italia, 3 vols. (Rome, 1964–92).

Scarabello, G., "Una organizzazione di assistenza dei carcerati veneziani: la fraterna del Santissimo Crocefisso di S.Bartolomeo dei poveri prigioni," in G. Cozzi (ed.), *Stato, società e giustizia nella Repubblica Veneta (secc. xv–xviii)* (Rome, 1980), 324–56.

Scentoni, G. (ed.), *Laudario orvietano* (Spoleto, 1994).

Schaub, J-F., review of B. Clavero, *Institucìòn historica del Derecho et a Hespanha, Poder e Instituçoes no Antigo Regime Revue d'Histoire Moderne et Contemporaine*, 42 (1995): 367–70.

Schiaffini, A. (ed.), *Testi fiorentini del Dugento* (Florence, 1926), 55–72.

Schinosi, F., *Istoria della Compagnia di Giesù appartenente al Regno di Napoli*, 2 vols. (Naples, 1706–11).

Schwarzfuchs, S., "Un episodio della Comunità di Roma nella prima metà del sec. XVI: nota a un documento," in D. Carpi, A. Milano and U. Nahon (eds.), *Scritti in memoria di Enzo Sereni: Saggi sull' Ebraismo romano* (Jerusalem, 1970).

Sebregondi, L., *Tre confraternite fiorentine. Santa Maria della Pietà, detta 'Buca' di San Girolamo. San Filippo Benizi. San Francesco Poverino* (Florence, 1991).

"A Confraternity of Florentine Noble Women," *Confraternitas*, 4/2 (Fall 1993): 3–6.

"Lorenzo de' Medici confratello illustre," *Archivio Storico Italiano*, 150 (1992): 319–42.

"La soppressione delle confraternite fiorentine: la dispersione di un patrimonio," in L. Borgia *et al.* (eds.), *Studi in onore di Arnaldo d'Addario*, vol. 3. (Lecce, 1995), 1041–9.

Segre, R., "Sephardic Settlements in Sixteenth-Century Italy," in A. Meyuhas Ginio (ed.), *Jews, Christians, and Muslims in the Mediterranean World After 1492* (London, 1992).

Sella, D., *Crisis and Continuity: The Economy of Spanish Lombardy in the Seventeenth Century* (Cambridge, MA, 1979).

Selwyn, J., "'Procur[ing] in the Common People These Better Behaviors': The Jesuits' Civilizing Mission in Early Modern Naples, 1550–1620," *Radical History Review* (1997): 5–34.

Sensi, M., "Fraternite disciplinati e sacre rappresentazioni a Foligno nel secolo XV," *Bollettino di Storia Patria per l'Umbria*, 71 (1974): 139–217.

Sergi, G., "Anscarici, Arduinici, Aleramici: elementi per una comparazione tra dinastie marchionali," *Bollettino storico-bibliografico subalpino*, 82 (1984): 301–20.

"La feudalizzazione delle circoscrizioni pubbliche nel regno italico," in *Structures féodales et féodalisme*, 251–61.

Settia, A. A., "Crisi e adeguamento dell'organizzazione ecclesiastica nel Piemonte bassomedievale," in AA.VV., *Pievi e parrocchie in Italia nel basso Medioevo (sec.XIII–XV)* (Rome, 1984): 609–24.

Shahar, S., "The Regulation and Presentation of Women in Economic Life (13th–18th centuries)," in S. Cavaciocchi (ed.), *La donna nell'economia secc. XIII–XVIII* (Prato, 1990), 501–22.

Shulvass, M., *The Jews in the World of the Renaissance* (Leiden and Chicago, 1973).

Siepi, S., "Descrizione di Perugia," in M. Roncetti (ed.), *Annotazioni storiche* (Perugia, 1994).

Sills, D., "Voluntary Associations: Sociological Aspects," in D. Sills (ed.), *Inter-*

national *Encyclopedia of the Social Sciences*, vol. 16 (New York, 1968).

The Volunteers: Means and Ends in a National Organization (Glencoe, 1957).

Silvestrini, M. T., *La politica della religione. Il governo ecclesiastico nello Stato sabaudo del XVIII secolo* (Florence, 1997).

Simonsohn, S., *History of the Jews in the Duchy of Mantua* (Jerusalem, 1977).

The Jews in the Duchy of Milan, 4 vols (Jerusalem, 1982–6).

"On the History of the Rieti Banking Family in Tuscany," *Festschrift in Honor of Dr. George S. Wise* (Tel-Aviv, 1981).

(ed.), *The Apostolic See and the Jews*: 8 vols. (Toronto, 1988–91).

Sodini, C., *Il Gonfalone del Leon D'Oro nel quartiere di S. Giovanni a Florence* (Florence, 1979).

Sola, J. C., "El P. Juan Bautista Eliano: un documento autobiográfico inédito," *Archivum Historicum Societatis Iesu*, 4 (1935): 291–321.

Solfaroli Camillocci, D., "Le Confraternite del Divino Amore. Interpretazioni storiografiche e proposte attuali di ricerca," *Rivista di Storia e Letteratura Religiosa*, 27 (1991): 315–32.

Sonne, I. (ed.), *Mi-Pavlo ha-Revi'i ad Pius he-Hamishi* (Jerusalem, 1954).

Spicciani, A., "The 'Poveri Vergognosi' in Fifteenth-Century Florence," in T. Riis (ed.), *Aspects of Poverty in Early Modern Europe* (Florence, 1981), 119–82.

Staaff, E. (ed.), "Le laudario de Pise, du ms. 8521 de la Bibliothéque de l'Arsenal de Paris, etude linguistique," *Skrifter utgivna av Kungl. Humastiska Veten-skaps-Samfundet I Uppsala*, 27 (1931–2): 1–295.

Starn, R., *Contrary Commonwealth: The Theme of Exile in Medieval and Renaissance Italy* (Berkeley, 1982).

Statuti di confraternite religiose di Padova nel Medio Evo, in G. De Sandre Gasparini (ed.), *Fonti e ricerche di storia ecclesiastica padovana*, 6 (Padua, 1974).

Stefani, M. di C., *Cronaca fiorentina*, in Niccolo Rodolico (ed.), *Rerum Italicarum Scriptores*, NS, vol. 30 (Città di Castello, 1903–55).

Stevens, K. M., "Vincenzo Girardone and the Popular Press in Counter-Reformation Milan: A Case Study (1570)," *Sixteenth Century Journal*, 26 (1995): 639–59.

Stierli, J., "Devotion to Mary in the Sodality," *Woodstock Letters* 82 (1953): 17–45.

Stow, K. R., *Catholic Thought and Papal Jewry Policy, 1555–1593* (New York, 1977).

"A Tale of Uncertainties: Converts in the Roman Ghetto," in *Shlomo Simonsohn Jubilee Volume: Studies on the History of the Jews in the Middle Ages and Renaissance Period*, ed. D. Carpi (Tel Aviv, 1991).

(ed.), *The Jews in Rome*, Vol. 1, 1536–1551 (Leiden, 1995).

Strocchia, S., *Death and Ritual in Renaissance Florence* (Baltimore, 1992).

Structures féodales et féodalisme dans l'occident méditerranéen (X–XIII siècles) (Rome, 1980).

Tacchi-Venturi, P., *Storia della Compagnia di Gesù in Italia*, 2 vols (Rome, 1951).

Tamburini, F., *Santi e peccatori: confessioni e suppliche dai Registri della Penitenzieria dell'Archivio Segreto Vaticano: 1451–1586* (Milan, 1995).

Terpstra, N., "Apprenticeship in Social Welfare: From Confraternal Charity to Municipal Poor Relief in Early Modern Italy," *Sixteenth Century Journal*, 27 (1994): 101–20.

"Confraternities and Public Charity: Modes of Civic Welfare in Early Modern Italy," in J. P. Donnelly and M. W. Maher (eds.), *Confraternities and Catholic Reform in Italy, France, and Spain* (Kirksville, 1999), 97–120.

"Confraternal Prison Charity and Political Consolidation in Sixteenth-Century Bologna," *Journal of Modern History*, 66 (1994): 219–48.

"Kinship Translated: *Confraternite maggiori* and Political Apprenticeship in Early Modern Italy," in D. Zardin (ed.), *Corpi, 'Fraternità', Mestieri nella storia della società europea* (Rome: 1998), 103–115.

Lay Confraternities and Civic Religion in Renaissance Bologna (Cambridge, 1995).

"Piety and Punishment: The Lay Conforteria and Civic Justice in Sixteenth-Century Bologna," *Sixteenth Century Journal*, 22 (1991): 679–94.

"Ospedali e bambini abbandonati a Bologna nel Rinascimento," in A. J. Grieco and L. Sandri (eds.) *Ospedali e città: L'Italia del Centro-Nord, XIII–XVI secolo* (Florence, 1997), 209–32.

"Women in the Brotherhood: Gender, Class, and Politics in Renaissance Bolognese Confraternities," *Renaissance and Reformation*, 24 (1990): 193–212.

Thiessen, V. D., "Hartmut von Cronberg's Statutes of the Heavenly Confraternity," *Confraternitas*, 8/2 (1997): 9–12.

Toccafondi, D., "L'Archivio delle Compagnie Religiose Soppresse: una concentrazione o una costruzione archivistica?," in C.Vivoli (ed.), *Dagli archivi all'Archivio. Appunti di storia degli archivi fiorentini. Archivio di Stato di Florence, Scuola di Archivistica Paleografia e Diplomatica*, 3 (Florence, 1991): 107–25.

Tognetti, G., "Sul moto dei Bianchi nel 1399," *Bullettino dell'Istituto Storico Italiano per il Medio Evo*, 78 (1967): 205–343.

Thompson, A., *Revival Preachers and Politics in Thirteenth-Century Italy: The Great Devotion of 1233* (Oxford, 1992).

Toniolo, A., "Gli esposti in collegio. Progetto e realizzazione di un istituto per illegittimi di talento (secc. XVI–XVIII)," *Sanità scienza e storia*, 2 (1989): 99–116.

Torre, A., "Confraria e comunità nella Bassa Valsesia (secoli XVI–XIX)," *De Valle Siccida*, 9/2 (1998).

Il consumo di devozioni. Religione e comunità nelle campagne dell'Ancien Régime (Venice, 1995).

"Feuding, Factions and Parties: The Redefinition of Politics in the Imperial Fiefs of Langhe in the Seventeenth and Eighteenth Centuries," in E. Muir and G. Ruggiero (eds.), *History from Crime* (Baltimore, 1994): 135–69.

"Percorsi della pratica, 1966–1995," *Quaderni storici*, 90 (1995): 799–829.

"Politics cloaked in worship: State, Church and local power in Piedmont 1570–1770," *Past and Present*, 134 (1992): 42–92.

"Società locale e società regionale: complementarità o interdipendenza?,"

Società e storia, 18 (1995): 113–24.

"Village Ceremonial Life and Politics in Eighteenth-Century Piedmont," in
 J. Obelkevich, L. Roper, and R. Samuel (eds.), *Discipline of Faith: Studies in
 Religion, Politics and Patriarchy* (London, 1987), 194–207.

"Le visite pastorali: altari, famiglie, devozioni," in Garrone, *et al.* (eds.), *Valli
 monregalesi*, 148–88.

Toubert, P., "Les statuts communaux et l'histoire des campagnes lombardes au
 xive siècle," *Mélanges d'Archéologie et d'Histoire, Ecole Française de Rome*, 72
 (1960): 397–508.

Trexler, R., "Charity and the defense of Urban Elites in the Italian Communes,"
 in F. C. Jaher (ed.), *The Rich, the Well-Born and the Powerful* (Urbana,1973),
 64–109.

Dependence in Context in Renaissance Florence (Binghamton, NY, 1994).

Public Life in Renaissance Florence (New York, 1980).

"Ritual in Florence: Adolescence and Salvation in the Renaissance," in C.
 Trinkaus and H. A. Oberman (eds.), *The Pursuit of Holiness in Late Medieval
 and Renaissance Religion* (Leyden, 1974): 200–64.

"A Widow's Asylum of the Renaissance: The Orbatello of Florence," in
 Dependence in Context, 415–48.

Tugwell, S. (ed. and trans.), *Early Dominicans: Selected Writings* (New York,
 1982).

Turi, G., *"Viva Maria." La reazione alle riforme leopoldine (1790–1799)* (Florence,
 1963).

Urbanelli, C., *Storia dei Cappuccini delle Marche*, 3 vols. (Ancona, 1978–84).

Vaccari, P., *La territorialità come base dell'ordinamento giuridico del contado nell'Italia
 medioevale* (Milan, 1962).

Valeri, E., *La fraternita dell'Ospedale di S. Maria della Misericordia in Perugia nei secoli
 XIII–XVII* (Perugia, 1972).

Valone, C., "Women on the Quirinal Hill, Patronage in Rome, 1560–1630,"
 Art Bulletin, 76/1 (1994): 129–46.

"Piety and Patronage: Women and the Early Jesuits," in E. A. Matter and J.
 Coakley (eds.), *Creative Women in Medieval and Early Modern Italy. A
 Religious and Artistic Renaissance* (Philadelphia, 1994).

Vaquero Pineiro, M., "L'ospedale della nazione castigliana in Roma tra
 Medioevo ed Età contemporanea," *Roma moderna e contemporanea*, 1 (1993):
 57–81.

Varanini, B., "Spunti per una indagine sull'economia della confraternita (Anni
 1484–1488)," in *Liturgia, pietà e ministeri al Santo* (Vicenza, 1978), 235–43.

Varanini, G. M. (ed.), *La Valpolicella nella prima età moderna* (Verona, 1987).

Varanini, G., L. Banfi, and A. C. Burgio with G. Cattin (eds.), *Laude cortonesi dal
 secolo XIII al XV*, 3 vols (Florence, 1981).

Vasaio-Zambonini, M. E., "Il tessuto della virtù. Le zitelle di S. Eufemia e di S.
 Caterina dei Funari nella Controriforma," *Memoria*, 11–12 (1984): 53–64.

Vattasso, M., *Per la storia del dramma sacro in Italia* (Rome, 1903).

Vauchez, A., *I laici nel Medioevo. Pratiche ed esperienze religiose* (Milan, 1989).

"Une campagne de pacification en Lombardie autour de 1233: l'Action politique des ordres mendiants d'après la reform des statuts communaux et les accords de paix," *Ecole Française de Rome: Mélanges d'archéologie et d'histoire*, 78 (1966): 519–49.

"La commune de Sienne, les ordres mendiants et le culte des saints. Histoire et enseignements d'une crise (novembre 1328–avril 1329)," *Mélanges de l'Ecole Française de Rome: Moyen Age–Temps Modernes*, 89/2 (1977): 757–67.

The Laity in the Middle Ages: Religious Beliefs and Devotional Practices, trans. M. J. Schneider, ed. D. Bornstein (Notre Dame, 1993).

Ventrone, P., "Thoughts on Florentine Fifteenth-Century Religious Spectacle," in Verdon and Henderson (eds.), *Christianity and the Renaissance*, 405–112.

Verdon, T. and J. Henderson (eds.), *Christianity and the Renaissance: Image and Religious Imagination in the Quattrocento* (Syacuse, 1990).

Villani, G., *Cronica*, 2 vols., ed. F. Dragomanni (Florence, 1844).

Villaret, E., *Les Congregations Mariales* (Paris, 1946).

Vincent, C., *Des charités bien ordonnées. Les confréries normandes de la fin du XIIIe siècle au début du XVIe siécle* (Paris, 1988).

Vittori, R., "Bonifacio dalle Balle e le Putte di Santa Croce (1547?–1612)," (Bologna: Tesi di Laurea, 1985).

Volpe, M., *I Gesuiti nel napoletano* (Naples, 1914).

Von Henneberg, J., *L'oratorio dell'Arciconfraternita del Santissimo Crocefisso di San Marcello* (Rome, 1974).

Weil, M., "The Devotion of the Forty Hours and Roman Baroque Illusion," *Journal of the Warburg and Courtauld Institutes*, 37 (1974): 218–48.

Weinstein, D., "The Myth of Florence," in N. Rubinstein (ed.), *Florentine Studies: Politics and Society in Renaissance Florence* (London, 1968).

Weissman, R., "Brothers and Strangers: Confraternal Charity in Renaissance Florence," *Historical Reflections/Réflexions Historiques*, 15 (1988): 27–45.

"Cults and Contexts: In Search of the Renaissance Confraternity," in K. Eisenbichler (ed.), *Crossing the Boundaries: Christian Piety and the Arts in Italian Medieval and Renaissance Confraternities* (Kalamazoo, 1991): 201–36.

"Lorenzo de' Medici and the Confraternity of San Paolo," in B. Toscani (ed.), *Lorenzo de' Medici: New Perspectives* (New York, 1993), 315–29.

Ritual Brotherhood in Renaissance Florence (New York, 1982).

"Sacred Eloquence: Humanist Preaching and Lay Piety in Renaissance Florence," in Verdon and Henderson (eds.), *Christianity and the Renaissance*, 250–71.

Weisz, J., "Caritas/Controriforma: The Changing Role of a Confraternity's Ritual," in Eisenbichler (ed.), *Crossing the Boundaries*, 221–36.

Pittura e Misericordia: the Oratory of San Giovanni Decollato in Rome (Ann Arbor, 1984).

Wickham, C., *Comunità e clientele nella Toscana dei secoli XII e XIII* (Rome, 1995).

Wicki, J., *Le Père Jean Leunis, S.I (1532–1584), fondateur des Congrégations Mariales* (Rome, 1951).

Wilson, B., *Music and Merchants: The Laudesi Companies of Republican Florence* (Oxford, 1992).

Wisch, B., "The Colosseum as a Site for Sacred Theatre: A Pre-History of Carlo Fontana's Project," in H. Millon and S. Scott Munshower (eds.), *An Architectural Progress in the Renaissance and Baroque: Sojourns In and Out of Italy* (Papers in Art History from the Pennsylvania State University, 1992), 92–111.

"The Passion of Christ in the Art, Theater, and Penitential Rituals of the Roman Confraternity of the Gonfalone," in Einsenbichler (ed.), *Crossing the Boundaries*, 237–62.

"The Roman Church Triumphant: Pilgrimage, Penance and Processions Celebrating Holy Year of 1575," in *Triumphal Celebrations of the Rituals of Statecraft* (Papers in Art History from the Pennsylvania State University, 1994), 83–93.

Young, W. (ed. and trans.), *Letters of St. Ignatius of Loyola* (Chicago, 1959).

Zardin, D., "Carità e mutua assistenza nelle confraternite milanesi agli inizi dell'età moderna," in M. Pia Alberzoni and O. Grassi (eds.), *La Carità a Milano nei secoli xii–xv* (Milan, 1989), 281–300.

"Le confraternite bresciane al tempo della visita apostolica di san Carlo Borromeo," *San Carlo Borromeo e Brescia. Atti del convegno di Rovato* (Rovato [Brescia], 1987), 123–51.

"Confraternite e comunità nelle campagne milanesi fra Cinque e Seicento," *La scuola cattolica*, 112 (1984): 698–732.

"Confraternite e 'congregazioni' gesuitiche a Milano fra tardo Seicento e riforme settecentesche," in A. Acerbi and M. Marcocchi (eds.), *Ricerche sulla chiesa di Milano nel Settecento* (Milan, 1988), 180–252.

"Le confraternite in Italia settentrionale fra xv e xviii secolo," *Società e storia*, 35 (1987): 81–137.

Confraternite e Vita di Pietà nelle campagne lombarde tra '500 e '600 (Milan, 1981).

"La 'perfettione' nel proprio 'stato': strategie per la riforma generale dei costumi nel modello borromaico di governo," in F. Buzzi and D. Zardin (eds.), *Carlo Borromeo e l'opera della 'grande riforma.'* (Milan, 1997).

"La riforma delle confraternite di Disciplinati ed una sconosciuta 'Regola della compagnia della Penitenza'," in D. Zardin, *San Carlo Borromeo*, 7–54.

Riforma cattolica e resistenze nobiliari nella diocesi di Carlo Borromeo (Milan, 1984).

"Il rilancio delle confraternite nell'Europa cattolica cinque-seicentesca," in C. Mozzarelli and D. Zardin (eds.), *I tempi del Concilio. Religione, cultura e società nell'Europa tridentina* (Rome, 1997), 107–44.

San Carlo Borromeo ed il rinnovamento della vita religiosa dei laici. Due contributi per la storia delle confraternite nella diocesi di Milano. Memoria, 21 (Legnano, 1982).

"Solidarietà di vicini. La confraternita del Corpo di Cristo e le compagnie devote di S. Giorgio al Palazzo tra Cinque e Settecento," *Archivio storico lombardo*, 118 (1992): 361–404.

(ed.), *La Città e I Poveri. Milano e terre lombarde dal Rinascimento all'età spagnola* (Milan, 1995).

Zarri, G., "Dalla profezia alla disciplina (1450–1650)," in L. Scaraffia and G. Zarri (eds.), *Donne e fede. Santità e vita religiosa in Italia* (Bari, 1994), 177–225.

Zdekauer, L. (ed.), *Il Costituto del comune di Siena dell'anno 1262* (1897) (Bologna, 1983).

Zimmerman, S. and R. F. E. Weissman (eds.), *Urban Life in the Renaissance* (Newark, 1989).

INDEX

Aristocrats in bourgeois Italy
The Piedmontese nobility, 1861–1930
ANTHONY L. CARDOZA

Italian culture in northern Europe
in the eighteenth century
Edited by SHEARER WEST

The politics of ritual kinship
Confraternities and social order in early modern Italy
Edited by NICHOLAS TERPSTRA